PRINT CULTURE AND MUSIC
IN SIXTEENTH-CENTURY VENICE

PRINT CULTURE AND MUSIC IN SIXTEENTH-CENTURY VENICE

Jane A. Bernstein

OXFORD
UNIVERSITY PRESS
2001

OXFORD
UNIVERSITY PRESS

Oxford   New York
Athens   Auckland   Bangkok   Bogotá   Buenos Aires   Cape Town
Chennai   Dar es Salaam   Delhi   Florence   Hong Kong   Istanbul   Karachi
Kolkata   Kuala Lumpur   Madrid   Melbourne   Mexico City   Mumbai
Nairobi   Paris   São Paulo   Shanghai   Singapore   Taipei   Tokyo   Toronto   Warsaw

and associated companies in
Berlin   Ibadan

Copyright © 2001 by Oxford University Press

Published by Oxford University Press, Inc.
198 Madison Avenue, New York, New York 10016

Oxford is a registered trademark of Oxford University Press

Library of Congress Cataloging-in-Publication Data
Bernstein, Jane A.
Print culture and music in sixteenth-century Venice / Jane A. Bernstein.
p. cm.
Includes bibliographical references and index.
ISBN 0-19-514108-3 (pbk.)
1. Music trade—Italy—Venice—History—16th century.   2. Music
printing—Italy—Venice—History—16th century.
3. Music—Publishing—Italy—Venice—History—16th century.
I. Title: Print culture and music in the 16th-century Venice.   II. Title.

ML3790 .B47 2001
070.5'794'094531—dc21   00-047898

1 3 5 7 9 8 6 4 2
Printed in the United States of America
on acid-free paper

FOR LEWIS LOCKWOOD
ON HIS SEVENTIETH BIRTHDAY

PREFACE

Nearly two decades ago, I embarked on an odyssey that would take me to fifty-six libraries and archives all over Europe and the United States to examine the music books issued by the sixteenth-century Venetian printer, Girolamo Scotto. The topic proved to be even more fascinating than I had anticipated, for it allowed me to explore various subjects beyond my own discipline. Every time I opened a sixteenth-century book, I discovered whole new areas of inquiry from printing and publishing, descriptive bibliography and iconography, to the history of books, philosophy, and medicine. Most important, by studying the Venetian book trade, I gained a great deal of insight into the cultural, political, and economic history of sixteenth-century Europe. The project culminated in the book, *Music Printing in Renaissance Venice: The Scotto Press (1539–1572)*, which appeared in 1998. Intended as a reference tool, it contains an introductory historical study and a catalogue detailing over 400 music editions brought out by the Scotto firm during its most productive period.

The present study emanates from the introduction to this much larger work. It is about the commerce of music and its connection to the printing and publishing industry in mid-Cinquecento Venice. While it incorporates much of the material presented in the original study, this book differs from the earlier work in its coverage and treatment. Technical analyses and tables dealing with various typographical issues have been omitted. Emphasis on the Scotto press has given way to a broader portrayal of the Venetian music book trade. Discussion of other sixteenth-century music presses, in particular the House of Gardano, has also been greatly amplified. Finally, detailed treatment of individual music editions found in the last chapters of the original study has been downplayed in favor of a more general exploration of business strategies that music printers followed in the marketing of musical repertories.

Parts of chapters 3, 4, and 5 appeared in preliminary versions as "Financial Arrangements and the Role of Printer and Composer in Sixteenth-century Italian Music Printing" in *Acta musicologica* 62 (1990): 39–56; "Girolamo Scotto and the Venetian Music Trade" in *Atti del XIV congresso della Società Internazionale di*

Musicologia, Bologna, 27 agosto-1 settembre 1987, ed. A. Pompilio, D. Restani, L. Bianconi, and F. A. Gallo (Turin, 1990), 1:295–305; and "Printing and Patronage in Sixteenth-century Italy" in *Actas del XV congreso de la Sociedad Internacional de Musicologia, Madrid, 1992* (Madrid, 1993), 2603–13. I thank the International Musicological Society for permission to reuse these materials here.

In addition to the many institutions, colleagues, and friends whom I thanked in my original book, I wish to express my gratitude, once again, to the staff at Oxford University Press, in particular Maribeth Payne, Nancy Hoagland, Jessica Ryan, and Maureen Buja for being so helpful in all matters of production. I also want to thank Paul Grendler for his helpful comments.

As ever, I owe a special debt of gratitude to my husband, James Ladewig, and my daughter, Lily, for their patience, love, and support.

CONTENTS

LIST OF ILLUSTRATIONS
AND TABLES

TABLES

ABBREVIATIONS AND GLOSSARY

AIM	American Institute of Musicology
ASV	Archivio di Stato, Venice
binder's volume	two or more different editions bound together into one large book.
CMM	Corpus mensurabilis musicae
chanson	secular polyphonic vocal music in French typically for four voices, but could be for two, three, or more than four voices.
choirbook	layout in which all vocal or instrumental parts for a musical work appear on the same page opening of one volume. It, thus, allows a group of musicians to perform from a single book.
colophon	publishing information, which might include name of printer, place and date of publication, printer's mark, and/or statement of privilege that appears at the end of the book.
compartment	a carved, single-piece, decorative enclosure with one or more spaces cut out of the center for insertion of type
DBI	*Dizionario biografico degli italiani*, 46 vols. to date (Rome, 1948–)
edition	all copies of a text printed from the same setting of type.
fol.	folio
font	a group of type-cast letters, numbers, and other symbols of any one size and design.
frame	a border made up of two or more decorative ornaments
imprint	information that identifies the printer, place and date of publication appearing on the title page
incunabulum	a book printed before 1501.
intabulation	an arrangement of a vocal composition for lute or keyboard, which appears in tablature (notation system using letters, numbers, or figures instead of notes on a staff); known as intavolatura, the term also denotes the notation for keyboard scores.
issue	copies of an edition that are deliberately planned as a distinct unit. Use of an altered title page or different dedication in an edi-

tion printed simultaneously in two forms constitutes a different issue.

JAMS *Journal of the American Musicological Society*

madrigal secular polyphonic vocal music with Italian text generally of a serious nature for three, four, five or more voices.

matrix an impression created when the punch strikes a small block of copper; constitutes the second stage in the process of making type.

MGG *Die Musik in Geschichte und Gegenwart*, ed. Friedrich Blume, 14 vols. (Kassel, 1949–86)

motet a solemn polyphonic vocal work in Latin, usually sacred, for four or more voices.

New Grove *The New Grove Dictionary of Music and Musicians*, ed. Stanley Sadie, 20 vols. (London, 1980)

Nuovo Vogel Emil Vogel, Alfred Einstein, François Lesure, and Claudio Sartori, *Bibliografia della musica italiana profana pubblicata dal 1500 al 1700. Nuova edizione interamente rifatta e aumentata con gli Indici dei musicisti, poeti, cantanti, dedicatari e dei capoversi dei testi letterari*, 3 vols. (Pomezia, 1977)

partbooks printed books that contain music for a single vocal or instrumental part of a musical work. A basic set of partbooks usually consists of four books designated: cantus or superius; contratenor or altus; tenor; and bassus. Works for five and six voices have additional partbooks designated quintus and sextus.

punch a piece of metal, the end of which contains an incised design for letter or symbol in mirror image.

ricercare an instrumental piece usually for solo lute or keyboard, which is contrapuntal in style.

RISM *Répertoire international des sources musicales*. A/I/1–9. *Einzeldrucke vor 1800*, ed. K. Schlager (Kassel, 1971–92); B/I/1. *Recueils imprimés XVIᵉ–XVIIᵉ siècles. Liste chronologique*, ed. François Lesure (Munich, 1960)

state an alteration in the content of an edition either during or after the printing process constitutes a different state.

type an individual piece of metal containing a letter or symbol; the casting of type occurs when the metal (e.g., lead or tin) is poured into a mold containing the matrix. The type appears in mirror image.

v verso

villanesca a light secular vocal form popular in Italy originally from Naples originally for three, then later four or five voices; also known as villota, canzone villanesca alla napolitana, or simply napolitana.

PRINT CULTURE AND MUSIC
IN SIXTEENTH-CENTURY VENICE

INTRODUCTION

From almost the earliest years of my childhood I strove with all my might, main, effort and concentration to assemble as many books as I could on every sort of subject. Not only did I copy many in my own hand when I was a youth, but I spent what I could set aside from my small savings on buying books. For I could think of no more noble or splendid possession, no treasure more useful or valuable, that I could possibly gather for myself. Books ring with the voices of the wise. They are full of the lessons of history, full of life, law, and piety. They live, speak, and debate with us; they reveal matters which are furthest from our memories, and set them, as it were, before our eyes. Such is their power, worth and splendor, such their inspiration, that we should all be uneducated brutes if there were no books.[1]

—Cardinal Bessarion, *letter accompanying the donation*
of his library to the Republic of Venice, 1468

 usic printing as a successful commercial enterprise began at a particularly propitious moment in Venetian history, for the years from 1540 until 1570 marked an era of unbroken peace and prosperity for the Most Serene Republic. The sense of stability and affluence prompted Venetians to turn their attention to external appearances. Proclaiming themselves the new Romans, they became concerned with ceremonial display and artistic endeavors, made manifest in the construction of new civic buildings and in an ambitious program of patrician patronage.[2] Architectural projects multiplied, commissions for paintings and sculpture proliferated, and music and literature flourished in both the public and private spheres.[3]

This atmosphere of economic and cultural growth provided the ideal stimulus for the burgeoning business of music printing. Girolamo Scotto and Antonio Gardano exemplified the new period of intense commercialism. Active as publishers, booksellers, and composers from the period around 1536 until 1572, they each issued more than four hundred music publications containing a huge repertory that ranged from Masses and motets to madrigals, chansons, and instrumental music by all the leading composers of the day. The influence of the Scotto press as printer and publisher moreover extended beyond music into other fields, in particular philosophy, medicine, and religion, where it published a number of books equal to the firm's music production.

For over a century, the Houses of Gardano and Scotto played an instrumental role in the international book trade. They marketed books throughout Europe, held interests in retail stores, and acted as publishers who underwrote the editions of other printers. Their prodigious output, the importance of the repertories they published, their business activities in indisputably the greatest center of sixteenth-century printing and publishing, and their impact on other areas of Renaissance thought made them a pivotal force reflecting the fascinating relationship between the worlds of commerce, culture, and scholarship in Cinquecento Venice.

Over the past four decades, a number of studies have appeared on sixteenth-century music printers. Claudio Sartori's catalogue of Petrucci and François Lesure and Geneviève Thibault's bibliographies of the Parisian firms of Le Roy and Ballard and Du Chemin were among the pioneering works.[4] Musicologists of the next generation expanded the format by including historical studies with their catalogues. Daniel Heartz broke new ground by placing the Parisian printer Pierre Attaingnant within his socio-cultural milieu.[5] Samuel Pogue in his book on Jacques Moderne dealt with music printers in Lyons, while Catherine Chapman explored Italian music printing at the time of Andrea Antico.[6] These studies served as prototypes for later catalogues. More recently, scholars of music print culture have brought to the field a variety of methodologies. They have examined typographical issues and production methods. They have also utilized archival evidence and the tools of descriptive bibliography in their work. Kristine Forney, Henri Vanhulst, and Robert Weaver have concentrated on music printers from the Low Countries.[7] Italian music printers have been the subject of works by Suzanne Cusick, Stanley Boorman, Mary Lewis, Richard Agee, and Thomas Bridges.[8] All of these musicologists have contributed a great deal to our knowledge of music print culture during the sixteenth century.

The present book differs from these previous works in that it will offer a broad view of the music printing industry in mid-Cinquecento Venice. By exploring the economics of the trade, I propose that commerce played a crucial role in every aspect of music printing. I stress the role of the entrepreneur, with the Scotto and Gardano presses serving as vehicles for the narrative. This book can be viewed, then, as a socio-economic study, in which the transmission of music is perceived primarily as a business phenomenon.

The idea of capitalistic enterprise as the modus operandi of the sixteenth-century book trade is certainly not a new one; it has already been advanced by several historians and bibliographers. Hirsch, Febvre and Martin, Voet, Lowry, Grendler, Chartier, and Quondam, to name a few, have dealt with this subject from different perspectives.[9] Above all, Eisenstein has emphasized economics as the moving force of the printing industry. She has also expressed concern that "one rarely gets a sense of its significance as a whole" given the fact that the topic of print culture has been "segmented, subdivided, and parcelled out" among economic and social historians, literary scholars, media analysts, bibliographers, librarians, and print designers.[10] To Eisenstein's list we must also add musicologists, for scholars of music print culture have only just begun to look beyond their specialty.

My aim is to broaden the picture. In the present study, I hope to bridge the gap between music and other disciplines. I have tried to incorporate music printing into the wider world of the printing industry, and to demonstrate that music printing was no different from any other specialty of the book trade. Within that framework, the singular theme of commercial enterprise runs throughout the book.

The book begins with a broad overview of the book trade. Who were the leading firms? How many books were published? Where were the presses located? The emphasis is on the community of printers and publishers. We observe how familial and personal relationships provided the structural underpinnings for most commercial activities, how the bookmen governed themselves, and what their connections were to the intellectual and artistic world of Venice. This chapter reveals how printing specializations became the basis for the marketing strategies of the industry. It concludes with a survey of those specializations with particular attention given to the field of music.

The book continues with an exploration of the multifaceted world of sixteenth-century music printing and the various activities of the trade. The manufacturing of a music book takes center stage in chapter 2. We experience, the organization of the workforce within the shop, how a music book was produced, and what materials and supplies were required. The chapter provides crucial details concerning editorial practices, typographical materials, formats, title pages, and printers marks used by the various presses. It also gives us a sense of how a typical music print shop operated in the sixteenth century.

Chapter 3 is concerned with the financial arrangements made in the publishing of music books, describing independent sponsorship and partnerships with other bookmen. Publications commissioned by composers and other third parties are also explained. In this chapter I attempt to define the close relationships that existed among Cinquecento Venetian music printers.

In chapter 4 we move away from the print shop into the international world of book distribution. Here, the complicated networks of agents, book carriers, and foreign printers are discussed. The chapter provides information on the trade routes used by the Venetians in their travels throughout the Italian peninsula, as well as across the Alps to northern Europe. It details the northern European book fairs and explains such marketing tools as book-fair trade lists and printers' broadside catalogues. The chapter concludes with a brief consideration of customers and collectors, both individual and institutional, who purchased music books.

Chapter 5 considers what influence the music-printing industry had upon its clients. We see how composers could augment their income by commissioning and then selling their own editions and, in some cases, even entering into the business of printing and publishing. The role of the patron and the involvement of the composer in the printing process are also addressed.

The last part of the book focuses on the two most important music printing dynasties of Cinquecento Venice: the Houses of Scotto and Gardano. Chapter 6 presents a history of the two firms, tracing their development through several generations of bookmen. The last chapter analyzes the musical repertories Antonio Gardano and Girolamo Scotto published. It examines previous hypotheses concerning possible rivalry or cooperation between the two printers. It then explores the various business strategies they observed in the acquisition and marketing of their music publications. These business strategies not only help define the relationship between the two Venetian music printing firms as it took place over a thirty-year period, they also throw some light on the wider issues of change and continuity that occurred in the musical world of Cinquecento Venice.

NOTES

1. "Equidem semper a tenera fere puerilique aetate omnem meum laborem, omnem operam, curam studiumque adhibui, ut quotcumque possem, libros in omni disciplinarum genere compararem. Propter quod non modo plerosque et puer et adolescens manu propria conscripsi, sed quidquid pecuniolae seponere interim parca frugalitas potuit, in iis coëmendis absumpsi. Nullam enim magis dignam atque praeclaram supellectilem, nullum utiliorem praestantioremque thesaurum parare mihi posse existimabam. Quippe pleni sunt libri sapientium vocibus, pleni antiquitatis exemplis, pleni moribus, pleni legibus, pleni religione. Vivunt, conversantur, loquunturque nobiscum, docent nos, instituunt, consolantur, resque e memoria nostra remotissimas quasi praesentes nobis exhibent et ante oculos ponunt. Tanta est eorum potestas, tanta dignitas, tanta maiestas, tantum denique numen, ut, nisi libri forent, rudes omnes essemus et indocti . . ." Transcription in Ludwig Mohler, *Kardinal Bessarion als Theologe, Humanist und Staatsmann* (Paderborn, 1942), 3: 541. English translation by Martin Lowry in *Venice: A Documentary History, 1450–1630*, eds. David Chambers and Brian Pullan, with Jennifer Fletcher (Oxford, 1992), 357.

2. On the Venetians patterning themselves on Ancient Rome see D. S. Chambers, *The Imperial Age of Venice*, 1380–1580 (London, 1970), 12–30.

3. An introduction to the subject of patronage of the arts in Venice appears in Oliver Logan, *Culture and Society in Venice, 1470–1790* (London, 1972). On architectural enterprises see Deborah Howard, *Jacopo Sansovino: Architecture and Patronage in Renaissance Venice* (New Haven, 1975). Discussion of patronage in the other visual arts appears in several sources, among them David Rosand, *Painting in Cinquecento Venice: Titian, Veronese, Tintoretto* (New Haven, 1982). Martha Feldman explores music and literature in the private sphere in *City Culture and the Madrigal at Venice* (Berkeley and Los Angeles, 1995).

4. Claudio Sartori, *Bibliografia delle opere musicali stampate da Ottaviano Petrucci* (Biblioteca di bibliografia italiana 18; Florence, 1948); François Lesure and Geneviève Thibault, *Bibliographie des éditions d'Adrian Le Roy et Robert Ballard (1551–98)* (Paris, 1955); "Bibliographie des éditions musicales publiés par Nicolas Du Chemin (1549–1576)," *Annales musicologiques* I (1953): 269–373.

5. Daniel Heartz, *Pierre Attaingnant, Royal Printer of Music* (Berkeley and Los Angeles, 1969).

6. Samuel Pogue, *Jacques Moderne: Lyons Music Printer of the Sixteenth Century* (Geneva, 1969); Catherine W. Chapman, "Andrea Antico" (Ph.D. diss., Harvard University, 1964).

7. Kristine K. Forney, "Tielman Susato, Sixteenth-Century Music Printer: An Archival and Typographical Investigation" (Ph.D. diss., University of Kentucky, 1978); Henri Vanhulst, *Catalogue des éditions de musique publiées à Louvain par Pierre Phalèse et ses fils 1545–*

1578 (Brussels, 1990); Robert Weaver, *A Descriptive Bibliographical Catalog of the Music Printed by Hubert Waelrant and Jan de Laet* (Warren, Mich., 1994).

8. Suzanne Cusick, *Valerio Dorico, Music Printer in Sixteenth-Century Rome* (Studies in Musicology 43; Ann Arbor, Mich., 1980); Stanley Boorman, "Petrucci at Fossombrone: A Study of Early Music Printing with Special Reference to the Motetti de la Corona (1514–1519)" (Ph.D. diss., University of London, 1976); Mary S. Lewis, *Antonio Gardano, Venetian Music Printer, 1538–1569: A Descriptive Bibliography and Historical Study*. Vol. 1: *1538–49*; Vol. 2: *1550–1559* (New York and London, 1988–1997); Richard Agee, *The Gardano Music Printing Firms* (Rochester, N.Y., 1998); Thomas W. Bridges, "The Publishing of Arcadelt's First Book of Madrigals," 2 vols. (Ph.D. diss., Harvard University, 1982).

9. Roger Chartier, *The Culture of Print: Power and the Uses of Print in Early Modern Europe*, trans. Lydia G. Cochrane (Princeton, 1989); Lucien Febvre and Henri-Jean Martin, *The Coming of the Book: The Impact of Printing 1450–1800*, trans. David Gerard, ed. Geoffrey Nowell-Smith and David Wooton (London, 1976). Originally published as *L'Apparition du livre* (Paris, 1958). Paul S. Grendler, *The Roman Inquisition and the Venetian Press, 1540–1605* (Princeton, 1977) and "Printing and Censorship" in *The Cambridge History of Renaissance Philosophy*, ed. Charles B. Schmitt and Quentin Skinner (London, 1973), 25–53; Rudolph Hirsch, *Printing, Selling and Reading, 1450–1550* (Wiesbaden, 1967); Martin Lowry, *Nicholas Jenson and the Rise of Venetian Publishing in Renaissance Europe* (Oxford, 1991) and *The World of Aldus Manutius: Business and Scholarship in Renaissance Venice* (Ithaca, N.Y., 1979); Amedeo Quondam, "Mercanzi d'onore, 'Mercanzia d'utile': produzione libraria e lavoro intellettuale a Venezia nel Cinquecento," in *Libri, editori, e pubblico nell'Europa moderna: guida storica e critica*, ed. Armando Petrucci (Rome, 1977), 51–104; and Leon Voet, *The Golden Compasses: A History and Evaluation of the Printing and Publishing Activities of the Officina Plantiniana at Antwerp*, 2 vols. (Amsterdam, 1972).

10. Elizabeth L. Eisenstein, *The Printing Press as an Agent of Change: Communications and Cultural Transformations in Early Modern Europe*, 2 vols. (Cambridge, 1979), 24.

One

PRINTERS AND PUBLISHERS

The Merchants of Venice

Venice may be called a summary of the universe, because there is nothing originating in any far-off country but it is found in abundance in this city. The Arabs say that if the world were a ring, then Ormuz, by reason of the immeasurable wealth that is brought thither from every quarter, would be the jewel in it. The same can be said of Venice, but with much greater truth, for she not only equals Ormuz in the variety of all merchandise and the plenty of all goods, but surpasses her in the splendor of her building, in the extent of her empire, and, indeed in everything else that derives from the industry and providence of men.[1]

—Giovanni Botero, *Della relatione della Republica Venetiana*, 1605

"he Venetians never wanted an empire," remarked Gore Vidal, "They just wanted to do business . . ."[2] and business did flourish in sixteenth-century Venice. Venice was indeed the marketplace of the world. Its location on the lagoons and its unique connection with the sea distinguished it among the great commercial centers of the Renaissance. A maritime power and trading emporium, it survived for a thousand years as an independent city-state protected from internal strife and foreign invasion. It gained its power and prosperity not from the quantity of lands owned by its patriciate, but from the mercantile activities of its residents.

It is in this larger context that we must begin our study, for commerce and trade played a central role in the development and achievements of music printing. Venetian merchants inhabited a cosmopolitan world, where they trafficked in a wide array of goods, dealt in high finance, and set the standard for international trade. They sold spices, salt, cotton, grains—items they had imported from the East for centuries. They also traded in commodities they manufactured themselves: woolen cloth, glassware, soap, and silks. In the late fifteenth century, these entrepreneurs created a whole new industry, the production of books.[3]

Venice offered an ideal center for the printing of books. It boasted the best and most advanced distribution system in the world. And because its printers and publishers could not all rely on the patronage of a ruler or the church but depended mainly on market forces in order to make their living, the Venetian printing industry, from its inception, became a capitalistic enterprise, producing books in larger quantities and distributing them much further afield than any other European center.

The first book was not printed in Venice until 1469 when a German immigrant named Johannes de Spira obtained a five-year monopoly from the Venetian Senate.[4] The monopoly did not last long, for Johannes died only a few months after his request was granted. Others quickly came to Venice to seek their fortune in the new industry, and by 1473 there were at least a dozen printers active in the city. Printing became a boom industry, in which many competed but few survived.[5] One of them, the Frenchman Nicolas Jenson, became the most celebrated publisher in Venice during this period.[6] Jenson and Johannes de Spira's firm, now headed by Johannes's brother Wendelin and by Johannes de Colonia, formed two syndicates that dominated the industry. Between them they produced some sixty-four editions during the period 1471–72—about half of the total for all Venetian presses.[7] A number of Italians from other cities came to Venice during the last two decades of the fifteenth century. These new arrivals succeeded the Germans and French who had dominated Venetian printing during its formative years. Several of them prospered and, in turn, established their own dynastic presses, some of which lasted for over a century.

Among these printers, the houses of Giunti, Giolito, and Manuzio became the preeminent publishers of Cinquecento Venice. To these illustrious firms we must add the presses of Scotto and Gardano, which, until now, have remained unrecognized as leaders of the Cinquecento book trade. During its 134-year history, the House of Scotto printed more than 1,650 editions, while the Gardano press, which endured for seventy-three years, produced some 1,425 titles. In both cases, these figures matched or exceeded the other great printing houses of Venice. Indeed, the Scotto and Gardano firms were not just important Venetian presses, they were the most renowned music publishing houses of Renaissance Europe.

Scholars of print culture have been at a loss for what to call the dynastic bookmen, in view of the wide repertoire of roles they played in the printing industry. Eisenstein designated them master printers; Lowry simply labeled them publishers.[8] Grendler noted that the terms *stampatore, libraio*, and *bibliopola* were commonly used to identify booksellers and printers.[9] But the Scotti, Giunti, and Gioliti belonged to a different class; they were men of distinction and reputation, who sometimes stylized themselves as *nobili*. Contemporaries did have a name for these early capitalists; they called them *mercatori* or merchants.

The Venetian *mercatori* dealt with all facets of their trade. They directed a complex mechanized operation that employed a highly skilled workforce and used expensive equipment and materials. They oversaw every aspect of the production of their books, from the acquisition of manuscripts to the setting of type, running of presses, and proofreading of copy. As merchant-capitalists, these men were responsible for all financial aspects of the business. They solicited other printers, publishers, and entrepreneurs to form syndicates or invest in their publications and, in turn, they underwrote the publication of books produced by other bookmen. They cultivated potential authors and clients, who might commission books. Above all, these dynastic printers supervised a complex distribution network that extended throughout Europe. They retained book carriers, who hawked their publications from town to town, formed alliances with foreign presses to sell their books, and employed book agents to look after their interests abroad. They owned or invested in bookshops, and, in several cases, maintained satellite offices in other cities.

GROWTH OF AN INDUSTRY

The rise of these publishing houses reflects the rapid development and success of the Venetian book business in general. Figures compiled by modern bibliographers show that printing and publishing reached its zenith in *La Serenissima* during the period from 1540 to 1575—an era of unbroken peace which came to an end with the disastrous plague. Scholars have conservatively estimated that in the sixteenth century, Venetian presses published around 7,560 to 17,500 editions.[10] Yet the total number is even greater than has been reckoned. The production of individual printers, in many cases, is three to twenty times greater than the figures first cited by Pastorello.[11] Surviving editions published by Venetian music printers demonstrate this point: Pastorello counted 347 Scotto editions for the entire sixteenth century, whereas extant titles number about 1,500. She cited twenty-nine editions by Antonio Gardano, while Lewis noted 438. Pastorello listed only two editions from Merulo's press, whereas thirty-four survive. Furthermore, Pastorello and Grendler deliberately presented conservative figures by not taking into account Cinquecento editions that no longer exist. Though an exact total cannot be determined until all significant Venetian presses have been studied, doubling the number to 35,000 individual editions seems a more reasonable estimate.[12]

The size of the pressrun for Venetian editions varied from title to title, depending on the type of publication. A "vanity" book commissioned and financed by an author or patron probably ran to about 500 copies, since the Venetian Senate refused to grant a privilege for a pressrun of fewer than 400 copies.[13] "Bestsellers" brought out by a major publisher might number as high as 2,000 to 3,000 copies. The pressrun for an ordinary edition was about 1,000 copies.[14] Pressruns in specialty areas such as music correspond to these figures.[15] The total number of copies printed also depended on whether a private party commissioned the edition or a syndicate financed it. In 1565 Girolamo Scotto printed 500 copies of the *Passiones, Lamentationes, Responsoria* of Don Paolo Ferrarese, an edition commissioned by the Monastery of San Giorgio Maggiore.[16] In 1516 Andrea Antico contracted in a partnership with Ottaviano II Scotto and other bookmen to print 1,008 copies of an anthology of Mass settings titled *Quindecim missarum*.[17] How many books did the Venetian printers produce? On the basis of the size of average pressrun and total number of editions, we can estimate that more than thirty-five million books were printed over the course of the sixteenth century.[18]

The locations of the bookmen's presses and shops emphasized the success of the Venetian printing industry. Unlike bookmen in Paris, who were generally confined to a single area on the Left Bank near the University,[19] Venetian printers and booksellers established their businesses in practically all the districts of the city. Most of the bookstores and presses were located in the *sestieri* of Castello, Cannaregio, and San Marco. Situated above the Grand Canal, these three districts were, in the sixteenth century as today, the commercial areas of the city, while Santa Croce, San Polo, and Dorsoduro, located below the Grand Canal, were more residential in nature. Bookshops and stalls filled the Merceria, the main thoroughfare linking the financial and commercial center at the Rialto to the Piazza San Marco, the political and intellectual hub of the city. The bookstores and presses stretched from the Rialto district as far east as the parish of Santi Giovanni e Paolo to the precinct of San Zacharia, to the north of the Piazza San Marco.[20]

The addresses of the music presses, as seen in the map in figure 1.1, reveal the widespread dispersement of printing concerns around the city. During its long history, the Scotto firm moved its press several times. Ottaviano Scotto established his firm in the district of San Marco in the parish of San Samuele (1). By the time his nephew Ottaviano took over the business, the press was situated in the parish of San Felice (2) in Cannaregio. After 1547 the firm returned to the district of San Marco, first to San Benedetto (3) and then to the Corte del Albero in the parish of Sant'Angelo (4). Antonio Gardano first owned a shop in the Calle de la Scimia (5) in the *sestiere* of San Polo near the Pescaria. In 1536 Francesco Marcolini's press was located in Cannaregio in the parish of Santi Apostoli (6) at the house of the Order of Crutched Friars (Frati Crosachieri). Francesco Rampazetto established his press in Castello in the Calle dalle Rasse (7) right off the Riva degli Schiavoni.

COMMUNITY OF BOOKMEN

Printers, publishers, and booksellers made up the main constituency of the Venetian book trade. They worked cooperatively, with the printer in charge of the presswork, the publisher financially responsible for the publication and distribution, and the bookshop selling the books. Distinctions among the occupations were often blurred, with the majority of bookmen carrying out two or more aspects of the trade. A printer who worked on consignment, or a bookseller who did not own a press, might occasionally finance a title on his own or in collaboration with a publisher. *Mercatori* such as the Scotti or Giunti took on all three professional roles at the same time.

Whatever their stature, Venetian bookmen maintained strong alliances with one another. Besides forming partnerships, they bought, sold, and lent typographical materials to one another, witnessed each other's contracts, and collectively carried

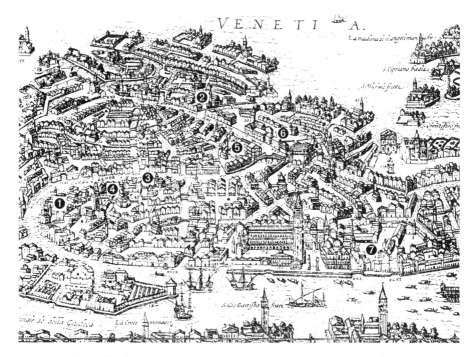

FIGURE 1.1 Detail of Venice showing locations of sixteenth-century music presses. After George Braun, *Civitas orbis terrarum* (1573). 1. Scotto firm ca. 1480; 2. Scotto firm ca. 1534; 3. Scotto firm ca. 1547; 4. Scotto firm after 1560; 5. Gardano firm ca. 1539; 6. Marcolini firm, 1536; 7. Rampazetto firm ca. 1562. Photo courtesy of The Edward E. Ayer Collection, The Newberry Library.

out other matters of the trade. The small presses relied on the large publishers for the distribution of their editions, while the larger firms subcontracted to the more modest presses the printing of some of their books.

Familial and personal relationships often formed the basis for commercial activities. Venice, as a great mercantile center, emphasized these connections. Family enterprises and workshops played a central role in defining the socioeconomic hierarchy, whether in the woolen cloth trade, the printing industry, or the artist's workshop.[21] Under Venetian law, upon the death of the head of a family, all of the male heirs shared jointly in the estate. Brothers or cousins would form a *fraterna* or family partnership, collectively operating their own business and often living together in the same house.[22] Nearly all of the leading publishing firms of Venice were run by *fraterne*. It was not uncommon even for distant relatives to work for the press. As in other industries, advantageous marriages within the book trade were used to strengthen the large presses.[23] Widows who inherited established firms would sometimes marry other bookmen in order to further the interests of the press. One fascinating case is that of Paola da Messina, whose second husband was Johannes de

Spira, Venice's first printer. After his death in 1470, she married another printer, Johannes de Colonia, who, by joining the press, made it a powerful syndicate that rivaled the firm of Nicolas Jenson. When Johannes de Colonia died, Paola married her fourth husband, another printer named Reynaldus de Novimagio, who promptly joined the company created by Johannes de Spira and strengthened by Johannes de Colonia.[24]

Journeymen and aspiring young printers would seek strategic marriages to the daughters of established bookmen. The Frenchman Antonio Gardano married the daughter of the Venetian printer Agostino Bindoni. Gardano may have worked as a journeyman at Bindoni's press when he first arrived in Venice.[25] Besides or in lieu of the usual cash gift, the dowry Bindoni provided his daughter conceivably could have contained material goods, such as books, presses, typographical equipment, and paper. Most important, it must have included the intangible assets of business connections and clients—all of which could facilitate the establishment of Gardano's own printing concern.[26]

Though business connections reduced the kind of cut-throat competition that might have destroyed the industry as a whole, it did not entirely eradicate disagreements among Venetian printers. Bookmen took out privileges from the Venetian Senate to protect their work from pirated editions. They could seek redress in court for infringement of their privileges or other business disputes but did so infrequently, choosing instead to govern themselves in an informal manner. Printers and publishers usually settled their legal conflicts privately, or if that failed, set up arbitration boards to deal with the disagreements. For every dispute, each of the opposing parties selected another bookman to serve as an adjudicator; the two chosen then named a third, and the three had the responsibility of reaching a binding decision.[27] The conflicts concerned all sorts of legal issues, and often involved printers from other cities. In one such case, the Milanese printers Pietro and Francesco Tini were awarded recompense by the arbitrators, Damiano Zenaro and Francesco Ziletti, for two bales of books which were water-damaged during transport by the book carrier Pietro Longo.[28]

As part of their governance, the bookmen maintained their own guild or *arte*.[29] Each industry had its own guild: the *Arte della Seta* for the silk weavers, the *Arte della Lana* for those involved in the woolen cloth industry. Even the painters belonged to a guild, the *Arte dei Depentori*, which in its membership not only included figure painters but also sign painters, mask makers, illuminators, gilders, leatherworkers, and embroiderers.[30] Every guild met on the premises of a church and placed itself under the protection of a saint.[31] The *Arte* (or *Università*) *delli Librari et Stampadori* convened their meetings at Santi Giovanni e Paolo in the chapel of Santa Maria del Rosario.[32] This was an appropriate place, since the Dominican church had a warehouse where bookmen occasionally stored their books.[33] The protectors of the Arte were Our Lady of the Rosary and St. Thomas Aquinas.[34]

Unlike the *arte* of several other Venetian industries, the guild of printers and booksellers played a relatively minor role in the internal affairs of the book trade.

It was not officially instituted until 1567, though bookmen must have had an informal organization before then. Membership was confined to master printers and booksellers and was not open to journeymen and apprentices. Brown estimated that the membership ranged from sixty-six to seventy-five, figures significantly lower than the 125 presses active at the end of the century. But the guild counted a number of distinguished printers of Venice among its members. These included the heads of the firms: Tomaso Giunti, Vincenzo Valgrisi, Andrea Arrivabene, Michele Tramezzino, and Giordano Ziletti. Girolamo Scotto was elected the first prior in 1571, with Gabriel Giolito, Zuan de Varisco, Giovanni Griffio, Pietro da Fino, and Gasparo Bindoni serving as officers.[35]

The guild offered limited social and welfare services, such as the granting of dowries to unprovided daughters of deceased members.[36] It also gave printers and booksellers a united voice in their negotiations with state and Church authorities. Even before the official promulgation of its regulations in 1567, the guild on several occasions sent representatives to petition the Venetian Holy Office against the Index of Prohibited Books, which threatened their business.[37]

Printers and booksellers forged important alliances with members of the intellectual world of Venice. Their business distinguished them from other merchants by bringing them into contact with writers, artists, and musicians. Academies established by patricians and men of letters in the Veneto formed close relations with the Venetian press. An academy was apparently founded at the Aldine press in 1502 for the purpose of promoting the study of Greek.[38] By mid-century, other Venetian academies with connections to presses also sprang up. The Accademia Pellegrina, a literary group founded in 1549, used Marcolini as their official printer.[39] The Accademia Veneziana or Accademia della Fama, established in 1557 by the patrician Federigo Badoer, operated its own printing establishment with the aid of Paolo Manuzio, then head of the Aldine press. The Academy set itself an extraordinary agenda of publishing some 300 titles, only twenty-two of which were printed before its disbanding in 1561.[40] The Accademia degli Infiammati of Padua, founded in 1540 by professors at the university and intellectuals from the Venetian patriciate, also provided an important bond between the scholastic world and the printing industry; the works of a few of its members were published by the Scotto press.[41]

The informal gatherings or *cenacoli* of Venetian intellectuals became valuable sources for publications. Discussions, debates, and performances by writers, artists, scholars, and musicians held at the homes of such Venetian noblemen as Domenico Venier, Antonio Zantani, Marcantonio Trevisan, and Paolo Paruta moved from the private sphere to the public arena with the printing of dialogues, letters, essays, poetry, and madrigals.[42]

Several *mercatori* were well educated in the fields they published, and a few gained a considerable reputation in the intellectual and artistic world. One of the first was Aldo Manuzio (1450–1515). As a distinguished man of letters in his own right, he wedded serious scholarship to the business of printing. He set himself the enormous task of printing Greek and Latin classical works from the best texts available and in so doing revolutionized the standards of the printing industry. Many of the great scholars of the day, including Pietro Bembo, Giambattista Egnazio, Marcantonio Sabellico, Marin Sanudo, and Desiderius Erasmus, collaborated with the Aldine press.[43]

Several leading publishers of the next generation also pursued scholarly interests. Printers of vernacular literature were particularly well connected with intellectuals and artists. Francesco Marcolini da Forlì, an architect, diplomat, printer, and secretary to the Venetian Accademia dei Pellegrini, enjoyed the friendship of such leading artists as Titian, Tintoretto, and Sebastiano del Piombo.[44] Marcolini's edition of Sebastiano Serlio's architectural treatises and his reprint of Vitruvius' *De archi-tectura* in Italian translation helped shape Venetian taste in architecture, as exemplified in the works of Jacopo Sansovino.[45] Some of the designs for the woodcut illustrations that accompany Marcolini's editions have been attributed to Titian.[46] Gabriel Giolito actively supported and encouraged such authors as Ortensio Lando, Lodovico Dolce, and Lodovico Domenichi, who served as editors, translators, and compilers of his editions.[47]

At the Scotto press, Ottaviano II and his brother Girolamo were both proficient in their publishing specialties. Ottaviano held a doctorate in medicine and was well versed in the field of natural philosophy. On occasion he edited Aristotelian commentaries for the press. He moved comfortably in the intellectual circles of Venice and was on good terms with several members of the renowned Accademia degli Infiammati in Padua. Girolamo, as well as another printer, Antonio Gardano, pursued an interest in music. Highly skilled as composers, they published several editions of their own music, including madrigals, motets, French chansons, and instrumental works in the contrapuntal idiom.

PRINTING SPECIALIZATIONS

The Venetian printers understood that their liaisons with the patriciate and the intellectual world provided them with commissions and other advantageous business opportunities. They were also keenly aware with their independently financed ventures, that books were merchandise to be bought and sold, and they knew that market demand determined what they should print. Venetian dominance of the European printing industry depended upon the marketing strategies of its bookmen. The most important practice was the concentration of subject matter in which each bookman published. The *mercatori* learned the significance of this strategy when an economic crisis hit the industry only four years after its inception in 1469. During the early 1470s, printers issued classical Greek texts only in Latin translation. They printed so many copies of the same titles that by 1473 they glutted the market. Many publishers and printers, particularly the small firms and transients, went bankrupt in this new venture.[48] The financial disaster made apparent to the Venetians the basic principles of supply and demand. Those who survived learned several lessons. The industry as a whole would have to diversify the subject matter it printed. At the same time, individual firms would have to create their own specialized fields, so as to avoid direct competition among themselves.[49] Yet when printers discovered titles that sold well, they cautiously reprinted them in a "follow-the-leader" fashion.[50]

These marketing strategies played an important role in the success of the industry for the next hundred years. The smaller firms, who usually worked on commission, printed almost anything. The dynastic presses published in many areas as well, but they also carved out their own specializations.[51] The House of Manuzio continued to publish classical literature in Greek as well as humanist commentaries in Latin translations. The Giolito press specialized in vernacular literature. The Giunti press held the market in liturgical volumes; they also printed legal, medical, and philosophical texts intended for the university market. Like Giunti, the Scotto firm maintained an interest in university textbooks; it also specialized in music. Gardano and his heirs restricted themselves to the field of music.

The bookmen even sub-specialized in branches of particularly large and lucrative subjects. For example, several printers divided up the sizeable university market for Aristotelian studies.[52] The Giunti concentrated on complete editions of the works of Aristotle in Latin translation, while the Aldine press continued to offer Aristotle in the original Greek. The Scotto firm focused on Aristotelian commentaries.[53] Printers even partitioned Aristotle's works and commentaries into separate subject areas. Works belonging to the field of classics and humanism, such as the *Rhetoric*, were issued in the original Greek by Giovanni Griffio in 1546 and in Latin translation by Comin da Trino in 1544.[54] Those texts concerned with natural philosophy, such as the *Physica* and the *Parva naturalia*, were mainly printed by the Scotto press. Almost all the smaller firms that issued these titles were in one way or another connected with the House of Scotto. These included the printers Giacomo Fabriano, Giovanni Griffio, Gasparo Bindoni, and Giovanni Maria Bonelli.

The business tactic of narrow specialization helped to establish Venice as the most important printing and publishing center for many different fields. The Latin texts for the academic market, the legal and medical professions, and the clergy, the primary subjects printed in the incunabular period, continued to dominate the Cinquecento book trade. With the preeminence of Aristotelian studies at the University, Padua became an important site for philological scholarship.[55] In the sixteenth century, a new wave of intellectuals issued countless translations, commentaries, *tabulae*, and indices of Aristotelian texts in Venice. Printers brought out a flurry of lexicons, grammars, and studies in orthography, meter, and prosody—all intended to elucidate the classical Greek and Latin publications. These books formed the basis of the lucrative university and school book trade, and were issued in various formats to fit the pocketbook of patricians, professors, and students.

Though Latin remained the *lingua franca* of the international scholarly community, publications in the *volgare* increased dramatically in the sixteenth century. Linguistic works in Latin gave rise to studies of Italian usage. Pietro Bembo's *Prose della volgar lingua* (1525) and Sperone Speroni's *Dialogo delle lingue* (1542), advocating a modern classicism in Italian based on Ciceronian rhetoric and Petrarchan poetic style, signaled a new phenomenon: the advent of the vernacular press. The firms of Marcolini, Giolito, Comin da Trino, Valgrisi, Tramezzino, and others responded to and encouraged the new enthusiasm for books in the *volgare*. They published volumes of sonnets, dialogue verses, and other poetic forms by such *literati* as Annibale Caro, Benedetto Varchi, Luigi Tansillo, Domenico Venier, and Gaspara Stampa. They introduced a new type of non-scholarly prose, the *Libro di lettere volgari*, which, inherited in part from Latin Ciceronian models studied and imitated by pre-university students,[56] became the publication par excellence of the Venetian press.[57] They issued chivalric romances or *libri de batagia* with great frequency,[58] making a handsome profit from the sales of successive editions of Ariosto's *Orlando furioso*, by far the most popular book of the Cinquecento.[59] Venetian bookmen printed the scurrilous letters, plays, and dialogues of Pietro Aretino and the other *poligrafi*, Ortensio Lando, Antonfranceso Doni, and Nicolò Franco. They made the *popolaresco* plays of Ruzzante, Andrea Calmo, and Antonio Molino, with their use of dialect for satiric and comic effects, widely available to eager readers.[60] The dazzling breadth of non-scholarly literature issued by the vernacular press was due in part to the relative freedom enjoyed by the printing industry—at least until the 1560s, when Church and state began to tighten their control over the press.[61]

A surge also occurred in vernacular publications of a scholarly nature. Historiography became an important genre, with examples ranging from the writings of Francesco Patrizi, Paolo Paruta, and Nicolò Contarini, to the popularized histories of Francesco Sansovino.[62] Didactic literature formed another category. Baldassare Castiglione's best seller, *Il Cortegiano* (1528), and Alessandro Piccolomini's *De la institutione di tutta la vita de l'homo nato nobile* (1542), for example, were devoted to the education of the young aristocrat[63] Books concerned with commercial arithmetic (*abbaco*) and accounting (*quaderni*) were used in the teaching of merchants. Bible translations and devotional books rounded out the titles offered in Italian. The most popular religious books of the Cinquecento were *Fior di virtù*, a medieval book of virtues and vices, and Thomas à Kempis's *Imitation of Christ*. Both texts were used as readers in Italian vernacular schools. They were also prescribed as devotional books for the home.[64]

Book illustration, though not exclusively a Venetian specialization, also enjoyed some measure of success. Printers and authors received privileges for a variety of illustrated books. The Venetian Senate approved Sebastiano Serlio's and Agostino di Mussi's request to publish woodcuts of Venetian architecture in their *Regole generali di architetura sopra le cinque maniere de gli edifici* of 1537. The book, published by Marcolini, contained 126 woodcuts, fifty-six of which were full-page illustrations. It was the first book on architecture in which illustrations assumed a prominent role.[65]

Gabriel Giolito sought a privilege in 1541 for several ornaments and designs that accompanied his 1542 edition of the *Orlando Furioso*. The forty-six woodcut illustrations, which appeared at the head of each canto in the edition, served as models for several future editions, Giolito used them for no fewer than twenty-eight succeeding editions. Other Venetian bookmen copied the illustrations for their editions, as did printers in Florence, Lyons, and Paris.[66]

Two books exclusively containing illustrations were intended for those dabbling in artistic crafts and collecting. The first was a book of lace patterns issued in 1546 by Florio Vavassore.[67] It contained forty-seven intricate designs, which were to be torn out and used by ladies in their needlework. The second book, *Le imagini con tutti i riversi trovati et le vite de gli imperatori*, reflects the predilection at that time by the Venetian nobility for antiquities. It was published in 1548 by the nobleman Antonio Zantani, an avid collector, music lover, and owner of an important medal collection. The book consisted of sixty-two copper plates illustrating coins and medals, all produced by the noted engraver Enea Vico.[68]

Venetian bookmen made vital contributions to the printing of specialized languages. Aldo Manuzio was renowned for his texts using Greek type. Over a period of twenty years he printed some 130 titles, including thirty first editions of Greek literary and philosophical works. Aldo brought out the works of Aristotle, Homer, Thucydides, Herodotus, Xenophon, and Sophocles. During the first two decades of the sixteenth century, he printed Demosthenes' *Orationes*, Plutarch's *Moralia*, the comedies of Aristophanes, Aesop's *Fables*, the tragedies of Euripides, and works by other ancient Greek authors.[69]

Aldo was also the first printer to experiment with Hebrew type, which appeared in his 1498 edition of Poliziano's *Opera*. Full-scale operation of a Hebrew press, however, did not take place until Daniel Bomberg's arrival in 1516. A Christian from Antwerp, Bomberg became the most prominent printer of Hebrew texts in Venice. From 1516 to 1548, he published some 200 titles, including a milestone edition of the complete Babylonian Talmud, issued over a four-year period.[70] During the 1540s other printers, including the two patricians, Marc'Antonio Giustiniani and Alvise Bragadino, followed Bomberg's lead. Under their aegis, the printing of Hebrew texts continued to flourish in Venice, only to fall into sudden decline when anti-Semitism and a papal order provoked the burning of the Talmud and similar Hebrew books in 1553 and again 1568.[71]

Bookmen sought privileges from the Venetian Senate for editions in other languages. In 1498 Democrito Terracini obtained a privilege for twenty-five years to print all books in "arabica, morescha, soriana, armenicha, indiana et barbarescha."[72] Terracini died before he could apply his privilege. The first five books printed in Armenian appeared in Venice between 1511 and 1513. Edited by Jacob Melapart, the titles included a missal, a book of religious and secular poetry, a horoscope and astronomy book, a book of prayers and magic spells, and a simplified calendar.[73]

The earliest-known Venetian book in Arabic dates from 1537–38; it was a Koran printed by Paganino Paganini and his son Alessandro.[74] The Paganinis sought to publish Arabic texts intended for export to the Islamic market. Their undertaking was apparently a failure, since no other book in Arabic survives from their press. Books using Cyrillic typography appeared in Venice early in the sixteenth century.

From 1519 to 1561, Božidar Vuković and later his son, Vicentije, specialized in Slavonic editions. Most of their publications were of liturgical books that used the Cyrillic alphabet. The Vuković press were the main suppliers of books to the Greek Orthodox church. Their distribution network stretched across the Levant from Dalmatia and Albania to Greece, and from Hungary and Romania to Turkey.[75]

Of greater interest to our study is the specialty of music. Though not the first Italian city to bring out a book with music notation printed from movable type,[76] Venice established itself by the 1480s as a world center, issuing more than seventy-six editions or more than half of all Italian music incunabula. Some seventeen Venetian printers participated in the production of music books. The two most important, Johann Hamman and Johann Emerich, were solely responsible for half of the total Venetian production.[77]

Most of the music incunabula were Roman missals intended for liturgical use. Venice continued as a major player in the publication of plainchant service books well into the next century. Several Venetian printers, including Petri Liechtenstein, Scotto, Griffio, and Varisco, issued such books. Giunti was the leading press of liturgical music books until 1569, when Pope Pius V granted to another printer an exclusive privilege to print the Tridentine missal.[78]

Of all typographies, music proved one of the most challenging. Besides requiring a different set of symbols, it presented technical difficulties not associated with other specialized languages. Several types of notation were used in the late fifteenth and sixteenth centuries. These included white mensural notation, black mensural notation, various lute and keyboard tablatures, and three different plainchant notations (Roman, Gothic, and Ambrosian). But the major obstacle facing the early music printer was how to align the music symbols on the lines and spaces of a fixed staff. During the incunabular period, bookmen solved this problem in two ways. One was the xylographic method, wherein the music notation was carved into wooden blocks. Music illustrations for late fifteenth-century theoretical treatises were, for the most part, produced in this manner. The second and more common procedure was to print music from movable type using a multiple-impression process in which the staves were printed first. The paper was then run through the press a second and sometimes a third time with type containing the notes, symbols, initials, and text. This procedure was generally used in liturgical chant books, in which the staves were printed in red ink with the notes superimposed in black ink.[79] Though exceedingly labor-intensive, the multiple-impression method continued to be used in the printing of chant books throughout the sixteenth century.

In 1501, Ottaviano Petrucci printed in Venice the first book of polyphony set from movable type. The method he used to produce his books was not revolutionary, for it was the same multiple-impression process employed by printers of music incunabula.[80] Petrucci's achievement lay not with the method he used but with the complexity of the white mensural notation he printed and the smallness of his type font.[81] Furthermore, unlike the earlier printers, whose books had relatively few pages of music, Petrucci's volumes consisted entirely of music. No one could equal the precision with which Petrucci aligned notes on the staff nor rival the elegant look of his music pages. Following the custom of the time, Petrucci purposely designed his printed music books to resemble manuscripts.[82] Aldo Manuzio, for example, claimed that the Greek type fonts he used in his books were "as good, if not better, than any written with a pen."[83] Petrucci's music editions were deemed an artistic success, but the process used to achieve that success had a serious disadvantage. The time it took to run each sheet of paper two or more times through the press with correct alignment was so great that only a relatively small number of copies could be produced with each pressrun.[84] The high cost of Petrucci's books prompted others to experiment with different techniques.

Andrea Antico, an Istrian musician working in Rome in the 1510s, reverted to the xylographic method of printing music. Skilled as an *intagliatore*, Antico carved all of the music notation into wood. Upon completion, the woodblocks were set in the forme along with movable type containing the text underlay, initials, and decorative typographical materials. This process appeared to be more economical than the multiple-impression method, for the paper went through the press only once. The lesser cost of the presswork made it feasible for Antico to produce larger pressruns than those of Petrucci. Throughout the 1530s, the woodcut procedure became the method of choice for polyphonic music publications, and Antico, who moved to Venice in 1520, remained the main producer, working either with or for the Scotto press.

But xylography proved an outmoded method. It is true that Antico's woodblocks could be reused for later editions and more copies could be produced per pressrun than with the multiple-impression process. However, the time it took to carve the notes and staves into the strips of wood was apparently so great that, when factored into the cost of printing, the technique turned out to be more expensive than multiple-impression printing.[85] In 1536, Francesco Marcolini da Forlì received a privilege from the Venetian Senate "to print or have printed both music and tablature with characters of tin or of other mixture."[86] The granting of a privilege suggests that he had discovered a new method for printing music. In reality, he had simply resuscitated the double-impression process previously used by Petrucci. Without a single-impression method using movable type, the printer's craft would not be truly profitable.

The single-impression method of printing polyphonic music was introduced in London.[87] The printer John Rastell apparently first used it in 1519–23 for the printing of broadside song sheets and part-songs for his play books.[88] Only three songs and one part-song survive. The ephemeral nature of the large single-page broadsides makes it difficult to determine whether Rastell's music-printing enterprise was a financial success. John Milsom suggests that in the England of the 1520s and 30s music printing might have been a more substantial trade than has previously been thought. But it was the Parisian printer Pierre Attaingnant who in 1528 realized the full commercial potential of the new technology. By using the single-impression method, Attaingnant propelled music printing into a moneymaking enterprise. During the 1530s, the new process was quickly adopted by other printers. It spread across northern Europe from Paris to Lyons to the German cities, and finally, in 1538, to Venice.

The single-impression process proved to be simple. Each music note or symbol was combined with a short vertical section of the staff on the same piece of type. The compositor could then set the type on his composing stick, just as he would for type containing letters for text. While the resulting line of type gave the illusion of a continuous row of music notes, the breaks in the staff lines between each piece of type looked crude in comparison with Petrucci's and Antico's editions. Yet despite this disadvantage, the problem of alignment that had plagued the multiple-impression method had been solved. The aesthetic appearance of earlier music books was sacrificed in favor of mass production. Music books could now be published more cheaply, more quickly, and in greater quantity than hitherto imagined.

The adoption of a single-impression process in Venice at the end of the 1530s radically changed the music-printing industry. It entered a new era—moving away from the artisan stage into the commercial period. The music printers Girolamo Scotto and Antonio Gardano exemplified this coming of age. Scotto, who was born into a renowned Venetian publishing firm, and Gardano, a French emigré who established his own dynasty, became the giants of the industry. For the next thirty years, they produced more than 850 music editions, a figure that surpassed the total output of all other European music printers combined. Thus, what began in 1501 with Petrucci's financially precarious venture turned into a prosperous business enterprise. Venice could now claim preeminence in music printing.

NOTES

1. ". . . Venetia si può chiamare sommario dell'universo, perche non è cosa, che in quantunque lontano paese nasca, in lei copiosamente non si ritrovi. Gli Arabi dicono, che se il mondo fosse uno annello, Ormuz per le infinite richezze, che da ogni parte vi si conducono, sarebbe la sua gioia: ma ciò si può molto piu veramente di Venetia affermare conciosia che ella non solamente pareggia Ormuz nella varietà delle merci, e nella copia d'ogni bene; ma l'avanza nella magnificenza della fabriche, nella ampiezza dell imperio, & in ogni altra parte che dalla industria, e dalla providenza de gli huomini procede," fol. 75ᵛ. English translation by Brian Pullan in *Venice: A Documentary History, 1450–1630*, 167–68.

2. Gore Vidal, *Vidal in Venice* (New York, 1985), 48.

3. For an overview of these industries see Frederick Lane, *Venice: A Maritime Republic* (Baltimore, 1973), 309–21. On the book trade, see Marino Zorzi, "Dal manoscritto al libro," in *Storia di Venezia dalle origini alla caduta della Serenissima*, vol. 4: *Il Rinascimento politica e cultura*, ed. Alberto Tenenti and Ugo Tucci (Rome, 1996), 817–958; and Claudia Di Filippo Bareggi, "L'editoria veneziana fra '500 e '600," in *Storia di Venezia dalle origini alla caduta della Serenissima,* vol. 6: *Dal Rinascimento alla Barocca*, ed. Gaetano Cozzi and Paolo Prodi (Rome, 1994), 615–48.

4. Rinaldo Fulin, "Documenti per servire alla storia della tipografia veneziana," *Archivio veneto* 23 (1882), 99, doc. 1. On the early years of printing in Venice, see Victor Scholderer, "Printing at Venice to the End of 1481," in *Fifty Essays in Fifteenth-and Sixteenth-Century Bibliography*, ed. Dennis E. Rhodes (Amsterdam, 1966), 74–89; Leonardas Gerulaitis, *Printing and Publishing in Fifteenth-Century Venice* (London, 1976); Neri Pozza, "L'editoria veneziana da Giovanni da Spira ad Aldo Manuzio. I centri editoriali di Terraferma," in *Storia della*

Cultura Veneta, vol. 3, pt. 2: *Dal primo Quattrocento al Concilio di Trento,* ed. Girolamo Araldi and Manlio Pastore Stocchi (Vicenza, 1980), 215–44; and Horatio Brown's pioneer study, *The Venetian Printing Press 1469–1800* (London, 1891).

5. From the one hundred or so printing firms established in Venice up to 1490, twenty-three continued into the next decade, and only ten outlived the century. Lowry, *The World of Aldus Manutius*, 9, as calculated by Hirsch, *Printing, Selling and Reading*, 42–43.

6. On Jensen, see Martin Lowry, *Nicholas Jenson and the Rise of Venetian Publishing in Renaissance Europe* (Oxford, 1991).

7. Scholderer, "Printing at Venice," 75.

8. Eisenstein, *Printing Press as an Agent of Change*, 1:56 n. 49.

9. Grendler, *Roman Inquisition*, 4.

10. Ester Pastorello, in her pioneering work, *Tipografi, editori, librai a Venezia nel secolo XVI* (Florence, 1924) based her total of 7,560 editions on the holdings of selected northern Italian libraries. Her unpublished catalogue listing the titles brought out by Cinquecento Venetian printers is located in the Sala dei Manoscritti of the Biblioteca Marciana in Venice. The higher total of 17,500 appears in Grendler, *Roman Inquisition*, 8. He arrived at this figure by doubling Pastorello's total, and then by adding the outputs of the firms of Manuzio, Gioliti, Giunti, and Marcolini, as cited in S. Bongi, *Annali di Gabriel Giolito de' Ferrari Da Trino di Monferrato Stampatore in Venezia* (Rome, 1890–97); Scipione Casali, *Annali della tipografia veneziana di Francesco Marcolini da Forlì* (Forlì, 1861–65); Paolo Camerini, *Annali dei Giunti* (Florence, 1962); and Antoine Renouard, *Annales de l'imprimerie des Alde, ou Histoire des trois Manuce et de leurs éditions*, 3d. ed. (Paris, 1834).

11. Pastorello's estimates are also questioned by Quondam, "Mercanzi d'onore," 56. Using different evidence, Conor Fahy, "The 'Index prohibitorum' and the Venetian Printing Industry in the Sixteenth Century," *Italian Studies* 35 (1980), 59–61, also arrives at a figure "in excess of 30,000."

12. As Grendler himself admits, his analysis of imprimaturs in *Roman Inquisition,* 8–9 as another method of deducing the total production of Venetian books is also flawed, since printers did not seek licenses for the vast majority of their books. See Richard J. Agee, "The Privilege and Venetian Music Printing in the Sixteenth Century" (Ph.D. diss., Princeton University, 1982).

13. Grendler, *Roman Inquisition,* 9.

14. Ibid. See also id., "Printing and Censorship," in *The Cambridge History of Renaissance Philosophy,* ed. Charles B. Schmitt and Quentin Skinner (London, 1973), 25–53.

15. On the pressrun of music books see the survey of extant contracts in Agee, "A Venetian Music Printing Contract in the Sixteenth Century," *Studi musicali* 15 (1986): 59–65. The contract discovered by Bonnie J. Blackburn, in "The Printing Contract for the *Libro primo de musica de la salamandra* (Rome, 1526)," *Journal of Musicology* 12 (1994): 345–56, should be added to Agee's list. On Spanish contracts, see John Griffiths and Warren E. Hultberg, "Santa Maria and the Printing of Instrumental Music in Sixteenth-Century Spain," in *Livro de homenagem a Macario Santiago Kastner,* ed. M. F. Cidrais Rodrigues, M. Morais, and R. Veiera Nery (Lisbon, 1992), 347–60.

16. Agee, *"Venetian Music Printing Contract."*

17. Chapman, "Andrea Antico," 448.

18. Again this figure is approximately double Grendler's estimate of 15 to 20 million books: *Roman Inquisition*, 12.

19. Elizabeth Armstrong, *Robert Estienne, Royal Printer* (Cambridge, 1954), 3, and Heartz, *Pierre Attaingnant*, 3–4.

20. Fernanda Ascarelli and Marco Menato, *La tipografia del '500 in Italia* (Florence, 1989), 321–470 provide the press locations for several of the Venetian printers.

21. David Rosand comments on this phenomenon in connection with artistic production in *Painting in Cinquecento Venice*, 7–9.

22. On the *fraterna* see Frederic C. Lane, "Family Partnerships and Joint Ventures," in *Venice and History: The Collected Papers of Frederic C. Lane* (Baltimore, 1966), 36–55.

23. For specific examples of marriages within the book trade, see Di Filippo Bareggi, "L'editoria veneziana," 621–22; 644–45, nn. 23–26.

24. The documents appear in Gustav Ludwig, "Contratti fra lo stampador Zuan di Colonia ed i suoi soci e inventario di una parte del loro magazzino," *Miscellanea di storia veneta, Reale deputazione veneta di storia patria*, 2d ser., 8 (1902): 45–48. See also Gerulaitis, *Printing and Publishing*, 21–24.

25. Claudio Sartori, "Una dinastia di editori musicali," *La bibliofilia* 58 (1956): 176–208.

26. Examples of dowries given by other printers appear in Grendler, *Roman Inquisition*, 18. Speculation on the Bindoni dowry is taken from Lewis, *Antonio Gardano*, 1:20 n. 22.

27. Grendler, *Roman Inquisition*, 18. Bridges, "Publishing of Arcadelt's First Book," i: 130, mentions that peer arbitration was apparently used by Venetian merchants in other trades besides printing. He cites Wilfrid Brulez, *Marchands flamands à Venise, I (1568–1605)* (Études d'histoire économique et sociale 6; Rome and Brussels, 1965), pp. xxxii–xxxiii.

28. Corrado Marciani, "Editori, tipografi, librai veneti nel regno di Napoli nel Cinquecento," *Studi veneziani* 10 (1968): 457–554 at 516.

29. The best general history and discussion of the guilds appears in Richard Mackenney, *Tradesmen and Traders: The World of the Guilds in Venice and Europe, c. 1250–c. 1650* (Totowa, N.J., 1987).

30. Rosand, *Painting in Cinquecento Venice*, 9–15; also Elena Favaro, *L'Arte dei Pittori in Venezia e i suoi statuti* (Florence, 1975).

31. The locations of churches, scuole, and altars used by the guilds appears in Mackenney, *Tradesmen and Traders*, 244–48, app. 1.

32. In either 1575 or 1582, the confraternity known as the *Scuola di Santa Maria del Rosario* acquired the chapel, which became the most famous chapel and center for art owned by any late sixteenth century *scuola piccola*. Giulio Lorenzetti, *Venice and its Lagoon: Historical-Artistic Guide*, tr. John Guthrie (Trieste, 1926; repr. 1975), 353. Franca Zara Boccazzi, *La Basilica dei Santi Giovanni e Paolo in Venezia* (Padua, 1965), 194–98.

33. Grendler, *Roman Inquisition*, 5.

34. The Virgin Mary is mentioned in the first rule of their by-laws. The complete by-laws or *Mariegole* appear in Venice, Museo Civico Correr, MS Cicogna 3044. A reproduction of the first page appears in Di Filippo Bareggi, "L'editoria veneziana," 619. A complete transcription occurs in Brown, *Venetian Printing Press*, 243–48, doc. 3. Brown also provides an English translation on pp. 83–87. An illustration of Our Lady of the Rosary and St. Thomas Aquinas as protectors of the guild also appears in the manuscript, and is reproduced in Grendler, *Roman Inquisition*, 7, pl. 1.

35. Brown, *Venetian Printing Press*, 83–91 details various aspects of the printers' guild.

36. Grendler, *Roman Inquisition*, 19 n. 65.

37. Ibid., 99–100.

38. While earlier scholars have made much of Aldo Manutio's "New Academy," Lowry, *World of Aldus Manutius*, 195–98, is more cautious in his interpretation of the evidence.

39. See Grendler, *Critics of the Italian World, 1530–1560: Anton Francesco Doni, Nicolò Franco, and Ortensio Lando* (Madison, Wis., 1969), 58–59; Michele Maylender, *Storia delle accademie d'Italia* (Bologna, 1926–30), 4: 244–48.

40. Paul Lawrence Rose, "The Accademia Venetiana: Science and Culture in Renaissance Venice," *Studi veneziani* 11 (1969): 191–242.

41. A summary on the early years appears in Richard S. Samuels, "Benedetto Varchi,

the *Accademia degli Infiammati*, and the Origins of the Italian Academic Movement," *Renaissance Quarterly* 29 (1976): 599–633.

42. On Venier and Zantani see Feldman, *City Culture*, 63–81, 83–119; Paruta's activities appear in Oliver Logan, *Culture and Society in Venice*, 54–59.

43. Lowry, *World of Aldus Manutius*, passim.

44. Casali, *Annali della tipografia veneziana di Francesco Marcolini da Forlì*, pp. ii–xvii.

45. Howard, *Jacopo Sansovino*, 3, 26.

46. Fabio Mauroner, *Le incisioni di Tiziano* (Padua, [1943]), 20–21; 42–44; and figs. 22–25.

47. Quondam, "Mercanzi d'onore," 96.

48. Scholderer, "Printing at Venice," 78; but see Lowry, *Nicholas Jensen*, 107–111 for a different interpretation.

49. Lowry, *World of Aldus Manutius*, 14.

50. Gerulaitis, *Printing and Publishing*, 9.

51. Grendler, *Roman Inquisition*, 5–6.

52. For an introduction to the Aristotelian tradition in the Renaissance see various writings by Paul Oskar Kristeller in *Renaissance Thought and its Sources*, ed. Michael Mooney (New York, 1979); see also Charles B. Schmitt, *Aristotle and the Renaissance* (Cambridge, Mass., 1983).

53. F. Edward Cranz, *A Bibliography of Aristotle Editions 1501–1600*, 2d ed., ed. Charles B. Schmitt (Baden-Baden and Geneva, 1984). For a list of Aristotelian commentaries issued by Girolamo Scotto see Jane A. Bernstein, *Music Printing in Venice: The Scotto Press (1539–1572)* (New York, 1998), app. D.

54. Cranz, *Bibliography of Aristotle Editions*, no. 108.094.

55. For an introduction to this field see Schmitt, *Aristotle and the Renaissance*; on the Paduan School see Bruno Nardi, *Saggi sull'aristotelismo padovano dal secolo XIV al XVI* (Florence, 1958).

56. On the use of Cicero's letters in the Latin curriculum see Grendler, *Schooling in Renaissance Italy: Literacy and Learning, 1300–1600* (Baltimore, 1989), 217–29.

57. Over 540 volumes of familiar letters were issued over a hundred-year period of 1538–1627; see Quondam, *Le "carte messaggiere": retorica e modelli di comunicazione epistolare, per un indice dei libri di lettere del Cinquecento* (Rome, 1981), 13–157.

58. The term is taken from Grendler, *Schooling in Renaissance Italy*, 289.

59. Daniel Javitch, *Proclaiming a Classic: The Canonization of Orlando Furioso* (Princeton, 1991).

60. On Aretino see Thomas Chubb, *Aretino, Scourge of Princes* (New York, 1940) and Christopher Cairns, *Pietro Aretino and the Republic of Venice: Researchers on Aretino and his Circle in Venice, 1527–1556* (Florence, 1985), and Giovanni Aquilecchia, "Pietro Aretino e altri poligrafi a Venezia," in *Storia della cultura veneta*, vol. 3, pt. 2: *Dal primo Rinascimento al Concilio di Trento* (Vicenza, 1980), 61–98. On Doni, Lando, and Franco, see Grendler, *Critics of the Italian World*; also on the vernacular press, see Claudia Di Filippo Bareggi, *Il mestiere di scrivere. Lavoro intellecttuale e mercato librario a Venezia nel Cinquecento* (Rome, 1988). On Ruzzante, Linda L. Carroll, *Angelo Beolco (Il Ruzante)* (Boston, 1990).

61. See Grendler, *Roman Inquisition*, 128–61; and id., "Printing and Censorship," 45–48.

62. On the formal histories see Logan, *Culture and Society in Venice*, 112–26. For histories in the more popular vein see Grendler, "Francesco Sansovino and Italian Popular History, 1560–1600," *Studies in the Renaissance* 16 (1969): 139–80.

63. A summary of the literature on the education for the *vita civile* appears in Grendler, *Critics of the Italian World*, 136–42.

64. Grendler clarifies the teaching of Italian literature and merchant skills as parts of the vernacular curriculum in *Schooling in Renaissance Italy*, 275–329.

65. See Brown, *Venetian Printing Press*, 103, and Ruth Mortimer, comp. *Harvard College Library, Department of Printed Books and Graphic Arts. Catalogue of Books and Manuscripts, Part II, Italian 16th Century Books* (Cambridge, Mass., 1974), 2: 651–61.

66. See Mortimer, *Italian 16th Century Books*, 1:35–37 for discussion of the illustrations.

67. Ibid., 2: 720.

68. Ibid., 2: 777–78.

69. Lowry, *World of Aldus Manutius*, 144–45; 150–51.

70. Grendler, *Roman Inquisition*, 90; see also David W. Amram, *The Makers of Hebrew Books in Italy, Being Chapters in the History of the Hebrew Printing Press* (Philadelphia, 1909) and Joshua Bloch, "Venetian Printers of Hebrew Books," *Bulletin of the New York Public Library* 36 (1932): 71–92.

71. For a summary of the repeated burning of Hebrew books in mid-century Venice see Grendler, *Roman Inquisition*, 89–93; 140–45 and id., "The Destruction of Hebrew Books in Venice, 1568," *Proceedings of the American Academy for Jewish Research* 45 (1978): 103–30.

72. Fulin, "Documenti," 133–34.

73. See Raymond H. Kévorkian, *Catalogue des "incunables" arméniens (1511–1695) ou Chronique de l'imprimerie arménienne* (Geneva, 1986). *Le livre arménien a travers les ages*, Catalogue de l'exposition tenue au Musée de la marine, Marseille, 2–21 octobre 1985 (Marseilles, n.d.), and E. Schütz, "The Evolution of Armenian Typographic Art in the West-European Period (16th–17th Centuries)," *Atti del quinto simposio internazionale di arte armena* (Venice, 1991), 449–58 at 450.

74. Angela Nuovo, "Il Corano arabo ritrovato (Venezia, P. e A. Paganini, tra l'agosto 1537 e l'agosto 1538)," *La bibliofilia* 89 (1987): 237–71 and id. *Alessandro Paganino* (Padua, 1990), 107–31 and figs. 15–19.

75. F. Leschinkohl, "Venedig, das Druckzentrum serbischer Bücher im Mittelalter," *Gutenberg Jahrbuch* (1957): 116–21 and Corrado Marciani, "I Vukovic tipografi-librai slavi a Venezia nel XVI secolo," *Economia e storia* 19 (1972): 342–62.

76. The Roman printer Ulrich Han issued in 1476 the first book, a *Missale Romanum*. See Mary Kay Duggan, *Italian Music Incunabula* (Berkeley and Los Angeles, 1992), 13.

77. Ibid., 17–21.

78. For the conflict that occurred in the printing of Tridentine liturgical texts between the Venetian bookmen and the Roman papacy see Grendler's fascinating account in *Roman Inquisition*, 169–81.

79. Duggan, *Italian Music Incunabula*, 14. She also notes that in some cases the black impression preceded the red impression (n. 10); also see Stanley Boorman. "A Case of Work and Turn Half-Sheet Imposition in the Early Sixteenth Century," *The Library*, 6th ser., 8 (1986): 301–21.

80. Duggan, *Italian Music Incunabula*, 38–41 goes further to hypothesize that the mensural type font used by Petrucci for his music books may have been crafted by the typecutter Jacomo Ungaro, who may have made the mensural music type used in Venice as early as 1480.

81. Boorman, "Petrucci at Fossombrone," 29–30.

82. Eisenstein, *The Printing Press as an Agent of Change*, 1:51, Lowry, *World of Aldus Manutius*, 116, and Hellmut Lehmann-Haupt, *Peter Schoeffer of Gernsheim and Mainz, with a List of his Surviving Books and Broadsides* (Rochester and New York, 1950), 37–38.

83. As quoted in Lowry, *World of Aldus Manutius*, 131.

84. Lewis, *Antonio Gardano*, 1: 5.

85. Cusick, *Valerio Dorico*, 14.

86. ". . . far stampare musica, et intabolature con charatteri di stagno over di altra mestura." Archivio di Stato (hereafter. ASV), Senato Terra, reg. 29 (1536–7), fol. 33ᵛ. Complete transcription and English translation in Agee, "The Privilege and Venetian Music Printing," 69; 207.

87. Stanley Boorman has discovered even earlier experiments with single-impression printing. Around 1507–10, two printers of liturgical chant books in Venice and Vienna used the method for specific musical notes in their Salzburg missals. See "The Salzburg Liturgy and Single-Impression Music Printing," in *Music in the German Renaissance: Sources, Styles and Contexts*, ed. John Kmetz (Cambridge, 1995), 235–53.

88. A. Hyatt King, "The Significance of John Rastell in Early Music Printing." *The Library*, 5th ser., 26 (1972), 197–214. John Milsom reviews the early use of single impression music printing in England in "Songs and Society in Early Tudor London," *Early Music History* 16 (1998), 235–93.

Two

INSIDE THE VENETIAN PRINT SHOP

The Manufacturing of a Music Book

Equipment of the printing shop.

A polyphonic music type known as La Pecorina with its matrices, punches, and forms.

Item: an ordinary music type for standard books with matrices, punches, and forms.

Item: a small music type for villotte books with matrices, punches, and forms.

Item: a large music type for royal format with matrices and punches.

Item: punches of lute intablature and matrices and forms.

Item: keyboard intablature: punches, matrices, and forms.

Item: two music types for chant books with matrices, punches, and forms.

Item: two printing presses.[1]

—From a 1575 inventory of the Gardano estate

ixteenth-century music publishing presents a rare opportunity to observe the interrelationship between an art form and a commercial enterprise. The roles played by printers and musicians in the cosmopolitan world of Renaissance Venice were not always mutually exclusive. Scholars have depicted the music printer as a member of intellectual circles, acting as a friend and colleague to the leading musicians and *literati* of his day. But music printers were also merchants involved in the day-to-day commerce of the industry. The manufacturing, financing, distributing, and promoting of books were all major concerns of the printer/publisher in this specialty trade.

When Antonio Gardano and Girolamo Scotto began to print music in the late 1530s, they entered a business already geared to standardized production. By applying manufacturing techniques perfected by the Venetian printing industry over the previous fifty years, the two music printers were able to mass produce music books from the very outset of their careers. This chapter will concentrate on the operation of a sixteenth-century Venetian music press by examining the main features of the print shop: the workforce and the materials used. The process of typesetting a music book and the typographical style unique to a music press will also be described.

The materials and physical features that comprised Venetian music publications—papers, formats, title pages, printer's marks, decorative initials, and typefaces—help us to identify what books came from the various presses. They also assume a greater significance in reflecting the changes in cultural taste and consequently the marketing strategies of music printers in mid-Cinquecento Venice.

THE ORGANIZATION OF A MUSIC PRESS

One of the essential components of the music book trade was the press itself. The initial cost of running a print shop required an enormous outlay of capital for printing presses and typographical equipment. Printers also needed, from time to time, to replenish their stock with new type fonts. Over the lifetime of the firm, they could accumulate an abundance of type fonts, as seen in the Gardano inventory given in the epigraph above.

Printers also had to tie up a great deal of capital in unsold inventory. Two different book catalogues issued by the Gardano firm and by the Scotto press, listing hundreds of titles, attest to the large build-up of inventory.[2] Publications dating back some fifty years appear in both catalogues. Large sums of money were also held up in unpaid balances created in the marketing process. It often took years to collect from agents and booksellers, as seen with the Carrara brothers, booksellers in the cities of Messina and Palermo, who owed Scotto the enormou sum of 1,305 ducats and 20 lire for books they had sold for him some eight years earlier.[3]

The cost of labor was also considerable. The workers employed ranged from young apprentices and piece-work journeymen to pressmen, compositors, and proof correctors.[4] Apprentices or *garzoni* came from a variety of middle-class backgrounds. Usually the regulations regarding apprenticeships required a knowledge of Latin, and most assuredly in the case of the music presses, the *garzone* had to read music notation. The age of the apprentice averaged between fifteen and twenty years old. In Venice, a bookman had to serve a five-year apprenticeship before he could join the guild as an independent printer.[5] In addition to teaching the *garzone* his craft, the master was required to provide room and board, clothes, and pocket money. The *garzone*, in return, had to obey the master printer and perform all the menial tasks of the shop.

Other members of the print shop might include a journeyman who, after serving his apprenticeship, traveled from town to town, often for several years. Native-born Venetians had to work as journeymen for three years, and foreigners, in turn, had to serve in a Venetian print shop for five years in order to join the guild.[6] Ranking above the journeyman were the trained laborers, who worked either as compositors setting type and preparing formes or pressmen who pulled the sheets of paper and operated the press. At the top of the workforce was the head compositor, who supervised the other workers and corrected the first proofs. Finally, the job of proof correction was usually assumed by the *mercator* or a member of the family. It also appears that in many cases, the composers themselves were obliged to read and correct proofs for their own publications.

The workforce usually divided into groups of four or five men, consisting of two compositors, two pressmen, and an apprentice. Each group operated one press, so that in the largest printing establishments, there might be as many as forty to fifty men on eight to ten presses.[7] The two printing presses in the 1575 inventory of the Gardano estate cited above, suggest that at least ten workers were employed at the shop. Similarly, Girolamo and Ottaviano Scotto declared ownership of two presses in their 1566 tax declaration.[8] The total number of editions issued by the Scotto press per year indicates that in good years the firm operated three or four printing presses rather than the two declared, so that up to twenty men might have worked at the shop during certain peak periods. In addition, the Scotto press contracted other independent printers in Venice to print their books.

PRODUCTION METHODS

The process of printing a music edition began with the preparation of the copy. In most cases, the copy was a composer's manuscript or fair copy prepared by another scribe.[9] On other occasions, it could be a printed edition.[10]

Upon receipt of the copy, the typesetter or master would cast off the copy, that is, calculate precisely how the contents of the book were to be laid out. The calculation of line-breaks and page layout differed according to the type of musical genre printed. Madrigal editions were most often set one piece per page, but on occasion three works could be spread over two pages. Motets, often divided into two parts, would fit onto two pages (not necessarily facing each other). An entire Mass setting, in contrast, took up the inordinately large number of around eight pages or one gathering of quarto format.[11]

With preparation and casting off completed, the copy was then ready to be set in type. The compositor took each piece of type from large type-cases, which housed the type in different compartments. He then set both the music and text type on a hand-held tray called a composing stick. When he completed a line of music with its text underlay, the compositor slid the contents of the composing stick onto a wooden tray or galley that usually held one page of type.[12]

On completion of the appropriate number of pages of type, the compositor was ready to impose the pages into a forme. The forme was the arrangement of the pages on one side of a sheet of paper. The outer and inner formes made up the back and front of the sheet when printed. The number and arrangement of the pages was determined by the format of the book. Several different formats were employed by Venetian printers but the one most common for music books was oblong quarto. In oblong quarto, the outer forme contained pages 1, 4, 5, and 8, while the inner forme held pages 2, 3, 6, and 7. Both outer and inner formes made up one gathering.[13]

The compositor created the forme on a flat slab of marble called an imposing stone. Next he set a wooden or metal frame known as a chase around the forme. He then filled the spaces between the forme and chase with furniture (large wooden inner frames) and locked the forme into the chase with thumbscrews attached to two sides of the chase.[14]

As Mary Lewis has discovered, Venetian printers apparently employed a special kind of furniture for their music publications. She has speculated that the wooden inner frame contained indentations or grooves that held each line of music type in place. This caused alignment of music staves that is remarkably consistent from one page to another not only within a given music edition, but also in all editions using the same music type font. Scotto employed this special mechanism in his earliest music editions of 1539, while Gardano began to use it around 1542.[15]

After the forme had been printed off, it was returned to the compositor, who cleaned off the ink and distributed most of the type back to the cases. Since the arrangement of every forme of a book remained the same, the compositor would retain certain typographical parts, in particular headings, repeated rules, and ornaments, known as standing type, along with the chase and furniture. All of these components made up what is called the skeleton forme.[16] The skeleton forme was then reused for successive formes. The use of standing type was a labor- and time-saving device in the production of all books, and, as Lewis notes, was particularly effective in the printing of music in partbooks.[17]

Title pages, headings containing composer's names, sectional indications, and pagination all remained as standing type to be used in the typesetting for all of the partbooks. Lewis suggests that in addition to the type for headings and border material, Gardano's compositors from 1542 on retained much of the text underlay of the page as standing type. She further speculates that the purpose of the specially notched furniture was not only to align the staves within an edition, but to keep the music type fixed in position while shifting around the text underlay, when setting the forme for successive parts.[18] This may have been true in the case of Gardano, but not with Scotto. A cursory examination of Scotto's music editions from representative years reveals discrepancies in the text type of the underlay and, in some cases, in the decorative initials from part to part. All of these deviations in the text between partbooks imply that compositors at the Scotto press did not retain the text underlay as part of the standing type. That setting both the music and the text underlay together on the composing stick one line at a time was the prevalent method of typesetting employed by Scotto and other Venetian printers for all partbooks may be seen in the tenor book of an unsigned edition of Ghibel's Motets of 1546. Here an error occurs in no. 17, *Ecce salvator mundi*, where lines two and three of both the music and the text underlay were switched around.[19]

Music partbooks presented the opportunity for a different method of typesetting for compositors accustomed to working with single-volume publications. Following the usual manner of typesetting for single-volume editions, compositors could set all the formes for each partbook before proceeding to the next book (all of the cantus book, then all of the tenor book, etc.) But, as Lewis has shown, they could also take advantage of standing type, by setting all the partbooks one gathering (i.e. one forme) at a time. Lewis has coined the term "vertical setting" to describe this technique, in contrast to the traditional order, which she calls "horizontal setting."[20] Apparently, Gardano's compositors employed vertical setting of all music publications dating from 1545 onwards. It is also clear that after 1544, the Scotto press followed the same practice, though not with the same consistency as the Gardano firm.

EMENDATIONS DURING PRODUCTION

After the compositor locked the forme into its chase, he gave the newly imposed formes to the pressmen, who printed them on paper. A reader would check one of the earliest sheets pulled from the press. The *mercator* or a professional proof-reader knowledgeable in music presumably did this task for many of the music editions, particularly the anthologies, but a composer or his representative was usually responsible for correcting commissioned publications of their own works.

In general the two music presses did not bother to correct errors deemed minor or insignificant. Certain mistakes, such as turned letters in the text, designation of the wrong vocal part in the heading, or errors in pagination and signatures, remained, in many instances, uncorrected. More blatant mistakes, particularly concerning the music itself, were corrected after the pressrun by a variety of methods.

One standard practice was the issuing of an errata sheet. If Scotto or Gardano printed errata sheets for their music publications, then none survives. Extant copies of music editions, however, do display other forms of emendation. One of them was the paste-over, whereby a slip of paper containing the printed correction was affixed over the error, as seen on the altus title page of the Verona copy of *Missae cum quatuor vocibus paribus decantandae, Morales Hispani, ac aliorum* . . . of 1542, where the word "TENOR" is pasted over with the correct voice part.[21]

The most common kinds of corrections were handwritten ones, which appear most frequently in the emendation of signatures. Sometimes the music presses would employ white ink to hide the error, as seen in Gardano's 1546 edition of Domenico Bianchini, *Intabolatura de lauto*.[22] Incorrect notes could also be stamped over with square woodblocks by hand, known as overprinting, as seen on page 4 of the tenor to a copy of Contino's Lamentations (1561).[23]

Larger errors required more complicated correcting methods. Sometimes during the printing process, the press was stopped to make corrections in the type, or printed corrections could be appended to a page containing an error after the forme was printed. In some cases, variant states exist in different copies of the edition. For example, an entire musical phrase was left out in the bassus part of the fourth piece in the unsigned edition of Perissone Cambio's *Madrigali a cinque voci* (1545).[24] The four surviving copies of the bassus partbook differ from each other with regard to the correction. The Rome copy contains the page unemended in its original state.[25] The copy in Wolfenbüttel also left the press uncorrected, but has the missing musical phrase handwritten in ink at the bottom of the page with indication of placement at the beginning of the second system. The Modena and Verona copies have different variant states of the edition. Both have a typeset addendum containing the musical phrase with text underlay overprinted at the bottom of the page. Only the Verona copy includes a small hand printed at the beginning of the second system to indicate the placement of the addendum. It is clear that these emendations were not stop-press corrections, but were changes that took place after the pressrun.

Having described the hierarchy of the workforce and the process of typesetting, we now turn to the materials and elements—the paper, formats, printer's marks, decorative initials, and typefaces—that made up the unique typographical style of each music press. Today these physical characteristics play an important role in the identification of unsigned or incomplete editions. In the sixteenth century, they signaled to the general readership the contents and intended function of the edition.[26] Music publications in octavo format with small typefaces that contained Neapolitan dialect songs or *canzone villanesca* were aimed at a universal audience. Large books in upright quarto or folio format with elaborately decorated initials and large typefaces often served as presentation editions for important personages.[27] Furthermore, alterations in formats, title-page designs, and typographical features of music books at both the Gardano and the Scotto press that occurred over three decades reflect the rapid changes that were taking place in the new print culture.

PAPER

The kind of paper used by printers determined the size and shape of the music book they produced. Paper was the most important and most expensive material. Printing shops consumed vast quantities of it—about three reams a day per press.[28] Venetian printers maintained close contact with paper manufacturers, depending on an industry that had developed long before the advent of the printing press.

Paper first appeared in Europe sometime around 1100, when it was first manufactured in the Spanish towns of Xativa, Valencia, and Toledo. The industry reached Italy at the end of the thirteenth century. The town of Fabriano, situated near Ancona, became the first Italian center for the manufacture of paper. Renowned for the quality and quantity of its paper, Fabriano retained its status as a major producer of paper for centuries. By the middle of the fourteenth century, paper mills spread to other Italian cities, notably Padua and shortly thereafter to Treviso.[29]

The paper industry expanded quickly with the spread of printing, and by the sixteenth century, large amounts of paper were produced all over Italy as well as in France and Germany. The location of paper mills in the Venetian Republic proved a boon to printers, who obtained their paper mainly from the surrounding environs of Padua, Treviso, and the Friuli, as well as the Riviera di Salò on Lake Garda.[30] Girolamo Scotto acquired most of his paper from Padua. One of his closest associates, Jacopo Fabriano, was not only a printer and bookdealer in Padua but was also described as a "cartolarius Patavinus."[31]

Paper came in several dimensions, which varied slightly according to the mold size. In the fourteenth century four sizes of paper were established as the standard measurements for papermaking in Bologna. They were *imperialle* (74 × 50 cm. or 29 × 19.5 in.), *realle* (61.5 × 44.5 cm. or 24 × 17.5 in.), *mezane* (51.5 × 34.5 cm. or 20.25 × 13.5 in.), and *rezute* (45 × 31.5 cm. or 17.7 × 12.5 in.)[32] These four sizes remained fairly standard throughout the fifteenth century. Toward the end of the century most books in folio format were printed on paper corresponding to the smaller sizes of *rezute* and *mezane*. Italian printers, however, reserved the largest, most expensive *imperialle* size for their special books.[33] Certain musico-liturgical books intended for the choir to share at a single lectern required *imperialle* paper. Indeed, the largest size paper used for any incunabulum appeared in the *Graduale Romanum* (1499/1500) and companion *Antiphonarium Romanum* (1503–4) printed by Johann Emerich of Speyer for Luc' Antonio Giunti in Venice.[34]

By the middle of the sixteenth century, *rezute* became the most common size paper used by Italian printers. Some extant printing contracts specify the paper size if it differed from the standard *rezute*. The Roman agreement between Andrea Antico and Ottaviano Scotto, for example, specifies that the *Liber quindecim . . .* must be printed on "regali folio."[35] So does another Roman contract between the composer, Cristóbal de Morales, Valerio Dorico, Antonio de Salamanca, and Giovanni della Gatta which stipulates that the paper used must be "carta reale." The measurements of extant copies of these two editions, falling in the range of 43.3 × 28.5 cm., verify that the paper used was indeed the royal or *realle* size stated in the contracts. As with the extra-large folios of the incunabular period, these editions of polyphonic Mass settings in choirbook format required a large paper size, since they were intended for ecclesiastical use by a choir singing from one book.

Girolamo Scotto employed *rezute* paper for practically all his music books. Antonio Gardano also used the *rezute* size, but printed a few specially commissioned editions on larger size sheets. The paper measurements for Adrian Willaert's *Musica nova* of 1559 and Pietro Giovanelli's *Novus Thesaurus* volumes, both in upright quarto, correspond to *mezane*, while those of the 1562 folio editions of Morales's Manificats and Jacobus de Kerle's Mass settings conform with *realle*.[37]

Each sheet of paper carried the distinctive pattern of the mold in which it was made. The mold consisted of a frame containing wires running vertically (laid lines) and horizontally (chain lines) to form a grid. Paper manufacturers constructed their own personal design or watermark from wire and then sewed it onto the grid of laid and chain lines. The direction of both the laid lines and chain lines as well as the position of the watermark on the leaf help determine the format of a finished book.

FORMAT

During the sixteenth century, books were printed in a variety of formats. The term refers to the relationship between an individual leaf of a book and the original printed sheet of paper, which can vary in the number of leaves it contains.[38] The arrangement of the printed pages on one side of the sheet of paper known as the forme and the subsequent folding of the original sheet determine the format of a volume.

The most common formats are folio, quarto, octavo, duodecimo, and sextodecimo. In folio format, two pages are printed on each side of a sheet of paper, which is then folded once along the shorter side (crosswise) to make a two-leaf, four-page gathering. A quarto is produced from a sheet containing four pages printed on each side folded twice, once crosswise and once along the longer side (lengthwise), thus creating a four-leaf or eight-page gathering (duerno). Printed sheets for octavo format have eight pages printed on each side; the paper is subsequently folded once crosswise, once lengthwise, and then crosswise again, making an eight leaf or sixteen-page gathering (quaderno).

The standard orientation of a format is upright. Some formats can also be oblong, whereby the horizontal axis is longer than the vertical. During the mid-sixteenth century, the most common format for music books was oblong quarto. The layout or imposition of the pages on the forme and folding sequence for an oblong format differs from that of an upright format. Figure 2.1 illustrates the page placement and folding scheme of oblong quarto. The position of the watermark and the direction of the chainlines on the leaf also differ between the two formats. As seen in figure 2.2, the chainlines run horizontally and the watermark appears in the middle of the spine fold in upright quarto. Oblong quarto, in contrast, has vertical chainlines with the watermark at the top center of the leaf.[39]

Venetian music printers used five basic formats at different times during the sixteenth century. In mid century, oblong quarto became the format of choice. Nearly all of Antonio Gardano's music publications, including editions containing lute and keyboard intabulations appeared in this format.[40] Only four editions printed by Gardano have atypical formats for Venetian music books. They include the "deluxe" editions of Willaert's *Musica Nova* (1559) and Giovanelli's *Novus Thesaurus* (1568), in upright quarto, and Morales's Magnificats (1562) and Kerle's Masses (1562) in large folio editions. As noted previously, the upright quarto titles were printed on larger size paper. As special commissions, they were intended more for private than public consumption. The deluxe features of the folio volumes, on the other hand, had a functional purpose. The large size of their format, paper, and musical and textual typographies, as well as their unusual "choirbook" layout, in which all voice parts appear in one volume on the same page opening, suggest that they were "custom-made" to fit specific ecclesiastical requirements.

Like Gardano, Scotto used oblong quarto from 1539 until the early 1560s for all his music publications. An exception occurred in 1544, when he reversed the orientation to upright quarto. The catalyst for this sudden change in format was

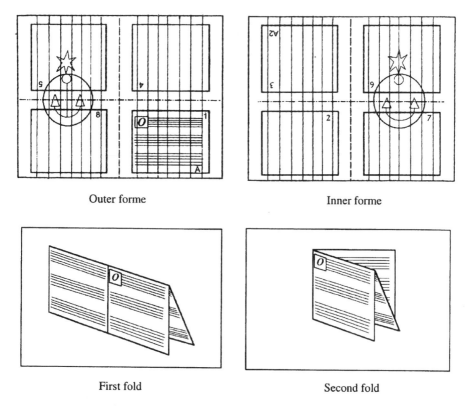

Outer forme   Inner forme

First fold   Second fold

FIGURE 2.1 Imposition and folding scheme of oblong quarto format

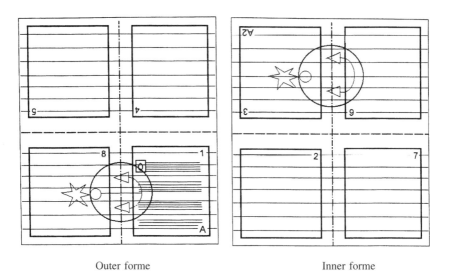

Outer forme   Inner forme

FIGURE 2.2 Imposition of upright quarto format

probably Antonfrancesco Doni, for whom Scotto printed both the *Dialogo di musica* and *Lettere*. The *Dialogo's* unusual conception as a hybrid musico-literary work presumably prompted the use of upright quarto. Upright octavo, traditionally employed for literary dialogic works, was too small to incorporate both music works and dialogue, while the oblong quarto of music editions was too wide and therefore wasted space for the texted portions. Scotto seemed to like the idea of the new format, for in that year he issued at least another six music editions in upright quarto.

The experiment, however, did not last. Girolamo ceased to print music from 1545 to 1547, and when he resumed his music-printing operations in 1548, he reverted to the traditional orientation of oblong format.[41] With one exception, oblong quarto continued as the favorite format until 1564, when upright quarto superseded it at the Scotto press. Scotto was, in fact, the first Italian music printer to change from oblong to upright quarto format. It took another twenty years for the upright orientation to become standard for all Venetian music printers.

The format of choice for the popular Neapolitan dialect song or *villanesche* editions by most printers was the smaller oblong octavo. Colonia in Naples, Dorico and Barré in Rome, Moscheni and Pozzo in Milan, Susato in Antwerp, and Le Roy and Ballard in Paris all used the diminutive format.[42] Gardano adopted it in 1560 for his *Villotte alla napolitana* series. Perhaps in response to Gardano's change in format, Scotto, in 1561, inaugurated another new format, upright octavo, for his music editions of *canzone alla napolitane, villote*, and other three-voice dialect songs. No other printer took up the upright orientation for their music books in octavo size. The diminutive dimensions of the format fit in well with the modest size and style of the pieces. Scotto adopted two different methods of presenting the poetry and music on the page. In most cases, he followed Gardano's lead by printing only the first stanza of text underneath the music and placing any additional strophes in a group at the bottom of the piece (see fig. 2.3). On rare occasions, Scotto copied the arrangement used by other printers, by placing the music with one stanza of text underlay on the verso page and the entire poem on the opposite page.

Only four of Scotto's music publications survive in folio format. They are single-volume lute books that were commissioned by their authors, Galilei and Barbetta and two chant books (*Missale Romanum* 1542; 1560). Unlike Gardano's editions, none of Scotto's sacred books appears in choir-book format. Only one volume, the *Villancicos* of 1556, is laid out in choirbook fashion. Unusual for this arrangement and upright quarto format, the *Villancicos* is the only music book with Spanish texts to be published in Cinquecento Venice.[43]

Venetian music partbooks generally followed the typical structure of four leaves per gathering in quarto format, and eight leaves per gathering in octavo. The average edition consisted of four or five gatherings (either sixteen or twenty leaves), but some editions, particularly of liturgical music, would run into more. Six staves of music were printed to the page in oblong quarto, but from 1564 to 1566, while experimenting with a larger music font, Scotto used five staves.[44] When he turned his quarto books upright, Scotto either employed eight or nine staves of music per

FIGURE 2.3 Venturi, *Il secondo libro delle villanelle a tre voci* (Venice: Scotto, 1571), bassus, pp. 88–89. Reproduced with permission of the Library, University of California, Berkeley.

page, depending on the size of the music and text fonts. His upright octavo books could accommodate up to six staves of music, but often contained only by four, leaving space at the bottom of the page for additional stanzas of text.

Venetian lute tablatures printed in oblong quarto contained four staves per page. Gardano's three editions of keyboard intablature also held four staves (in two systems) per page.

PAGINATION AND SIGNATURES

In the sixteenth century, methods of numbering leaves varied with the printer. Gardano used pagination for almost all his editions,[45] Scotto tended to be inconsistent in his numbering system, especially in the early years. He preferred pagination for his madrigal editions, foliation for his liturgical publications and lute books, and simply numbered each piece in his early motet editions. By the 1550s pagination became standard in Scotto publications. Whatever the numbering system, Roman numerals appeared in the majority of Scotto's music editions until the 1550s, when they were superseded by arabic numbering.

Signatures appear on the bottom right-hand corner of the recto of at least the first and second leaves of a gathering. They almost always consist of a letter from the Latin alphabet and sometimes a brief phrase or signature title identifying the work. Signatures assisted the printer in assembling the book by enabling him to identify the order of the gatherings and the correct way to fold them. Since books were shipped and sold in unbound gatherings, signatures and signature titles also helped booksellers and their customers in distinguishing between different publications.

The signatures for a set of partbooks presented a unique problem. They had to be similar in order to show that the set belonged together, but they also had to differentiate each of the partbooks. Several methods were devised by music printers. One system consisted of starting all the partbooks with the same letter, but distinguishing among them by using a different font or doubling the letters (A–F for cantus, *a–f* for tenor, AA–FF for altus, etc.).[46] Scotto utilized this method for all of his pre-1545 music publications. Another method favored by Gardano and other Italian printers was to letter the partbooks consecutively (e.g., A–D for cantus, E–H for the tenor, I–M for the altus, etc.).[47] This scheme became the predominant system employed by the Scotto press from 1548 until 1572. A third system, in which each partbook contained the same signature in upper-case letters (e.g., A–E; A–E; A–E etc.), proved untenable, since it did not differentiate the partbooks. Scotto used this method for the brief period 1554–55, and only sporadically thereafter.[48]

TITLE PAGES

The development of the title page ran parallel to the history of printing as a whole. Deemed "one of the most distinct, visible advances from script to print,"[49] the title page not only played a substantive role in facilitating the organization of libraries and catalogues, but it also made a crucial contribution to the commercialization of the book trade.[50] It acted as an advertisement for the book, author, patron, and publisher all in one. It also offered convenience by providing the necessary data upon which consumers could base their decision whether or not they wished to purchase a book. This was especially crucial in the field of music, where the consumer more than likely did not have the musical expertise to browse through and comprehend a music edition laid out in separate partbooks.

Soon after the advent of the printing press, bookmen began to print short titles on the blank front leaf of the book. At the end of the fifteenth century, practically all books had title pages. At first the title page consisted of only a brief designation with all publishing information retained in the colophon at the end of the book. By the second decade of the sixteenth century, printers realized its marketing potential and soon presented prolix titles detailing the various sections of the book, identifying the author, editor, commentator, and/or translator, and displaying the printer's mark.[51]

The title pages of Venetian music editions took a longer time to evolve than those of other fields. Petrucci, at the beginning of the century, employed generic titles that simply identified the number and kind of pieces contained in the volume. This practice continued through the 1530s. Only in the early 1540s, with the commercialization of music printing, did the title page catch up with other fields. Both Gardano and Scotto quickly adopted more elaborate titles promoting the fame of the composer, the novelty of the music, and, most significantly, the correctness of the edition. Their earliest music publications reflected the new marketing approach, as seen in the title page to Gombert's first book of four-voice motets:

> Of the most excellent Gombert, by his skillful genius chief among those in the
> art of music, *maestro di cappella* of Emperor Charles V, Music for four voices
> (commonly called motets), apt for viols and for shawm band. Recently com-
> posed with great diligence, never before published, but with great accuracy
> newly brought to light. Book one . . . [52]

PRINTER'S MARKS

Originally intended for the convenience of the book carriers, printer's marks became a visual advertisement for the publisher. They not only served a decorative function on the title page, but also acted as a trademark, attesting to the quality of the book. These symbols were considered so crucial to the identity of a press that they were regulated by the government. In Paris, François I banned the use of any printer's mark that might be mistaken for one of an existing press,[53] and in Venice the Magistrato alla Giustizia Vecchia oversaw the recording and exchanging of printer's marks.[54]

Devices began as simple monograms of the publishing house, as seen with Ottaviano Scotto I's printer's marks (see fig. 2.4). Soon printers and publishers

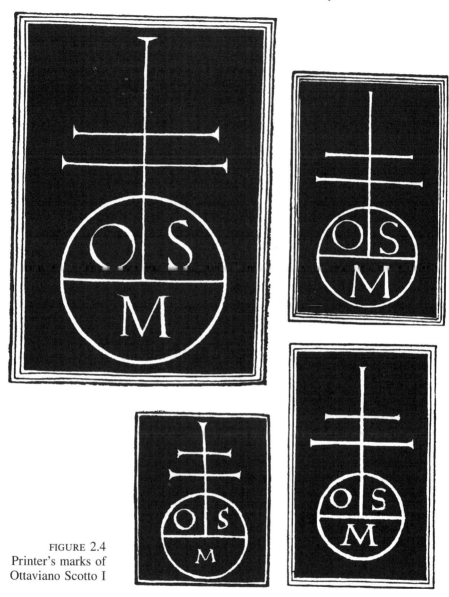

FIGURE 2.4
Printer's marks of
Ottaviano Scotto I

created woodcuts depicting animals, allegorical figures, and emblems to signify their press. Francesco Rampazetto's device portrayed two cherubs holding laurel wreaths with the motto "Et animo et corpore." Giacomo Vincenti, both in partnership with Ricciardo Amadino and later by himself, used the pine cone as his device. After his separation from Vincenti, Amadino adopted the organ with the motto "Magis surdo quam organo" for his own printer's mark. Claudio Merulo chose a tree trunk with an upright, leafless branch containing the motto, "Simili frondescet virga metallo"

("Let a bough in the same metal [i.e. gold] put forth leaves"). Derived from a passage in Vergil's *Aeneid* (VI, 144), the branch represents Proserpina's golden bough with which Aeneas is advised to arm himself prior to his descent into Hades.[55] Marcolini's device also contained a complex allegory depicting three naked figures. An old winged man with an hour glass grabs the left arm of a young woman, who is ascending out of an abyss; the third figure, a creature with human body and serpent's tail, pulls the young woman's hair with his left hand, while in his right he holds a number of snakes. The motto "Veritas filia temporis" ("Truth as the daughter of time") informs us that the young woman represents truth, the old man time, and the figure with serpent's tail calumny (see fig. 2.5).[56]

Francesco Rampazetto

Giacomo Vincentti and Ricciardo
Amadino, then Vincenti alone

Ricciardo Amadino

Claudio Merulo

FIGURE 2.5 Printer's marks of various music printers

Francesco Marcolini da Forlì

Pietro Pietrasanta; also Francesco Rampazetto

FIGURE 2.5 (*continued*)

The Gardano press, during its long history, used no fewer than fifteen printer's marks, all of which portray a lion and bear clutching a rose with a fleur-de-lys at its center. A banner draped around the animals accommodates the motto "Concordes virtute et naturae miraculis." The lion and bear symbolize the name of Gardano's early patron, Leone Orsini, Bishop-elect of Fréjus, and the rose was part of the Orsini coat of arms (see fig. 2.6.)

In sixteenth-century Venice, a complicated iconography developed in the devices employed by some presses that coincided with emblems associated with the Most Serene Republic itself. The central themes of peace, justice, fame, virtue, victory, and wisdom all symbolized the power and wealth of Venice and became part of a propaganda campaign that in the sixteenth century grew into what is known as the "myth of Venice."[57] These symbols, along with other attributes representing Venice, appeared in the sculpture and paintings that decorated the public buildings of Venice, in particular the Ducal Palace.[58]

Some of the publishing houses of Venice appropriated these emblems for their own printer's marks. The dolphin and anchor, maritime symbols of speed and stability, became the device of the famed Aldine press. Justice with her sword and balancing scales appeared on the title pages of books issued by the Bindoni firm. Virtue, another central theme of the Venetian Republic, appears holding palm frond and banner containing the motto "Virtus Dei donum" ("Virtue, gift of God") on the

Lion and bear I

Lion and bear II

Lion and bear III

FIGURE 2.6 Lion and bear printer's marks of Antonio Gardano

Lion and bear IV

Lion and bear V

Lion and bear VI

Lion and bear VII

FIGURE 2.6 (*continued*)

title pages of music books issued by Pietro Pietrasanta and later by Francesco Rampazetto (see fig. 2.5).

The symbolic connection between printer's marks and the Most Serene Republic was no more evident than in a series of printer's marks belonging to the Scotto press. Three of the emblems representing the Scotto firm during Girolamo's directorship were intrinsically linked with the new iconography of Venice. The main device of the press depicted an anchor surrounded by a palm frond and an olive branch with the initials S.O.S. (Signum Octaviani Scoti) all set into a log. A banner above the anchor proclaims the motto: "In tenebris fulget" ("In darkness he shines"), a reference to the Scotto name, of which the Greek, *skotos*, means darkness.[59] The anchor and log, symbols of political stability both on sea and land, refer directly to Venice, the great maritime power with dominions on the Italian mainland. The olive branch represents peace, while the palm frond as we have seen symbolizes victory or virtue.[60] The Scotto press used nine different printer's marks containing the anchor design (see fig. 2.7).

Fame and peace, prominent symbols of the Venetian Republic, appear in two other series of Scotto printer's marks. The image of Fame occurs in five different printer's marks used by Girolamo (fig. 2.8). In all of them, Fame is personified with her trumpet standing atop a winged sphere inscribed with the monogram O.S.M. In some cases, the motto "Famam extendere factis est virtutis opus" ("To spread fame by deeds is the work of virtue") frames the printer's mark. The motto, a rewording of "sed famam extendere factis hoc virtutis opus" from Vergil's *Aeneid* (Book X, lines 468–69), had a twofold connotation. It represented the printing press as an important vehicle, which offered to composers immortality or lasting fame.[61] As a central symbol of the Republic, the word "virtutis" also depicted Venice as a virtuous state.

Along with virtue, the concept of political peace was an important aspect of the myth of Venice. Both themes figure prominently in a third emblem used by the Scotto press. In two different printer's marks, Peace appears seated atop a globe of Europe and Africa (Peace I) or the celestial skies (Peace II) inscribed with the initials O.S.M. (fig. 2.9). She holds her symbol, an olive branch, in her right hand, while in her left hand she unfurls a banner declaring *Fiat pax in virtute tua* ("Let peace be in thy strength").[62]

Sometimes in commissioned editions a different device would substitute for a mark. A few display the heraldic device of a patron, such as the emblem of the dolphin for Giovanni Ferro, count of Macerata, in the *Corona della Morte* (1568) (fig. 2.10) or the "palle" of Cosimo de' Medici, duke of Florence, found in Corteccia, *Libro primo de madriali a 4* (Venice: Scotto, 1544; Gardano, 1547). Others exhibit the printer's mark of another bookman, presumably the underwriter of the edition. This is particularly the case with a series of music editions printed by Scotto, dating from 1565–68, where several different devices appear, such as Giacomo Anielli Sanvito's device of an eagle (fig. 2.11), Giovanni Maria Bonelli's printer's mark of Minerva, and Pietro da Fino's emblem of a rooster.[63]

In a few instances, music printers employed woodcut illustrations that had no connection with a dedicatee or another printer, but instead represent fanciful titles given to the edition, such as the circular labyrinth found in the Scotto *Motetti del Laberinto* series of 1554–55 (see fig. 2.12) Illustrations were sometimes recycled from earlier non-music publications. The labyrinth first appeared in Scotto's 1543 edition of Ovid's *Heroides*, where it depicted both the story of Theseus and the Minotaur (Book X) and Hermione and Orestes (Book VIII).

Sometimes woodcuts found on title pages had hidden meanings, such as those appearing in a series of three music editions, that make reference to a quarrel between two printing firms. In September 1538, Antonio Gardano published his first motet anthology for five voices, which he entitled *Motetti del frutto*. Appropriately, the title page contains a custom-made woodcut illustrating an arrangement of fruit.

Anchor I

Anchor II

Anchor III

Anchor IV

Anchor V

FIGURE 2.7 Anchor printer's marks of Girolamo Scotto

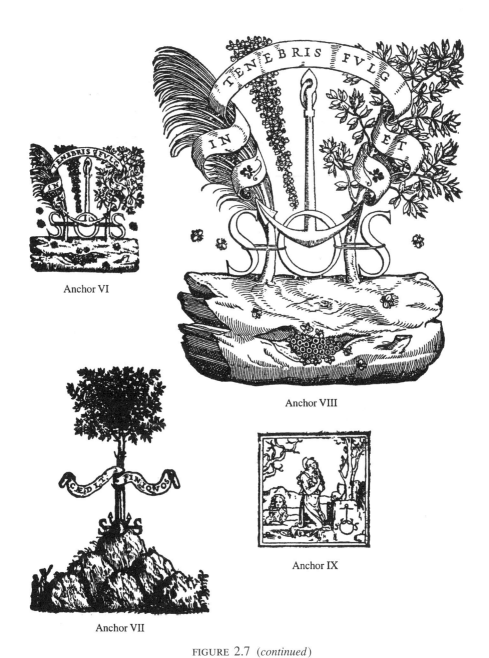

Anchor VI

Anchor VIII

Anchor VII

Anchor IX

FIGURE 2.7 (*continued*)

Fame I

Fame II

Fame III

Fame V

Fame IV

FIGURE 2.8
Fame printer's marks
of Girolamo Scotto

In January 1539, the Ferrarese firm of Johannes Buglhat, Antonio Hucher, and Henrico de Campis brought out a different collection of motets, the *Moteti de la Simia* with a titlecut depicting a monkey eating fruit. The monkey obviously refers to the title of the volume, but the illustration contains a further connotation, for the fruit that he is eating alludes to Gardano's earlier *Motetti del frutto* edition. Later that year Gardano responded with yet another collection of six-voice motets as part of his *Motetti del frutto* series. The title page displays an even stranger woodcut than the one found in the *Moteti de la Simia*. Here, a monkey surrounded by half-eaten fruit is being attacked by a lion and bear (see fig. 2.13). Gardano explains in his dedication that an incautious monkey has tried to steal his fruit, which has been

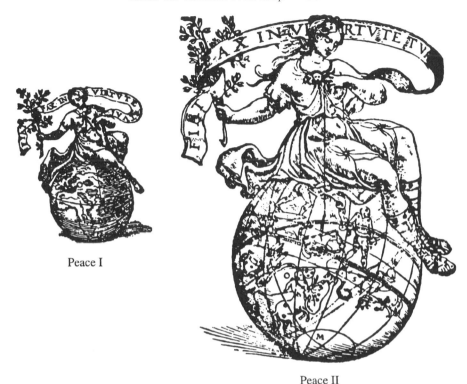

Peace I

Peace II

FIGURE 2.9 Peace printer's marks of Girolamo Scotto

vigilantly guarded by the ferocious lion and the cruel bear. The fruit, of course, symbolizes the motets in his original *Motetti del frutto* collection, while the monkey signifies the *Moteti de la simia* of the Ferrarese printers. Finally the lion and bear, who protect the fruit from the monkey, are an obviously reference to Gardano's own printer's mark.

Since all three editions survive, we can piece together the meaning of this allegory. Unfortunately, no evidence has come to light to assist us in the interpretation of another enigmatic title cut that appears in the cantus partbook of Anselmo Reulx's *Madrigali a quatro voci* (Venice: Scotto, 1543). Depicting a man being ravaged by two horses, this arcane woodcut might also refer to a conflict between hostile printers. Without further evidence, however, we can only suggest that it might be a simple representation of the Hercules story, where King Diomedes of Thrace is eaten by his wild mares (fig. 2.14).

On rare occasions, an extremely elaborate title cut would appear with or without a printer's mark in Venetian music publications. Two such examples occur in Willaert's *Musica nova* (Venice: Gardano, 1559) and Stefano Rossetto's *Lamento di Olimpia* (Venice: Scotto, 1567). Each contains a large pictorial compartment with

FIGURE 2.10 *Corona della morte* (Venice: Scotto, 1568); basso title page. Reproduced with permission of the Civico Museo Bibliografico Musicale, Bologna.

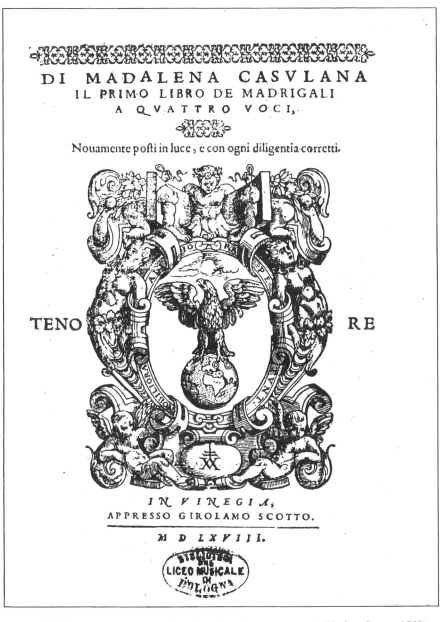

FIGURE 2.11 Casulana, *Il primo libro de madrigali a quattro voci* (Venice: Scotto, 1568), tenor title page. Reproduced with permission of the Civico Museo Bibliografico Musicale, Bologna.

TENOR

MOTETTI DEL LABERINTO,
A quatro Voci Libro Secondo.

Sacrarum Cantionum siue Motettorum,

THOME CRICQVILLONIS:

CLEMENTIS NON PAPÆ,

Aliorumque Præstantissimorum Auctorum.

CHOEO.

ILLVSTRISSIMI AC REVERENDISSIMI DOMINI,
D. Christophori Madruutij S. E. E. Cardinalis, Episcopi,
Principis Tridentino , & Brixiensis.
Paulus Caligopœus dedicauit.

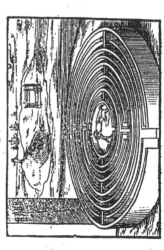

Venetiis apud Hieronymum Scotum
MDLIIII.

Motetti del Frutto (1538)

Moteti de la Simia (1539)

Motetti del Frutto, 6 vv (1539)

FIGURE 2.13 Woodcuts used on title pages of the *Motetti del Frutto* and *Motetti della Simia*

FIGURE 2.14 Anselmo Reulx, *Madrigali a quattro voci* (Venice: Scotto, 1543), cantus title page. Reproduced with permission of the Civico Museo Bibliografico Musicale, Bologna.

C A N T V S

DI ANSELMO REVLX

MADRIGALI A QVATTRO VOCI

NVOVAMENTE DAL PROPRIO AVTTOR

COMPOSTI ET MANDATI

IN LVCE.

Venetijs apud Hieronymum Scotum.

1 5 4 3.

holes at the top and/or center into which type was inserted for title and publishing information (see figs. 2.15 and 2.16). The richly decorative compartments were custom-made specifically for these expensive editions; as far as we know, they were only used one more time by their printers. Scotto employed the Rossetto compartment for the title page of *I dolci frutti: Primo libro de vaghi et dilettevoli madrigali* (1570), and Gardano's heirs recycled the *Musica nova* compartment in their edition of Fiorino's *Libro secondo: Canzonelle a tre e a quattro voci* (1574).[64]

DECORATIVE INITIALS

One of the important typographical distinctions between music and other printing specializations was the inordinate number of woodcut initials needed to produce a set of partbooks. A normal music edition demanded one and sometimes two woodcut initials for every page, while only a handful of initials were required for an entire volume of a standard text edition. During the period 1538–72 the Gardano firm employed fourteen different sets of decorated initials, while the Scotto press utilized seventeen (see figs. 2.17 and 2.18). Some series included a complete alphabet with a few duplicate letters, while others contained only of a handful of letters. The sets varied in size to accommodate different formats. In general, the designs of the initial sets were unique to the press in which they were employed. One exception, however, were the "Putti" initials containing small boys playing in and out of the letters that appeared in publications issued by Gardano (series VI) and Scotto from the early 1540s through at least the 1560s (see figs. 2.17 and 2.18).

The design of initials employed by the music presses reflected what was in vogue at the time.[65] In their first year or two of operations, Antonio Gardano and Girolamo Scotto used fanciful calligraphic Gothic initials (Gardano Series I and II) commonly found in manuscripts and books printed up until the 1530s. By 1540–41, the two printers abruptly changed to descriptive or decorative initials. The symbolic shift from the calligraphic Gothic of the manuscript tradition to "humanist" iconographic initials went hand in hand with the introduction of the single-impression method of music printing. These woodcut initials illustrate many of the decorative styles commonly used in Cinquecento books from 1540 onwards. Floral or stylized botanical decoration appears in several sets of initials (Gardano's series III-V and Scotto's series of "White" and "Dark florals"). Gardano's series VIII depicts uninhabited landscapes. Several sets are inhabited in style, such as the "Putti" initials mentioned above; Scotto's "Ghosts" series, containing naked boys, whose arms and legs often go through the letters; Gardano's "Animals" (Series XII), where each initial depicts a different whimsical creature, such as the snail, griffin, or turtle; and Scotto's "Centaurs" series, portraying mythical half-human, half-animal figures such as centaurs, satyrs, and mermaids (see figs. 2.17 and 2.18)

Scotto and Gardano also possessed their own distinctive sets of historiated initials. These iconographic initials represent a character or a scene that often has no

FIGURE 2.15 Stefano Rossetto *Il Lamento di Olimpia* (Venice: Scotto, 1567); tenor title page. Reproduced with permission of the Civico Museo Bibliografico Musicale, Bologna.

FIGURE 2.16 Willaert, *Musica nova* (Venice: Gardano, 1559), bassus title page;
Reproduced with permission of the Civico Museo Bibliografico Musicale, Bologna.

Large Bible   Dark floral I   Dark floral II   Dark floral III

Small Bible   Putti   White floral I   White floral II   Ghosts

Medium Bible   Centaurs   Calligraphic Gothic   Trees

Virtues   Large knight

Large myth   Crest

FIGURE 2.17 Decorative initials found in Girolamo Scotto's music editions

I: Calligraphic Gothic

II: Calligraphic Gothic

III: White floral

IV: White floral

V: White floral

VI: Putti

VII: Inhabited
landscape

VIII: Landscape

IX: Inhabited

X: Knight

XI: Animals

XIV: Myth

FIGURE 2.18 Decorative initials found in Antonio Gardano's music editions. Note: Roman numerals refer to "Series" described by Lewis, *Antonio Gardano*, 1:50.

connection with the music text. Narrative initials on biblical and mythological subjects appear in varying sizes. Both printers had different "Myth" sets, portraying classical scenes. They also possessed larger "Knight" initials (Gardano's Series X) illustrating chivalric stories. Scotto also owned very large "Virtue" sets depicting the cardinal virtues (see fig. 2.17).

Quite often the characters or scenes portrayed in these "parlanti" initials correspond to the letter they decorate, a common feature among initials dating from the middle of the sixteenth century.[66] Some depict mythological figures, such as Venus with Cupid for the letter *V* in Scotto's "Tree series" and Gardano's Series XIV (see figs. 2.17 and 2.18) or Bacchus for the letter *B* for Scotto's "Large myth" series (see fig. 2.17). Other initials narrate a particular mythological story, such as Hercules (Ercole) fighting the lion of Nemea for the letter *E* or the drowning of Thisbe for the letter *T*. In some cases, the iconographical reference to the letter is not obvious. Apollo chasing Daphne for the letter *L* connotes the laurel tree (Lauro) into which Daphne is transformed.

Historiated initials also portray biblical figures and scenes. As seen in figure 2.17, the letter *I* of Scotto's "Small Bible" set depicts John on the island of Patmos. King David appears in the letter *D* of his "Medium Bible" set. Scotto's "Large Bible" series includes the dramatic scene of David slaying Goliath for the letter *G*.[67] The letter *M* of Scotto's Virtue initials illustrates the cardinal virtue of moderation.

Another type of decorated initial illustrates heraldic coats of arms. Most of the letters in Scotto's Crest set depict the oak tree atop six mounts emblem of the Cesi family, sometimes with the six "palle" of the Medici coat of arms.

TYPE FONTS

The 1575 inventory cited in the epigraph at the beginning of this chapter informs us of the variety of music type fonts Antonio Gardano owned during the thirty years he operated his press.[68] It lists eight different music type fonts, including four for polyphonic music, one for lute intabulation, one for keyboard intabulation, and two for Roman chant books. The polyphonic music fonts are grouped according to the particular size and book format for which they were utilized. The first of the four, "Un Canto figurato ditto della Pegorina," can be identified with the music font Gardano had made especially for Willaert's *Musica nova* (1559).[69]

The second font, "un Canto comun ordinario," describes the music typeface used in regular quarto books (either oblong or upright). According to Lewis, during the thirty years Antonio Gardano directed his press, he employed four different music typefaces for his quarto publications. "Un Canto comun ordinario" could then refer to more than one type face in that size category lumped together, or more likely, it might actually describe a single typeface, since three of the four typefaces utilized by Gardano disappeared from his publications after 1546.[70]

Among the remaining music typefaces listed in the inventory, "un Cantino pi-colo delle Villotte" and "un Canto grande per real forma" were used for the small octavo and the large folio choirbook editions, respectively. The "ponzoni de Inta-bolatura de lauto et madre et forme" and the "Intabolatura d'organo ponzoni madre et forme" undoubtedly refer to the typefaces Antonio employed for his lute and keyboard publications. The 1575 inventory also lists two Roman plainchant fonts ("Doi Canti fermi con madre ponzoni et forme"). Although no plainchant editions from Antonio Gardano tenure at the press have come to light, his heirs did publish at least three liturgical books containing plainchant in 1587 and 1591.[71]

Scotto, in turn, used four polyphonic typefaces over the course of his profes-sional career. He also employed two typefaces for lute tablature, and three for Roman plain chant. The polyphonic music typeface with which Girolamo inaugurated his music printing enterprise remained in use for twenty years (see fig. 2.19). A number of other printers employed this elegant font at one time or another. It appeared in the limited output of music editions by the Ferrarese firm of Buglhat and Hucher. Gardano used it for several brief periods from 1538 to 1547. Even the Roman printer Antonio Blado employed it in an undated collection of madrigals by Hubert Naich entitled *Exercitium seraficum*. It has been suggested that since all of these printers utilized the same music typeface, they must have owned only the matrices, while the craftsman who created the type kept the punches.[72] Yet as noted above, only Scotto consistently made use of this typeface for over twenty years. It is highly unlikely that a wealthy publisher, who owned numerous typefaces, would have con-tinued to purchase matrices for such a long period of time. Scotto, as the most established printer of the group, must have bought the punches, possibly at the inception of his music-printing career; he then could have sold or rented the matrices, in particular to Gardano, who reverted to this font in 1542–43 and again in 1546–47. Blado might also have bought or borrowed the matrices of this font from Scotto during a possible trip to Venice or in Rome. A connection between Scotto and the Roman printer is not unlikely since the Scotto press maintained close ties with printers in Rome as far back as 1516.[73]

In 1554–56 Scotto experimented with new music type font of larger proportions. They had bigger, wider note heads, which opened up the page and gave it more legibility than his smaller type face. He called his new music type font "stampato grosso" to distinguish it from the smaller typeface. Now a client wishing to have a work printed by the Scotto press had a choice between the firm's standard music typeface and the new "stampato grosso." Publications of sacred music, in particular, apparently dictated the need for the larger music font, as Palestrina noted: "It would require a great deal of expense especially were the larger notes and letters used, as church publications properly demand."[74] Indeed, all but three of the sacred publications issued by Girolamo Scotto after 1554 display the larger music fonts.[75]

The Scotto press also owned three music fonts designed for roman plainchant notation. Two of them were multiple-impression type fonts; in which the pieces of

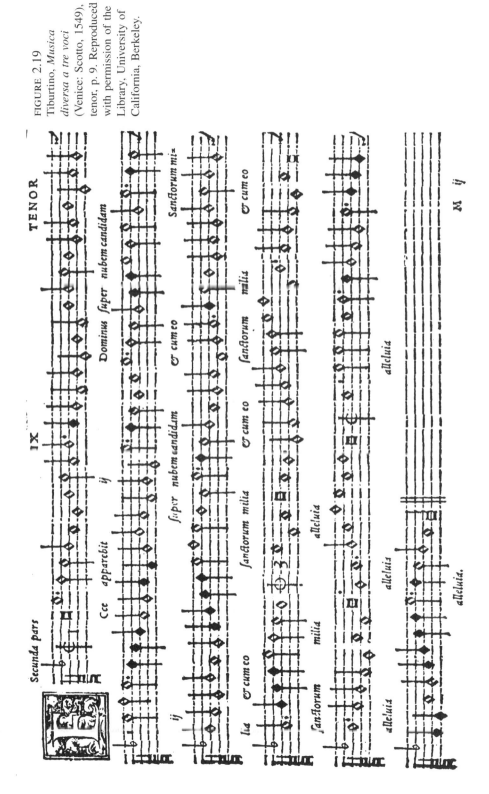

FIGURE 2.19
Tiburtino, *Musica diversa a tre voci* (Venice: Scotto, 1549), tenor, p. 9. Reproduced with permission of the Library, University of California, Berkeley.

type contained notes without their staves. Following the tradition of printing plain-chant, Scotto would print the music staves first in red ink; the paper would then go through the press a second time with the notes and text underlay printed in black ink[76] A third typeface was specially created as a single-impression font. It was utilized in only one extant missal printed by Scotto, the folio edition of a *Missale Romanum* of 1560.

In 1536, Johannes Sultzbach brought out in Naples Francesco da Milano's *Intavolatura de viola o vero lauto . . . libro primo della Fortuna e libro secondo*, the first lute publications produced by a single-impression method.[77] The technique differed from that of mensural notation in that a single piece of type contained both one character and a single segment representing only one line of the six-line staff. These pieces of type were then lined up vertically on top of each other to create the six-line staff of the lute tablature. Rhythmic symbols, mensuration signs, text, and other miscellaneous type then completed the forme, which was then run through the press once.[78]

This method of printing lute tablatures, though more labor-intensive and time-consuming than the single-impression technique devised for mensural notation, was commercially more viable for lute publications than either the earlier woodblock or multiple-impression technique.[79] It thus became the primary one used for printing lute intabulations throughout the sixteenth century.

The single impression process for tablature was not employed in Venice until 1546, when a series of six unsigned editions financed by the Scotto press and eight lute books printed by Gardano appeared. The wide separation between segments of the staff reveals that during the 1540s Scotto used individual pieces of type for every character, rhythmic symbol, and line of the staff in his lute books. By the 1560s Scotto and Gardano improved the technique by utilizing rules for the blank staves which extended over the width of several characters instead of a single character font (see fig. 2.20). The longer rules had several advantages over the previous system. First, they helped stabilize the smaller character pieces of the forme, creating an interlocking jig-saw puzzle pattern; they also decreased the number of blank staff fonts needed, and finally they improved the visual appearance of the music page with neater and smoother-looking staves. This kind of single-impression type, known as "nested" type, was employed by Susato and other Netherlandish and German music printers for their mensural notation rather than the traditional pieces of type containing a five-line staff favored by Italian and French printers.[80]

Whereas both Venetian printers issued books in lute tablature, only Gardano ventured into the specialized area of keyboard music, when, in 1549, he produced his first keyboard edition, Jacques Buus's *Intabolatura d'organo di recercari . . . Libro primo*. The format of Gardano's edition, noted in the 1575 inventory as intavolatura, is similar to modern mensural keyboard notation. It employs two staves, the upper containing five lines, the lower six lines. The notation denotes hand-division between upper and lower staves; it includes bar-lines and relatively good vertical alignment of the notes (see fig. 2.21). This edition was not only the first

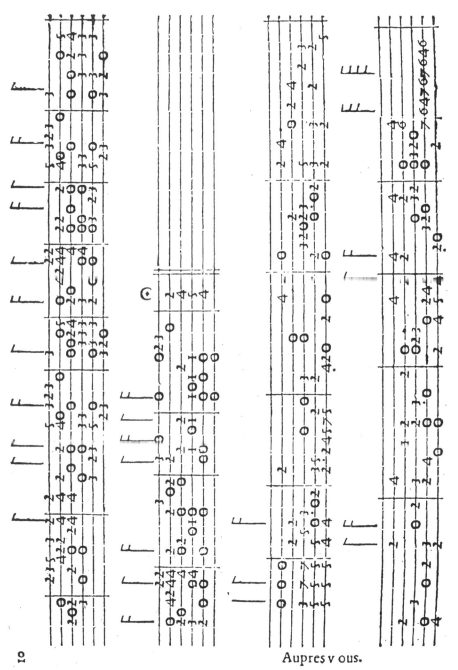

Aupres v ous.

FIGURE 2.20 Bianchini, *Intabolatura de lauto* (Venice: Scotto, 1563), p. 10. Reproduced with permission of the Musiksammlung der Österreichischen National bibliothek, Vienna

66

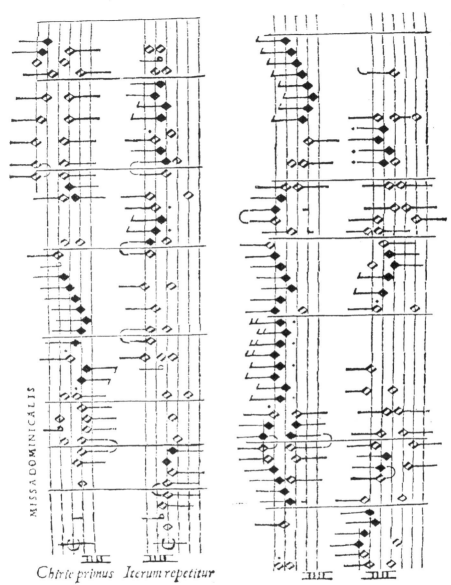

FIGURE 2.21 Cavazzoni, *Intabolatura d'organo* (Venice: Gardano, ca. 1555), fol. 12ᵛ. Reproduced with permission of the Civico Museo Bibliografico Musicale, Bologna.

keyboard intavolatura issued by Gardano, but also the first keyboard publication in Italy to use the technique of single-impression movable type, as Gardano proudly proclaimed on his title page: "novamente stampata con carateri di stagno" (newly printed with tin type).[82]

Buus presumably commissioned the edition. He dedicated the book to Paolo di Hanna, who was a member of a notable Flemish family with Venetian citizenship. Another relative (his father?), Giovanni da Hana, was a close friend of Titian. He commissioned three paintings from the artist, one of which, an *Ecce Homo*, was owned by Paolo.[83] Buus refers to Paolo as a youth ("Giovane"), which points to the instructional purpose of the edition.[84] The format of keyboard intavolatura, compared with partbooks and open score, was easier to play from, and thus was aimed at those who "are inexperienced and do not possess the art of Music."[85]

Both lute tablature and keyboard editions must have been very expensive to produce. Only three keyboard editions survive from the period of Antonio Gardano's tenure at the press,[86] and neither Girolamo Scotto nor his heirs appears to have issued any editions using keyboard intavolatura.

Paper, formats, title-page styles, typefaces, decorative initials, and printer's marks were all an important part in the shaping of the marketing process. Public taste dictated subtle changes that occurred in the physical features of music books. Gardano and Scotto remained cognizant of this fact, by operating printing shops whose organization and working habits embodied the attributes of thriving sixteenth-century music presses. The production of music books, however, was only one aspect of the business. In order to succeed in the marketplace, each of the music printers had to direct a multifarious operation. Financial contracts, marketing of books, distribution routes, composers, and patrons all played an important role in the intricate world of music printing and publishing, as we shall see in the chapters that follow.

NOTES

1. "Idem ordegni di stamparia. / Un Canto figurato ditto della Pegorina con le sue madre ponzoni et forme. / Item un Canto comun ordinario con le madre ponzoni et forme. / Item un Cantino picolo delle Villotte con madre ponzoni et forme. / Item un Canto grande per real forma con madre et ponzoni. / Item ponzoni de Intabolatura de lauto et madre et forme. / Item Intabolatura d'organo ponzoni madre et forme. / Item Doi Canti fermi con madre ponzoni et forme. / Item Doi torcoli da stampar." Transcription extracted from Claudio Sartori, "Una dinastia di editori musicali," *La bibliofilia* 58 (1956), 182.

2. See fig. 4.2 and discussion of publisher's book lists in chap. 4. An annotated catalogue of the Gardano book list appears in Agee, *Gardano Music Printing Firms*, 360–83. For modern transcriptions of both lists see Oscar Mischiati, *Indici, cataloghi e avvisi degli editori e librai musicali italiani dal 1591 al 1798* (Florence, 1984), 83–92; 99–106; see also Geneviève Thibault, "Deux catalogues de libraires musicaux: Vincenti et Gardane (Venise 1591), *Revue de musicologie* 11(1930), 8–18, for another transcription of the Gardano *Indice*.

3. ASV, Notarile Atti B. Solian, b. 11876, fols. 185ʳ–186.

4. Since little evidence about the day-to-day operation of a Venetian press survives,

information on the workforce of French and Netherlandish presses in Febvre and Martin, *Coming of the Book*, 129–30 and Voet, *The Golden Compasses*, 2: 343–53 have been used in this section.

5. Brown, *Venetian Printing Press*, 88.

6. Ibid.

7. As was the case with the Plantin press; see Voet, *Golden Compasses*, 2: 335.

8. "Stampa in ditta casa con doi torcoli." ASV, Dieci Savii sopra le Decime in Rialto, Condizione di Decima, 1566, San Marco, b. 126, no. 115.

9. In requesting a privilege on 6 May 1542, Girolamo Scotto mentions a copy made of Piccolomini's *De la institutione di tutta la vita de l'homo*. ASV, Senato Terra, Registro 32, fol. 29 (new fol. 50).

10. The term "edition" used throughout this study is defined as including all copies of a text printed from the same setting of type. For a more detailed description see Fredson Bowers, *Principles of Bibliographical Description* (New York, 1962), 42–77 and Stanley Boorman, "Edition," pt. 3 glossary of *Music Printing and Publishing*, ed. D. W. Krummel and Stanley Sadie (New York, 1990), 503–7.

11. In the case of smaller presses, the organization of the musical works in the book was determined by the decorative initials. If a press owned only one set of decorative initials, then the compositor had to plan one piece of music beginning with a particular letter to be set in each forme; see Forney, "Tielman Susato," 147. Since both Gardano and Scotto owned several sets of decorative initials, this was not a factor in the sequence of the contents of their music books.

12. Philip Gaskell. *A New Introduction to Bibliography* (Oxford, 1972), 40.

13. For an explanation of formats, see the section on format further on in this chapter.

14. According to Gaskell, *New Introduction*, 80, Italian printers used chases with thumbscrews instead of quoins (small wooden wedges driven between the furniture and chase) up until the eighteenth century.

15. Lewis, *Antonio Gardano*, 1:66, theorizes that the patent Gardano received in 1542 for the discovery of a new way of printing music was for this special grooved furniture. Scotto's employment of the same mechanism three years before Gardano proves this hypothesis to be untenable.

16. Gaskell, *New Introduction*, 109.

17. *Antonio Gardano*, 1:64.

18. Ibid., 1:66.

19. J. Bernstein, *Music Printing in Venice*, 334–37.

20. Lewis, *Antonio Gardano*, 1:68.

21. J. Bernstein, *Music Printing in Venice*, 278; for other examples see Lewis, *Antonio Gardano* 1:300; 439.

22. Lewis, 1:512.

23. J. Bernstein, 564.

24. Ibid., 322.

25. I am using the term "state" to mean an alteration of a book where a change in content is made. See Bowers, *Principles of Bibliographical Description*, 42–77 and Boorman, "Edition," pt. 3 glossary of *Music Printing and Publishing*.

26. On this point see Paul F. Grendler, "Form and Function in Italian Renaissance Popular Books," *Renaissance Quarterly* 46 (1993): 451–85.

27. For discussion of the relationship of the appearance of music books and their intended purpose, see Lewis, "The Printed Music Book in Context: Observations on Some Sixteenth-Century Editions," *Music Library Association Notes* 40 (1990): 899–918.

28. Febvre and Martin, *Coming of the Book*, 40.

29. Carlo Castellani, "Watermarks," in *Early Venetian Printing Illustrated* (New York, 1895), 3. See also Febvre and Martin, *Coming of the Book*, 33–44.

30. Giuseppe Fumagalli, *Lexicon Typographicum Italiae* (Florence, 1905), p. xxvi.

31. *Index Aureliensis: Catalogus Librorum Sedecimo Saeculo Impressorum* (Baden-Baden, and Geneva, 1962), 1: 47, no. 108.120.

32. Charles Briquet, *Les Filigranes* (Paris, 1907), 1:2–3; A. F. Gasparinetti, "Notes on Early Italian Papermaking," *The Paper Maker* 27 (1958): 25–32 at 25; and Gaskell, *New Introduction*, 67.

33. Konrad Haebler, *The Study of Incunabula*, trans. Lucy Eugenia Osborne (New York, 1933), 49. A perusal of the leaf measurements of Italian music incunabula listed in the catalogue in Duggan, *Italian Music Incunabula*, confirms this statement.

34. Duggan, 130.

35. Chapman, "Andrea Antico," 3: 448–53, pls. 13 and 14. See chap. 3 for a fuller description of this contract.

36. Cusick, *Valerio Dorico*, 172.

37. Lewis, *Antonio Gardano*, 1:39.

38. Boorman, Glossary in *Music Printing and Publishing*, 510–13; Gaskell, New Introduction, 80.

39. Krummel, "Oblong Format in Early Music Books," *The Library*, 5th ser., 26 (1971): 312–24 at 312; Forney, "Tielman Susato," 164–68; and Lewis, *Antonio Gardano*, 1:37.

40. Lewis, *Antonio Gardano*, 1:35–36.

41. On the unsigned music publications printed during these years see J. Bernstein, "Burning Salamander," 483–501.

42. Donna Cardamone, *The Canzone villanesca alla napolitana and Related Forms, 1537–1570* (Studies in Musicology 45; Ann Arbor, Mich., 1981), 1:7. Earlier printers such as Petrucci, Antico/Scotto, and Attaingnant also employed the format.

43. See J. Bernstein, *Music Printing in Renaissance Venice*, 495–97.

44. The use of five staves only lasted for two years; Scotto then reverted back to the more economical six staves of music.

45. Lewis, *Antonio Gardano*, 1:36.

46. This scheme was employed by the Parisian printer Attaingnant. See catalogue to Heartz, *Pierre Attaingnant*. It also appears on rare occasions in later Scotto editions.

47. These included Petrucci, Dorico, Antico/Scotto, and Gardano. See Lewis, *Antonio Gardano*, 1:38, and catalogues in Cusick, *Valerio Dorico*, and Boorman, "Petrucci at Fossombrone."

48. This method was commonly used by Moderne and Susato.

49. S. H. Steinberg, *Five Hundred Years of Printing* (London, 1955), 105.

50. Eisenstein, *Printing Press*, 1:52.

51. See Mortimer, *Harvard College Library . . . Italian 16th Century Books* for examples in the transformation of the title page.

52. "Gomberti excellentissimi, et inventione in hac arte facile principis, chori Caroli quinti imperatoris magistri, musica quatuor vocum (vulgo motecta nuncupatur), Lyris maioribus, ac Tibiis imparibus accomodata. Nuper maximo authoris studio composita, nulli hactenus visa, sed noviter accuratissime in lucem edita. Liber primus . . ." This unusual word order is part of the advertising for the volume, giving greatest prominence to the composer and less to the actual contents, Music for four voices. Scotto printed the first edition of Gombert's First Book of Four-Voice Motets in 1539; Gardano issued another edition with the same title in 1541. For details on these two editions see J. Bernstein, *Music Printing in Venice*, 228–29 and Lewis, *Antonio Gardano*, 1: 289–94.

53. Steinberg, *Five Hundred Years of Printing*, 63.

54. A register of printers and their emblems appears in ASV, Magistrato alla Giustizia Vecchia, Constituti, b. 49, reg. 79. See Giacomo Moro, "Insegne librarie e marche tipografiche in un registro veneziano del '500," *La Bibliofilia* 91 (1989): 51–80.

55. Rebecca A. Edwards, "Claudio Merulo: Servant of the State and Musical Entrepreneur in Later Sixteenth-Century Venice" (Ph.D. diss., Princeton University, 1990), 186–87.

56. For further information on Marcolini's device and motto, see Fritz Saxl, "Veritas Filia Temporis," in *Philosophy and History: Essays Presented to Ernst Cassirer*, eds. Raymond Klibansky and H. J. Paton (Oxford, 1936), 197–202.

57. For more on the myth of Venice see Ellen Rosand, "Music in the Myth of Venice," *Renaissance Quarterly* 30 (1977): 511–37; Myron Gilmore, "Myth and Reality in Venetian Political Theory," in *Renaissance Venice*, ed. John R. Hale (London, 1973), 431–44; and Logan, *Culture and Society in Venice*, 1–19.

58. Juergen Schulz, *Venetian Painted Ceilings of the Renaissance* (Berkeley and Los Angeles, 1968), 104–16.

59. Hugh William Davies, *Devices of the Early Printers* (London, 1935), 500–1, and Bridges, "Publishing of Arcadelt's First Book," 1: 144.

60. James Hall, *Dictionary of Subjects and Symbols of Art* (New York, 1974), 144.

61. This quotation from the *Aeneid* was well known in musical circles. Tinctoris, for example, used it to glorify music and composers in his *Expositio manus*, chap. 19, lines 6–12. The Tinctoris passage is cited in Rob Wegman, "From Maker to Composer: Improvisation and Musical Authorship in the Low Countries, 1450–1500," *JAMS* 49 (1996), 409–79 at 461.

62. The frame to a woodcut found on several Scotto publications dating from the late 1560s also contains a motto referring to virtue: "Virtus in omni re dominatur" ("Virtue rules in all matters") (see fig. 2.10 below). This motto reappears in one of Melchiorre Scotto's printer's marks depicting the three graces (see fig. 6.2).

63. The Bonelli and da Fino printer's marks are reproduced in Giuseppina Zappella, *Le marche dei tipografie degli editori italiani del Cinquecento* (Milan, [1986]), nos. 845 and 579. For further information on these editions and these other printers see chaps. 5 and 7.

64. Agee, *Gardano Music Printing Firms*, 109.

65. Terms used to describe initial styles are those of Steven Harvard, *Ornamental Initials: The Woodcut Initials of Christopher Plantin, a Complete Catalogue* (New York, 1974), 1–3. The names of specific initial series are my own.

66. Lamberto Donati, "Le iniziali iconografiche del XVI secolo," in *Studi bibliografici* (Florence, 1967), 219–39. The term "parlanti" is used by Franca Petrucci Nardelli, *La lettera e l'immagine: le iniziali "parlanti" nella tipografia italiana (secc. XVI–XVII)* (Florence, 1991).

67. Petrucci Nardelli, *La lettera*, 38–39, reproduces twenty-one letters from the "Medium Bible" and "Trees" series of Scotto initials.

68. A description of the technical process of how music type was produced appears in several music-printing studies such as D. W. Krummel, *English Music Printing 1553–1700* (London, 1975), 5–9; Heartz, *Pierre Attaingnant*, 46–48; and Lewis, *Antonio Gardano*, 1:51–52.

69. "La Pegorina" refers to Polisena Pecorina, a renowned Venetian singer who originally owned the manuscript that served as the source for Willaert's *Musica nova*. Willaert's publication, in turn, was also known by the name *La Pecorina*. For a summary of the vast literature on the *Musica nova*, see Richard J. Agee and Jessie Ann Owens, "La stampa della 'Musica nova' di Willaert," *Rivista italiana di musicologia* 24 (1989): 219–305; and also Lewis, *Antonio Gardano*, 2: 16–17.

70. *Antonio Gardano*, 1: 52–58.

71. Agee, *Gardano Music Printing Firms*, 122.

72. Lewis, *Antonio Gardano*, 1:52.

73. See chap. 6.

74. ". . . praesertim si adhibeantur maiores quaedam notae, et litterae, quas Ecclesiasticae res maxime requirunt." Dedication to Pope Sixtus V in *Ioan, Petri Aloysii Praenestini Lamentationum Hieremiae Prophetae Liber Primus* (Rome: Alessandro Gardano, 1588).

75. The three editions in question are Jacquet of Mantua's *Motteti a 4 Libro Primo, Motetti a 5 Libro Primo,* and *Motetti a 5 Libro secondo* of 1565; see J. Bernstein, *Music Printing in Venice*, 658–62.

76. See chap. 1 for a fuller description of the process.

77. The two books were first described by Yves Giraud, "Deux livres de tablature inconnus de Francesco da Milano," *Revue de musicologie* 55 (1969): 217–19. See also the preface by Arthur Ness to Francesco da Milano, *Intavolatura de viola o vero lauto*, I–II, facs. ed. (Geneva, 1988).

78. Charles P. Coldwell, "The Printing of Lute Tablature" (paper delivered at the annual meeting of the American Musicological Society, Louisville, Kentucky, 28 October 1983).

79. Publications for the lute must have still been fairly expensive to produce, as demonstrated by the small percentage of lute editions brought out by the large music presses. Only 22 lute publications out of 409 extant music editions survive from Girolamo Scotto's press, 33 out of 1,071 extant music editions from Antonio Gardano's press (Lewis, *Antonio Gardano,* 1:96), 18 lute, cittern, and guitar intabulations out of 320 from the Parisian firm of Le Roy and Ballard (Lesure and Thibault, *Bibliographie des éditions d'Adrian Le Roy et Robert Ballard,* 22), and 28 out of 189 from the press of Pierre Phalèse of Louvain (Vanhulst, *Catalogue des éditions de musique*, p. xxxi).

80. For an excellent description of "nested" music type and a plate picturing two music matrices see Forney, "Tielman Susato," 112–13; 264.

81. A reproduction of a music page from Cavazzoni's *Il primo libro de intabolatura d'organo* also appears in Lewis, *Antonio Gardano,* 1: pl.41.

82. Lewis, *Antonio Gardano,* 1:629.

83. Logan, *Culture and Society,* 312.

84. See Robert F. Judd, "The Use of Notational Formats at the Keyboard: A Study of Printed Sources of Keyboard Music in Spain and Italy c. 1500–1700" (D.Phil. thesis, Oxford University, 1988), 2:7–9.

85. Preface to Giovanni Piccioni, *Concerti ecclesiastici* (Venice: Vincenti, 1610), quoted by Judd, "The Use of Notational Formats," 1:94.

86. In addition to the Buus edition, Gardano printed an anthology, *Intabolatura nove di varie sorte de balli* (1551), and an undated reprinted edition of Girolamo Cavazzoni's *Libro secondo* under the title *Il primo libro de intabolatura d'organo dove si contiene tre messe* from about 1555 (see Lewis, *Antonio Gardano,* 2: nos. 163 and 200).

Three

THE FINANCING OF
VENETIAN MUSIC BOOKS

I, Don Benedetto Venitiano, monk of S. Giorgio Maggiore of Venice, as the procurator of the said monastery, promise to give to messer Girolamo Scotto eighty-eight ducats and five lire . . . whenever the said messer Girolamo gives me five hundred copies of the music of Don Pauletto Ferrarese.[1]

—Music book contract, 1565

enetian music printing during the sixteenth-century was a complicated and multifaceted business. It involved many financial risks and required substantial sums of money. As a specialty aimed at an elite audience, music printing demanded an expertise on the part of the printer and his pressmen. In comparison with other fields, the music book trade did not generate an impressive income. Yet the music publisher/printer had to have good business sense, for in order to be successful he not only had to gain entrance into intellectual circles, but also had to remain, first and foremost, a businessman who could carry on his trade in the international marketplace.

At the heart of the business were the financial arrangements made for the publication and sale of an individual book. These varied from one title to the next. Essentially there were two different strategies that Venetian publishers could follow in the financing of their publications. First, they could fund their books either independently or in partnership with other bookmen as a business venture. Second, they could accept books on a commission basis, taking no financial risk for the enterprise.

Independent sponsorship of publications by printers was a highly risky enterprise. Only the large Venetian presses had the necessary capital and contacts to finance their own publications. They not only issued their own editions, but also operated as publisher-underwriters to other printers, owned retail stores, and marketed books through international trade networks. These publishers or *mercatori* were willing to speculate on a popular textbook, liturgical book, or literary best seller such as Lodovico Ariosto's *Orlando furioso*, for after taking a gamble on the first edition, they could make a good return on capital investments with successive reprints.

In the field of music, didactic editions such as Jhan Gero's *Il primo libro de' madrigali italiani et canzoni francese a due voci* and Bernardino Lupacchino and Gioan Maria Tasso's *Primo libro a due voci* were probably initiated by the printer/publisher.[2] The marketability of these instructional publications was not lost on Scotto or Gardano; both printers were composers in their own right, and both issued editions of their own duos and trios early in their printing careers.[3] The large number of reprinted editions of these didactic titles, published well into the seventeenth century, attests to the popularity of the genre.

FINANCIAL BACKERS AND PATRONS

Unfortunately, evidence concerning independent funding by printers of their music editions remains admittedly sparse. Indeed, we must be cautious in claiming that printers furnished all the capital for some of their publications, since the absence of contractual agreements does not necessarily exclude the possibility that silent partners might have provided financial assistance for many best-selling publications, including the lucrative reprints. Dedications signed by Venetian printers, in fact, lend support to the notion that printers acquired or at least requested assistance from various patrons, particularly during the early stages of their printing careers. This was certainly the case with Claudio Merulo, who dedicated his 1566 reprint of Philippe Verdelot's *Madrigali del primo & secondo libri a 4* to Don Pellegrino Filarmonico degli Stellini, one of the original financial backers and silent partners of Merulo's printing venture.[4] Antonio Gardano's dedications to Bishop-elect Leone Orsini in early editions of Arcadelt's *Primo Libro a 4* and *Venticinque Canzoni Francese* strongly imply that the Venetian printer received financial assistance from Orsini at the outset of his printing career.[5] Even a well-established publishing firm might have requested aid from patrons. Girolamo Scotto turned to Alfonso d'Avalos, the marquis of Vasto and governor-general of Milan, for sponsorship of at least two of his early publications.[6]

PARTNERSHIPS AMONG BOOKMEN

Venetian music printers, in their speculative dealings, resorted to another kind of financial arrangement—the *societas* or *compagnia*. The high expense of printing and marketing specialized books required printers to band together and form partnerships so that they could spread the risks among themselves. A variety of intricate printing contracts emerged from such dealings. Some involved only short-term partnerships for the printing of one or two editions. Girolamo's brother Ottaviano formed such a partnership with Andrea Antico and Antonio Giunta in the publishing of *Liber Quindecim Missarum*. The partnership is described in two Roman contracts. The first, a statement of debts dated 26 May 1516, lists Ottaviano Scotto, a "merchant accepting the jurisdiction of the Roman *curia*," as the financial backer of the print. He or his agent, the Ferrarese printer Giovanni Mazzocchi, was to advance Antico the sum of 604 ducats and 59½ bolendini. Scotto was then entrusted with the press-run of 1,008 copies. Antico and Scotto were to share equally in the profits made from the sale of the books. The contract stipulated, however, that Antico could not collect his profits until Ottaviano recouped his investment as well as the money Antico owed him.

Under the terms of the agreement, Ottaviano Scotto financed the publication and was in charge of the sales and distribution of the pressrun, Antico prepared the woodcuts and edited the music, and another bookman, Antonio Giunta, printed the book. Giunta did not share in the profits, but was paid a flat fee for the printing.[7] The agreement was signed in a Roman bookshop jointly owned by Ottaviano Scotto and Adriano de Bave located in the district of Parione.

This contract between Scotto, Antico, and Giunta exemplifies the typical financial agreement made by the House of Scotto in which the firm participated as the underwriter and silent partner. In addition to their activities as printers, the Scottos tended to emphasize the marketing of books in their business activities. A second contract drawn up between Ottaviano Scotto and Antico, dated 20 August 1516, in fact deals with this aspect of the book trade. Scotto was to sell the pressrun of about 1,000 copies. The books were priced at 20 giulii retail per copy or 15 giulii wholesale for multiple copies. The revenues from books sold in Italy, France, and other northern countries were to be shared by Scotto and Antico. Thus, the Scotto firm financed and took charge of distribution and selling of the books, while other partners, such as Antico, were mainly responsible for book printing and production.

Other documents reflect more long-standing commitments. The well-known request of 24 June 1514 for a renewal of Ottaviano Petrucci's monopoly on music printing records a partnership among Girolamo Scotto's uncle Amadio then head of the Scotto press, Nicolò di Raffaele, and Petrucci that had begun with the establishment of Petrucci's press some fifteen years before. From this petition we gather that Scotto and Raffaele underwrote the original venture while Petrucci did the press-work.[8]

Although music-book contracts that identify partnerships and spell out the terms of the agreement are rare, other kinds of documentation, particularly the privileges and the prints themselves, provide evidence of consortia among Venetian publishers. In 1548 Domenico Splendor applied for a privilege to publish "Li moteti, et madrigali a 4 et a 5 voci, d'Henrico Scafen."[9] The next year Girolamo Scotto issued

Schaffen's four-voice madrigals *con gratia et privilegio*. Another privilege of 1563 names Zuan Battista and Marchio Sessa in a request for permission to print, among other things, Paolo Aretino's Lamentations.[10] In that same year, Scotto issued an edition of this sacred work. Again no documents survive connecting Scotto with the Sessa firm, but since the House of Sessa did not specialize in music printing, it must have financed this publication jointly with Scotto or commissioned the music printer to print it for a fee.

The music publications themselves also hint at partnerships among bookmen. Title pages and colophons sometimes indicate the underwriter of the publication. The colophon of the 1533 edition of Verdelot's First Book of Four-Voice Madrigals stated that Andrea Antico prepared the woodblocks, the firm of Giovanni Antonio da Sabio and his brothers did the presswork, and the House of Scotto financed the edition.

Unfortunately, very few Venetian music prints dating from after 1540 include a colophon which might identify the parties involved in the production of the book; to complicate matters further, the imprint on the title page usually designates only the printer and not the underwriter of the publication. Other physical characteristics of the book, in particular typography and printer's marks, do on occasion indirectly point to the existence of partnerships. Such is the case with a group of twenty-two unsigned music publications dating from 1545 to 1547 issued by a *societas* of book-men including Girolamo's cousin Ottaviano di Amadio, the Paduan printer Jacopo Fabriano, and possibly others all connected in one way or another to the House of Scotto.[11]

Typographical features of two music editions published by Scotto—Jacquet Ber-chem's and Giovanni Battista Melfio's First Book of Four-Voice Madrigals of 1555 and 1556, respectively—indicate a connection between Girolamo Scotto and another music printer, Francesco Rampazetto.[11] No contracts or privileges survive to docu-ment such a collaboration, and the editions contain no colophons that might name the co-printer. A close examination of these editions, however, reveals that, although Scotto's name appears on the title page, the music type font and initials belong to Rampazetto. It is tempting to speculate that Rampazetto and Scotto shared a part-nership in the Melfio and Berchem editions. More likely, Rampazetto, the less ex-perienced of the two, was subcontracted to print these books for Scotto, as he did for other publishers. He might, in fact, have apprenticed at the Scotto firm, for on several occasions during his printing career, Rampazetto borrowed typographical materials from the Scotto press. Decorated initials belonging to Scotto appear in the younger printer's publications.[12] At least two books issued by Rampazetto, Vergil's *Aeneid* of 1560 and Ariosto's *Orlando furioso* of 1554, contain woodcut illustrations which originally occurred in Scotto editions of a decade earlier.[13]

Dedications in music editions can also indicate business connections in the printing industry. The 1541 edition of Jhan Gero's *Il primo libro de madrigali ital-iani et canzon francese a due voci*, for example, though printed by Gardano, contains a dedication signed by Girolamo Scotto.[14] This edition proves valuable since it is the only known document that establishes a liaison between the two most important music printers of mid-sixteenth-century Venice.[15] In the dedication Girolamo Scotto implies that he underwrote the project. It would appear, then, that Scotto subcontracted Gardano to print this volume for a fixed fee or that the two formed a partnership and shared in the profits. Both the dedication and Scotto's position in the early 1540s (unlike that of Gardano) as the head of a wealthy publishing house suggest the former.

Two copies of an undated and unsigned tenor partbook of the Gero duos in Palermo and Munich further confirm Scotto's authoritative role in the publishing of this work. Both tenor partbooks were previously thought to be copies of the 1541 Gardano edition and the 1552 Scotto edition, respectively.[16] Lorenzo Bianconi was the first to speculate that the Palermo copy was an unknown first edition dating from 1539.[17] Recognizing it as the work of Scotto, Mary Lewis brought the partbook to the attention of Lawrence Bernstein and James Haar, who, in turn, concluded that it was "brought out by Girolamo Scotto between 1541 and 1543," that is, after the 1541 edition by Gardano.[18] Bianconi's hypothesis, though conjectural, actually comes closer to the date of publication, for typographical evidence reveals that Scotto could only have printed the tenor partbook in 1540. It is, therefore, the earliest surviving edition of the Gero duos. Since the cantus partbook, which customarily contains the dedication, is lost, we do not know whether Gardano pirated the earlier Scotto edition, dedication and all, or if sales encouraged Scotto to have Gardano reprint it for him. The former seems highly unlikely, since Gardano and Scotto, when reprinting each other's first editions, rarely if ever included the same dedication. At any rate, it appears that Scotto and Gardano, at least in the early years of their publishing careers, maintained some kind of business relationship.[19]

COMMISSIONED PUBLICATIONS

While independent production and partnerships represented financially risky ventures for bookmen, another type of agreement, the commissioned work, offered music printers a safe and steady income. Surviving contracts, dedications, and privileges indicate that many Venetian music editions were paid for by others both inside and outside the printing industry. In these cases, the printer would publish the book for a fixed fee, taking no financial risk for the publication at all. This type of agreement seems to have been popular especially in the highly specialized world of music printing, for it assured a steady influx of funds and protected the printer against the immediate problems of cash flow. Editions devoted exclusively to the works of one composer, many of which went through only one printing run, fall into this category. Certain turns of phrases such as "da lui composti & stampati," "novamente da lui composti rivisti & posti in luce," or "dal proprio auttor composti & mandati in luce" found on the title pages of madrigal editions assert only that the composer authorized the publication of their works, but in their dedications composers sometimes remark, as did the Florentine Francesco Corteccia in his *Libro primo de madriali* [sic] *a 4* (1544)[20] or Baldassaro Donato in his *Secondo libro de madrigali a 4* (1568),[21] that they were financially responsible for the publication of their madrigals.

Printers might have also profited financially from the sales of certain single-composer editions that proved successful. Reprints of single-composer works not bearing a dedication or privilege by the composer suggest that the printer brought out the composer's work on his own. Printers apparently also benefited from the trafficking of first editions. In some cases, they either legally or illegally issued extra copies of a commissioned book beyond the pressrun stipulated in the contract. Most extant music-printing contracts spell out whether or not a printer could issue extra copies. The contract between the composer Carpentras and the printer Channey of 1531, for example, states that the printer "must give up all the copies of what he prints . . . reserving only four of each [edition] to himself, under pain of L. 300 penalty."[22] A Madrid contract of 1598 drawn up by the Spanish composer Tomás de Luis Victoria stipulates that the printer may issue an additional 100 copies for himself which he could only begin to sell twelve months after publication.[23]

Interested parties other than composers also assumed the expenses of music publications. One lucrative source of funding was the Church. Various Orders commissioned music printers to issue responsories, hymnals, Magnificats, Lamentations, and other musico-liturgical books on a fee-for-service basis. While dedications written by clergymen for sacred publications, such as the 1567 Scotto edition of Jacquet of Mantua's *Orationes complures ad officium*, only allude to this type of agreement, an actual contract of 1565 between Girolamo Scotto and the Monastery of San Giorgio Maggiore in Venice offers concrete evidence concerning church support of music publications. This document proves very valuable as one of a handful of extant contracts concerning the printing of music, and the only one of its kind to survive from Cinquecento Venice. Since it provides in remarkable detail what must have been a typical agreement between private parties and printer, it will be considered here in detail.[24]

Dated 8 March 1565, the contract was drawn up between Girolamo Scotto and Don Benedetto Venetiano for the Benedictine monastery of San Giorgio Maggiore, situated on the island facing the Piazza San Marco.[25] In the contract, Scotto is paid for printing in "stampa grosetta" (the larger of the two music fonts employed in his music editions during this period) 500 copies of a music work by Don Pauletto Ferrarese.[26] He must use fine, white paper, unspotted and without flaws. Scotto is also responsible for all expenses and must correct without charge any errors or deviations from the exemplar. He is to print at least one folio per day, and the work must begin on 12 March. The contract stipulates that if Scotto does not live up to the agreement in any way, the document shall be declared null and void. For his labors, Scotto is to be paid a set fee of 550 lire or 88 ducats and 5 lire upon completion of the work.

Scotto completed the printing of the edition three months later, on 10 June. He apparently satisfied the procurator of San Giorgio Maggiore, since on that day Girolamo deposited the books at the monastery and collected 450 lire for his efforts. Girolamo's nephew Melchiorre received the remaining 100 lire from Don Benedetto nine days later.

This contract sheds light on several aspects concerning the production of music publications. First, it tells us the size of the pressrun. Although five hundred copies may appear to be a small number, it was probably average for a commissioned work of this type.[27] Secondly, the agreement specifies the production schedule. Scotto had to adhere to the completion of one folio per day; in this case, 176 folios (each of the four partbooks contains forty-four folios), which translated into 176 working days or a little over eight months (the average month consisted of twenty working days). This apparently gave Scotto more than ample time to complete the project, and allowed him to deliver the partbooks five months ahead of schedule.[28] Finally, the fee mentioned in the contract offers us some idea of how much profit a music printer might anticipate. The fee of 88 ducats and 5 lire, or 550 lire, came to about one lira per set of partbooks. The account books of the Accademia Filarmonica of Verona dating from the 1540s inform us that the average retail price for a set of four partbooks with five gatherings each was one lira and four soldi.[29] The set of four partbooks ordered by the monks of San Giorgio, however, contained the unusually large number of eleven gatherings. Scotto's fee of one lira per set of partbooks of the Paolo Ferrarese edition was clearly a wholesale price, since the retail price for this particular publication could not be less than two lire. Since Scotto was presumably still making a profit on this contract, the price for his music books sold in the retail market had to be more than double his cost of production, or, to put it another way, the gross profit per unit was at least 100 per cent.[30]

In addition to outside parties, Venetian publishers not specializing in music printing, formed another important group who contracted books from music printers. As we have seen in chapter 1, the tremendous expense and highly competitive nature of the industry forced bookmen to specialize in the subject matter they published. Thus, if publishers of non-music books received an order from a third party or wanted to publish a music work that they owned outright, they had to consign their presswork to a music printer. Francesco Rampazetto, who owned a small printing press, generally worked on consignment, issuing many of his books for other publishers. The bookman Giovanni Comencino, for example, hired Rampazetto to print Pietro Vinci's *Il secondo libro de madrigali a cinque voci*, as noted both on the title page of the edition and in the privilege that Comencino took out in 1567.[31]

Publishers and booksellers from Italian cities lacking a well-established music press also called on the services of Venetian music printers. The Neapolitan bookseller Scipione Riccio on 4 June 1587 signed a contract to have printed in Venice 200 copies of a book of sacred music by Giovanni Battista Racchiano, for which he paid 43 ducats.[32] Even an important regional center such as Florence did not have a printer specializing in music until the 1580s. As the Florentine publishers Jacopo and Filippo Giunti ruefully remark in a 1563 petition to the Medici court: ". . . when we have had to print a book of importance and requiring expense . . . we have had them printed in Venice."[33] Indeed, only four months after submitting this petition, the Giunti brothers commissioned Francesco Rampazetto to print Serafino Razzi's collection of Laudi Spirituali on their behalf.[34]

CONNECTIONS AMONG MUSIC PRINTERS

Music printing fostered close relationships among bookmen working in this highly specialized field. The supposition that fierce rivalries chronically occurred among Venetian music printers is not born out by existing evidence, for it appears that throughout the sixteenth century practically all Venetian music printers were connected in one way or another with the Scotto firm. We have already noted the important role played by the House of Scotto as underwriters to both Petrucci and Antico in the early sixteenth century. During Girolamo's tenure as head of the Scotto firm, a younger generation of bookmen presumably gained their start by either apprenticing or working for the press. As noted above, Francesco Rampazetto printed two of Scotto's music editions in the mid-1550s, and after establishing his own press, borrowed typographical materials from the Scotto firm.

Another music press associated with the Scotto firm was that of Claudio Merulo and Fausto Bethanio. In 1566 Claudio Merulo da Correggio, composer and organist at San Marco, joined together with Fausto Bethanio, Bolognino Zaltieri, an established non-music printer, and Don Pellegrino Stellini, a priest from Ravenna, to form a music-printing firm. Each partner contributed a specific expertise to the *compagnia*: Merulo, the composer and musician, supplied the music and read the proofs; Zaltieri must have acted as the retail agent and distributor for the firm; while Stellini underwrote the operation.[35] The fourth partner, Fausto Bethanio, whose life until now has remained a mystery, was apparently in charge of the actual printing of music. Two years before the formation of this partnership, Bethanio, as a witness to the last will and testament of the writer Veronica Franco, refers to himself as a printer at the Scotto press ("stampator in venetia alla d[itta] Scotti").[36] It is clear from this document that Bethanio had learned the technique of music printing by working either as a journeyman or apprentice at the Scotto firm.

Rampazetto and Bethanio were not the only music printers we can link with Girolamo. Ricciardo Amadino, an important music publisher from 1583 until 1617, witnessed Girolamo's will in 1569, and might also have worked at the Scotto press.[37] Amadino and his partner Giacomo Vincenti sold a considerable number of books issued by the Scotto firm, as seen in an extant trade list of 1591 issued by Vincenti after the breakup of his partnership with Amadino.[38] Whether the use of Ottaviano IV and Brandino Scotto's printer's mark by Pietro Pietrasanta, who published a handful of music editions in 1557—the year in which no Scotto music publications survive—connects this bookman with a minor branch of the Scotto firm remains highly speculative.[39] A more shadowy figure, Antonio dell'Abate, who published along with Antico the important 1536 edition, *La Courone et fleur des chansons a troys*, might be the Antonio dell'Abbate da Rovigo whose name appears in numerous contracts as Scotto's agent and debtor.[40]

Independent production, partnerships, and commissions—all these arrangements illustrate how complicated the economics of producing a music edition were in the sixteenth century. Yet financial agreements were only the first step in the production of music books. Music printers and publishers had to deal with other aspects of the book trade. One of them, the marketing of their books, as we shall explore in the next chapter, remained a constant and central preoccupation of the Venetian bookmen.

NOTES

1. "Prometto Io Don Ben[tto] Venitiano Monaco di .S.° Giorgio Maggiore di Venetia, come procuratore del detto Monasterio, di dare à M. Girolamo Scotto Ducati ottanta otto, et lire cinque . . . che il detto M. Girolamo mi darà . . . cinquecento opere della Musica di .D. Pauletto Ferrarese." Extracted from transcription in Agee, "A Venetian Music Printing Contract," 59.

2. In his dedication of the Gero "Duos," Scotto specifically states that the works were "completed at my request by the excellent musician Gian Gero." See Jhan Gero, *Il primo libro de' madrigali italiani et canzon francese a due voci*, ed. Lawrence Bernstein and James Haar (Masters and Monuments of the Renaissance 1; New York, 1980), pp. xxii–xxiii, which lists a total of twenty-five extant editions of the Gero Duos. On the Lupacchino and Tasso Duos see J. Bernstein, *Music Printing in Venice*, 558–59.

3. Gardano issued his *Canzoni francese a due voce* in 1539, while Scotto countered with his publication *Il primo libro de i madrigali a doi voci* in 1541. Haar, *Essays on Italian Poetry and Music in the Renaissance, 1350–1600* (Berkeley and Los Angeles, 1986), 102 n. 12, suggests that Scotto may not have been the composer of the madrigal editions that appeared under his name. This seems unlikely, not only because of the numerous reprints of the duos, and of Scotto's insistence on the title pages that the madrigals were printed *ipso authore*, but also because a selected number of works by him appeared in other collections. Furthermore, these musical works, in particular the duos, though technically capable, do not show great creativity on the part of the composer.

4. See Rebecca A. Edwards, "Claudio Merulo," 176–77.

5. For further details about Orsini and the Gardano press see chap. 6.

6. See chap.7 for more information on d'Avalos and Scotto.

7. Reproductions, transcriptions, and English translations of the contractual documents appear in Chapman, "Andrea Antico," 3: 448–53, pls. 13 and 14.

8. A transcription of the petition appears among other places in Sartori, *Bibliografia . . . Petrucci*, 19; for further discussion see Boorman, "Petrucci at Fossombrone," 21–22.

9. For the full privilege, see Agee, "The Privilege and Venetian Music Printing," 221.

10. Ibid., 258.

11. A detailed account of these editions appears in Bernstein, "Burning Salamander."

12. One particular decorated initial, a floriated S, which Rampazetto used in his 1554 edition of Ariosto's *Orlando furioso*, suggests a connection between Rampazetto and the group

of unsigned music prints from 1545–47 cited above. See Bernstein, "Burning Salamander," 493.

13. The Vergil edition is described in Mortimer, *Harvard College Library . . . Italian 16th Century Books*, 2: 731. A woodcut of the Trojan horse taken from Scotto's 1545 edition of Luigi Pulci, *Morgante maggiore*, and employed by Rampazetto in his Vergil edition is reproduced in Leo S. Olschki, ed., *Choix de livres anciens rares et curieux* (Florence, 1940), 12: 5064.

14. Haar was the first to mention this connection in "The *Note nere* Madrigal," *JAMS* 18 (1965): 22–41. For a detailed description of this edition see the preface to Jhan Gero, *Il primo libro*.

15. Although Antonio Gardano is not mentioned in any of Scotto's notarial documents, his father- and brother-in-law Agostino and Marcantonio Bindoni appear as witnesses to a Scotto contract of 1557 (ASV, Notarile Atti B. Solian, b. 11868, fols. 32–33).

16. The Munich copy is incorrectly cited in *Nuovo Vogel*, 730 as a copy of the 1552 edition, while the Palermo copy is listed in the RISM *Einzeldrucke* as a copy of the 1541 edition.

17. "Weitere Ergänzungen zu Emil Vogels 'Bibliothek der gedruckten weltlichen Vocalmusik Italiens, aus den Jahren 1500–1700' aus italienischen Bibliotheken," *Analecta musicologica* 9 (1970): 142–202 at 162 n. 22.

18. Jhan Gero, *Il primo libro*, p. xxvi.

19. For more on the relationship between Gardano and Scotto see chap. 7.

20. "io habbia fatto stampare questo primo libro de i miei Madriali"; see dedication in J. Bernstein, *Music Printing in Venice*, 301.

21. "Per il che li ho fatti stampare, & come parto destinato a lei innanzi, che 'l nascesse, li ho publicato co 'l titulo del suo honorato nome"; see dedication in Ibid., 742.

22. "Item sera tenu led. De Chennay rendre . . . tous les livres qu'il aura imprimé sans en réserver pour son fortz que quatre de chescune sure peinne de IIIC livres." Complete transcription in Pierre Pansier, *Histoire du livre et de l'Imprimerie d'Avignon*, 3:125. English translation taken from Heartz, *Pierre Attaingnant*, 111.

23. Tomás Luis de Victoria, *Opera omnia*, ed. F. Pedrell (Leipzig, 1902–13), 8: lxxxv.

24. A transcription of the contract appears in Agee, "A Venetian Music Printing Contract," 59–65; see also id., *Gardano Music Printing Firms,* 41–42.

25. In 1562 Scotto also published a *Breviarium Monasticum* in accordance with the Cassinese Congregation of the Benedictine order (to which S. Giorgio Maggiore belonged; possibly it was commissioned by the monastery) see J. Bernstein, *Music Printing in Renaissance Venice*, app. D, no. 301.

26. The publication in question, Don Pauletto Ferrarese's *Passiones, Lamentationes, Responsoria, Benedictus, Miserere, Multaque alia Devotissima cantica*, was issued by Girolamo Scotto in 1565; Ibid., 666–70.

27. Opinions on what was the average pressrun for a sixteenth-century music publication appear in Lewis, *Antonio Gardano*, 1: 87–89; Heartz, *Pierre Attaingnant*, 122; Pogue, *Jacques Moderne*, 45, and Agee, "A Venetian Music Printing Contract," 61–65.

28. Since it took Scotto less than half the time allotted, his compositor must have set at least two folios per day, a figure that coincides with the number of formes of literary text that a northern European compositor could set per day. See D. F. McKenzie, "Printers of the Mind: Some Notes on Bibliographical Theories and Printing-House Practices," *Studies in Bibliography (Papers of the Bibliographical Society of the University of Virginia)* 22 (1969): 1–75 at 8, and Voet, *Golden Compasses*, 2: 33.

29. Several inventories and account books of the Accademia Filarmonica from 1543 onwards specifying the titles of music editions and their prices appear in Giuseppe Turrini,

L'Accademia Filarmonica di Verona dalla fondazione (maggio 1543) al 1600 e il suo patri-monio musicale antico (Atti e memorie della Accademia di Agricoltura, Scienze e Lettere di Verona 18; Verona, 1941), 30–40, 44–45, 56–68, 81–82, and 87–92.

30. Grendler, *Roman Inquisition,* 15 comes up with a comparable figure.

31. A transcription of the privilege appears in Agee, "The Privilege and Venetian Music Printing," 265–67.

32. This contract is mentioned in Angelo Pompilio, "Editoria musicale a Napoli e in Italia nel Cinque-Seicento" in *Musica e cultura a Napoli dal XV al XIX secolo,* ed. Lorenzo Bianconi and Renato Bossa (Florence, 1983), 79–102 at 94; Keith Larson, "Racchiano, Giovanni Battista" in *The New Grove,* 15: 524; and Gaetano Filangieri, *Documenti per la storia, le arti e le industrie delle provincie napoletane,* 6 (Naples, 1891), 354–55.

33. "Che quando fino ahora havemo hauto a stampare qualche libro d'importanza e di grande spesa, . . . noi gli haviamo tutti stampare, . . . in Venezia." Transcription and English translation taken from Tim Carter, "Music-Printing in Late Sixteenth- and Early Seventeenth-Century Florence: Giorgio Marescotti, Cristofano Marescotti and Zanobi Pignoni," *Early Music History* 9 (1989): 27–72 at 34.

34. Both the printer's mark and the name of the house of Giunti appear on the title page and the colophon. The dedication, signed by the Giunti brothers, is dated 30 July 1563.

35. Edwards, "Claudio Merulo," 171–84.

36. ASV, Notarile testamenti, not. Antonio Maria Vincenti, b. 1019, no. 806, as cited by Margaret F. Rosenthal, *The Honest Courtesan: Veronica Franco, Citizen and Writer in Sixteenth-Century Venice* (Chicago, 1992), 76.

37. Bridges, "Publishing of Arcadelt's First Book," 1: 231.

38. Mischiati, *Indici, cataloghi e avvisi,* 93–98.

39. See J. Bernstein, "Burning Salamander," 491.

40. ASV, Notarile Atti B. Solian, b. 11875 (1567), fol. 23; 11876 (1569), fols. 77–79 and fol. 122^{r-v}. Bridges, "Publishing of Arcadelt's First Book," 1: 91 also suggests this correlation. Considering the close relationship between Abbate, Scotto, and Antico, it is tempting to speculate that the Scotto press might have had a hand in the publication of *La Courone.*

Four

THE DISTRIBUTION OF
VENETIAN MUSIC BOOKS

SALARINO: Your mind is tossing on the ocean;
There where your argosies, with portly sail,—
Like signiors and rich burghers of the flood,
Or, as it were, the pageants of the sea,—
Do overpeer the petty traffickers
That curt'sy to them, do them reverence.
As they fly by them with their woven wings.
  —Shakespeare, *The Merchant of Venice*

eal money in music publishing lay not with the printing of books, but with their distribution. As highly successful book merchants, Gardano and Scotto maintained efficient marketing systems involving established networks of publishers, printers, and booksellers that stretched far beyond the confines of Venice. The relationships among these bookmen formed the basis for the European book trade.

In order to reach an international market, the music printers relied on a group of business associates and employees different from the men who worked in their printing shops to distribute books. The most important members of this workforce consisted of the *procuratori* or agents, who traveled to or resided in cities outside of Venice. Their duties concerned all aspects in the transport of books, including the receipt of book shipments, the selling of books either in their own bookshops or to other bookdealers, and the collecting of money and bills of exchange from other bookmen for the *mercatori*. In addition to employing their own agents, Scotto and Gardano entrusted independent book carriers to transport their books to the northern book fairs where they bought and sold books for several publishers. At the final destination point were the *librarii* or *bibliopolae*, who sold the Venetian printers' books in their retail shops.

The success of this entire organization depended on familial relationships. Publishing houses were often made up of extended families whose members could be entrusted to carry out the duties of the firm both in and outside of Venice. Partnerships between the resident merchant and a brother, son, or nephew were common. Relatives would often serve as resident agents in other cities, managing stores or distributing books for the main firm. The House of Scotto proved no exception. Although Girolamo ran the press by himself, he actually co-owned the firm with his brother Ottaviano. More distant relatives worked for the press in other Italian cities. Girolamo's nephew Giovanni Maria Scotto maintained a branch in Naples, where he ran a bookshop and acted as an agent.[1] Two other nephews, Gian Andrea and Gian Michele Maldura, were resident agents in Milan and Mantua. Girolamo's second cousin Ottaviano di Amadio Scotto, an independent printer in Venice, made trips as far afield as Rome to collect debts for the main branch of the firm.[2] Girolamo's nephew Melchiorre helped as agent and manager in Venice as early as 1565 until Girolamo's death in 1572, when he inherited the business.

In addition to family members, Scotto had a highly developed syndicate of contacts all over the Italian peninsula. Notarial contracts name *libraii* or *bibliopolae* from Perugia, Ferrara, Brescia, Siena, Cremona, Milan, Mantua, Rome, Florence, and Padua. The intricacy of the relationship between the Venetian printer and a *bibliopola* would vary according to the status of the bookman and the nature of the task performed. Large firms would reciprocate favors, for example, the Florentine printers Filippo and Jacopo Giunti, who, in 1559, acted as intermediaries for Scotto in the collection of funds from another Florentine bookman.[3] Other agreements concerned the appointment of distributors outside of Venice. In August 1566 Scotto designated the Roman printer Marco de Amadoro as his agent "to seek, demand, and receive whatsoever quantities of money, things, and goods and all which the said principal [i.e., Scotto] ought to have and could demand from whatsoever persons in the said city of Rome for whatever reason and cause, and give quittances for the receipts."[4] Many of Scotto's notarial documents deal with the establishment of such agents or *procuratori*.

As a wealthy *mercator,* Scotto also acted as a broker in the transport of books issued by smaller Venetian printers to other cities. In May 1569 Domenico and Angelo Pederzano, printers at the sign of the Tower, gave Scotto 207 ducats to ship books to their brothers in Palermo to be sold in their store.[5] Scotto not only shipped books for other printers, he also apparently eliminated the middlemen and acquired his own barges and ships, or at least bought interests in the shipping industry. He might even have gone a step further in the buying and selling of wood for the purpose of shipbuilding, as seen in an agreement made with two other Venetians to form a company in order to purchase oak and ash, the primary woods used to build ships.[6]

At the other end of the marketing process were the distribution centers and retail stores. Owners of modest presses tended not to have sufficient capital. They had to rely on the larger publishing houses to distribute their books. Wealthy firms would take a percentage of the book sales or buy up books printed by these small firms and market them at various outlets. They often held interests in the retail bookshops where their books were sold. The type of partnership varied from store to store. As early as 1516, the Scotto firm co-owned a bookshop in Rome.[7] They also maintained a store in Naples. Often the financial arrangements of these partnerships were intricate, as is seen in a contract dated 2 October 1559 between Scotto and the owner of a small Venetian bookstore. Baldo Sabini, whose shop was located at the sign of the Colombina at San Bartolomeo, agreed to sell a quantity of Scotto's books for which Sabini would receive the usual commission of 15 percent. As part of the contract, Scotto had to pay half the annual rent of 37 ducats for Baldo's shop, giving Scotto a share in the store.[8]

THE TRADE ROUTES

Gardano and Scotto relied on trade networks already established by Venetian bookmen. They also sought out new avenues in the dissemination of their music books. Their first sales outlet was the Most Serene Republic itself. Venice held a unique position in the commercial world as the principal crossroad between East and West. Tourism was then as now an important part of Venice's economy. Along with foreign mariners and merchants, pilgrims setting off for the Holy Land flooded the streets and shops of the city. The Rialto, the financial district of Venice, was the starting point of the Mercerie, which extended all the way to San Marco; this street and the Frezzeria, which stretched from the churches of San Moisè to San Fantin, would tempt sixteenth-century passers-by with stalls and shops filled with books. Travelers included foreign aristocrats such as Henry Fitzalan, the duke of Arundel, who bought music books for his library at Nonesuch Castle or a German woman possibly on a pilgrimage named Maria Pfaffenperg, who proudly inscribed on the flyleaf of her music purchase: "Anno 1577 In Venedig Dis buech gehört mir."[9]

Yet even a large cosmopolitan city such as Venice could not absorb an entire pressrun of 500 to 1,000 copies per music book. When one figures that the population of Venice by 1540 numbered 170,000 people, it is clear that the music printers had to look beyond their city and export their music editions to other places.[10] Their market extended throughout the Italian peninsula and even further to Spain and northern Europe. Scotto and Gardano exported their music editions in small consignments, packing them with a wide assortment of other books in large wooden crates. Printed books "desligadi e diverse sorte," that is without bindings and representing a variety of titles, comprised each bale, which might include only one or two copies of a particular music title. The shipments were then dispatched to their destination by boat, wagon, or a combination of both. The crates, though sturdy, ran the risk of water damage, particularly at the bottom of a ship's hold.[11] Any ruined books were the responsibility of the distributor, as we learn from a bill of exchange dated 5 October 1558 between Scotto and his nephew, Giovanni Maria, where Girolamo subtracts 8 ducats for *libri bagnati* damaged during transport to Naples.[12]

The music printers sent their cargoes of books via Venice's traditional land and maritime trade routes. Books and other merchandise were sent whenever possible by water, since transport by sea and inland waterways was considerably cheaper than by land. Local transport occurred by barge along the coast of the Adriatic and up the rivers of the plain to Padua, Vicenza, Verona, Trent, and other northern Italian cities. Larger carracks or round boats were used for long-distance travel.[13] They followed some of the old trade routes of the fifteenth-century state galleys. Some traveled at least part of the Acque Morte route, heading south down the Adriatic into the Mediterranean between Sicily and the toe of Italy out to Spain.

Among the local cities, Padua provided an important outlet for music books. Lute publications, though few in number, were probably intended for Padua and other university towns. Foreign students from northern Europe could sample a variety of genres, including intabulations of chansons, madrigals, motets, and Masses, as well as dances and ricercars by *oltremontani* and native Italians. Often these foreign students returned home with their book purchases. The German Peter Peuch, who received his doctorate in medicine from Padua and then became medical officer for the town of Zwickau, brought back several Venetian music publications now preserved in the Ratsschulbibliothek in Zwickau.[14] The international repertory contained in these lute editions made them the most catholic of all sixteenth-century music publications. Scotto certainly had the Paduan market in mind in 1546 when he requested a privilege to print two volumes of lute intabulations by the Paduan lutenist Antonio Rotta.[15] Although only the first book of Rotta's intabulations appeared, it became the lead volume in Scotto's first series of ten lute publications, containing five volumes of lute music by another Paduan, Melchiore de Barberiis.

Two of the major staging points for Venetian book distribution were the Kingdom of Naples and Sicily.[16] Although they might seem distant for the trafficking of books, these southern points were made more accessible to Venice by boat routes than the closer inland Italian cities. It is clear from archival documents that Naples and Sicily were crucial outposts for the Scotto firm. Girolamo's nephew Giovanni Maria was in charge of operations in Naples. Scotto's notarial contracts name some nine bookmen alone in the cities of Messina and Palermo.[17]

The Italian peninsula clearly provided Scotto and Gardano with their most valuable market. This is evident not only from the intricate distribution system but also from the music repertory issued by the Venetian printers. They dominated Italian music printing; thus music with a "national" bias, both light and serious music with Italian texts, became the mainstay of their musical output.

BOOK TRADE WITH NORTHERN EUROPE

While catering to the Italian market, the Venetian printers also had an eye on the international book trade to the north, for their primary aim was to secure as wide a market for their music books and as great a demand as possible. Their commercial relations with the north were well established and extensive. They had business contacts in both the Catholic and the Protestant transalpine centers. In order to reach the northern centers, Gardano and Scotto had to transport their books overland by way of the more expensive transalpine routes. The route to Flanders taken by the Venetian State galleys a century before, which went north up the Atlantic coast to the city of Bruges, was abandoned by 1530 because of the perils of piracy and wars. Accessibility to the German centers lay north by barge up the Adige, Piave, Brenta, and Tagliamento rivers and through the Brenner and other eastern passes. Books traveled to French and Swiss centers via the plain rivers and then by land through the western Alpine passes (see fig. 4.1). Independent book carriers made the long journeys to Lyons, Geneva, Strasbourg, Basel, and Zurich, as well as to the German towns of Munich, Augsburg, Nuremberg, Wittenberg, Leipzig, Erfurt, and Cologne, where they would buy and sell books for several publishers at one time. The music editions were then sold in the bookshops of northern European cities. The daily account books of the famed Plantin press in Antwerp, for example, record among its purchases and sales music books from Venice.[18]

Important outlets for the Venetian booksellers were the northern European fairs, which served as focal points for the international book trade. From the late fifteenth century until the mid-1560s, the most successful fairs were held at Lyons.[19] The French city was ideally situated on a direct route from Italy to Paris. Venetians made their way to Lyons by taking the overland route across Lombardy over the Alps by way of the Great St. Bernard Pass, with a stopover in Geneva. The fairs occurred four times a year for a period of fifteen days each. The French king granted liberal privileges to the foreign traders, who were issued safe-conducts to and from the fairs, exempted from taxes on goods bought or sold, and permitted to use foreign currency at its fair market value. Merchants from all over Europe and the Middle East attended the fairs. Italians from Venice, Florence, Lucca, Genoa, Bologna, and

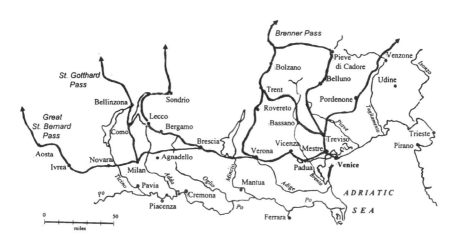

FIGURE 4.1 Map of transalpine routes used by Venetian bookmen

Milan came to trade in literally every commodity known to Renaissance Europe. Lyons became an international center for the book trade, particularly for the importation of Italian books, which their printers would then copy and issue in pirated editions. The importance of the French market was such that some of the major Italian publishers such as the Giunti opened up permanent branches of their firm in Lyons.[20]

By the mid-sixteenth century, book fairs in the German towns of Frankfurt and later in Leipzig came to eclipse those held in Lyons.[21] The Frankfurt fair had become the commercial center of the Rhineland, where dealers from England and the Low Countries traded their commodities with merchants from German-speaking cities, France, and Italy.[22] A directory of the 1569 Autumn Fair listing eighty-seven book-dealers indicates the thriving book trade. Among this international group were three representatives of the Venetian book trade—Gasparo Bindoni, Pietro Valgrisi, and Pietro Longo.[23] All three were carriers who transported books to and from the fairs for other publishers as well as for private clients. Bindoni and Valgrisi were members of two prominent families in the printing trade. Bindoni, who was related by marriage to Gardano, also had close business connections with the Scotto firm, maintaining at least one partnership with Scotto and several other bookmen for the publication of law books.[24] Longo and Bindoni traveled together many times, often stopping on their return from Frankfurt for additional books in Basel.[25]

BOOK FAIR LISTS AND PUBLISHER'S CATALOGUES

The most significant by-product of the Frankfurt fairs were the trade lists of books available at the fair.[26] They provide us not only with the titles of lost editions, but also with invaluable documentation as to the number and types of music publications that the Italian publishers sent to Frankfurt. In light of their small delegation, the Venetian publishers were represented by a disproportionately large number of music editions. Of a total of 154 music titles listed in the catalogues during the period 1565–70, ninety-one were of Italian origin. The 1565 catalogues, for example, list thirty-two from Venice, one from Rome, one from Louvain, and one from Wittenberg.

The Italian editions listed in the 1565–70 catalogues divide equally into sacred and secular music, suggesting that there was just as much a market for Italian madrigals as for sacred music in northern Europe. A closer examination of both the publisher's output and the specific titles in the fair catalogues, however, clarifies the northern European taste in Italian music prints.

Among the sacred music publications listed in the Frankfurt fair catalogues, half are devoted to polyphonic settings of liturgical music, such as Masses, magnificats, hymns, and psalms, while the other half contain motets. Several of the publications are by lesser-known composers, suggesting that the Venetian printers shipped as many sacred music titles as they could. The list of secular editions, on the other hand, tends to be more selective. One-third of them contain the popular *canzoni villanesche alla napolitana*. Many of the remaining madrigal editions feature best-selling composers such as Cipriano de Rore, Arcadelt, and Verdelot, works by such northerners as Orlando di Lasso, Hubert Waelrant, and Philippe de Monte, and anthologies. Yet even though one-half of the music editions in the Frankfurt catalogues include Italian secular music, this figure remains misleading when viewed against the Venetian printers' entire music output for the period. Between 1560 and 1569, Venetian printers brought out a total of 402 extant music editions. 307 of the publications contain madrigals and instrumental music, as opposed to only ninety-five sacred editions. Thus even though three-quarters of the editions issued by the Venetians consisted of Italian music, they deliberately catered to northern European taste by emphasizing music with Latin texts, particularly Masses and other liturgical genres, in the publications they exported to the Frankfurt fairs.

The fair trade lists evolved from book catalogues put out by individual booksellers. As early as 1460, publishers printed broadsides containing announcements to prospective customers of their forthcoming publications. Printers seem to have issued hundreds of these single-sheet "flyers" during the incunabular period, but due to their ephemeral nature only a handful of them survive today.[27] What began as advertisements for one or two books led to full-fledged sales catalogues. Lists of books for sale were an early feature of the Venetian publishing trade. One of the first, brought out by Johannes de Colonia and Manthen, appeared sometime before 1476.[28] Aldo Manuzio issued a book list in 1498 and another dated 1513. His catalogues not only enumerate the publications available at his press, but also specify the prices for each edition.[29]

While it is likely that the music presses periodically issued catalogues of their books, only two such book lists dating from the 1590s survive.[30] The *Indice de libri di musica stampati dalli magnifici Scoti cioè quelli che sino al presente anno 1596 si ritrovano* (see fig. 4.2), lists music books printed by the House of Scotto up until 1596. The other catalogue, the *Indice delli libri di musica che si trovano nelle stampe di Angelo Gardano*, records music books still available at the Gardano press in 1591.

The Scotto catalogue includes 256 entries, and the Gardano *Indice* lists about 360 titles.[31] The entries in both book lists are methodically organized according to genre and number of voices, and in the Scotto book list, are also arranged within each subheading in alphabetical order by composer. Both catalogues offer clear details concerning the title, composer, and number of voices. They do not, however, provide dates of publication. Early printers rarely if ever included this information in their book catalogues, since they did not wish to advertise the fact that several of the items listed were old—some even dating as far back as fifty years.[32]

Unlike the Gardano *Indice*, which is printed in small octavo format, the Scotto book list appears as a broadside, that is, on one side of a single, unfolded sheet of paper. One of the benefits of the inordinately large broadside format, as seen in fig. 4.2, was that all the entries in the *Indice* could be accommodated on one side of a single piece of paper. This would allow both bookseller and buyer to view at a

INDICE DE LIBRI DI MVSICA
STAMPATI DALLI MAGN. SCOTI
Cioè quelli che fino al presente Anno 1596. si ritrouano.

Musica a due voci.

Ieronymo Scoto lib. primo & 2.	L. l.	f
Pietro Vincio	L.	f 10
Agostino Licino.	L.	f 10
De diuersi Antichi.	L.	f 10
Afula.	L.	f 10
Lupachino.	L.	f 10

Madrigali A Tre Voci.

Abcadelti. lib. Primo.	L.	f 10
Constantio Festa.	L.	f 10
Gaudio De diuersi.	L.	f 10
Iyeronimo.Scoto Lib. 1.& 2.	L. l.	f
Idem Vergine.	L.	f 10
Musica De diuersi.	L.	f 10
Pietro Vincio.	L.	f 10

Canzone & Napolitane A Tre Voci.

Arpa Lib. Primo.	L.	f 6
Bonagionta Lib.Primo & 2.	L.	f 10
Corona De diuersi.	L.	f 10
Corona del Abbate Francese.	L.	f 10
Iustiniane De diuersi Lib.Primo.	L.	f 10
	L.	f
Iacobo Celano.	L.	f
Mazzone Lib.Primo & 2.	L.	f 12
Maximo Troiano Lib. Primo.& 2.	L.	f
Luca Marenzio Lib.1.2.3.	L. l.	f
Idem.Lib. 4.5.	L. l.	f
Pinelli. Lib.2.3.4.	L.	f 18
Policreti.	L.	f 8
Pompilio Ventura.Lib.2.& 3.	L. l.	f 4
Primauera Lib.1.2.4.	L.	f 8
Zapasforgo .Lib.Primo & 2.	L.	f 10

Madrigali A Quatro Voci.

Adriano Villaert.	L.	f 12
Aierosi De diuersi Lib.1.& 2.	L. l.	f 8
Amorosi Concenti De diuersi	L.	f 10
Archadelti.	L.	f 16
Baldefar Donato Lib.Primo.	L.	f 10
Antonio Bonauita Lib. Primo.	L.	f 10
Battaglia Francese.	L.	f 10
Camillo Borghese.	L.	f 12
Correccia lib.Primo.	L.	f 12
Cipriano Lib.Primo.	L.	f 12
Cauatone lib.Primo.	L.	f 12
Ippol Camatero lib.Secondo.	L.	f
Ioan.Contino lib.Primo & 2.	L. l.	f 10
De diuersi Lib.Primo.2.& 3.	L.	f
Desiderio De diuersi Lib.Primo & 3.	L. l.	f 4
Scipion Ceretto Lib. Primo.	L.	f 12
Ioan.Andrea Dragone lib.Primo.	L.	f 15
Fama Lib.Primo	L.	f 10
Filippo de Monte lib.Primo 2.3.	L. l.	f 7
Filippo Duca	L.	f 15
Giulio Schiauetto	L.	f 15
Giulio Fiescho lib.1.	L.	f 12
Iachet Mantua lib.1.	L.	f 15
Iacomo Orfino	L.	f 15
Lamberto	L.	f 12
Marc'Antonio Mazzone lib.1.	L.	f 12
Martinengo.	L.	f 12
Marc'Antonio d' Maio.	L.	f 12
Mascoretta	L.	f 12
Orlando Lasso. lib.1.	L.	f 12
Francesco Portinaro.lib.1.	L. l.	f 10
Paulo Ragazzo	L.	f 10
Palestina lib.1. & 2.	L. l.	f 10
Rocco Rodio lib. 2.	L.	f 10
Paulo Ragazzoni	L.	f 15
Matheo Ruffulo	L.	f 15
Simon Baelano lib.1.2.	L. l.	f
Theodoro Riccio.	L.	f 15
Tutaualla Menon.	L.	f 12
Vincio lib.1.	L.	f 15

Canzone, & Napolitane A Quatro voci.

Alex.Romano lib.1.2.	L.	f 15
Baldifar Donato.	L.	f 8
Eliseo Bonizoni.	L.	f 8
Gio.Domenico da Nolla.	L.	f 8
Giouan Nasco.	L.	f 8
Giouan Pizzone lib. 1.	L.	f 8
Mercurio Iacouelli.	L.	f 16
Primauera De diuersi lib.1.	L.	f
Francesco Adriano.	L.	f

Madrigali A Cinque Voci.

Adriano Villaert lib.1.	L.	f 15
Antonio Martello.	L.	f 15

Alberigo Maluezi lib.1.	L.	f 15
Antonio Bonauitta lib. 1. 2.	L.	f 10
Ascanio Meo lib.1.2.	L.	f
Alexandro Striggio lib. Primo	L.	f 8
Idem lib.2.	L.	f
Idé Ci calamenti delle Donne.	L.	f 10
Anibal Stabile lib. Primo & 3.	L. l.	f 10
Biagio Pisciolino.	L.	f
Baruaba Ceruo.	L.	f
Benedetto Serafico Lib. 2. & 3.	L.	f 10
Concenti De diuersi lib. 1. 2.	L. l.	f 10
Cipriano Cromatici lib.Primo.	L.	f 8
Idem lib. 4.	L.	f
Christoforo Maluezzi Tib. Primo	L.	f 15
Dolci Frutti De diuersi.	L.	f
Dolci Afferti de Diuersi.	L.	f 15
Egidio Napolitano.	L.	f 15
Franc.Vecoli.lib.Primo.	L.	f
Filippo de Monte lib. Primo 2.3.4.	L. 3	f
Idem lib. 8. 9. 10.	L. 3	f
Francesco Adriano. lib. Primo. & 2.	L. 2	f
Gio.Andrea Dragoni	L.	f 10
Gio.Battista Moscaglia lib. 3. 4.	L. 2	f 10
Gio. Pizzone lib. 3.	L.	f 15
Gio.Pizzone. & Spontone.	L.	f 15
Gio.Thomaso del Benedicto.	L.	f
Gio. Francesco Surentino. lib. 3.	L.	f 15
	L.	f 5
Iacobo Fogliano. lib. 1.	L.	f 15
Ippolito Bachufi.lib.1.	L.	f
Ippolito Camateró. lib. 2. 3. 4.	L. 2	f 5
Luca Marenzio. lib. 5.	L.	f 4
Idem Spirituali.	L.	f 15
Leonardo Meldert. lib. 2.	L.	f
Leonardo Primauera. lib. 1. 2	L.	f
Idem lib. 4.6.7.	L. 4	f
Marc'Ant.Mazzone. lib.2.	L. 1	f 10
Muse De Diuersi.lib.1.2.	L. l.	f 10
Michel Comis.	L.	f 10
Marcello Tortora lib. 1.	L.	f 15
Nicolo Dorato.	L.	f
Oratio Scalletta lib. Primo & 2.	L. l.	f 10
Orlando Lasso lib. 1. 2. 3.	L. 2	f 5
Prima Stella De Diuersi.	L.	f 15
Paulo Lagudio.	L.	f 15
Paulo Clerico. lib.1.2.	L. l.	f 10
Paulo Ragazzo	L.	f 10
Paulo Belafio lib.1. 2.	L. 2	f 10
Paulo Cauatone.	L.	f 12
Paulo Caraciolo.	L.	f 15
Pasqual Tristaboca.	L.	f 15
Pietro Vinci lib. Primo	L.	f
Idem lib. 2. 3. 4.	L. 2	f
Idem lib. 6. 7.	L. l.	f
Idem Spirituali.	L.	f
Rinaldo del Mel lib.1.	L.	f
Scipion Ceretto lib.2.	L.	f 15
Simon Florio lib. 1.	L.	f 15
Stefano Felis. lib. 6. 7.	L.	f 15
Spirito da Reggio lib. 1.	L.	f
Spirituali Da diuersi.	L.	f 5
Spoglia Amorosa De diuersi.	L.	f
Tagglia.	L.	f 4
Vicenzo Bellauer. lib.2.	L.	f 15
Vicenzo Bastini.	L.	f 15
Vicenzo Pozzo.	L.	f 15

Canzone & Napolit. A Cinque Voci.

Alexandro Romano lib.1.2.	L.	l 10
Gio.Andrea Dragone. lib.1.	L.	f 8
Gio. Feretti.lib.1.2.3.4.5.	L. 3	f
Gio.Pizzone.lib.2.3.4.5.	L.	f 8
Francesa.	L.	f 15
Ieronymo Conuersi.	L.	f 15

Madrigali A Sei Voci.

Alexandro Marino.	L.	f
Armonia Celeste De diuersi.	L.	f
Alexandro Striggio.lib.Primo.	L.	f
Idem lib.Secondo.	L.	f 4
Corona De diuersi.	L.	f
Christoforo Maluezzi.	L.	f
Filippo de Monte lib. 1. 2.	L.	f
Francesco Adriano.	L.	f
Ippolito Bachufio.lib.2.	L.	f
Iacobo Cosfino.	L.	f
Ieronimo Conuersi.	L.	f
Luca Marenzio lib. 1.2.3.4.5.	L. 5	f
Pietro Vinci.lib.Primo & 2.	L. 1	f
	L.	l

Canzon & Napolitane A Sei Voci

Gio.Feretti.lib.Primo.	L.	l f
Idem lib.2.	L. 1	f 4

Messe A Quatro & A Cinque Voci.		
Afula à 4.	L.	f 15
Bachufio à 5.	L.	l f
Camatero à 5.	L.	l f
Gio.Contino à 4.	L.	l f
Gasparo Alberti à 4.	L.	l f
Gio.Pizzone à 4.	L.	f 15
Gio. Rouelli à 5.	L.	l f
Pietro Poncio à 4. lib. 1. 2.	L. l	f 10
Idem lib.2.3. à 5.	L. l	f 10
Pietro Vinci à 4.	L.	l f
Idem à 5. & 6.	L.	f 15
Pasquale Tristaboca à 4.	L.	f 15
Michaele Varotto à 6.	L.	l f 4
Palestina à 4 & à 8.	L.	f 15
Idem à 4. 5. 6. lib. 5.	L.	l f
Paulo Isnardo à 6.	L.	f 15
Idem à 8.	L.	f 15

Motetti A 4.5.6. & 8.

Andrea Pietra Santa à 5.	L.	f 15
Bernardino Garulli à 5.	L.	f 15
Cipriano à 4.	L.	f 12
Clemens. à 4.	L.	f 12
Don Françis de Lasso à 5. lib. 1	L. l	f 10
Enriche Scafen à 5. lib. 1. 2.	L. l	f 10
Filippo di Monte. lib. 5.	L. l	f 10
Francesco Vecoli à 5.	L. l	f 10
Frutti à 4.	Ll	f 15
Francesco Londariti à 6.	L. l	f 4
Gio. Baptistæ Racani à 5.	L. l	f 4
Gio. Gero à 6.	L. l	f 4
Iachet Mantua à 4.	L.	f 10
Idem à 5.lib.1. 2.	L. l	f 10
Iaches VVert à 5.lib. 2.	L. l	f
Idem à 6.lib. 1.	L. l	f
Ioan Contino à 5.	L.	f 15
Iullio Schiauetto. à 5.	L. l	f
Iacobo Corsino. à 6.	L. l	f
Ioan.Contino. à 6.	L. l	f
Luca Marenzio à 4	L.	f 15
Palestina à 4. lib. 1 & 2.	L. l	f
Idem à 5. lib. 2. & 3.	L. 3	f
Idem à 5. 6. lib. 3.	L. l	f
Idem à 5. lib. 4. & 5.	L. l	f
Pietro Poncio.à 5. lib. 1. 2. 3.	L. l	f 10
Pauli Macri à 5.	L.	f
Pietro Vinci à 8.	L. l	f 4
Idem à 5.lib. 2.	L.	f

Vesperi & Salmi.

Matthei Afulz à 6.	L.	l f
Idem à 8.	L.	l f
Alexandro Marini à 4.	L.	l f
Bonifacio Pasquale. à 5.	L.	l f
Domenici Finot. à 4.	L.	l f
Floriani Canali. à 4.	L.	l f
Lambertini à 4.	L.	l f
Pietro Poncio à 4.	L.	l f
Paulo Ferrario à 4.	L.	l f
Vicenzo Isnardo.à 5.	L.	l f
Paulo Isnardo à 5.	L.	l f
Vicenzo Ruffo à 5.	L.	l f
Ippolito Camateró à 8.	L.	l f

Lamentationi p la Septimana Sancta.

Iachet Mantua à 5.	L.	f 15
Marc' Ant. Mazzone à 5.	L.	l f
Alex.Romano à 5.lib. 1. 2.	L.	l f
Paulo Isnardi à 4.	L.	l f
Pietro Poncio à 4.	L.	f 15
Pietro Poncio. à 4.	L.	f 15
Palestina à 4.	L.	f 10

Completorij.Afula. à 6.	L.	l f
Paulo Ferrari à 4.	L.	l f
Magnificat Camatero à 5.	L.	l f
Pauli Isnardi à 5.	L.	f 15
Pietro Poncio à 4.	L.	f
Vincenti Ruffi à 4.	L.	l f
Introiti Camateró à 5.	L.	l f
Imnij Palestina à 4.	L.	l f
Imnij Iachet à 4.	L.	l f
Intauolatura de Lauto Galilei.	L 3	f 10
Francesco da Milano lib.1.2.	L. l	f 16
Gabriel Falamero.	L.	f 8
Iacobo Gorzanis à Cantare	L.	f 8
	L.	l f
Nobilta di Roma p Cantare	L.	f 12
Intauolatura Cittara Virchi.	L.	f 10
Contrapuncti Don Ferrandi	L.	f 12
Vergine Francisco Portinaro à 6.	L.	f 10
Vergine Ieronimo Scoto.à 5.	L.	f 10

FIGURE 4.2 *Indice de libri di musica stampati dalli magn[ifi]ci Scot.* [Venice: Heirs of Girolamo Scotto, 1596]. Shelfmark Broxbourne 97. 10(2. Reproduced with permission the Bodleian Library, Oxford

glance all the titles available from that particular printer. The use of the broadside format also suggests that this music book list was intended to serve as a poster, a circular, or possibly even a handbill. While both catalogues were used as advertisements in the sixteenth century, they now aid modern scholars in the recovery of lost editions, as well as the reconstruction of a musical repertory.

BUYERS AND COLLECTORS

In light of the widespread distribution of music books throughout Europe, one wonders about the potential market for these new publications. What type of person or organization purchased music books? Who were the bibliophiles and private collectors?[33]

The first and most obvious parties were royal monarchs and aristocrats who in some cases helped finance the publication of individual titles. Philip II of Spain, for example, owned several Venetian publications, according to a 1606 inventory of the Spanish royal chapel at El Escorial.[34] At least two binder's volumes containing Scotto and Gardano editions in the cathedral in Valladolid were presumably purchased when the Imperial court resided there in the sixteenth century.[35] The Royal library of John IV of Portugal contained a phenomenal assemblage of sixteenth-century printed music, all of which was destroyed in the great earthquake that struck Lisbon in 1755.[36] Venetian music books made their way to England, as seen in the Arundel–Lumley library, which contained several Gardano and Scotto prints.[37]

Throughout the German-speaking provinces, dukes as well as patrician collectors procured Venetian music editions for their libraries. Surviving collections, some containing a great number of books, others now consisting of only a few sets of partbooks, are scattered throughout the libraries and archives of Europe, sometimes far from their place of origin. Duke Albrecht V (1550–79) and his son Wilhelm II (1579–97) of Bavaria owned an important collection of music books containing many Venetian editions that now make up the nucleus of the music section of the Bavarian State Library in Munich. A collection of partbooks in the University Library in Cracow once belonged to Duke Wilhelm of Lüneburg (1559–92) and his cousin, Duke Julius of Brunswick-Lüneburg (1568–89), the founder of the first ducal library at Wolfenbüttel.[38]

Ecclesiastical institutions also bought and even financed the printing of music publications. Archival documents concerning the *cappella* of San Antonio Basilica (known as "Il Santo") in Padua and the Monastery of San Giorgio Maggiore in Venice, for example, reveal that these organizations either rewarded individual composers or paid outright for the publication of music.[39] Other ecclesiastical establishments purchased numerous Venetian music publications, such as the Palatine Basilica of Santa Barbara in Mantua, constructed in the 1560s by Duke Guglielmo Gonzaga (1550–87), an avid music lover and composer. The bulk of the extensive Santa Barbara collection survives today in the Milan Conservatory Library.[40] The Jesuit

Colleges in Palermo[41] and Regensburg,[42] and the Monastery of Saints Ulrich and Afra in Augsburg,[43] also had impressive music collections. A number of ecclesiastical institutions in Bologna contained choral libraries rich in Venetian music publications, for example, the Scuola Pia, an *ospedale*, which taught music to the orphans,[44] and the Monastery of San Salvatore, where the theorist Giovanni Maria Artusi (ca.1540–1613) was a canon.[45] The choir school of the Carmelite Convent of St. Anna in Augsburg possessed one of the most extensive music collections of all church establishments. A group of no fewer than forty different sacred sixteenth-century music editions now located in several northern European and American libraries contain on their title pages a stamp with the monogram SANA, identifying these publications as part of the St. Anna collection.[46]

Secular institutions, including academies and universities, also purchased music books for their membership. Sixteenth-century Italian academies played an important role in the intellectual and cultural life of their time. Antonfrancesco Doni describes a circle of *dilettanti* devoted to the study of poetry and music in Piacenza in his *Dialogo* of 1544.[47] The surviving inventories and account books of the Accademia Filarmonica in Verona document the purchase of individual music editions directly from Venice.[48] Still other volumes in the collection were given by individual donors. Bartolomeo Cartero, a composer and member of the academy, donated at least eight sets of partbooks to the academy.[49] Another five editions once belonged to Count Giovanni Severino.[50]

Universities constituted another type of secular institution that acquired music publications. The University of Jena, for example, which maintained its own church and library, owned a large collection of music manuscripts and prints, given to the university by its founder, Elector Johann Friedrich der Großmütige, in 1548 for use by the university choir.

In addition to aristocrats and institutions, individual owners from professional and merchant classes also bought music publications. Augsburg, an important German commercial center with close ties to Venice, had several patrician collectors of music. Two of them were Johann Georg von Werdenstein and Hans Heinrich Herwart (1520–1583), whose libraries were later purchased by the duke of Bavaria.[51] Various members of the well-known Fugger family also owned impressive libraries containing music publications. Most of the collections assembled by the brothers, Raimund (1528–69) and Georg (1518–69), and Georg's son, Philipp Eduard (1546–1618), in 1655, passed into what is now the Austrian National Library in Vienna.[52]

Only a handful of surviving Venetian publications attest to the music collections once owned by individual composers. Twelve Venetian editions belonged to the Augsburg composer Gregor Aichinger, who may have obtained them when he studied with Giovanni Gabrieli in Venice.[53] The early seventeenth-century Hamburg composer Thomas Selle acquired a collection of Venetian music editions dating from the 1540s. The title page to a Venetian edition of Lasso madrigals now in the Civico Museo Bibliografico Musicale in Bologna bears the signature of the famous madrigalist Luca Marenzio.[55]

With ownership of music publications by composers, we come full circle—from the creation and printing of music to its dissemination into the hands of other composers. The role of the composer in the book trade was not just limited to that of consumer. The commercialization of music printing had a profound influence on the lives of composers as well as their patrons in Cinquecento Italy.

NOTES

1. He was also an independent printer, who issued over 35 of his own publications; see Pietro Manzi, "Annali tipografici di Giovanni Maria Scotto (1559–1566)," in *La tipografia napoletana nel '500.* [3] *Annali di Giovanni Paolo Suganappo, Raimondo Amato, Giovanni de Boy, Giovanni Maria Scotto et tipograft minori (1533–1570)*, 159–206 (Florence, 1973), 159–206.

2. On the connection between Girolamo and Ottaviano di Amadio see J. Bernstein, "Burning Salamander," 495–97.

3. ASV, Notarile Atti B. Solian, b. 11870, fol. 277^{r-v}.

4. "Ad ipsius nomine et pro eo petendum exigendum et recipiendum quas pecuniae ac rerum bonorum quantitates ac totum id quod dicta constituens habere debet et petere posset a quibuscumque personis in dicta alma urbe Rome quauis ratione uel causa et receptis quietandum." ASV, Notarile Atti B. Solian, b. 11875, fol. 123. My thanks to Leofranc Holford-Strevens for his assistance with the transcription and translation of this document.

5. ASV, Notarile Atti B. Solian, b. 11876, fols. 106–10.

6. ASV, Notarile Atti B. Solian, b. 11874, fols. 16–17^{v}.

7. Chapman, "Andrea Antico," 448–52.

8. ASV, Notarile Atti B. Solian, b. 11870, fols. 261–62^{v}.

9. The inscription appears in the altus partbook of the British Library copy of Paolo Ferrarese's *Passiones, Lamentationes, Responsoria . . .* (Venice: Scotto, 1565)

10. Eugene Rice, "Recent Studies on the Population of Europe, 1348–1620," *Renaissance News* 18 (1965): 180–87.

11. A general description of the distribution of books appears in Febvre and Martin, *Coming of the Book,* 222–44.

12. ASV, Notarile Atti B. Solian, b. 11869, fol. 230^{v}.

13. An account of the round boat, state galleys, and trade routes appears in Lane, *Venice: A Maritime Republic,* 336–89.

14. Emil Herzog, *Chronik der Kreisstadt Zwickau* (Zwickau, 1839), 2: 371.

15. For a transcription of the privilege see Agee, "The Privilege and Venetian Music Printing," 220. In 1560, Canon Scardeonius wrote that Antonio Rotta was virtually unrivaled as a lutenist in Italy and was also an excellent teacher who had grown quite rich by giving lessons on the lute [to university students, *literati,* academicians]. See Hans Radke, "Rotta, Antonio," in *New Grove* 16: 260.

16. Marciani, "Editori, tipografi, librai veneti."

17. ASV, Notarile Atti B. Solian. b. 11866 fol. 325^{v}; 11867 fol. 63; 11868 fol. 32; 11869 fol. 159; 11873 fol. 156; 11875 fol. 59; 11876 fol. 185^{v} mention the following Sicilian bookmen: Tomaso della Porta, Antonio Bertoleno, Simon de Franco, Giovanni Franco and Lodovico Carrara, Giovanni Battista Calegaris, Sebastiano de Paladini, Francesco Patavino, Agostino Canella, and Battista de Bonadio.

18. Henri Vanhulst, "Suppliers and Clients of Christopher Plantin, Distributor of Polyphonic Music in Antwerp (1568–1578)," in *Musicology and Archival Research. Colloquium Proceedings Brussels 22–23.4.1993*, ed. B. Haggh, F. Daelemans, and A. Vanrie (Archives et

Bibliothèques de Belgique 46; Brussels, 1994), 558–604 at 584, 596. He suggests that "Moralis Hispani Missae 4° Venetiis" sold by Plantin in 1568 might have been a copy from the 1563 edition printed by Rampazetto or Scotto and a copy of "Jachet Motetti" bought by the Jesuit College in Bruges might be from one of the 1565 Scotto editions.

19. A detailed account appears in Henri Brésard, *Les Foires de Lyon au XVe et au XVIe*
siècle (Lyons, 1914).

20. Two documents in the *Bibliographie Lyonnaise*, sixièmes série, 389, dated December 2 and 5, 1584, reveal Angelo Gardano's trade connections with the north. They mention a packet of eleven books addressed to Gardano, and a commission which Gardano apparently gave to a Parisian bookseller named Nicolas Nivelle to buy some books printed in red and black ("si ledit Gardon n'aurait pas donné commission a Nicolas Nivelle, m^t libraire de paris, d'acheter quelques livres imprimés en rouge et en noir."); cited in Bridges, "Publishing of Arcadelt's First Book," 1:221.

21. Although the Lyons book fairs declined by 1560, a brisk trade between Lyonnais and Venetian printers continued well into the late sixteenth century. Archival documents show that in August 1583, Melchiorre Scotto received three or four bales of books from Lyons which went through Venetian customs without being inspected by the Inquisition. See Grendler, *Roman Inquisition*, 105.

22. See the contemporary account of the fair by Henri Estienne, *The Frankfurt Book Fair*, trans. J. W. Thompson (Chicago, 1911).

23. Friedrich Kapp, *Geschichte des deutschen Buchhandels* (Leipzig, 1886), 1: 772–74.

24. ASV, Notarile atti, B. Solian, b. 11875, fols. 25^v–26^v.

25. Apparently the Frankfurt fair was not only an important center for the dissemination of books in general, but also for the clandestine trade in titles placed on the Index of Prohibited Books. Pietro Longo turned out to be a smuggler of banned books and was eventually put to death by the Venetian Inquisition for trafficking in prohibited titles and possibly for holding Protestant beliefs. See Grendler, *Roman Inquisition,* 186–89.

26. A facsimile edition of all the complete catalogues from 1564–73 appears in Georg Willer, *Die Messkataloge Georg Willers Herbstmesse 1564 bis Herbstmesse 1573,* vol. 1 of *Die Messkataloge des sechszehnten Jahrhunderts*, ed. Bernhard Fabian (Hildesheim and New York, 1972). For a modern transcription of the music books only see Albert Göhler, *Verzeichnis der in den Frankfurter und Leipziger Messkatalogen der Jahre 1564 bis 1769 angezeigten Musikalien* (Leipzig, 1902).

27. Albert Ehrman and Graham Pollard, *The Distribution of Books by Catalogue from the Invention of Printing to A.D. 1800* (Cambridge, 1965), 23.

28. Ibid.; the book list is reproduced in *Gutenberg Jahrbuch* (1961), 43–48.

29. The complete catalogue appears in Renouard, *Annales de l'imprimerie des Alde*, 329–31.

30. Conrad Gesner in compiling his *Bibliotheca universalis* (1545) and *Pandectae* (1548) made use of printed catalogues supplied by such firms as Manuzio and Estienne; see Hans Fischer, "Conrad Gesner (1516–1565) as Bibliographer and Encyclopaedist," *The Library*, 5th ser., 21 (1966): 119–33. Since the Swiss bibliographer lists in the *Pandectae* music books published by Gardano and Scotto, he presumably acquired book lists printed by the two presses. Gesner's choice of Scotto as one of the scholar-printers to whom he dedicated a section of the *Pandectae* further supports this premise; see Lawrence F. Bernstein, "The Bibliography of Music in Conrad Gesner's *Pandectae* (1548)," *Acta musicologica* 45 (1973): 129.

31. Agee, *Gardano Music Printing Firms*, 74.

32. Ibid., 77, where Agee provides a tabulation of entries from the Gardano book list by year.

33. Only a brief survey of owners and collectors of printed music books is offered here. A more detailed discussion occurs in Jane A. Bernstein, "Buyers and Collectors of Music

Publications: Two Sixteenth-Century Music Libraries Recovered," in *Music in Renaissance Cities and Courts: Studies in Honor of Lewis Lockwood*, ed. Jessie Ann Owens and Anthony Cummings (Warren, Mich., 1997), 21–34.

34. Edmond vander Straeten, *La Musique aux Pays-Bas avant le XIXe siècle* (Brussels, 1867–88), 8: 365–83.

35. Higinio Anglés, "El Archivo musical de la Catedral de Valladolid," *Anuario musical* 3 (1948): 59–108 at 60–61.

36. Joachim Vasconcellos, ed. *Primeira parte do index da livraria de musica muyto alto, e poderoso do Rey Dom João o IV . . . Por ordem de sua Mag. Por Paulo Crasheck. Anno 1649* (Porto, 1874–76).

37. John Milsom, "The Nonsuch Music Library," in *Sundry Sorts of Music Books: Essays on the British Library Collections presented to O. W. Neighbour on his 70th birthday*, ed. Chris Banks, Arthur Searle, and Malcolm Turner (London, 1993), 146–82.

38. On the discovery of this collection see Bernstein, "Buyers and Collectors," 23–24. The contents of the collection appears on pp. 29–30.

39. On Il Santo see Jessie Ann Owens, "Il Cinquecento," in *Storia della musica al Santo di Padova*, ed. Sergio Durante and Pierluigi Petrobelli, *Fonti e studi per la storia del Santo Padova* 6 (Vicenza, 1990), 27–92 and 285–338.

40. On the original library see Iain Fenlon, *Music and Patronage in Sixteenth-Century Mantua* (Cambridge, 1988), 201–8. On the part of the collection that survives see Gilda Grigolato, comp., and A. Zecca Laterza, indexer, *Musiche della Cappella di Santa Barbara in Mantova* (Conservatorio di Musica "Giuseppe Verdi," Catalogo della biblioteca . . . Fondi speciali I; Florence, 1972).

41. An example from the Palermo collection appears in Palermo, Biblioteca Nazionale, Rari 1.a.29–32. The core of the rare music collection in the Biblioteca Nazionale of Palermo comes from the library of the Jesuit College. See Lewis, *Antonio Gardano*, 1: 147.

42. A set of five partbooks (Regensburg, Proskesche Musikbibliothek AR 284–290) contains the inscription: "Collegij Societatis Jesu ad D. Paulum Ratisponae." See Lewis, *Antonio Gardano*, 1: 150.

43. Clytus Gottwald, *Die Musikhandschriften der Staats- und Stadtbibliothek Augsburg* (Handschriftenkataloge der Staats- und Stadtbibliothek Augsburg 1; Wiesbaden, 1974).

44. For more on the *ospedale* see Carlo Vitali, " 'La scuola della virtù delle Zitelle': insegnamento e pratiche musicali fra Sei e Ottocento presso il Conservatorio degli Esposti di Bologna," in *I Bastardini: patrimonio e memoria di un ospedale bolognese* (Bologna, 1990), 134 n. 4. I wish to thank Craig Monson for bringing this article to my attention.

45. On San Salvatore and its manuscript collection see Oscar Mischiati, *La prassi musicale presso i Canonici regolari del Ss. Salvatore nei secoli XVI e XVII e i manoscritti polifonici della Biblioteca musicale "G. B. Martini" di Bologna* (Rome, 1985).

46. For further details on the identity of the collection and a list of editions from the collection see Bernstein, "Buyers and Collectors," 27–28 and 31–33.

47. A modern transcription of the complete edition appears in Antonfrancesco Doni, *L'opera musicale*, ed. Anna Maria Monterosso Vacchelli (Instituta e monumenta, ser. 2, vol. 1; Cremona, 1969).

48. Turrini, *L'Accademia Filarmonica*, 30–40, 44–45, 56–68, 81–82, and 87–92.

49. Ibid., 145–46. See also Paganuzzi, "Il Cinquecento," in *La musica a Verona*, ed. E. Paganuzzi et al. (Verona, [1976]), 135; the portrait appears as fig. 90.

50. Turrini, *L'Accademia Filarmonica*, 144–45.

51. H. Colin Slim, "The Music Library of Hans Heinrich Herwart," *Annales musicologiques* 7 (1964–77): 67–79.

52. Richard Schaal, "Die Musikbibliothek von Raimund Fugger d.J.: Ein Beitrag zur Musik-überlieferung des 16. Jahrhunderts," *Acta musicologica* 29 (1957): 1–137.

53. The set of partbooks is now in Augsburg, Staats- und Stadtbibliothek, 4° Tonkunst Schletterer 411–415; for a description see Lewis, *Antonio Gardano*, 1: 128–29.

54. An elaborately bound set of partbooks in the Hamburg, Staats- und Universitätsbibliothek (shelfmark Scriv. A594). See ibid., 1: 133–34.

55. A reproduction of the titlepage with Marenzio's autograph signature appears in James Chater, "'Such sweet sorrow'; the *dialogo di partenza* in the Italian Madrigal," *Early Music* 27 (1999), 584. Gaetano Gaspari, *Catalogo della biblioteca del Liceo Musicale di Bologna* (Bologna, 1943), 3: 88.

Five

COMPOSERS, PATRONS, AND THE VENETIAN MUSIC PRESS

> I have composed and published many works, but have far more in my possession, in publishing which I am delayed by the (financial) constraints I spoke of. A great deal of expense is needed, especially should larger notes and letters be used, as church music above all requires.[1]
>
> —Giovanni Pierluigi da Palestrina, Dedication
to Pope Sixtus V, Lamentations, 1588

omposers quickly became aware of the possibility of addressing a larger audience through the press. With the commercialization of music printing, they no longer had to rely solely on their immediate circle of patrons for the circulation of their music. In addition to retaining the existing patronage system as their primary means of support, they could now seek out other patrons to supplement their income. They could use their publications to "advertise" for another position, or they could act as entrepreneurs by selling their own editions. Not just established musicians but also rank amateurs tried to reach the public at large through the print medium, as the German theorist Hermann Finck lamented:

> Moreover, many of those whom I have mentioned even dare to claim for themselves the title of composer. After managing, in the space of half a year, to produce with much sweat a little song, such as it may be, with scarcely three consonances in it, they immediately get it printed, so that their great and glorious name may become known to the whole world.[2]

Nowhere was this felt more clearly than in Venice, where, unlike its northern counterparts, editions devoted to the works of an individual composer outnumbered music anthologies or *recueils*, as they were more commonly known in the north. Musicians understood the influence of the new industry and tried to use it to their advantage in several ways. They eagerly sought out reliable and competent publishing houses that would issue their works quickly and correctly, as we learn from Heliseo Ghibel, who praised Ottaviano Scotto for bringing out his motets.[3] At times publishers are thanked for their generosity, as in the unusual circumstance of the composer Claudio Veggio, who in his 1540 Book of Four-Voice Madrigals acknowledged Girolamo Scotto for donating six pieces by Arcadelt to complete his own book of madrigals.[4]

Composers could now augment their fixed income either by selling their works outright to printers, or by getting involved in the actual publishing and marketing of their own works. Evidence regarding the type of payment authors received in the sixteenth century remains ambiguous at best. Sources dealing with literary publications suggest that, for the most part, printers did not pay authors a flat fee for their works, but instead furnished them with complimentary copies of their publications.[5] The handful of documents concerning payments to composers, however, offer a conflicting view. The Englishman Thomas Whythorne, who visited Italy in the 1550s, noted that in order to obtain new music, printers "do fee the best musicians that they can retain, to the end that when they do make any new songs their printers may have the only copies of them to print; which encourageth the musician to employ and give his mind and endeavour the more to his study therein."[6] Though from a different country and time period, a court case concerning the publishing of John Dowland's Second Booke of Songs in 1600 reveals that Dowland's wife was paid a fee of £20 for the manuscript.[7]

As early as 1536, Costanzo Festa apparently attempted to sell his music outright to a printer. In a letter addressed to Filippo Strozzi, the composer requested the Florentine nobleman to find an unnamed Venetian printer to whom he could sell his hymns, Magnificats, and *basse* for the enormous sum of 200 scudi.[8] Festa either was unsuccessful in selling his sacred works or, more likely, changed his mind, for two years after he wrote this letter he took out a privilege from the Venetian Senate to print "messe, mottettj, madrigali, basse, contraponti, lamentation et qualunq[ue] delle composition sue." This privilege and an unsigned edition of Festa's *Madrigale . . . Libro primo* dated 1538 have led James Haar to conclude that Festa went into the publishing business as an *editore*, that is, underwriting the entire edition, hiring a printer on a fee-basis to do the presswork, and profiting from the sales of the book.[9] If this indeed were the case, then Festa did not make use of his privilege to publish further volumes of his music. This would also explain the lacuna in music editions devoted to Festa's music, while whole series of books substantially devoted to the music of Festa's contemporaries Verdelot and Arcadelt emerged from Venetian presses.[10]

Festa's brief foray into the publishing world occurred in the same year that the single-impression method of music printing was first used in Venice. The composer's belief that he could make a quick profit from this new process might in fact have turned into a disastrous loss, for even with contacts and marketing experience, an underwriter could not be assured of selling the entire pressrun. Yet Festa was undoubtedly a visionary among musicians in recognizing the economic possibilities of the music-printing trade, for payment of a flat fee for a composer's works was presumably not nearly as lucrative as the earnings one could acquire from the marketing of one's own books.[11]

Though a printing contract between a music publisher and a composer in Cinquecento Venice has yet to be unearthed, extant agreements of this sort originating in other cities might also apply to Venice as well. Composers apparently entered into temporary partnerships with printers and other third parties for a share of the profits made from the sales of their works. Often they were obliged or chose to put up part or all of the production capital. The amount of money the composer was required to pay and the terms of the contract depended upon the circumstances as well as the relationship between composer and printer.[12] Sometimes composers assumed the entire expense of the pressrun, as did Tomás Luis de Victoria in the printing of his *Missae, Magnificat, motecta, psalmi* of 1600.[13] At other times they paid a share of the cost of production. Morales, for example, financed about half of the printing expenses for *Missarum Liber Primus*,[14] as did Matteo Bosca for the now lost *Libro primo de musica de la salamandra*,[15] and Philippe de Monte was obliged to advance a portion of the production costs to Plantin for the publication of his *Liber I. Missarum* of 1587.[16] In return they received all or part of the pressrun. The profits they reaped came from the copies they sold to patrons, to friends, and on the open market. In agreements where parties shared in the expenses, certain sales restrictions could apply. Morales, in his 1543 contract with the Roman printer Valerio Dorico, and the two *editori*, Antonio de Salamanca and Giovanni della Gatta, was allowed to sell as many of the 275 copies he received in Spain, but only fifty on the Italian peninsula, so long as the transaction did not involve any merchant or bookstore.[17]

It appears that certain composers did very well on the sales of their music. Victoria, for example, turned out to be quite a businessman, sending his publications to various churches, institutions, and noblemen as far afield as Graz, Urbino, and Bogotá, Colombia. He even recruited relatives in Spain to sell his publications during the years he worked in Rome. His *Missae, Magnificat, motecta, psalmi* of 1600 apparently realized a profit equivalent to the annual income he earned from all his Spanish benefices.[18]

Several composers evidently sought to profit from the printing not only of their own works but also of those by their more illustrious colleagues. Hermann Mathias Werrecore, the choir master of the Duomo of Milan, sent "a treasury of songs of greatest value from Italy," including works by Josquin des Prez, to the Strasbourg music printer Peter Schoeffer, who issued them in his *Cantiones quinque vocum selectissimae* of 1539.[19] In 1548 Perissone Cambio and Paolo Vergelli presumably underwrote two separate editions of Rore's *Terzo libro di madrigali a cinque voce*[20] Francesco dalla Viola, with the help and influence of Prince Alfonso of Ferrara, commissioned the printing of Willaert's *Musica nova*.[21]

One of the most successful of these musician-underwriters was the relatively unknown composer Giulio Bonagiunta. A singer at St. Mark's in Venice, Bonagiunta composed Italian madrigals and *canzoni alla napolitana*. From 1565 to 1568, he chose to supplement his income by sponsoring some seventeen editions, all but two of which were printed by Girolamo Scotto. Although it has been generally thought that Bonagiunta acted merely as an in-house music editor and proofreader for Scotto, the publications state consistently that Bonagiunta underwrote the editions.[22] They also intimate that the financing of the Bonagiunta series was more complicated than the usual contractual agreement between composer and printer, for all but three editions contain printers' marks not associated with the Scotto firm. Thus, Bonagiunta provided, edited, and proofread the music (and possibly put up some of the money), Scotto printed it, and a different publisher financed the edition. Significantly, not one but several printers' marks unrelated to those of the House of Scotto appear in the Bonagiunta prints. The title page of the first edition of Alessandro Striggio's *Il cicalamento delle donne al bucato* of 1567 cites Girolamo Scotto as the printer, but the device, an elaborate woodcut depicting Minerva holding a lance atop a lion and containing the initials "Z M B V," turns out to be that of the Venetian printer Giovanni (i.e. Zuan) Maria Bonelli il Vecchio.[23] Another printer's mark, illustrating an eagle atop a globe with the motto "Nobiliora altiora petunt" and the initials "A V" surmounted by a patriarchal cross, appears on the title pages of Bonagiunta's three-volume madrigal series, *Il Desiderio*. This woodcut can be identified with the bookman Giacomo Anielli Sanvito (see above, fig. 2.11)[24] The title pages of Bonagiunta's edition of Giovanni Ferretti's *Canzone alla napolitana a cinque voci* of 1567 and his anthology *Il Gaudio. Primo libro de madrigali de diversi eccellen. musici a tre voci* of 1566[25] contain yet a third woodcut, a rooster with the motto "Excubo ac vigilo," which is associated with the printer Pietro da Fino.[26]

PATRONAGE AND PRINTING

Patrons also saw the potentials of the printing press as a means of public recognition. Dedications abound with metaphors extolling the culture, erudition, and generosity of the benefactor. In some cases, public recognition of the patron went beyond the dedication page. Music or poetry written by the dedicatee or another member of the honored family would appear in the publication, such as three madrigals by Scipione Gonzaga in Clerico's *Secondo libro de madrigali a 5* (Venice: Scotto 1562), a madrigal by Guglielmo Gonzaga in Oratio Faà's *Libro primo de madrigali a 5* (Venice: Gardano, 1569), or a canzone by Ferdinando de' Medici set to music by Rossetto in his *Lamento di Olimpia* (Venice: Scotto, 1567).

Some ardent patrons went even further in promoting themselves and the music they loved through the print medium. The most remarkable case was Prince Alfonso d'Este, later duke of Ferrara (1559–97), who went to great lengths to publish Willaert's *Musica nova*. During the 1580s and 90s Ferrara even had its own music printer, Vittorio Baldini, who issued beautifully executed music publications by composers either connected to the Este court or who paid homage to its various members.[27]

The printing press had a profound effect upon traditional patronage by democratizing the system to include benefactors from classes other than royalty and the highest of nobility. People with more modest incomes, who could not afford to maintain the services of musicians in their household, could now commission or simply pay for the publication costs of a music book. Indeed, for a relatively moderate sum, a patron could achieve some measure of fame as a worthy benefactor.

DEDICATIONS

Most of our information regarding this new kind of patronage may be gleaned from dedicatory pages. Though one or two dedications appeared in music publications of the incunabular period, they did not emerge in Italy in great numbers until around 1538–40. Significantly, the dedication page began to flourish at precisely the same time that the notorious writer Pietro Aretino introduced a new literary form into the Italian language, the *libro di lettere* or book of letters. The development of both genres at the same time was not a mere concidence, for the dedication was directly related to the art of letter writing.

To whom were these dedications addressed and what kind of information do they provide? The list of dedicatees of over 400 Italian music editions dating from 1536 to 1572 in appendix B reveals a wide assortment of both dedicators and dedicatees. As we might expect, many were addressed to monarchs and ruling nobility. Royalty outside of Italy include King Philip II of Spain; Emperor Maximilian II; Archdukes Ferdinand and Charles of Austria; and Dukes Albrecht and Wilhelm of Bavaria, to name a few. Within Italy, music patronage by the Gonzagas and the Estense has been well documented.[28] The names of other signorial families, in particular the Farnese in Parma, the Medici in Florence, and to a lesser extent the della Rovere in Urbino, appear as dedicatees, as do members of the ruling families of Sicily and Naples, the Santa Pau, Moncada, and heirs of the House of Aragon.

Yet these signorial patrons account for only a quarter of the dedicatees. The remaining 75 percent of dedications were not addressed to famous rulers but to lesser-known nobility, members of the Church, academies, wealthy merchants, *literati*, and even to other composers. Minor nobility, too numerous to name, from cities and towns all over the Italian peninsula appear once or twice as dedicatees. In a few instances, their patronage extended beyond the occasional publication by a local composer. The name of Giovanni Ferro, count of Macerata, occurs in five different publications dating from the late 1560s, and Count Mario Bevilacqua of Verona, later in the century, was the dedicatee of no fewer than twelve publications (see app. B).[29]

Dedications also honor members of the Church. Support for music publications came from entire ecclesiastical institutions such as the canons of the cathedrals of Brescia, Padua, and Fanestri, as well as St. Peter's Basilica. Specific cardinals, archbishops, bishops, abbots, deacons, and other churchmen also sponsored publications. One of the most prominent was Cardinal Cristoforo Madruzzo, bishop of Trent and Bressanone, who was involved during the early years of the Tridentine Reform.[30] Other important names include Cardinal Otto Truchsess von Waldburg, bishop of Augsburg, a friend of Madruzzo and also an ardent music lover; Cardinal Ercole Gonzaga,[31] and the reformers Domenico Bollano, bishop of Brescia, Cardinal Carlo Borromeo, and Cardinal Giovanni Morone, bishop of Novara, who, briefly in 1537 and 1538 while bishop of Modena, took the extreme position of abolishing all sacred polyphony in the cathedral of Modena.[32]

In addition to the Church, Italian academies also sponsored music publications. Several of these secular institutions, which sprang up in many cities, were mentioned in dedications, either as dedicatees or in passing. The musical activities of the Accademia Filarmonica in Verona are well known.[33] No fewer than ten music publications contain dedications to the membership of this venerable society.[34] But there were many other academies in Italy that maintained an interest in music. Giovanni Contino addressed the dedication of his *Primo libro de' madrigali a cinque voci* (1560) to Barbara Callina, an important figure of the Accademia degli Occulti of Brescia; Gasparo Fiorino honored the Accademia of Rossano with a three-voice villanella from his *La Nobiltà di Roma*; Nasco and Portinaro both dedicated their 1557 editions to the Academy in Vicenza;[35] Antonfrancesco Doni described a circle of *dilettanti* devoted to the study of poetry and music in Piacenza in his *Dialogo* of 1544, while Portinaro dedicated his *Quarto libro de madrigali a cinque voci* (Gardano, 1560) to the Accademia degli Elevati in Padua.

Dedications by musicians living in areas of the Veneto suggest that there was a greater degree of independence in the patronage system of the Venetian Republic than in other Italian city-states. In addition to members of the patriciate and clergy, we find high government officials, foreign ambassadors, merchants, intellectuals, university professors, and even composers listed among the dedicatees. Giovanni da Lezze, procurator and treasurer of St. Mark's, was chosen at least twice as a dedicatee.[36] The name of Georg Uttinger, a German whose father was consul of the Fondaco dei Tedeschi, the residence of German merchants in Venice, appeared in the dedications of three Gardano editions.[37] Other prominent foreigners in Venice, García Fernando, secretary of King Philip of Spain, and Vito Dorimbergo, Imperial Ambassador to the Venetian Republic, were also honored as dedicatees. The Paduan lutenist Melchiore de Barberiis chose Marcantonio Passeri da Genova, a scholar who taught natural philosophy at the University of Padua, as the dedicatee of his fifth book of lute tablatures (Venice: Scotto, 1546). Giulio Bonagiunta dedicated his *Canzone napolitane a tre voci secondo libro* (Venice: Scotto, 1566) to three patrons, one of whom, Marco Milano, was a merchant of precious stones.[38]

Dedications to writers and intellectuals also appeared in a few publications. Perissone Cambio paid tribute to the renowned poet Gaspara Stampa in his *Primo libro di madrigali a quatro voci* (Venice: Gardano, 1547), while he dedicated his edition of Rore's Third Book of Madrigals (Venice: Gardano, 1548) to the writer, bishop, and papal diplomat Giovanni della Casa. The literary figure Girolamo Fenarolo is commemorated in a dedication by Antonio Barges.[39] Then there is the unusual case of two dedications addressed to the composer Maddalena Casulana— one by the playwright, actor, and composer Antonio Molino, and the other by the Venetian printer Angelo Gardano.[40]

Besides identification of patrons, what else does the dedication page tell us? A perusal of dedications reveals that the vast majority are written in an artificial, almost formulaic style. They tend to contain the same imagery and turns of phrases found in published literary letters. Composers refer to their music works as fruits to be enjoyed by the dedicatee, who, in turn, is endowed with the divine qualities of virtue, kindness, and courtesy (*la virtù, la gentilezza, & la cortesia*). Allusions to antiquity and nature often round out what turns out to be a carefully crafted yet contrived text. One must be cautious in taking the contents of these dedications too literally, for, as Lorenzo Bianconi has noted, sixteenth- and early seventeeth-century dedi- cations belonged to the particular literary genre or topos of epistles. Secretaries and other literary figures published dedicatory letters in their *libri di lettere*; these letters were intended to serve as models for others to imitate.[41] Indeed, in many cases, composers and printers commissioned men of letters to write or revise their own dedications.[42]

There are several examples cited in the literature. One of the earliest is Antonio Gardano's dedication of his *Canzone francese a due voci* (1539), which was written by his friend Nicolò Franco, who issued a paraphrased version of the text the same year in his *Pistole vulgari*.[43] The most striking documentation concerning this prac- tice is a series of letters written by Giovanni de Macque, in which his original dedication of *Ricercate et Canzoni francese a quattro voci* (1586) appears along with the revised version he requested from the humanist Giovanni Francesco Peranda.[44] Other examples include Luzzasco Luzzaschi's dedication of *Madrigali per cantare e sonare* (1600), found in Alessandro Guarini's *Prose* (1611);[45] and Filippo Paruta's dedication of Antonio Il Verso's Twelfth Book of Five-Voice Madrigals.[46]

Despite literary conventions, dedications sometimes provide important infor- mation concerning relationships among composer, patron, and printer. In rare in- stances, a composer might explain how he arrived at dedicating his book to a par- ticular patron, as in the case of Baldassare Donato, who in his *Secondo libro de madrigali a quattro voci* (1568) explains that his friend Giulio Bonagiunta proposed that he dedicate his book to the patron since he was the most worthy to receive this gift.[47] Dedications can also document connections between composers and printers, such as Marc'Antonio Mazzone, who explains in the *Corona delle napolitane* of 1570 that Scotto gave him the music of several composers (all friends of Mazzone) to emend and publish.[48]

TYPES OF PATRONAGE

Why would a composer choose a particular person as a dedicatee? The most obvious answer was for financial gain or the hope of some other reward. Patrons selected for this reason fall into three distinct categories. The first and most traditional relationship concerns a composer in the service of a particular patron who would pay either part or all of the printing expenses for the edition. Archival documents confirm that patrons awarded payments to composers for the specific purpose of having their music printed. Cardinal Pietro Aldobrandini granted a bonus of 100 scudi to Ruggiero Giovanelli two weeks before the publication of the composer's *Terzo libro de madrigali a cinque voci* (Venice: Vincenti, 1599).[49] The deputati of Il Santo in Padua bestowed rewards upon composers in order to pay for the printing of music, and, in turn, were named as dedicatees.[50] Composers might also dedicate an edition to their patron for gratitude in procuring a position or for extra remuneration. Vincenzo Ruffo, only a year after his appointment as *maestro di cappella* at the cathedral of Pistoia, received such a reward.[51]

Composers might dedicate a book to a potential patron with whom they sought employment. In 1563 Biagio Pesciolini, while *maestro di cappella* at the cathedral in Volterra, dedicated his first book of madrigals to the provost of the cathedral in Prato, where nine years later the composer became canon and *maestro di cappella*. In the same year Michele Varoto dedicated his book of Masses to the bishop of Novara; one year later he was appointed *maestro di cappella* at the cathedral.

The third kind of patronage moved beyond the traditional realm of patronage into the market system, whereby the musician composed something "ready-made" and then sought out an individual patron.[52] In these cases, the composer was neither employed by nor sought a position with the dedicatee, but only hoped for a substantial subvention to pay for the publication. Lasso obviously sought a substantial reward from Duke Alfonso d'Este, to whom he dedicated and presented his *Libro quarto de' madrigali a cinque voci* during his trip to Italy in 1567.[53] In 1572 Palestrina dedicated his Second Book of Motets to Duke Guglielmo Gonzaga in hopes of placing his eldest son, Rodolfo (a contributor to the volume) at the Mantuan court. For his effort Palestrina received the generous sum of 25 scudi from the duke, and an appointment for his son.[54]

Composers would sometimes solicit financial support from potential donors before the publication their works. Marc'Antonio Mazzone requested permission through the Mantuan ambassador to dedicate his 1591 book of *Canzoni* to Duke Vincenzo Gonzaga (1587–1612) and in return received 28 scudi.[55] Orazio Angelini was not so fortunate; the funding he requested for "tre mute di madrigali a sei voci" from the grand duke of Tuscany in his *Canzone* of 1577 apparently did not materialize.[56]

The concept of patronage expanded when music printing became a successful commercial venture; the industry offered new financial incentives for composers. A composer could earn additional money by presenting copies of his publication to nobles and prelates other than the dedicatee of his book. This was evidently a common practice, as seen with Vincenzo Galilei, who, in 1581, presented to the duke of Mantua a copy of his *Fronimo Dialogo*, which was originally dedicated in 1568 to Duke Wilhelm of Bavaria.[57] In 1602 the Spanish composer Tomás Luis de Victoria sent to the duke of Urbino a copy of his Masses, Magnificats, Motets, and Psalms of 1600 (*Missae, Magnificat, motecta, psalmi*), which he had dedicated to King Philip II. A year later, having received no reply from the duke, Victoria sent from Madrid the following letter:

Most Serene Lord,

Last year I sent your highness ten little music books with a thousand things [in them] and among others there was a Battle Mass that gave my Lord the King much pleasure and since your highness has not had me advised of the receipt I have determined to send more to your highness and to beg that you will receive them together with my service. And may your highness condescend to give me some largesse to help with the printing, and for whatever will be given I shall be thankful all my life.[58]

While composers expected substantial remuneration from aristocrats and churchmen, they anticipated different kinds of rewards from middle-class dedicatees. Merchants, writers, and friends appear to have had more complicated connections with composers, as seen with Don Pellegrino Stellini, the dedicatee of Claudio Merulo's edition of Verdelot's First and Second Books of Madrigals (1566). Stellini had been one of Merulo's original partners in their music-printing firm. He apparently relinquished his share of the business to Merulo when the partnership broke up.[59] The composer's primary motive for honoring poets and literary figures was not direct reward, but, as in the case of Perissone Cambio's dedication to Gaspara Stampa, entry into the inner circle of Venetian academies, which included among their membership wealthy patrician dilettantes.[60]

SUPERVISION OF THE PRINTING PROCESS

Composers even made the move from underwriter of their own publications to music printer. As we have observed, Claudio Merulo da Correggio, the famous organist and composer, from 1566 to 1570 in partnership and later alone, issued some thirty-four music books. The printing venture was mainly a financial one, but Merulo might have set up his own print shop so that he could have complete control over the printing of his own music. Indeed, a number of documents reveal that composers were greatly concerned with the accurate transmission of their music. We learn from Francesco Corteccia in the dedication of his *Libro primo de madriali* [sic] *a quattro voci* of 1544 that he was forced to have his music printed as a result of misattributions of his works to other composers in earlier editions. Furthermore, Corteccia continued, "to these reasons one might add that my works, as well as the others, were full of the ugliest mistakes and of the gravest errors, both in words and music."[61] Jacquet Berchem voiced the same complaint in his *Madrigali a cinque voci* of 1546.[62]

We have evidence of other composers whose possible concern for errors prompted them to reprint their works with a different printer immediately after the publication of the first edition. The French composer Guillaume Boni, for example, was granted a special privilege by the French King Henri III "to assign the printer of his choice to print faithfully and correctly . . . his own music books . . . in order to correct the printing heretofore made by another and not yet issued."[63]

Concern for accurate transmission of their works (and possibly contractual obligations) led to the supervising and proofreading by composers of their music publications. There are several cases of composers given permission from their employers to travel to Venice or Rome for the printing of their music. Alessandro Striggio made such a request in a letter to his patron Cosimo de' Medici dated 25 February 1560 in order to oversee the printing of his two books of five- and six-voice madrigals in Venice.[64] The Spanish composer Francisco Guerrero also traveled to Venice in 1589 for the publication of his Second Book of Motets and his *Canciones y villanescas espirituales*.[65] If a composer could not be present, then he would appoint a surrogate. Ludovico Balbi, a student of Costanzo Porta, supervised the printing of Porta's book of motets in 1579,[66] and Benedetto Pallavicino acted as the proofreader for Guglielmo Gonzaga's 1586 edition of Magnificats.[67] Even the renowned Orlando di Lasso was concerned with the accurate transmission of his music. For Lasso, this led to his presence during the printing of several of his publications. He was apparently in Antwerp in 1555, where he acted as proofreader for Susato's first editions of the so-called "Opus 1."[68] During his stay in Paris in 1571, he not only received a printing privilege from the French king but also oversaw Le Roy and Ballard's publication of his *Livre de chansons nouvelles a cinc parties* and *Moduli quinis vocibus nunquam hactenus editi Monachii Boioariae compositi*.[69] He might also have witnessed the printing of his music in Venice, for in May 1567, Nicolò Stoppio, a bookdealer and agent for Duke Albrecht in Venice, wrote to Hans Jakob Fugger that "Orlando is here [in Venice] and is well . . . in eight days he wishes to leave for Ferrara with a book of madrigals which he has had printed and dedicated to the duke."[70] The publication to which Stoppio referred is the *Libro quarto de madrigali a cinque voci . . .* , issued by Gardano in 1567 and containing Lasso's dedication to Alfonso. Thus, Lasso must have supervised the printing of the book in Venice.

In many instances, Lasso could not be present during the printing of his first editions, especially if there were several being printed at the same time in different cities. The famous composer's concern for accuracy in the transmission of his works led him to another means of control. In an extraordinary letter of 1581 to the Emperor Rudolph II, Lasso requested a privilege granting him the sole rights to all his works printed in German territories. He insisted that his works be published as correctly as possible. He also maintained that his music must be presented to the public exactly as he wrote it and urged that his directions be respected for the first edition of all his music works. In order to put an end to all the errors, he requested that all privileges related to his compositions be accorded to himself, so that he could make the final judgment as to which firm he would entrust his pieces.[71]

The privilege that Lasso received went much further than contemporary Venetian privileges in that it did not specify any limit of time; it also applied to the whole of his compositions, whether they were published or not. Furthermore, Lasso regained the rights to all of his works that were printed in German territories since 1562 and was assured of retaining the rights to each of his works published in the future. Lasso's supplication to Rudolph II, then, documents an economic phenomenon that is of crucial importance to our study: a privilege granting a composer a complete monopoly on the printing of his works for an indefinite time period by any printer in any city of the German territory.

Lasso's intended monopoly on the publications of his music, however, appears to have gone even further afield than his native domain. Some ten years before his request to Rudolph II, Lasso received from the French King Charles IX a privilege bestowing upon him a monopoly similar to the German privilege (though with a limitation of time). When combined with the German privilege, the French *lettres patentes* established an important precedence, for not only could Lasso be counted among the few sixteenth-century composers who sought a foreign privilege,[72] but now he distinguished himself by becoming the first composer to acquire what might be considered a quasi-international copyright for the publication of all his music.

On the whole, the advent of music printing did not drastically alter the connection between composer and patron, but offered new avenues to make the composer's voice heard and the patron's name known. Composers played a more integral role in the printing process. They paid for the privilege of having their works printed, and in so doing became partners in the printing venture. Venetian music printers, furthermore, did not always assume a dominant role in the creation of music editions, but in many cases acted merely as agents and middlemen for composers, patrons, and other interested parties who sought fame or financial gain through this new industry.

NOTES

1. "Multa composui, edidique, multo plura apud mesunt: a quibus edendis retardor ea, quam dixi angustia. Sumptu non mediocri opus est; praesertim si adhibeantur maiores quaedam notae, et litterae, quas Ecclesiasticae res maxime requirunt."

2. "Praeterea multi ex illis, quorum mentionem feci, audent etiam Componistarum titulum sibi arrogare, cumq[ue] intra spacium dimidij anni multo sudore qualemcumq[ue] cantiunculam, quae vix tres concordantias habeat fabricarunt, statim typis illam excudi curant, quo etiam ipsorum magnum & gloriosum nomen in universa terra notum fiat." *Practica musica* (Wittenberg, 1556), sig. Ooiii^v. I am grateful to Jessie Ann Owens for drawing this source to my attention and for her aid with the translation.

3. *Motetta super plano canto cum quinque vocibus et in festis solennibus decananda. Liber primus* (Venice, 1546).

4. "vengono accompagnati da sei altri della misura a breve, donativi dal cortesissimo Messer Hieronimo Scotto, che con quelli desidera habbiate memoria di lui." *Madrigali a quattro voci di Messer Claudio Veggio . . .* (Venice, 1540).

5. See Febvre and Martin, *Coming of the Book*, 159–61; Voet, *Golden Compasses*, 2: 283–85; and J. Hoyoux, "Les Moyens d'existence d'Erasme," *Bibliothèque d'Humanisme et Renaissance* 6 (1944): 7–59.

6. J. M. Osborn, ed., *Autobiography of Thomas Whythorne* (London, 1962), 207; cited in Tim Carter, review of Lewis, *Antonio Gardano*, in *Journal of Musicological Research* 12 (1992): 119.

7. M. Dowling, "The Printing of John Dowland's Second Booke of Ayres," *The Library*, 4th ser., 12 (1932): 365–80.

8. Richard J. Agee, "Filippo Strozzi and the Early Madrigal," *JAMS* 38 (1985): 227–37 at 232–35.

9. "The 'Libro Primo' of Costanzo Festa," *Acta musicologica* 52 (1980): 47–55. The same device of two lions facing each other and holding a laurel wreath with the initials "C. F.," appearing on the title page of this edition, occurs in a Cappella Sistina manuscript devoted to sacred works by Festa and copied by Johannes Parvus around 1535. See Mitchell P. N. Brauner, "The Parvus Manuscripts: A Study of Vatican Polyphony (c. 1535–1580)" (Ph.D. diss., Brandeis University, 1982), 123–26.

10. Iain Fenlon and James Haar, *The Italian Madrigal in the Early Sixteenth Century: Sources and Interpretation* (Cambridge, 1988), 73. There is also the possibility that Festa had other volumes of his music printed either in Venice or Rome, but they do not survive.

11. The court case concerning the publishing of John Dowland's *Second Booke of Songs* in 1600 reveals that the fee of £20 given to Dowland's wife for the manuscript was negligible in comparison with the profit the publisher could make in selling the entire pressrun of 1,000 copies at two shillings per copy. See Dowling, "The Printing of John Dowland's Second Booke," 365–80.

12. The difference in stature among composers and printing firms apparently influenced the terms of agreement. A composer of prominence who initiated and financed a printing venture with an inexperienced printer could dictate very strict terms, as in the anomalous case of the contract for Frescobaldi's First Book of Toccatas (See A. Morelli, "Nuovi documenti frescobaldiani: i contratti per l'edizione del primo libro di Toccate," *Studi musicali* 17 (1988): 255–63, which should be read in conjunction with the critical report by Étienne Darbellay, ed., *Le Toccate e i Capricci di Girolamo Frescobaldi: genesi delle edizioni e apparato critico* (Monumenti musicali italiani 2–4, supplement; Milan, 1988), 37–39. The large Venetian publishing firms, on the other hand, were in a better position to dictate what they wanted to print, as is seen in the case of Angelo Gardano, who, miffed by a remark made by Guglielmo Gonzaga, informed the duke of Mantua that he did not have the time to print his Magnificats. See Richard Sherr, "The Publications of Guglielmo Gonzaga," *JAMS* 31 (1978): 118–25 at 123.

13. Albeit a Spanish contract dating from the end of the century, the agreement signed between Victoria and the Madrid printer Julio Junti de Modesti, conforms to the few contracts we have encountered in mid-sixteenth-century Italy. In it, Victoria commissioned Modesti to print 200 copies of a collection of polychoral Masses, Magnificat settings, motets, and psalms in ten partbooks. The printer received a set fee of 2,500 reales paid in three installments. While the contract was signed on 1 October 1598, the edition did not appear until 1600. For more information, see Victoria, *Opera omnia*, 8: p. lxxxv. Financial terms of other sixteenth-century Spanish music book contracts also agree with the Victoria one; see Griffiths and Hultberg, "Santa Maria," 347–60.

14. Cusick, *Valerio Dorico*, 95.

15. See Blackburn, "The Printing Contract," 353.

16. A summary of the correspondence between Plantin and Monte concerning this particular edition appears in Forney, "Tielman Susato," 216–17. Transcriptions of the full letters are found in M. Rooses and J. Denucé, eds., *Correspondance de Christophe Plantin* (Antwerp 1833–1918), 8: 1185, 1211, 1302.

17. Cusick, *Valerio Dorico*, 95.

18. See Robert Stevenson, *Spanish Cathedral Music in the Golden Age* (Berkeley and Los Angeles, 1961), 368. The Spanish composer evidently began this practice early in his career with his first publication of motets (1572), of which he sent (and sold) a copy to San Giacomo degli Spagnoli in Rome. His uncle was less fortunate in obtaining payment for another copy of the print from the Cathedral in Ávila. Ibid., 355, 465 n. 6.

19. "Thesaurus cantionum summi pretij ex Italia." Taken from Schoeffer's dedication to his edition. See Bonnie J. Blackburn, "Josquin's Chansons: Ignored and Lost Sources," *JAMS* 29 (1976): 30–76 at 62.

20. For more information on the Rore editions see Alvin H. Johnson, "The 1548 Editions of Cipriano de Rore's Third Book of Madrigals," in *Studies in Musicology in Honor of Otto E. Albrecht*, ed. John W. Hill (Kassel, 1980), 110–124, and Mary Lewis, "Rore's Setting of Petrarch's 'Vergine Bella': A History of its Composition and Early Transmission," *Journal of Musicology* 4 (1985–86): 365–409.

21. A compilation of the documents appears in Jessie Ann Owens and Richard J. Agee, "La stampa della 'Musica nova' di Willaert," *Rivista italiana di musicologia* 24 (1989): 219–305.

22. "Di novo posti in luce per Giulio Bonagionta da San Genesi." For more information on Bonagiunta see Giulio Ongaro, "Venetian Printed Anthologies of Music in the 1560s and the Role of the Editor," in *The Dissemination of Music: Studies in the History of Publishing*, ed. Hans Lenneberg (Lausanne, [1994]), 43–69 at 47–51.

23. Apparently, Scotto and Bonelli collaborated on other non-musical publications; see Pastorello, *Tipografi, editori, librai*, 14, 79. For a reproduction of this printer's mark, see Zappella, *Le marche dei tipografie*, no. 845.

24. Zappella, *Le marche*, no. 113. According to Bridges, "Publishing of Arcadelt's First Book," 157, Sanvito underwrote at least one non-musical book printed by Scotto: *Lombardus, Synopsis eorum, quae de balneis aliisque miraculus puteolanis scripta sunt . . .* (Venice, 1566). The British Library copy of this edition does not identify Scotto as the printer on the title page nor does it contain a colophon. The printer's device of a small griffin occasionally used by Scotto, as well as the woodcut initials and other typographical features clearly link it to the Scotto press.

25. This anthology appears neither in RISM-B nor in Vogel–Einstein. A unique copy of the tenor partbook is located in the Torrefranca collection of the Conservatorio di Musica Benedetto Marcello, Venice. See J. Bernstein, *Music Printing in Renaissance Venice*, 727–29.

26. This device occurs on the title page of the first edition of G. Zarlino, *Le istitutione harmoniche* (Venice, 1558). The same rooster, but with a different motto, "Tota Nocte Excubo," appears as the colophon to both Scotto prints. It is also used on the title page of *Dante con l'espositione di M. Bernardino Daniello da Luca, sopra la sua Comedia*, printed by Pietro da Fino in 1568. This printer's mark is reproduced in Zappella, *Le marche*, no. 579.

27. Adriano Cavicchi, "Baldini, Vittorio," in *Music Printing and Publishing*, 158–59; see also Anthony Newcomb, *The Madrigal at Ferrara, 1579–1597* (Princeton, 1980), 1: 28.

28. Lewis Lockwood, *Music in Renaissance Ferrara 1400–1505* (Cambridge, Mass., 1984); Newcomb, *Madrigal at Ferrara*; William Prizer, *Courtly Pastimes: The Frottole of Marchetto Cara* (Ann Arbor, Mich., 1980); and Fenlon, *Music and Patronage*.

29. Paganuzzi et al., eds., *La musica a Verona*, 179–89.

30. Romano Vettori, "Note storiche sul patronato musicale di Cristoforo Madruzzo cardinale di Trento (1512–1578)," *Rivista italiana di musicologia* 20 (1985): 3–43, and Renato Lunelli, "Contributi trentini alle relazioni fra l'Italia e la Germania nel Rinascimento," *Acta musicologica* 21 (1948): 41–70.

31. Fenlon, *Music and Patronage*, 47–78.

32. Lockwood, *The Counter-Reformation and the Masses of Vincenzo Ruffo* (Vienna, 1970), 78–79.

33. Turrini, *L'Accademia Filarmonica.*

34. Most of them appear in Paganuzzi, *La musica a Verona* 133–40.

35. Nasco, *Il segondo libro d'i madrigali a cinque voci* (Venice: Gardano, 1557), and Portinaro, *Il terzo libro di madregali a cinque & a sei voci* (Venice: Gardano, 1557)

36. Boyleau, *Motetta quatuor vocum* (Venice: Scotto, 1544) and Padovano, *Il primo libro de ricercari a quattro voci* (Venice: Gardano, 1556).

37. Rore, . . . *Motectorum . . . liber primus quinque vocum* (1544); Buus, *Recercari . . . libro primo a quatro voci* (1547); and Buus, *Il secondo libro di recercari . . . a quatro voci* (1549); see Lewis, *Antonio Gardano*, 1:425; 557; 628.

38. Giulio Ongaro, "The Chapel of St. Mark's at the Time of Adrian Willaert (1527–1562): A Documentary Study" (Ph.D. diss., University of North Carolina at Chapel Hill, 1986), 207.

39. *Il primo libro de Villotte a quatro voci* (Venice: Gardano, 1550).

40. Molino's *Il dilettevoli madrigali a quattro voci* (Venice: Merulo, 1568), and Monte's *Il primo libro de madrigali a tre voci* (Venice: Gardano, 1582).

11. "Il Cinquecento e il Seicento," in *Letteratura italiana*, ed. Alberto Asor Rosa (Turin, 1986), 6: 319–63 at 320.

42. See Amedeo Quondam, *Le "carte messagiere"*, 120.

43. Bridges, "Publishing of Arcadelt's First Book," 1: 99–100.

44. See Friedrich Lippmann, "Giovanni de Macque fra Roma e Napoli: nuovi documenti," *Rivista italiana di musicologica*, 13 (1978): 245–79; the complete letters are transcribed in the appendix to Ruth DeFord, "Ruggiero Giovanelli and the Madrigal in Rome 1572–1599" (Ph.D. diss., Harvard University, 1975).

45. Luzzasco Luzzaschi, *Madrigali per cantare e sonare, a uno, due e tre soprani* (1601), ed. Adriano Cavicchi (Monumenti di musica italiana, ser. 2: Polifonia, 2; Brescia and Kassel, 1965), 12.

46. Antonio Il Verso, *Madrigali a tre e a cinque voci (libro XV, opera XXXVI, 1619)*, ed. Lorenzo Bianconi (Musiche rinascimentali siciliane 8; Florence, 1978), p. xxv.

47. J. Bernstein, *Music Printing in Renaissance Venice*, 742.

48. Ibid., 833.

49. Claudio Annibaldi, "Il mecenate 'politico': ancora sul patronato musicale del cardinale Pietro Aldobrandini (1571–1621)," pt. 1, *Studi musicali* 16 (1987): 33–93 at 65; p. 81, app. 1, 1598, no. 14; p. 92, app. 2, no. 10.

50. Owens, "La cappella musicale della Basilica del Santo: alcune forme di mecenatismo," in *La cappella musicale nell'Italia della controriforma: Atti del Convegno internazionale di studi nel iv Centenario di fondazione della Cappella Musicale di S. Biagio di Cento, 13–15 ottobre 1989*, ed. Oscar Mischiati and Paolo Russo (Florence, 1993), 251–63.

51. An archival document dated 5 February 1574 states that Ruffo presented "a printed edition of four Masses addressed and dedicated to the Chapter . . . the Chapter recognized the said Vincentio with twelve bushels of grain and twelve barrels of wine each year so long as he remains in the service of the Chapter in Pistoia. The wine and grain shall be given him over and above his regular salary as a token of recognition for his gift." Lockwood, *The Counter-Reformation*, 64.

52. Peter Burke, *Culture and Society in Renaissance Italy, 1420–1540* (London, 1972), 88.

53. Wolfgang Boetticher, *Orlando di Lasso und seine Zeit* (Kassel, 1958), 164.

54. Alberto Cametti, *Palestrina* (Milan, 1925), 158. See also J. Bernstein, *Music Printing*, 888.

55. See David Bryant, "Alcuni osservazioni preliminari sulle notizie musicali nelle re-

lazioni degli ambasciatori stranieri a Venezia," in *Andrea Gabrieli e il suo tempo. Atti del convegno internazionale (Venezia, 16–18 settembre 1985)*, ed. Francesco Degrada (Florence, 1990), 181–92 at 183–84; also Marc'Antonio Mazzone, *Il primo libro delle canzoni a quattro voci*, ed. Maria Antonietta Cancellaro (Musiche del Rinascimento italiano 2; Florence, 1990), 8.

56. Bianconi, "Il Cinquecento e il Seicento," 343 n. 23.

57. Antonino Bertolotti, *Musici alla corte dei Gonzaga dal secolo XV al XVIII* (Milan, [1890]), 60–61, and Fenlon, *Music and Patronage*, 88.

58. English translation taken from Piero Weiss, *Letters of Composers through Six Centuries* (Philadelphia, 1967), 31.

59. Edwards, "Claudio Merulo," 176–77. See also above, chap. 3.

60. Perissone Cambio, *Madrigali a cinque voci* (Venice, 1545), ed. Martha Feldman (Sixteenth-Century Madrigal 2; New York and London, 1990), pp. xiii–xiv. See also J. Bernstein *Music Printing*, 321.

61. "A queste cose s'aggiugneva, che gli miei, & gl'altri erano cosi nelle note, come nelle parole pieni tutti di scorrezzioni bruttissime & importantissimi errori . . ." Complete dedication and English translation in Francesco Corteccia, *The First Book of Madrigals for Four Voices*, ed. Frank A. D'Accone (CMM 32, vol. 8; AIM, 1981). See also J. Bernstein, *Music Printing*, 301.

62. The dedication appears in Lewis, *Antonio Gardano*, 1: 509.

63. "Par privilege du Roy, donné à Paris, le quinzième jour de Septembre, l'an mil cinq cens soixante & seise, il est permis à Guillaume Bony, Musicien, de commettre tel Imprimeur qu'il voudra choisir, pour fidellement & correctement imprimer, ou faire'imprimer les livres de musicque de son invention: tant de celle qu'il a puis naguere reveüe pour en corriger l'impression cy devant faicte qu'autre non encor par luy mise en lumière." The first printer here was Nicolas Du Chemin, who published Boni's *Sonets de P. de Ronsard* early in the year 1576. A new edition came out later that same year by Boni's chosen printer, Le Roy and Ballard.

64. David Butchart, "The First Published Compositions of Alessandro Striggio," *Studi musicali* 12 (1983): 17–33 at 26.

65. Stevenson, *Spanish Cathedral Music*, 169.

66. See a letter from Balbi to Porta in Antonio Garbelotto, *Il Padre Costanzo Porta da Cremona, O.F.M. Conv., grande polifonista del '500* (Rome, 1955), 50. My thanks to Jessie Ann Owens for drawing this document to my attention.

67. Sherr, "Publications of Guglielmo Gonzaga," 124–25.

68. Forney, "Orlando di Lasso's Opus 1: The Making and Marketing of a Renaissance Music Book," *Revue belge de musicologie* 39–40 (1985–86): 33–60 at 33–35, and Donna Cardamone and David L. Jackson, "Production with Multiple Formes in Susato's First Edition of Lasso's 'Opus 1'," *Music Library Association Notes* 46 (1989): 7–24 at 8.

69. Horst Leuchtmann, *Orlando di Lasso: Sein Leben* (Wiesbaden, 1976), 51, 155–58.

70. "Orlando e qui et sta bene . . . partia fa 8 [giorni] di [qui] per ferrara con una muta de madrigali, che l'ha fatto stampare e dedicato a quel duca . . ." Quoted in Boetticher, *Orlando di Lasso*, 164; see also Leuchtmann, *Orlando di Lasso*, 138–39.

71. Henri Vanhulst, "Lassus et ses éditeurs: remarques à propos de deux lettres peu connues," *Revue belge de musicologie* 39–40 (1985–86): 80–100.

72. Ibid., 85.

Six

THE HOUSES OF SCOTTO
AND GARDANO

Two Printing Dynasties

To Girolamo Scotto, famous printer of Venice.... So numerous are
the excellent books in every branch of philosophy, most distinguished
Girolamo, that your workshop, which once belonged to your father
[sic] Ottaviano of happy memory, has published, greatly to the glory
of both of you, so that the name of Girolamo Scotto has long been
most famous everywhere in the world.... [1]

—Conrad Gesner, *Pandectarum . . .* 1548

s the towering figures of the Venetian music printing trade, Antonio
Gardano and Girolamo Scotto had a tremendous impact on the dissemination of music throughout continental Europe. During the
course of the sixteenth century, the two presses published over two
thousand music editions—a figure representing more than the total
output of all contemporary Italian and northern European music printers combined.
The dynasties mirrored the growth of the Venetian book trade as it progressed from
its inception in the latter decades of the fifteenth century through its years of ex-
pansion and commercial success in the sixteenth century. In order to understand the
major influence the Scotto and Gardano presses had on music printing and the
Venetian printing industry as a whole, we must first examine the history of the two
firms.

By the closing decades of the fifteenth century, a wave of "foreigners" arrived
in Venice to try their hand at the burgeoning printing industry. The imprints and
colophons of their books show that they came from all parts of the Italian peninsula—Bernardino Benalio from Bergamo, Andrea Torresano from Asola, and
Luc'Antonio Giunti from Florence. One such émigré was Ottaviano Scotto. He arrived prior to 1479 and very quickly gained prominence as a printer and publisher.

The press he established was to flourish for over a century. Making a name for itself as a publisher of Latin texts, the Scotto firm also acted as a primary player in the development of music printing in Italy before the advent of the single-impression method.

THE FOUNDING OF THE SCOTTO PRESS

Ottaviano Scotto came from Monza, a small town not far from Milan.[2] He presumably went to Venice in the 1470s, to seek his fortune in a new industry, where "the glitter of gold was more inviting than anywhere in fifteenth-century Europe."[3] How and where Ottaviano learned the printing trade remains unknown. He set up a shop in the parish of San Samuele,[4] where, in 1479, he printed his earliest surviving book, *Ordo compendii diurni iuxta Romanae Curiae.*[5] For the next nineteen years, Ottaviano was active as a printer, underwriter, and bookdealer, producing no fewer than 220 books.[6] Scotto did not break new ground in the subjects in which he chose to print, but instead followed the patterns already set up by Venetian printers in the 1470s, who targeted their production toward an established readership of doctors, clergy, lawyers, teachers, and students. He published a variety of subjects ranging from theology, law, astronomy, and medicine to vernacular texts, but his strength lay in the areas of philosophy and classical literature in Latin translation. These subjects were aimed at the academic market of the universities. While students in Bologna, Pavia, Perugia, Siena, and Ferrara all bought their books from Venice, Scotto's main outlet for his academic texts was Padua, a university town ruled and frequented by the Venetians. It was considered an important center for Aristotelian studies during the sixteenth century. This academic market, as we shall see, became the bread and butter of the Scotto press, which throughout its long history, was one of the foremost printers of Aristotelian commentaries.

Ottaviano made several contributions to the history of printing. He was the first printer to use quarto and octavo formats for liturgical books. These small formats not only made liturgical books more affordable, but also allowed greater portability for the clergy, since the bulk and weight of large folio volumes required them to remain stationary on lecterns.[7] Ottaviano was the first Italian to print music from movable type.[8] His first effort in music printing occurred in 1481, when he completed a *Missale Romanum* in quarto format containing blank spaces for music on 29 December. Both the staves and the note heads were to be filled in later by hand.[9] The next year, on 31 August 1482, Ottaviano brought out a *Missale Romanum* in folio format; this time the book contained music printed from movable type. In this and two other later missals, Scotto employed the double-impression method, whereby the staves printed first in red ink were overlaid with the notes in black ink.[10] Ottaviano printed four missals before 1484 and published another three in the 1490s with music printed by Johann Hamman.[11]

Ottaviano used his monogram, O.S.M. (Octavianus Scotus Modoetiensis), as his device. Initials placed within an orb and surmounted by a double cross was a favorite symbol among Venetian printers during the incunabular period.[12] Ottaviano employed it in four printer's marks of varying sizes (see fig. 2.4 above). This monogram and its modified version S.O.S. (Signum Octaviani Scoti) continued to be used by his heirs throughout the life of the firm.

By 1484, only five years after his first publication, Ottaviano abandoned his work as a printer to become a publisher-underwriter whose books were printed by others. Among the ten or more printers who worked for Scotto, the most important one was Boneto Locatelli, a priest from Bergamo, whose long association with the firm lasted well into the next century.[13] During this time Ottaviano concentrated his efforts on the commerce of bookselling. Noted as a *mercator* who underwrote the publications of other printers, he was mainly involved with the international distribution of books. His commercial relationships extended from Italian bookmen throughout the entire peninsula to printers and publishers as far away as Valencia, Spain.[14]

On 24 December 1498, Ottaviano died in Venice. He was buried in the Franciscan church of San Francesco della Vigna, where his tombstone on the floor of the cloister still remains today with the inscription: "Nobilis Octavianus Scotus de Modoe[t]ia Mercator Libror[um] Imp[re]ssor sibi et successoribus qui obiit XXIIII Decembri[s] 1498." His coat of arms, a crest containing a dove in the upper left-hand section and his monogram printer's mark on the right-hand side, is carved in the middle of the marble slab.[15]

THE HEIRS OF OTTAVIANO SCOTTO (1500–1533)

Only months after Ottaviano's death, Venice succumbed to one of the worst financial crises in its entire history. Political enemies threatened the Most Serene Republic on two fronts: to the east, the Ottoman Empire endangered its naval supremacy in the Mediterranean by capturing nearly all of the Venetian ports in Greece, while to the west, the shifting alliances of France, Spain, Germany, and the Pope jeopardized both its newly acquired and established territories on the mainland. In order to finance its military operations on land and sea, the Venetian state imposed forced loans in the form of government bonds upon the taxpayers. Excessive demands for money compelled Venetians to withdraw their own funds from the banks, which, in turn, caused a run on all the banks in Venice. The panic that ensued prompted the failure of two banks.[16] The shortage of cash and credit during the crash of 1499 had a profound effect upon all commercial enterprises. It caused a major catastrophe for the relatively new printing industry. Of the twenty-three firms active in the 1490s, fewer than ten survived the century.[17]

The Scotto press turned out to be one of the fortunate few. In 1499 editions continued to be issued under Ottaviano's name, but during the following year the imprint of the firm was changed to the "Heirs of Ottaviano Scotto" (Heredes Octaviani Scoti). In accordance with Venetian law, the estate apparently did not pass solely to the eldest surviving male heir, but was shared jointly by all male heirs. Since Ottaviano died without male issue, the inheritance of the firm reverted to the sons of his three brothers, Brandino, Antonio, and Bernardino (see table 6.1). The heirs, who probably held financial shares in the press, included Ottaviano's nephews: Amadio, son of Brandino Scotto; Giovanni Battista, son of Antonio Scotto; and Paolo and Ottaviano II, sons of Bernardino Scotto. All of these nephews lived in Venice. They presumably formed a *fraterna* or family partnership, designating one of them, perhaps the oldest, to serve as manager of the firm.

Although Ottaviano Scotto's last will and testament no longer survives, we learn from a contract dated 27 November 1499 that Amadio di Brandino Scotto had been named Ottaviano's beneficiary.[18] We know that Amadio soon assumed the directorship of the firm, for in 1500 he requested a privilege from the Venetian Senate to print the unedited works of Galen, the *Continens*, a medical encyclopedia by the medieval Arabic scholar called Rasis, the problems of Aristotle, a "Descrizione di Terra Santa," and "Cesario de exemplis."[19] The fact that Amadio did not use his own name in the imprints to the books issued by the Scotto firm also points to joint ownership of the press by the nephews. Divisiveness among the heirs might have prompted the collapse of the firm, but the soundness of the business and the acumen of its new director helped guide the press through these perilous years of financial instability in Venice.

Amadio moved the press to the parish of San Felice, where he lived with his cousins, Giovanni Battista, Paolo, and Ottaviano II. They continued to publish subjects that their uncle had established as specialties of the House of Scotto. The total output of the heirs during the thirty-five-year period exceeded 280 books.[20] By 1531 Amadio was proud to declare in a petition to the Venetian Senate that the House of Scotto was "famosissimi impressori di opere nove non piu stampate precipue della sacra teologia, de logica et philosophia et medicina."[21] As with his uncle, most of his books were either printed by others or published with the help of a consortium of bookmen.

During the early years of the century from 1500 to around 1509, Boneto Locatelli, who served as the principal printer for Ottaviano Scotto, continued in that capacity. His colophon can be found on practically all the non-liturgical Scotto books from this period. Shortly thereafter, other printers, such as Giorgio Arrivabene and the firm of Francesco Bindoni and Maffeo Pasini, replaced Locatelli as printers for the Scotto press.

From 1513, editions issued with the Scotto imprint included the added phrase, "na Sociorum." This meant that the Scottos joined with others to form partnerships. The scarcity of printing agreements among sixteenth-century bookmen prevents us from knowing all the partners who helped finance these books, but a contract dated

TABLE 6.1 Genealogy of the Scotto family

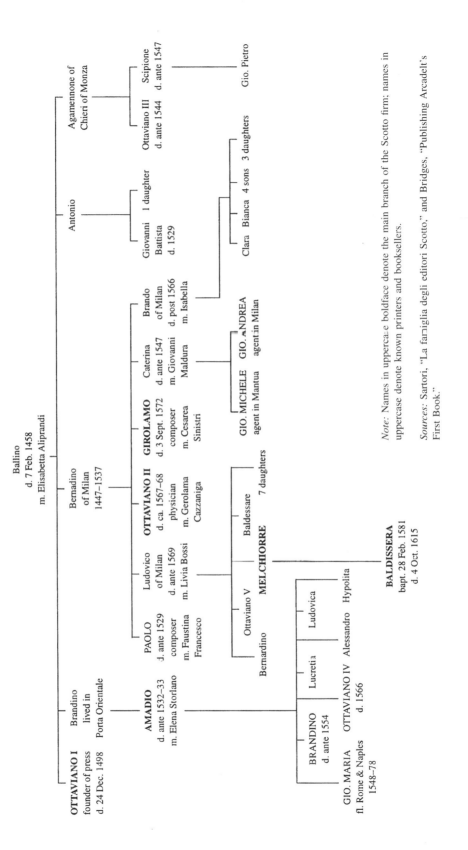

Note: Names in uppercase boldface denote the main branch of the Scotto firm; names in uppercase denote known printers and booksellers.

Sources: Sartori, "La famiglia degli editori Scotto," and Bridges, "Publishing Arcadelt's First Book."

25 June 1507 does name Luc'Antonio Giunti, Zorzi (Giorgio) Arrivabene, the brothers Battista and Silvestro de Tortis, and Antonio Moreto as partners with Amadio Scotto to print several books.[22]

We cannot be sure how many of these titles were actually issued, for only two years after the contract was signed, an alliance of all the great European powers known as the League of Cambrai plunged Venice into a war that threatened her very existence. On 9 May 1509 Venice suffered a disastrous defeat at Agnadello; in a matter of weeks, French and Habsburg forces overwhelmed nearly all of her possessions on the Italian mainland. Venice was forced to cede the empire she had carefully built up during the previous century. Only in her darkest hour was the Most Serene Republic saved by the loyalty of her citizens in the neighboring towns of Padua, Vicenza, and Treviso, and by the Pope and Spanish king, who decisively switched their allegiance away from the French and the Habsburgs to the Venetians. *La Serenissima*, after seven years of war, regained most of her territory. The war with the League of Cambrai, however, took its toll on the Republic; it became a turning point in Venetian history.

The years 1509 to 1513 were difficult ones for the Venetian printing industry. Several printers went bankrupt, while others were forced to suspend operation. The total output of all twenty firms still in business amounted to only fifty editions per year.[23] In 1509 the great Aldine press dissolved temporarily, and its director Aldo Manuzio was forced to leave Venice and to travel around northern Italy for the next three years.[24] Little is known about the Scotto press during this time period. Though it survived these turbulent years of war and financial instability, the firm's production declined drastically. In 1508 the Scotto firm issued at least fifteen editions, while their output for the next four years dwindled down to a total of only six publications.

That the wars had a devastating effect on the printing industry may be observed in a request made by Ottaviano Petrucci to the Venetian Senate. In his petition dated 24 June 1514, Petrucci appealed for a renewal of his monopoly on music printing. He stated that he and his partners were unable to benefit from his invention, since the war had disturbed business and they were unable to recoup their initial capital investment.[25] The Venetian Senate granted Petrucci and his partners a five-year renewal. This petition turns out to be a seminal one for our study, since one of Petrucci's silent partners was Amadio Scotto. Scotto's connection with Petrucci and his other partner, Nicolò di Raffaele, apparently began with the establishment of Petrucci's music press some fifteen years before. The fact that the House of Scotto acted as publisher-underwriter and bookseller for several printing enterprises suggests that Amadio Scotto helped finance the original venture that allowed Petrucci to be the first to print polyphonic music from movable type.

With the end of the war in 1513, the Scotto press resumed its printing and publishing activities at a normal level, and the firm prospered once again, as is evident from the properties Amadio Scotto purchased. In that year, he rented a house that was explicitly not used for the business of printing,[26] and in 1522 he acquired ten fields with buildings and farmland.[27] Several documents refer to Amadio not only as a "libraro" but also as a "mercadante di libri." He was clearly well respected by other Venetian bookmen; his name appears as executor of the estates of Bernardino Benalio and Lazzaro di Soardi, two important Venetian printers of the incunabular period.[28]

Amadio probably died around 1533, the year the imprint of the firm changed back from "Heredes Octaviani Scoti" to "Octaviani Scotti." Upon the deaths of the other heirs, ownership of the main branch of the firm passed to Ottaviano II, son of Bernardino Scotto.

LEADERSHIP UNDER OTTAVIANO SECONDO (1533–1539)

Ottaviano II took over the press sometime during the latter part of 1533. The colophon to an edition of Verdelot's First Book of Four-Voice Madrigals of 1533 contains the phrase "Ad instantia deli Scotti," suggesting that Amadio was still alive. By the end of year, however, Ottaviano brought out his own publications; his very first independent publication may have been an edition of Gabriele Zerbo's *Anathomie* dated 1 October, 1533.[29]

Ottaviano kept the press at the same location in the district of San Felice, where it remained until 1547, if not later. He continued to employ many of the printer's marks used by his predecessors as well as a few of his own, in particular a figure representing Fame carrying a trumpet atop a winged globe with the initials O.S.M. (see fig. 6.1). The monogram O.S.M. in this device as well as the earlier orb and double cross printer's marks referred to his uncle Ottaviano (Octavianus Scotus Modoetiensis), but it also applied to Ottaviano II, who was from Milan (Octavianus Scotus Mediolanensis).

For the next six years, Ottaviano Scotto carried on the tradition of the firm by publishing over sixty texts in fields that had established the reputation of the House of Scotto, particularly philosophy, medicine, and religion. Ottaviano held more than a passing interest in at least the first two subjects, for he was a Doctor of Medicine and was conversant in the field of philosophy. On more than one occasion, Ottaviano served as editor of the Aristotelian commentaries that his firm published. In his dedication to an edition of Aristotle's *De Physica* printed in 1540, Ottaviano stated that he had emended the commentary and "tried to cleanse it of errors." He may even have made his own translation of the Commentaries to Aristotle's *Topica*, a work on logic.[30]

Ottaviano's abilities in both of these fields should not surprise us since within the faculty of arts of Italian universities, logic and natural philosophy played an integral role in the curriculum, being considered preparatory subjects for the study of medicine.[31] He clearly moved in academic circles and was well known by the *literati* not only of Venice, but also at the University of Padua, from whence he most

FIGURE 6.1 Printer's marks of
Heirs and Ottaviano Scotto II

assuredly received his doctorate in medicine. In his preface to Alessandro Piccolo-mini's *De la Institutione*, Ottaviano extolled the virtues of the Sienese humanist's book and cited his own participation in the famed Accademia degli Infiammati in Padua. He addressed his preface to Alfonso d'Avalos, the marquis of Vasto and governor-general of Milan,[32] and his wife Maria d'Aragona, important patrons of the Scotto press during the early 1540s.

Besides publishing in the areas of philosophy and medicine, Ottaviano intro-duced publications of polyphonic music to the Scotto book list during his tenure as director of the press. From 1533 until 1538 he issued, in collaboration with the woodcarver-musician Andrea Antico, a series of at least sixteen music editions. Ottaviano's connection with Antico and with music printing did not start in the 1530s, but went as far back as 1516, when Scotto acted as a financial underwriter for Antico's *Liber quindecim missarum*.

The first cooperative music publication of the 1530s between Antico and the Scotto press was Verdelot's First Book of Four-Voice Madrigals of 1533. The col-ophon at the back of the Bassus partbook states that the Scotto firm, acting as the financial backer, requested the press of Giovanni Antonio Nicolino de Sabio and his brothers to print the edition, while Andrea Antico prepared the woodcuts. Ottaviano II published no fewer than fifteen other editions containing works by Verdelot, Wil-laert, Festa, Arcadelt, and others. All of them used woodblocks cut by Antico.

Whether Antico acted as an equal partner with the Scotto press or worked as a hired artisan whom Ottaviano commissioned on a fee-for-job basis to prepare the woodblocks for his music publications is impossible to ascertain.[33] Antico might simply have supplied Ottaviano with the woodblocks, which then became the prop-erty of the Scotto press. It is also hard to determine if Ottaviano printed any of the editions himself; he might not have had any musical expertise. His interest in music printing could have been limited only to the publishing and marketing side of the trade. If Ottaviano Scotto could not edit music, and Antico was only commissioned to prepare the woodblocks, then who at the Scotto press had the technical and musical knowledge to see the editions through the press? The obvious candidate was Ottaviano's brother, Girolamo Scotto.

GIROLAMO SCOTTO AND THE PRESS (1539–1572)

Practically nothing is known about the early life of Girolamo Scotto. The colophon to his 1557 edition of Giovanni Pico della Mirandola's *Opera omnia* indicates that he was originally from Milan ("Apud Hieronymum Scotum Mediolanensem"). Pre-cisely when Girolamo became involved in the activities of the printing firm and when he arrived in Venice remain mysteries. Although his name does not appear on any publication issued by the Scotto press until 1539, he was certainly involved in the business before that time.

The first known document naming Girolamo is a petition to the Venetian Senate dated 20 October 1536, in which a "hier[onymo] scoto mercadante de libri" requests a privilege to print "le correttioni, tauole et digressioni d[e]l q[uondam] ex[cellente] M. Marcantonio cimara sop[ra] li testi de aristotele con il commento de Aueroys."[34] The House of Scotto published a folio edition of the Zimarra "Tables" in 1537. The privilege requested by Girolamo is mentioned on the title page to the edition, but the colophon names Ottaviano as printer. Two printer's marks identified with the Scotto press also appear in the edition. The O.S.M. monogram in an orb surmounted by a cross within a large rectangular floral frame, usually identified with Ottaviano and his predecessors at the press, appears in the colophon (see fig. 6.1), while Fame V, a device later employed by Girolamo, appears on the title page (see above, fig. 2.8). This edition has been attributed to Ottaviano, since his printer's mark and name appear in the colophon, but Girolamo could easily have been responsible for the publication. Other printer's marks later used by Girolamo occur in Ottaviano's publications beginning in 1535, suggesting that Girolamo might have been active at the press at this time, if not from the very beginning of Ottaviano's tenure as director.[35]

Girolamo might have been responsible for a handful of music editions dating from 1536. Chapman hypothesizes that perhaps Girolamo rather than Ottaviano printed the *Intavolatura de li madrigali di Verdelotto da cantare et sonare nel lauto, intavolati per messer Adriano*, since a colophon naming the printer does not appear at the end of the edition, and Girolamo used the same woodblocks when he reprinted the edition in 1540.[36] Furthermore, the printer's mark of fame (Fame IV) on the title page is one that Girolamo frequently utilized in his music books from 1558 until 1563 (see fig. 2.8). Another edition of Verdelot's Second Book of Five Voice Madrigals dating from 1538 also shows signs of Girolamo's work. Again the colophon and printer's name are lacking, but the title page contains the same design layout as several music editions printed by Girolamo in 1539–41. The printer's mark, an anchor with palm frond on left and olive branch on right (Anchor I), was also one that Girolamo used on the title page or colophon of all but one of his music editions of 1539.[37]

Whether or not Girolamo was responsible for some or all of the music prints issued by the Scotto press in the mid 1530s, he did not make his mark in the field of music until he took over the active management of the Scotto firm in 1539. Why Ottaviano II relinquished control of the firm to his brother remains unclear. That he drew up two separate wills in 1544 and again in 1547 suggests that he may have been ill. Indeed, by this time Ottaviano must have already been in his fifties. In light of his other professional interests as a physician and philosopher, he might simply have had neither the time nor the inclination to continue directing the day-to-day operations of the business. He did execute his own publications of mainly Aristotelian commentaries on a sporadic basis; the last imprint bearing his name appears in the colophon of a 1552 commentary on Aristotle's *Posterior Analytics*, a work of logic issued jointly with Girolamo.[38] Yet even though he was not an active participant at the press, Ottaviano did remain a partner in the business until his death, sometime between 10 April 1567, when he witnessed a notarial contract for his brother Girolamo,[39] and October 1569, when Girolamo mentions his inheritance from Ottaviano in his own will.

Whatever Girolamo's role was in the printing firm from 1533 to 1538, by 1539 his position had changed dramatically. From that time onwards, nearly all of the books published by the main branch of the House of Scotto contained Girolamo's imprint. Scotto became one of the most prolific music printers of the Renaissance. From 1539 until his death in 1572, he issued over four hundred music editions. This prodigious output made him a major figure in music printing, rivaled only by his contemporary, Antonio Gardano. Yet unlike Gardano, Scotto also published books on other subjects, which comprised half of his output.[40] Girolamo Scotto's production was truly enormous; during a thirty-three year period, he published over 800 books.

As the firm continued to grow, the Scotto family, like other publishing clans, increasingly became absorbed in investing their capital in mainland properties.[41] Girolamo mentioned in his joint tax declaration with Ottaviano of 1566: "that little money which is raised from trade in the said goods [i.e., books] I have withdrawn into these small pieces of real estate . . ."[42] In this they emulated the Venetian nobility who, in the sixteenth century, gradually shifted their income from commercial to landed interests.[43] Girolamo Priuli noted in 1509: "Venetian merchants, given that voyages are few, without spices and hardly profitable, have retired from trade and have invested their money in property . . ."[44] Girolamo, along with other members of his family, owned property in Venice and the neighboring provinces of Padua and Treviso.

We can get an idea of the size of their wealth by piecing together information gleaned from wills, rental contracts, and tax declarations.[45] Beginning with the tax census of 1566, Girolamo and Ottaviano reported in their joint statement that they rented a house in the Corte dell'albero in the district of Sant'Angelo from the magistrate Domenico Priuli, for the enormous sum of 120 ducats per year; here, they operated two printing presses.[46] They also owned three rental properties in Padua along with a woodland containing thirty-two cultivated fields as well as another thirty-two and one-quarter fields, all located in the environs of Padua, which generated an income of ninety-nine ducats.[47] In addition, Girolamo along with his cousin, Francesco, bought property in Treviso in 1550.[48]

The acquisition of cultivated land and residential property turned into a lucrative passive investment for the Scotto family, for sixteen years later, Girolamo's heir, Melchiorre, declared that he owned two houses in Padua and from 110 to 120 fields, which produced an income of 276 ducats.[49] These properties represented only a fraction of the family's wealth, since other income generated from business concerns such as residences, shops, and other properties outside the jurisdiction of the Venetian republic were excluded from the *Decima*.[50]

Wills and contracts reveal additional sources of income. In his will of 1547, Ottaviano mentions real estate inherited from his father in Milan and Monza, as well as business property in Naples, Siena, and Bologna. Added to these investments were interests in bookshops in at least Venice, Rome, and Sicily. The Scottos enjoyed investment income not only comparable to the larger printing houses, but also to members of the professional class, such as lawyers, doctors, and secretaries, whose property generated 100 to 150 ducats annually.[51] Needless to say, this does not take into account the income generated from their most lucrative source—their printing and publishing establishment. All of these business activities led the Scotto firm to financial prosperity.

Along with wealth came praise by contemporaries. In his *Pandectae* of 1548, the Swiss bibliographer Conrad Gesner selected eighteen printers from all over Europe as dedicatees of various parts of his bibliography. He dedicated his section on politics to Girolamo Scotto (see epigraph above). Only three other Venetians, Vincenzo Valgrisio, Tomaso Giunta, and Paulo Manuzio—all from eminent dynastic presses—receive such a tribute. Scotto was also honored by his peers, when, in 1571, the guild of printers and booksellers elected him their first *priore*.

Girolamo Scotto died on 23 September 1572. He was buried in Venice at San Francesco della Vigna, the same monastic church as his uncle, Ottaviano I. In his will, he appointed his wife Cesaria Sinistri as executor of his estate. Since he had no children,[52] Girolamo bequeathed the firm and all his property in the Veneto to his nephew, Melchiorre.[53]

DIRECTORSHIP UNDER MELCHIORRE SCOTTO (1577–1613)

Melchiorre or Marchio Scotto joined his uncle at the press around 1565, if not before. He was the son of Girolamo's eldest brother Ludovico, who lived in Milan. In 1565 Melchiorre signed an agreement to act as agent for Girolamo.[54] The following year he negotiated a printing contract between the Scotto press and the Monastery of San Giorgio Maggiore, under which he signed the agreement, collected money, and delivered books on behalf of his uncle.[55] The increased output of the press during the latter half of the 1560s, particularly in the field of music, suggests that Melchiorre played an active role in the business at this time. Girolamo named Melchiorre in his will as his sole heir to the press on the condition that his nephew renounce his inheritance from his father Ludovico. In a notarial document issued after Girolamo's death in 1572, Melchiorre relinquished his portion of Ludovico's property in Milan to his brothers, Baldiserre, Ottaviano V, and Bernardino. When he took over the firm after Girolamo's death, he employed Girolamo's imprint until 1573, after which he changed it to "Herede di Girolamo Scotto." He continued to use the elaborate anchor printer's mark (Anchor V) found on Scotto music editions dating from the 1560s.[56] When the original woodcut wore out, Melchiorre replaced the mark with an exact duplicate. He also employed other devices, including one depicting the three graces within an elaborate compartment containing personifications of justice, fame, and peace (see fig. 6.2).

Melchiorre carried on the firm's tradition, issuing titles in philosophy, law, religion, medicine, classical literature, and music, but his output declined sharply to half the former level. Unlike his uncle, he tended to rely more on music publications. Of the 375 editions that survive, 291 or three-quarters of Melchiorre's publications were in the field of music. This contrasted with the parity between music and non-music publications that existed in the catalogue of books issued by Girolamo Scotto. The change in the balance of the press could reflect a personal interest in music or possibly indicate greater competition from other presses in the other subjects.

FIGURE 6.2 Printer's mark of Melchiorre Scotto

For the next forty years, Melchiorre issued first editions and reprints of works by new composers and those already established with the Scotto press in the 1560s and 70s, such as Monte, Palestrina, Striggio, and Marenzio. The Scotto firm was the exclusive press for such composers as Pietro Vinci, Giovanni Ferretti, Giovanni Piccioni, and Giovanni Andrea Dragoni. Melchiorre also published several first editions of Pietro Pontio, Paolo Isnardi, and Girolamo Conversi. He printed a wide variety of genres, including Masses, motets, madrigals, *canzoni alla napolitana*, and instrumental pieces in mensural notation as well as in lute intabulation. The press tended to specialize in the lighter secular genres, in particular the *canzona alla napolitana*.

By 1588 the majority of music publications brought out by the Scotto press consisted of reprinted editions. From 1592 until 1596 Melchiorre's output decreased dramatically. After a brief revival, production at the press came to a halt in 1610, and then resumed only for the year 1613. Melchiorre had an illegitimate son Baldissera, born 28 February 1581. Girolamo's widow Cesarea Sinistri named Melchiorre in her will of 1589, where she also stated that in the event of Melchiorre's death, his natural son Baldiserra would be her heir. Baldissera presumably apprenticed with his father at the press. We do not know when Melchiorre died, but a hiatus in publications in 1610 coupled with the fact that Baldissera made out his own will that same year[57] suggests that Melchiorre had died at that time. Baldissera might have taken over the firm, printing only a handful of music publications in 1613. On 4 October 1615 Baldissera died in the town of Montà near Padua. Since he was illegitimate, Baldissera could not be buried in the Scotto family tomb in the church of San Francesco della Vigna, nor was his will recognized by the Venetian authorities, who sold his property at public auction.

Baldassera's death signaled the end of a publishing dynasty that had endured for 134 years. It also marked the passing of one of the two leading music printing firms of Cinquecento Venice. The other Venetian music press, which flourished concurrently with the Scotto firm, was the House of Gardano.

On the surface, Antonio Gardano and Girolamo Scotto appear to have paralleled each other in their publishing careers: they were almost exact contemporaries; both lived in Venice; and both produced an impressive output of over four hundred music publications each. Yet despite these obvious similarities, many differences set these two great music publishers apart from each other. Whereas Girolamo Scotto was born into one of the distinguished Venetian publishing dynasties of the Renaissance, Antonio Gardano had to set up his own firm. Arriving in Venice as an immigrant, Gardano quickly established himself as a printer specializing in music publications. The dynasty that he founded in 1538 endured under his name for nearly seventy-five years. It continued to rise in prominence, so that by the end of the sixteenth century, the House of Gardano became the most prolific publisher of music in Renaissance Europe.

Almost nothing is known about Gardano's background before his arrival in Venice.[58] He was born in 1508 or 1509, since the *Necrologi Sanitari* in the Venetian archives tell us that on "28 October 1569, Antonio Gardan, bookseller, [died] at the age of sixty."[59]

Gardano's birthplace and his early training in music and printing remain a mystery. The first privilege he received from the Venetian Senate, dated 11 May 1538, refers to him as "Antonio Gardane musico francese."[60] Nicolò Franco also mentions in a literary letter to Bonifatio Pignoli, private secretary to Leone Orsini, that "my friend, messer Antonio Gardane, . . . [has] been born like yourself in France."[61] That Gardano was a Frenchman is further supported by the original spelling of his surname, "Gardane," which the printer used in his imprints up until 1555. French, moreover, was the only vernacular language that Gardano, as a composer, set to music.

François Lesure has theorized that the printer came from the Midi in the south of France, noting a Gardane family in Carpentras during the sixteenth century. A town with the name Gardanne lies further south between Aix-en-Provence and Marseilles.[62] Mary Lewis has also remarked that Fréjus, whose bishop-elect Leone Orsini was Gardano's early patron, is situated nearby on the Côte-d'Azur.[63]

Before the inception of his career as a printer in Venice, Gardano was regarded mainly as a musician and composer. In 1532, when he was about twenty-two years old, his first published work, a Mass setting entitled *Missa super Si bona suscepimus*, appeared in the *Liber decem missarum* printed in Lyons by Jacques Moderne. During his lifetime, Gardano composed a considerable number of works, including sixty-nine French chansons, ten motets, two Masses, and one French psalm. Surprisingly, he printed only about a third of his own works. The rest of his extant output appeared in anthologies brought out by all the major French music printers as well as other northern continental firms.[64]

By 1538 if not earlier, Gardano married the daughter of Agostino Bindoni, a successful Venetian printer-bookseller. They had four sons and two daughters (see table 6.2). The oldest child, Alessandro, was born before 1539; the birth of Angelo, the second child, soon followed in 1540. Some fifteen years later, Matthio was born. There was a fourth son, whose baptismal name and birthdate remain unknown. He became a monk in the Capuchin order, taking the name Fra Pacifico. Of the two daughters, Angelica married in 1569, and Lucieta, the youngest child, was born around 1561.[65]

Unfortunately, few archival documents concerning the Gardano press during the years under Antonio's directorship have come to light. To make up for the scant evidence, scholars have relied on sixteenth-century literary publications for biographical information. The most important source is Nicolò Franco's *Pistole vulgari*. Franco was a writer who arrived in Venice in 1536. He found work at the Marcolini

TABLE 6.2 Genealogy of the Gardano family

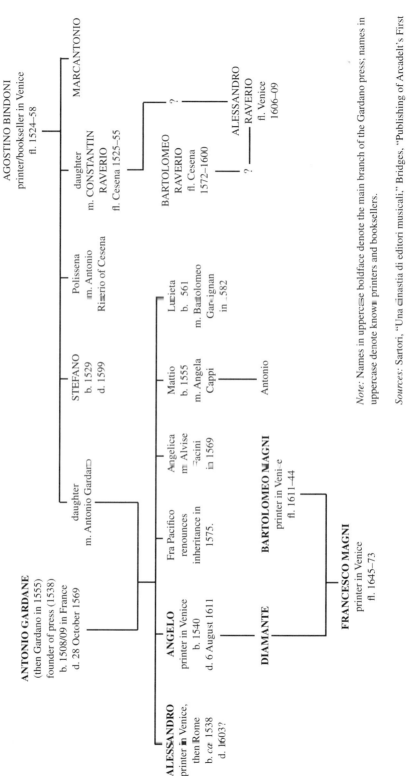

Note: Names in uppercase boldface denote the main branch of the Gardano press; names in uppercase denote known printers and booksellers.

Sources: Sartori, "Una dinastia di editori musicali;" Bridges, "Publishing of Arcadelt's First Book," and Agee, *Gardano Music Printing Firms.*

press and soon after became secretary to Pietro Aretino, the most notorious literary figure in Venice. At the end of 1537, Aretino had his *Lettere* printed by Marcolini, which Franco copied and prepared for publication. Having witnessed the success of Aretino's publication, Franco decided to try his hand at this genre. He contracted Gardano to print his own *Pistole vulgari*, which first appeared in November 1538 without a publisher's name, and then as a reissue in April, 1539 with Gardano's name and device appearing in the colophon.[66]

Franco addressed his letters to a wide assortment of people ranging from such highly placed individuals as Francis I, King of France, the Duke of Urbino, the Cardinal of Lorraine, and the Duke and Duchess of Mantua to a common prostitute ("puttana"). Most were directed to Venetian friends and acquaintances, many of whom played an important role in the intellectual and artistic life of the city, such as Domenico Venier, Girolamo Molino, Daniele Barbaro, Speroni Sperone, Jacopo Sansovino, and Titian.

Some of the letters mention Antonio Gardano by name. In the letter to Bonifatio Pignoli, cited above, Franco implies that Gardano, at least at the beginning of his printing career, had difficulties writing in Italian and had to rely on the writer to act as his translator.[67] Other letters praise Gardano as a composer. Franco writes about four of Gardano's motets in a letter of 1 May 1537 addressed to the printer:

> I know that in my mouth sings a voice so awkward and coarse as to make even the chorus of paradise fall apart, and yet your pieces have the power to make it sound capable of something. Were that devilish fellow Nero alive today he would no doubt give you his empire.[68]

Besides commenting on Gardano as a musician, Franco also implies in a letter to Valerio Negron dated 20 June 1537 that Gardano directed a [music] school ("scola") in Venice.[69]

Perhaps the most significant information the letters provide concern the friendship between Gardano and Franco and the patronage they both briefly received from Bishop-elect Leone Orsini. Orsini clearly gave Gardano considerable financial support at the inception of his printing career. As the dedicatee of *Le pistole vulgari*, he presumably also helped Franco with his publication expenses. From Franco's letters we gather that Gardano made Orsini's acquantance, possibly as early as 1537;[70] he then introduced his young friend to the biship-elect. In a letter dated 20 September 1538, Franco writes to Orsini's secretary, Pignoli: "And yet, I have more than you reason to bless the boat that brought me to these waters, where I first saw you, and the great science [i.e., music] of Gardano, since by means of his music I became your friend and servant."[71]

We must remain cautious in our use of literary sources for biographical evidence.[72] As a work of fiction, this collection of letters inevitably contains fabrications in the events it reports. Yet, as Bridges notes, "Franco appears to have been genuinely sincere in his friendships, and we may suppose that *Pistole* which touched on his closest friends must have had some kernel of truth—the more so in that Gardane, as printer of the letters, was in a position to protest any essential falsification."[73]

While Franco's letters speak of Gardano as a friend and musician, they reveal nothing of him as a printer. Several scholars have speculated on the source of the Frenchman's knowledge of music printing. Both Moderne in Lyons and Attaingnant in Paris have been named as possible mentors.[74] Some have suggested that Gardano arrived in Venice sometime late in 1537 or early 1538, presumably after he learned his craft as a printer in France.[75] It is, I believe, highly unlikely that as a foreigner, Gardano could have arrived in Venice, married into an important Venetian printing dynasty, and established his own press all in the same year. He must have worked in the Venetian printing trade before that time—arriving in *La Serenissima* possibly as early as 1532, that is five years before he founded his own business.

Regulations established by the Venetian guild of printers and booksellers in 1572 lend credence to this theory. They state that any foreigner who wished to set up a printing press had to serve first for five years in a shop in Venice, after which time he would be examined and approved by the guild.[76] Although made explicit years after Gardano's arrival, this practice could have been observed by Venetian printers some forty years earlier.

If Gardano did come to Venice in the early 1530s, then from whom did he learn his trade? The logical choice, as Bridges speculates, is Gardano's future father-in-law, Agostino Bindoni.[77] Bindoni, however, never printed music books. So if Gardano did begin as a journeyman at Bindoni's printing shop, he might have gone to another Venetian press to learn the specialty of music printing. Could he have worked for the Scotto firm during the late 1530s? His connection with Girolamo during the early stages of his press and the fact that the House of Scotto was the only Venetian firm to issue music editions consistently throughout this crucial period argue in favor of this supposition. But Gardano's friendship with Franco and other circumstantial evidence suggests an even stronger link between Gardano and another press with an interest in music printing: the firm of Francesco Marcolini da Forlì.

Marcolini, as noted in chapter 1, was a prominent printer of vernacular literature, serving as the principle publisher for such writers as Pietro Aretino and Antonfrancesco Doni. His abilities in the arts went beyond the typical sixteenth-century printer. He numbered among his friends Titian, Jacopo Sansovino, Tintoretto, and Sebastiano del Piombo. An accomplished architect, he designed the "Ponte Longo" (now known as the Ponte Vivarini), the bridge across the widest canal on the nearby island of Murano in 1545. He was a connoisseur of antiquities, in particular the writings of Vitruvius, and as an expert goldsmith might have designed and engraved some of the illustrations found in his own publications. He later gained a prominent position as secretary and official printer to the Venetian Accademia Pellegrina.[78]

Arriving in Venice sometime around 1527 Marcolini established his own press in 1535 in the precinct of Santo Apostolo (see fig. 1.1 above). The publications he brought out during the early years of his press exemplify his wide-ranging intellectual and artistic interests. He initiated a series of architectural volumes by Sebastiano Serlio in 1537 with the printing of Book 4 (*Regole generali di architetura sopra le cinque maniere de gli edifici*), and then in 1540 brought out Book 3 (*Il terzo libro nel qual si figurano, e descrivono le antiquita di Roma*). The Serlio books appeared in deluxe folio with custom-made woodcuts for the title pages. The title cut of the *Regole* contains the first use of an architectural title-border with caryatids and fruit. Even more elaborate is the title cut of Roman ruins for the *Terzo libro*.[79] As noted in chapter 1, these two volumes were the first architectural publications where illustrations took prominence over the text.

For the next few years Marcolini printed several other books of high artistic quality. His 1537 edition of Aretino's *Stanze*, for example, includes a dedication by Titian as well as a chiaroscuro title cut attributed to the artist.[80] But Marcolini's most unusual illustrated book is *Le sorti intitolate Giardino di pensieri* of 1540, a folio volume containing some one hundred woodcuts that portray abstract personages (virtues, vices, etc.) and philosophers atop of charts with playing cards. The title cut, signed by Giuseppe Porta, Salviati depicts a complex study of men and women engaged in discussion. A portrait of Marcolini, also attributed by some scholars to Titian, appears on the verso side of the title page.[81]

In addition to his printing interests in architecture and literature, Marcolini entered into the music printing business only one year after he established his own press. As previously noted, Marcolini not only requested from the Venetian Senate a privilege to print specific music editions, but also a patent to revive Petrucci's double-impression method for printing music. In his application he writes:

> It is about thirty years since Ottaviano [de' Petrucci] of Fossombrone first printed music in the manner in which letters are printed and about twenty-five years since such works were [last] done . . . I, Francesco Marcolini . . . have labored many days and with no little expense to rediscover this method.[82]

In light of his expertise as a goldsmith, it is tempting to speculate that Marcolini himself designed and executed his own music typeface.

He chose for his first music publication a book of lute intabulations by Francesco da Milano. It is clear from the preface to the 1536 edition that he planned to print several music editions, for he named a second lute book with works by Francesco da Milano, Alberto da Ripa, and Marco Dall'Aquila, as well as "a volume of Masses, and one of motets, and one of madrigals composed by the stupendous Adriano [Willaert]."[83] The edition of Willaert's Masses, brought out in September 1536, is the only polyphonic music publication to survive from his press. His choice of Francesco da Milano, the most celebrated lutenist of the sixteenth century, and Adrian Willaert, the *maestro di cappella* at San Marco, for his first two music publications was impressive, as was the artistry of his editions.

Gardano might have joined Marcolini's press as early as 1536 if not before. Indeed, the Frenchman's musical expertise could have prompted Marcolini to enter the specialized world of music printing. Marcolini's printing shop might have also been the place where Gardano and Nicolò Franco first became acquainted. As noted previously, Franco joined Marcolini's press shortly after his arrival in Venice in 1536 and was employed there as a corrector until he moved to Aretino's house the following year.

Whether or not Gardano worked for Marcolini, it appears that the Italian printer had an influence upon the young Frenchman. Gardano clearly viewed himself as a printer of vernacular literature and music when he set up his own press. He must have observed like his friend, Nicolò Franco, Marcolini's success as the publisher of Aretino's *Lettere* and tried to emulate if not surpass the achievements of the Italian printer.

Like Marcolini, who issued Aretino's *Lettere* in folio format, Gardano deliberately printed Franco's *Pistole vulgari* in large folio. This format, usually reserved for deluxe publications, was the one Marcolini employed for his illustrated architecture books. Certain typographical features found in *Pistole* suggest that Gardano modeled his edition after Marcolini's architecture publications. Most obvious is the engraved title page, where an architectural border with pediment supported by two terminal figures directly imitates the title cut compartment found in Marcolini's 1537 edition of Serlio's *Regole generali di architetura*.[84]

The woodcut of the lion and bear holding the Orsini rose found in the colophon on the last page of *Pistole* also connotes a competitive spirit on the part of the printer. The mastery of the design and boldness of the figures matches if not overshadows Marcolini's elegant device (see figure 2.5 above). Gardano probably had it specially made for the Franco edition, since the device is inordinately large for oblong quarto format. Yet despite its size, it was Gardano's favorite printer's mark and was used not only in his early music prints in quarto oblong, but also in publications throughout the life of the firm. As noted in chapter 2, the Lion and Bear I device served as the prototype for all of Gardano's printer's marks created thereafter. It was also the largest and boldest printer's mark employed by any Venetian printer in a quarto oblong music book (see figure 2.6 above).

Gardano's publication of Franco's *Pistole vulgari* did not go unnoticed by either Aretino or Marcolini. Aretino grumbled in a letter dated 7 October 1539 to Lodovico Dolce, appearing in his second book of *Lettere* that

> I do not deny that they [Franco's *Pistole vulgari*] surpassed mine in number, in their title page, in the style of printing, in the haste in which they were written, in their paper, their illustrations and in the way in which they were touted, but not in their being alive . . . When Marcolini, that loyal friend, heard that the tosspot, chortling to see his trifles published, had said, "I have the man from Forlì's [Marcolini's] bread and Aretino's reputation," he thus made answer: "If my bread and Aretino's reputation had not been handy, Franco would have been a scullion."[85]

If Gardano viewed himself as a competitor to Marcolini in the subject of Italian literature, then he very quickly changed his mind, for, as we shall see, certain events that took place only two years after his opened his printing shop put an end to his plans. Although he failed to become an important publisher of vernacular literature, he did succeed in putting Marcolini out of business in his other specialization by employing a new process of printing music in Venice.

When Gardano set up his own press in 1538, he was evidently the first in Venice to adopt the single-impression method of printing—a technique, which, as we have seen, had already been employed several years earlier in London, Paris, Lyons, and a few German cities.[86] He was not, however, the first in Italy to utilize the single-impression technique; in 1537 the Roman printer Valerio Dorico brought out the earliest Italian music edition to employ the process. In 1538 the Ferrarese firm of Johannes de Buglhat, Henrico de Campis, and Antonio Hucher also utilized the single-impression method, and one year later Girolamo Scotto followed suit.

After only two years as an independent printer, Gardano might have experienced financial difficulties. In 1540 he published only one edition. Mary Lewis has suggested that Gardano's printing shop possibly sustained physical damage because of his publication of Nicolò Franco's *Pistole vulgari*, not to mention his personal friendship with the author.[87] The publication apparently had dire consequences for Franco, and possibly for Gardano, too. In the letter cited above, Aretino denounced Franco as a "sodomite who from copyist became imitator of my letters. He made a book of them and because he did not sell a single copy he ruined the French printer Gradana [*sic*] who lent him money to print them."[88] Franco was forced to leave Venice after having been expelled from Aretino's house and badly beaten in the street. It is possible that Gardano also might have been roughed up and his printing shop smashed for his role in this episode, for upon resuming printing in 1541 he employed new type and music fonts. Henceforth, Gardano confined his publishing activities almost entirely to the "safe" field of music.

By 1548 the Gardano press relocated to the Merceria near San Salvador, where it remained for the life of the firm.[89] In addition to his press, Gardano owned a bookshop. Unlike Scotto, who is named in archival documents as a *mercator*, Gardano consistently referred to himself as *libraro* (bookseller). While we have no notarial documents to verify the extent of his business connections, we must assume that they were similar to those of Scotto, though perhaps smaller in scale. He must have had agents working for him in various cities in the Italian peninsula as well as beyond the Alps.

His tax declaration of 1566 states that he owned twenty-six fields in the small town of Morelle on the *Terraferma*, which earned an income of thirteen ducats.[90] During the late 1560s and early 1570s, the Gardano family continued to acquire additional properties on the mainland. In 1575, when their assets were divided, they owned fifty-four fields in various villages, as well as a house in Padua.[91] Angelo Gardano, in the *Decima* of 1582, declared an income of fifty-four ducats from fifty fields.[92] The Gardano family had prospered, quadrupling the earnings they derived from their mainland properties.

The income the Gardano family generated from mainland properties may seem modest in comparison to that of the Scotto clan, whose tax statements of 1566 and

1582 declare earnings of ninety-nine and 276 ducats, respectively. It must be re-
membered, however, that at least during the first thirty years of operation the Gardano press was not as large an enterprise as the Scotto firm. The total extant titles
it published during this period numbered about half that of the House of Scotto.
Furthermore, the Scotto press had been in business for over half a century before
Antonio Gardano founded his firm. Only in the last decades of the sixteenth century
did the Gardano dynasty come into its own.

On 28 October 1569, Antonio Gardano died of a fever at the age of sixty. He
may have been ill for a while, for five months before his death the family began
making arrangements to purchase space for a tomb in the church of San Salvador.[93]
Since the Gardano firm was located in the precinct of San Salvador, it was natural
that the family worshipped at the church. Antonio's sons, Alessandro and Angelo,
moreover, were members of a religious confraternity, the *Scuola Grande di San
Teodoro*, which kept an altar in the church as well as buildings next to it.[94] A
memorial stone with the inscription, "ANTONIO | GARDANO AC POST. | VSQ. AD NO-
VISSIMVM | DIEM. | OBIIT ANN M.D.LXVIIII | MEN. OCT. | DIE XXVIII" on the floor of
the church to the right of the main entrance can still be seen today.[95]

THE HEIRS OF ANTONIO GARDANO (1569–75)

The year 1569 witnessed not only the death of a distinguished music printer, but
also the end of the long, uninterrupted peace that had brought wealth and prosperity
to the merchants of Venice. Famine along with a typhus epidemic overcame the city.
In February of the new year war broke out with the Turks, and Cyprus quickly fell
into the hands of the enemy. In 1570–71 Venice became embroiled in a bitter struggle
with the Turks. The Republic joined forces with Spain and the Papacy forming a
Holy League. The war against the Turks culminated with the Battle at Lepanto,
which led to a great victory for Venice and her allies—a victory that did not save
Cyprus, but at least restored Venice's naval reputation.

These first years after Antonio's death must have been difficult ones for the
press, but the transfer of leadership to the heirs seems to have gone smoothly. The
two older sons, Alessandro and Angelo, most assuredly took an active role in the
firm during the late 1560s, just as Girolamo's nephew, Melchiorre, did at the Scotto
press. When the two brothers joined the religious confraternity of the *Scuola Grande
di San Teodoro* in 1566, each one was listed in the *mariegola* as a *liberer* or bookseller.[96]

Upon Antonio's death, the estate was shared jointly by his children in accordance with Venetian law. Two of the six were not included in the bequest: Fra
Pacifico, who renounced his inheritance, and Angelica, who was already provided
for with a dowry when she married a mercer named Alvise Facini in 1569.[97] The
four remaining siblings, Alessandro, Angelo, Matthio, and Lucieta, continued to run
the press at the same location in the Merceria. All held equal shares in the family

partnership or *fraterna compagnia* with Alessandro and Angelo overseeing the financial interests of Matthio and Lucieta, who were still minors. Although the two eldest brothers assumed joint directorship of the firm, it appears that Angelo, the younger of the two, played a more dominant role in the managing of the business.[98]

For the remaining three months of 1569, publications were still issued under Antonio's name, but by 1570 the imprint of the firm changed to "li figliuoli di Antonio Gardano." Production at the Gardano press began to increase from an average of sixteen editions per year for the preceding decade to twenty editions per year during the next five years.[99]

From 1575 to 1577 two critical events took place that had an important effect upon the House of Gardano. The first was Alessandro Gardano's withdrawal from the *fraterna compagnia*. A series of notarial documents dating from April through November of 1575 record the amicable division of family assets. These documents prove valuable for they are among the very few extant sources to provide accurate biographical evidence concerning various members of the Gardano family. They also shed light on the value of the printing press at that time. Finally, they contain the only inventory to specify in remarkable detail the contents of a Venetian music print shop.

Alessandro requested and received one-quarter of the property the family owned on the *Terrafirma*. He was also alotted a quarter of other family possessions, including clothing, furniture, and other household things as well as merchandise and equipment from their bookshop and press. The Gardanos drew up an inventory listing all of the belongings of the family. From it, we can not only gain some insight into the private home life of a Venetian middle-class family, but can also reconstruct the basic contents of a Venetian music printing shop. Among the items listed for the shop were two printing presses with four tympans ("tellari") and other components; seven different music type fonts with their matrices, punches, and forms; the matrices of various letter type fonts; wood block miniatures containing various illustrations and coats-of-arms; 1,000 pounds of old tin or cast type ("stagno vecchio") with type cases ("casse da componer"); tables used to set up the formes ("tavole da forme"); several tables used for the assembling of books ("tavole diverse da meter libri insieme"); and an assortment of stools, benches, shelves, boxes, and buckets. The shop also contained 110 bales of books in good and bad condition as well as lutes and lute parts.[100]

Alessandro took his portion of household items from the family residence. Curiously though, he chose nothing from the shop, but instead agreed to accept 300 ducats. The Gardano family, thus, valued their business at 1,200 ducats, a substantial sum of money. Given that Alessandro set up his own printing press only two years later, it is surprising that he did not take his share of the business in tangible goods. The reason might have to do with the *fraterna's* concern to keep the Gardano firm intact at all costs. This was one of the underlying principles of family-owned businesses. Ottaviano II Scotto, for example, rewrote his will naming his brother Girolamo as sole heir to the press, for the express purpose of keeping the business together in its entirety.[101] In 1579, when Lucieta Gardano drew up her will, she stipulated that her assets should be divided between her two brothers Angelo and Matthio, but if in the future Matthio was to leave the *fraterna*, that he should only receive 100 ducats.[102] Decades later, Angelo Gardano, in a dispute with Matthio's widow, declared his intention for her son Antonio (who was his only male heir) to continue the family business of printing and bookselling, rather than deplete the wealth of the *fraterna* by giving her Matthio's share of the business.[103]

Alessandro's agreeing to leave the printing shop intact might account for the friendly division of the family assets among the heirs. After his withdrawal from the *fraterna*, Alessandro remained in Venice where he established his own printing firm around 1577–78. His printer's mark, similar to that of his father and brother, depicted two lions holding a globe. The ribbon that entwines the lion and bear contains the motto: "Aeque fortes aeque concordes" ("Equally strong, equally concordant") (see fig. 6.3). Unlike the main branch of the firm, Alessandro did not confine himself to the specialty of music, but printed other subjects as well. His printing concern in Venice lasted for only about four years. By 1583 he moved to Rome, where he ran a press in partnership with Francesco Coattino. With the financial assistance of Giacomo Tornieri and Bernardino Donangeli, the Roman *compagnia* issued no less than ninety-four editions between 1583 and 1591.[104]

Around the same time that Alessandro left the Gardano press, a catastrophic plague struck Venice. It began in 1575 and did not cease until the summer of 1577. Killing more than a quarter of the population, the epidemic placed a stranglehold on the city. Shops closed; businesses ceased operations. Rich and poor alike sought refuge on the mainland during the worst periods. From time to time, a quarantine was placed upon the city in an effort to contain the disease, thus crippling Venetian commerce and trade.[105]

The printing industry was not immune to the devastation. As the plague dragged on, book production declined sharply at most presses. Music publications issued at the Scotto firm, for example, dropped from sixteen in 1575 to five in 1577. At the

FIGURE 6.3 Printer's marks of Alessandro and Angelo Gardano

Gardano press, it decreased from an average of twenty to sixteen editions in 1576, and then slipped dramatically to only three titles in 1577. That same year, privileges granted by the Venetian Senate came to a temporary halt.[106]

In 1578 the Gardano press fortunately resumed its printing activities at a normal level. It continued to prosper over the next thirty-three years, bringing out, during the 1580s and early 1590s, an average of twenty-eight titles per year. Under Angelo's aegis, the firm grew in size to become the most prolific music press in sixteenth-century Europe.

Angelo Gardano continued to use the same lion and bear emblem that was created by his father when the press was established. After his brother's withdrawal from the press until his death, Angelo employed no fewer than eleven printer's marks.[107] All of them contained the same elements as the original device, but with one exception: the direction of the ends of the banner in Angelo's printer's marks pointed downward, while the seven of his father's turned upward (see fig. 6.3 and fig. 2.6).

From 1575 until 1611, Angelo Gardano produced at least 813 music editions—a figure that nearly doubled the output of his father.[108] He issued reprints and first editions of works by such prominent composers as Giovanni Matteo Asola, Claudio Merulo, Claudio Monteverdi, Luca Marenzio, Giovanni Pierluigi da Palestrina, Giaches de Wert, and Luzzasco Luzzaschi. Other composers such as Andrea Gabrieli, Marco da Gagliano, Don Carlo Gesualdo, Ruggiero Giovanelli, Marc' Antonio Ingegneri, Philippe de Monte, Costanzo Porta, Orazio Vecchi, and Camillo Zanotti used the Gardano press exclusively or almost exclusively for their Venetian publications. Angelo printed all the musical genres previously offered by his father, including madrigals, lighter Italian secular forms, motets, Masses and other liturgical settings, and instrumental pieces in mensural notation and in lute and keyboard intabulation. In addition, he brought out liturgical books containing plainchant, and in 1577 he issued the two earliest extant publications in score or partitura notation: *Musica de diversi autori la Bataglia francese et Canzon delli ucelli* and the complete four-voice madrigals of Cipriano de Rore.

Angelo Gardano died on 6 August 1611 at the age of seventy-one. His will stipulated that the printing firm be divided in accordance with an agreement drawn up in 1606 with his brother Matthio's widow.[109] He left 1,000 ducats to his son-in-law Bartolomeo Magni, who had worked at the Gardano press from as early as 1606, and bequeathed the remainder of his estate to his natural daughter Diamante.

The Gardano press did not cease operations upon the death of Angelo, but survived for most of the seventeenth century under the name of Magni.[110] Diamante's husband, Bartolomeo Magni, printed music editions as the "heir of Angelo Gardano" until his death sometime in the 1640s or 1650s. His son Francesco took directorship of the firm around 1651; he published sacred and instrumental music as well as nonmusic books until his death in 1673. The Magni press continued to use the lion and bear printer's mark to indicate their connection with the Gardano family. In 1685, the Magni firm disappeared and with it the legacy of the Gardano dynasty.

Enduring throughout the sixteenth century, the Houses of Gardano and Scotto together became the primary force in the commercialization of the Venetian music printing industry. They played a remarkable role at every step in the development of music printing. Ottaviano, founder of the Scotto press, was the first Italian to print music from movable type. Amadio Scotto acted as a silent partner to Ottaviano Petrucci, providing the financial backing to the first printer who published polyphonic music using the multiple-impression method. Ottaviano II underwrote Andrea Antico's *Liber quindecim missarum* and collaborated with the *intagliatore* on a series of sixteen xylographic music books. Angelo Gardano became the most prolific music printer of sixteenth-century Europe. Nonetheless, it was Antonio Gardano and Girolamo Scotto who boldly switched to the single-impression method of music printing, thus making the publication of music books a money-making enterprise. Their contributions to the commercialization of music printing along with their prodigious outputs established the Houses of Scotto and Gardano as the two most important music publishing firms in Renaissance Europe.

NOTES

1. "Tantus est optimorum in omni philosophia libroru[m] numerus, Hieronyme vir clarissime quos officina tua & felicis memoriae patris tui Octaviani, magna cum gloria vestra in lucem protulit, ut nomen tuum ubique gentium iam dudum celeberrimum." Conrad Gesner, *Pandectarum sive Partitionum Universalium . . . Libri XXI* (Zurich, 1548), fol. 311.

2. The origins of the Scotto family of Monza are summarized in J. Bernstein, *Music Printing in Renaissance Venice*, 30; see also Giovanni Scotti, "L'antica famiglia verennate degli Scotti," *Periodico della Società Storica della Provincia e antica Diocesi di Como* 22 (1915), 65–97; Anton Francesco Frisi, *Memorie storiche di Monza e sua Corte* (Milan, 1794), 3: 140; Carlo Volpati, "Gli Scotti di Monza, tipografi-editori in Venetia," *Archivio storico lombardo* 49 (1922), 365–82; and Claudio Sartori, "La famiglia degli editori Scotto," *Acta musicologica* 36 (1964): 19–21.

3. Lowry, *World of Aldus Manutius*, 8.

4. An endorsement of a will dated 1 March 1481 mentions one Battista, son of Andrea de Dentis of Bellano, as an "impressore librorum de confinio S Samuelis in domibus ser Ottaviani Scotti." See B. Cecchetti, "Altri stampadori ed altri librai," *Archivio Veneto* n. ser., 29 (1885): 412–13 at 413.

5. British Museum, *Catalogue of Books Printed in the XVth Century now in the British Museum. Part V. Venice*, ed. Julius Victor Scholderer (London, 1924), 275.

6. Bridges, "Publishing of Arcadelt's First Book," 1: 134.

7. In popular literature, Aldo Manuzio has often been credited with the invention of the so-called portable book. As Lowry, *World of Aldus Manutius*, 142–43, notes, octavo format had already been used in manuscripts and in printed books of a religious or devotional nature.

8. German printers working in Italy issued books with music notation printed from movable type before Scotto. See Duggan, *Italian Music Incunabula*, 102 and Sartori, "La famiglia," 22.

9. Duggan, *Italian Music Incunabula*, 102–5; a plate of a folio from the missal appears as fig. 39.

10. Ibid., 103.

11. William H. J. Weale and Hans Bohatta, *Bibliographia liturgica: catalogus missalium ritus Latini, ab anno M.CCCC.LXXIV impressorum* (London, 1928), nos. 870, 875, 877, 926,

938, 1815, 1822 (no. 1821 is a ghost); Kathi Meyer-Baer, *Liturgical Music Incunabula* (London, 1962), nos. 126, 127, 152, 156, 212, 215; and Duggan, *Italian Music Incunabula*, nos. 55, 60, 62, 95, 104, 131, 136.

12. See Zappella, *Le marche* 2: no. 53, "Cerchio et croce," for several examples of this sign.

13. British Museum, *Catalogue of Books Printed in the XVth Century*, 5: xxii.

14. ASV, Serenissima Signoria, Lettere sottoscritte, Mar. I I.a 164 dal 12 marzo al novembre 1492, as cited by Volpati, "Gli Scotti di Monza," 369.

15. Other members of the Scotto family, including Girolamo, are buried in the same church. Only Ottaviano I's tombstone survives in the cloister; a sketch of the stone appears in Sartori, "La famiglia," 20[bis]. According to a Franciscan monk of the church, the remaining family stones were destroyed during the Napoleonic occupation.

16. Frederic C. Lane, "Venetian Bankers, 1496–1533," in *Venice and History*, 69–86 at 69–79.

17. Hirsch, *Printing, Selling and Reading*, 42.

18. ASV, Quattro Ministeriali: strida e clamori, Registro 79, c. 108. Parts of the document are quoted in Sartori, "La famiglia," 22 n. 20.

19. ASV, Notat. Collegio 28, c. 28; as cited in Fulin, "Documenti," 142–43. Aristotle's *Problemata* appeared in 1501 (a copy of this book is located in London, British Library).

20. This estimate is calculated from a number of published and unpublished catalogues that list the holdings of several European and American libraries. To mention a few: Herbert Mayrow Adams, ed., *Catalogue of Books Printed on the Continent of Europe 1501–1600 in Cambridge Libraries*, 2 vols. (Cambridge, 1967); British Museum, *Short-Title Catalogue of Books Printed in Italy and of Italian Books Printed in Other Countries from 1465 to 1600 now in the British Museum* (London, 1958); Richard J. Durling, comp., *A Catalogue of Sixteenth-Century Printed Books in the National Library of Medicine* (Bethesda, 1967); *Le edizioni italiane del XVI secolo: censimento nazionale*, ed. Maria Sicco and M. A. Baffio, 4 vols. to date (Istituto centrale per il catalogo unico delle biblioteche italiane e per le informazioni bibliografiche; Rome, 1985–); *Index Aureliensis*; Ester Pastorello, handwritten catalogue of books printed in Venice, 1469–1600, held in selected northern Italian libraries. Sala dei Manoscritti, Biblioteca Nazionale Marciana, Venice; *Primo catalogo collettivo delle biblioteche italiane*, ed. Centro nazionale per il catalogo unico delle biblioteche italiane e per le informazioni bibliografiche, 9 vols. (Rome, 1962–79); RISM; *Short-Title Catalogue of Books Printed in Italy and of Books in Italian Printed Abroad 1501–1600 Held in Selected North American Libraries*, ed. Robert G. Marshall, 3 vols. (Boston, 1970); M. A. Shaaber, ed., *Sixteenth-Century Imprints in the Libraries of the University of Pennsylvania* (Philadelphia, 1976); Margaret H. Jackson, ed., *Catalogue of the Francis Taylor Pearson Plimpton Collection of Italian Books and Manuscripts in the Library of Wellesley College* (Cambridge, Mass., 1929).

21. ASV, Senata Terra, Registro 126, fol. 184; as cited in Volpati, "Gli Scotti di Monza," 372.

22. ASV, Miscellanea Gregolin, b. 32; transcribed in Fulin, "Nuovi documenti per servire alla storia della tipografia veneziana," *Archivio veneto* 23 (1882): 390–405 at 401–5.

23. Georg Panzer, *Annales typographici ab artis inventae origine ad annum 1500* (Nuremberg, 1800), 8: 410–24.

24. Lowry, *World of Aldus Manutius*, 160–61.

25. ASV, Registro Notatorio XXV, 1512–1514, c. 92. A transcription of the petition appears among other places in Sartori, *Bibliografia delle opere musicali*, 19. For further discussion see Boorman, "Petrucci at Fossombrone," 21–22.

26. Volpati, "Gli Scotto di Monza," 371.

27. ASV, Dieci Savi Decime, reg. 1233, 64; also ASV, Dieci Savi, Condizioni di decima, b. 92, no. 57.

28. ASV, Notarile Testamenti, B. 974, no. 7. Benalio's two wills date from 1516 and 1517. Soardi died in 1517; his will appears in ASV, Notarile Testamenti, B. 999, no. 145. Cited in Volpati, "Gli Scotto di Monza," 369 n. 4.

29. "Impressum Venetiis apud Octavianum Scotum Anno Domini 1533 Kal. Octobris." A copy of the edition is located in the library of the University of Pavia.

30. *Catalogus translationum et commentariorum: Medieval and Renaissance Latin Translations and Commentaries*, ed. Paul Oskar Kristeller ([Washington, 1960]), 1: 103.

31. Kristeller, "The Aristotelian Tradition," in Renaissance Thought, 42.

32. See chapter 7 for further information on d'Avalos.

33. Chapman, "Andrea Antico," 134, supports the latter view. See also Martin Picker, ed. *The Motet Books of Andrea Antico* (Monuments of Renaissance Music 8; Chicago, 1988), 4, and Beth Miller, "Antico, Andrea," in *Music Printing and Publishing*, ed. D. W. Krummel and Stanley Sadie (New York and London, 1990), 145.

34. ASV, Senato Terra, reg. 29, fol. 81ᵛ (new fol. 102ᵛ). Marc' Antonio Zimarra (c. 1475–1532) was a professor of logic and, later, natural philosophy at the University of Padua and elsewhere. The book in question, *Tabula dilucidationum in dictis Aristotelis et Averrois*, became the standard indices to the works of Aristotle and Averroes. See *The Cambridge History of Renasissance Philosophy*, ed. Charles B. Schmitt and Quentin Skinner, 841, for a capsule biography.

35. Certainly by 1537, the year of his father's death, Ottaviano, who inherited his father's noble title, might have begun to ease himself out of his role as manager of the day-to-day operations of the firm.

36. Chapman, "Andrea Antico," 145.

37. Anchor I is reproduced in fig. 2.7. Fenlon and Haar, *Italian Madrigal*, 306, also speculate that Girolamo might have been responsible for *Libro secondo a cinque*, stating that the device found on the Cantus partbook was one preferred by Girolamo. This statement is slightly misleading since it implies that this particular printer's mark (Anchor I) was used quite often by Girolamo. As we have seen in chap. 2, the Scotto firm employed at least eight different printer's marks depicting the anchor with palm frond and olive branch. Anchor I was, in fact, used by Girolamo for only one year (and only in his music editions); he replaced it with a smaller anchor in which the palm frond and olive branch are reversed.

38. *Aristo. posteriorum libri una cum linconiensi atque Burleo fidelissimis interpretibus his adiecimus Pamphili Montij Bononiensis glossemata, in marginalibus apposita . . . Venetiis*, Apud Hieronymum Scotum. M. D. LII.

39. ASV, Notarile Atti, Benedetto Solian, b. 11875, fols. 60ᵛ–61ᵛ.

40. A catalogue of short titles of his non-music publications appears in J. Bernstein, *Music Printing in Renaissance Venice*, app. D.

41. A summary of properties owned by other printers appears in Claudia di Filippo Bareggi, "L'editoria veneziana fra '500 e '600," 623–25.

42. "quelli pochi denari che soleva traficar in ditta mercantia li ho retirati in questi pochi stabili . . ."; ASV, Dieci Savii sopra le Decime in Rialto, Condizione di Decima, 1566, San Marco, b. 126, no. 115.

43. Brian Pullan, "Occupations and Investments of the Venetian Nobility," in Renaissance *Venice*, ed. John R. Hale (London, 1973), 379–408.

44. As quoted in Ugo Tucci, "The Psychology of the Venetian Merchant in the Sixteenth Century," in *Renaissance Venice*, ed. John R. Hale (London, 1973), 346–78 at 352.

45. A census for the purpose of tax collection was taken by the Dieci Savii sopra le decime in Rialto in 1514, 1537, 1566, 1581, and 1661. Taxes were only levied on investment

property within the Venetian Republic; income from the Scottos' business, the house in which they lived, and property outside the state were exempt. Although "Ottaviano and Girolamo Scotto, stampadori," are listed in the book of summaries for the 1537 Decima (Dieci Savii sopra le decime, red. 1537, reg. 1475, c. 560), the actual statement (*condizione*) in nuove or stravaganti, no. 457 is missing from the archives.

46. During Girolamo's tenure, the press moved at least twice. It was located in the district of San Felice until at least 1547. By 1561 the firm had moved to the parish of San Benedetto, and in 1564 it was established in the Corte dell'Albero at Sant'Angelo; see fig. 1.1 for locations.

47. ASV, Dieci Savii sopra le Decime in Rialto, Condizione di Decima, 1566, San Marco, b. 126, no. 115.

48. ASV, Serenissima Signoria, Lettere sottoscritte, Terra, Filza 10, 19 dic. Cited in Volpati, "Gli Scotto di Monza," 379 n. 2.

49. ASV, Dieci Savii sopra le Decime in Rialto, Condizione di Decima, 1582, San Marco, b. 158, no. 859.

50. Grendler, *Roman Inquisition*, 19 n. 67.

51. Ibid., 20.

52. Remo Giazotto, *Harmonici concenti in aere veneto* (Rome, 1954), claims that Girolamo Scotto had a daughter named Laura, who, in 1568, he endowed with a printing shop upon her marriage to Alessandro Gardano, son of Antonio. No daughter is mentioned in Girolamo's will. Furthermore, the document referred to by Giazotto has not turned up in any archive in Venice.

53. ASV, Notarile Testamenti, not. Benedetto Solian, b. 899, n. 233. A partial transcription of Girolamo Scotto's will appears in Sartori, "La famiglia," 27 n. 33.

54. ASV, B. Solian Notarile Atti, b. 11874, fol. 10^{r-v}.

55. Agee, "A Venetian Music Printing Contract," 61. For further discussion of this contract see chap. 3.

56. See fig. 2.7 in chap. 2.

57. ASV, Cancelleria Inferiore, Cedole, b. 68, no. 216. A transcription of parts of Baldissera's will appears in Sartori, "La famiglia," 29 n. 34. In the will, Baldissera mentions his inheritance from Girolamo's widow, Cesarea Sinistri, further suggesting his father's death by that date.

58. Biographical information on the Gardano family appears in Claudio Sartori, "Una dinastia di editori musicali," *La Bibliofilia* 58 (1956): 176–208. See also Lewis, *Antonio Gardano*, 1:17–34; Bridges, "Publishing of Arcadelt's First Book," 96–99; Agee, *Gardano Music Printing Firms*, 51–89; and Elisa Bonaldi, "La famiglia Gardano e l'editoria musicale veneziana (1538–1611), *Studi veneziana* new ser. 20 (1990): 273–302.

59. "Die 28 Ott. 1569: M. Antonio Gardan libraro d'anni 60 da febre, et medicho Picholomini, et medicine al S. Jerolimo S. Salvador." Cited in Claudio Sartori, "Dinastia," 176.

60. ASV, Senato Terra. Reg. 30 (1538–39), fol. 21 (new fol. 41). A transcription of the full document appears in Agee, "Privilege and Venetian Music Printing," 209.

61. "il mio M. Antonio Gardane, il quale per essere nato in Francia non men che voi" in Nicolo Franco, *Le Pistole vulgari* (Venice: Gardano, 1539), fol. 14^v. A partial English translation as well as a transcription of the complete letter appear in Bridges, "Publishing of Arcadelt's First Book," 1: 101; 2:375.

62. Ed., *Anthologie de la chanson parisienne au XVIe siècle* (Monaco, 1953), p. vii.

63. *Antonio Gardano*, 1: 17.

64. A complete list of Gardano's compositions appears in Bridges, "Gardano," *New Grove* 7: 159. For a modern edition of all his chansons published by Le Roy and Ballard, see

J. Bernstein, ed. *Adrian Le Roy, Premier livre de chansons en forme de vau de ville (1573),
Nicolas de la Grotte, Chansons de P. de Ronsard, Ph. Desporte, et autres (1580), Premier
livre de chansons à deux parties (1578), Chansons by Antonio Gardane Published by LeRoy
and Ballard.* Sixteenth-Century Chanson 15 (New York and London, 1992).

65. The ages of Mattio and Lucieta appear in ASV, Atti notaio Zuanne Figolin, f. 5624,
vol. I, fols. 181–83. A complete transcription of the notarial document appears in Sartori,
"Dinastia," p. 179.

66. All the copies of *Le pistole vulgari* cited in Lewis, *Antonio Gardano,* 1:218–19,
which contain a colophon dated April 1539 with Gardano's imprint and printer's mark, have,
until now, been regarded as the only issue of the first edition. A second copy of *Le pistole*
located in Houghton Library, Harvard University (shelfmark: f*IC5. F8485. 538p), however,
displays on its last folio a different unsigned colophon with an earlier date of November 1538.
An examination of the two copies reveals that the unsigned copy is the original issue of the
first edition. The copies signed by Gardano, therefore, represent a reissue with two canceled
leaves (GG1 and GG4), the last of which contains the newly printed colophon with Gardano's
name.

67. Bridges, "Publishing of Arcadelt's First Book," 1: 101; 2: 375.

68. "In so che mi conto in bocca una voce si sgangherata, che farebbe sconcertare la
cappella del paradiso, e pure le cose vostre han forza; da farla parere da qualche cosa. Do-
vrebbe vivere a i di nostri quella indiavolata anima di Nerone, che senza dubbio vi donarebbe
l'Impero." Franco, *Pistole,* fols. 33ᵛ–34. Translation from Bridges, 1: 102; transcription of full
letter appears in id., 2: 376–77.

69. Ibid., 1: 103.

70. Lewis, *Antonio Gardano,* 1: 21.

71. "E però, ho io piu di voi cagione di benedire, e la barca che mi condusse in queste
acque, ove prima vi viddi, e la somma scienza del Gardano, poiche per mezzo de la sua
musica vi divenni quell' amico e servo che già vi sono," Franco, *Pistole,* fol. 104; transcription
of the full letter appears in Bridges, 2: 384–85; Both Bridges, 1: 102 and Lewis, 1: 21 translate
"barca" as bark instead of boat.

72. Another literary source, the *Nuove rime di diversi eccellenti auttori le quali si leg-
gono sparse hora raccolte e scelte con cura e abbondantia* (Padua, 1546), appearing in Remo
Giazotto, *Harmonici concenti in aere Veneto* (Rome, 1954), contains sonnets that cite Gardano.
One of them is addressed to the music printer, who is depicted as a friend of the composers
Girolamo Parabosco, Perissone Cambio, Cipriano de Rore, and possibly Costanzo Festa. The
poem also indicates a personal connection between Gardano and such important literary figures
as Gaspara Stampa, Domenico Venier, Domenico Michiel, Leonardo Emo, Girolamo Molino,
and Francesco Sansovino.

This sonnet has been used by Lewis, *Antonio Gardano,* 1:25–30, as proof of Gardano's
membership "within the favored circles of [Venice's] literary and musical elite." Unfortunately,
as Lewis has noted (1:23 n. 38), several scholars have been unsuccessful in their efforts to
locate the original 1546 print. In light of the difficulty in corroborating the existence of *Nuove
rime,* it seems prudent not to use it as a source for biographical evidence until a copy of the
sixteenth-century publication surfaces.

73. Bridges, "Publishing of Arcadelt's First Book," 1: 101.

74. Pogue, *Jacques Moderne,* 73 and Heartz, *Pierre Attaingnant,* 158–59.

75. Lewis, *Antonio Gardano,* 19.

76. As cited in Brown, *Venetian Printing Press,* 88.

77. "Publishing of Arcadelt's First Book," 1:99. Bridges refrains from suggesting Gardano's date of arrival in Venice.

78. Biographical information on Marcolini is derived from Luigi Servolini, new intro-

duction and Scipione Casali, original introduction to *Annali della tipografia veneziana di Francesco Marcolini da Forlì* (Bologna, 1953).

79. See Mortimer, *Italian 16th Century Books*, 2: 651–55.

80. Ibid., 1: 32–33.

81. Ibid., 2: 409–13.

82. "esser circa xxx. Anni che fu uno Ottaviano da Fossanbrono, che stampava musical nel modo, che se imprimono le l[etter]e, et è circa xxv. Anni che tal opera non si fa, . . . Io Franc[esc]o Marcolini . . . essendomi affaticato molti giorni, e non con poca spesa in ritrovar tal cosa." English translation taken from Chapman, *Andrea Antico*, 149. A transcription of the privilege appears in several sources, most recently in Agee, "Privilege and Venetian Music Printing," 207.

83. Translation taken from Chapman, *Andrea Antico*, 147–48.

84. Grendler reproduces the title page to Franco's *Pistole vulgari* in *Critics of the Italian World*, 41. The Serlio title page appears in Mortimer, *Italian 16th Century Books*, 2: 651.

85. "Non nego di esser vinto da lui di numero, di titolo, di stile, di prestezza, di bella carta, di pittura, e di fama, ma non di umanità. . . . Intendendo il marcolino lealtà de l'amicizia che il Briaco sgongolando nel vedere stampate le sue bagatelle haveva detto al Forlivese il pane, e a lo Aretino il credito haggio tolto loco, rispose se il mio pane, e il credito del compar non fosse stato, il Franco sarebbe guattero." *Del secondo libro de le lettere di M. Pietro Aretino* (Paris: Matteo il Maestro, 1609), fols. 98; 99ᵛ. English translation from Thomas C. Chubb, *The Letters of Pietro Aretino* (New York, 1940; reprint, Hamden, Conn., 1967), 151–52.

86. See chapter 1 for a brief synopsis.

87. Lewis, *Antonio Gardano*, 1:23 n. 35.

88. "il sodomito di scrittore ed le mie lettere ne divenne emulo; onde ne fece il libro, che col non se ne vender pur una ha rovinato il Gradana Francese, che gli prestò i denari per istamparle." *Del secondo libro*, fol. 98. The letter and incident are also described by Bridges, "Publishing of Arcadelt's First Book," 1:104

89. The sonnet honoring Gardano in Giazotto, *Harmonici concenti*, implies that Gardano's press had moved from the Calle de la Scimia to the area of San Zaccaria in the early 1540s ("Che reca al grande torchio e mi conceda sosta a San Zaccaria"). As mentioned previously, without confirmation of the existence of the original print, we cannot ascertain the authenticity of this source.

90. ASV, Dieci Savii sopra le Decime in Rialto, Condizione di Decima, 1566, San Marco, b. 126, no. 56, as cited by Grendler, *The Roman Inquisition and the Venetian Press*, 23, and Lewis, *Antonio Gardano*, 1:23.

91. Details of the various purchases appear in Agee, *Gardano Music Printing Firms*, 55.

92. ASV, Dieci Savii sopra le Decime in Rialto, Condizione di Decima, 1582, San Marco, b. 157bis, no. 767, as cited by Grendler, *The Roman Inquisition*, 23, and Lewis, *Antonio Gardano*, 1:23. See Agee, *Gardano Music Printing Firms*, 66–67, for detailed discussion on this tax declaration.

93. Agee, *Gardano Music Printing Firm*, 51–52.

94. Ibid.

95. A photograph reproduction of the stone appears in Sartori, "Dinastia," 208, and Antonio Gardano, *Canzoni francesi*, 73

96. Agee, *Gardano Music Printing Firms*, 51.

97. Sartori, "Dinastia," 201.

98. Agee, *Gardano Music Printing Firms*, 52.

99. Ibid., 56.

100. ASV Archivio notarile, Atti Zuanne Figolin, f. 5624, vol. 1, 12th gathering (Extravaganza Iᵒ [fols. 32ᵛ–34ᵛ], as cited by Agee, *Gardano Music Printing Firms*, 56 n. 26. A

transcription of the inventory as well as other documents pertaining to the 1575 division of assets appears in Sartori, "Dinastia," 180–89.

101. The two wills appear in ASV Notarile Testamenti, not. Angelo Calvi, b. 307, no. 308 and ASV, Notarile Testamenti, not. Giacomo Formento, b. 413, no. 359, respectively. They are partially transcribed in Sartori, "La famiglia degli editori Scotto," 25–27, nn. 29, 30.

102. ASV Notarile Testamenti, not. Giacomo Carlotti, b. 277, no. 255. A transcription of the will appears in Sartori, "Dinastia," 192.

103. ASV, Giudici di Petizione, Dimande, b. 21. Transcribed in Sartori, "Dinastia," 199; also cited by Agee, *Gardano Music Printing Firms*, 80.

104. Agee, *Gardano Music Printing Firms*, 63–65. A preliminary checklist of his publications appears in id., 343–59.

105. Brian Pullan, *Rich and Poor in Renaissance Venice: The Social Institutions of a Catholic State to 1620* (Oxford, 1971), 314–26.

106. Agee, *Gardano Music Printing Firms*, 17. Brown, *Venetian Printing Press*, 239 lists no applicants for the year 1577 in his table of monopolies, patents, and copyrights. Agee, *Gardano Music Printing Firms*, 17 n. 6 mentions that while no privileges were granted, the *Riformatori dello Studio di Padova* and the Venetian Council of Ten continued to issue book licenses.

107. Of the eleven printer's marks, three had already been employed by Angelo's father, Antonio; the remaining eight were new.

108. Ibid., 4.

109. A transcription and photographic reproduction of the will appear in Sartori, "Dinastia," 205–6.

110. On the Magni family, see Stanley Boorman, "Magni," in *Music Printing and Publishing*, ed. D. W. Krummel and Stanley Sadie (New York, 1990), 329–30.

Seven

SCOTTO AND GARDANO

Marketing a Musical Repertory

uring the three decades they operated their presses, Girolamo Scotto and Antonio Gardano printed almost every musical genre offered by Italian and *oltremontane* composers. Their production not only expressed the catholic taste of cosmopolitan Venice, it also reflected the interests of a wide-ranging international audience. The musical repertory they published and the effect it had upon their relationship remain central to any study devoted to sixteenth-century music printing.

The final part of the study concentrates on the marketing of this musical repertory. It will examine the specific business strategies Gardano and Scotto observed in the acquisition and promotion of their music publications. By exploring the music editions from an economic perspective, a new view concerning the relationship between the Venetian printers and the kind of repertories they produced will emerge. But first, we begin with an overview of the genres issued by the two presses.

The Italian madrigal, as might be expected, dominated the output of both printers. Figure 7.1 illustrates this point: almost half of Scotto's and nearly 60 percent of Gardano's extant editions are comprised of madrigals. Tastes within the Italian peninsula, the main marketplace for both bookmen, dictated the proliferation of this vernacular genre.

Lighter Italian secular forms, the *canzone villanesca alla napolitane, villote, moresche,* and *mascherate,* were also an important part of the trade. Both Venetian printers published a substantial number of collections in this genre, with Scotto producing nearly double that of Gardano. Editions of instrumental music took up a small but significant part of the output of the two printers. They brought out an equal number of lute intabulations, but only Gardano tried his hand at printing the more complex keyboard intabulations as well as ricercars for ensembles.

Latin as the *lingua franca* for all of Europe made sacred music more exportable than the vernacular genres. Sacred publications claimed a good share of the Venetian

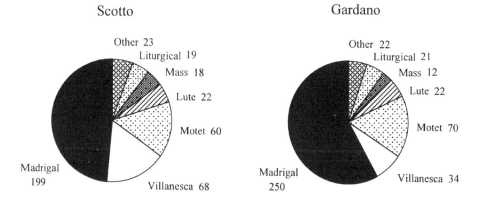

Total editions: Scotto=409   Gardano=431

FIGURE 7.1   Scotto and Gardano editions by genre

printers' *opere*, taking up nearly 25 percent of the total surviving music books of both presses. Motet publications made up the bulk of this group. Editions of polyphonic liturgical settings, including responsories, introits, hymns, psalms, and Lamentations, also were printed in encouraging numbers. In addition, the Scotto press issued missals containing plainchant—a printing interest of the firm since its inception. Mass settings complete the picture, with Scotto producing almost double the number of publications brought out by Gardano.

COOPERATION OR COMPETITION?

Much has been made of the rivalry between the two printers, with attention paid most notably to the extensive reprinting of each other's editions. On occasion, one or the other has been accused of piracy. Scholars have theorized about connections, competition, and contention between Scotto and Gardano, particularly during the early stages of their publishing careers. Eitner was presumably the first to portray Scotto and Gardano as rivals who did not observe each other's privileges. He stated that when one issued a successful edition, the other would print a pirated edition, often in the same year.[1] Einstein went one step further by declaring that Girolamo Scotto "was essentially a pirate, even though many musicians came to him with their original works."[2] He probably based his opinion on the caustic remarks Gardano made in the dedications and title pages of his early editions, where he accused other printers of plagiarism. The charge of piracy Einstein leveled against Scotto became established as fact in the secondary literature. Claudio Sartori, in particular, declared that Scotto frequently stole editions from Gardano.[3]

Daniel Heartz was the first to express a different viewpoint. By examining the typeface used by Scotto and Gardano in their early editions, he recognized that it was manufactured from the same punches and matrices. He suspected collusion rather than competition between the two printers. Heartz furthermore named Gardano as the originator of the typeface, who possibly created it himself or commissioned it from "craftsmen [brought] with him to Venice."[4] As noted in chapter 2, at least four different printers employed the same music typeface. Of the four, only Girolamo Scotto made consistent use of the typeface for over twenty years, suggesting that he must have bought the punches, and possibly sold or rented the matrices to Gardano and the other printers.

More recently, several other scholars have argued in favor of cooperative enterprise. Agee used privileges as evidence, noting that "the two printers seem to have respected each other's privileges in most cases." He further speculated that in the few instances where Gardano and Scotto republished each other's privileged edition, they could have obtained permission from the original holder of the privilege.[5]

Bridges noted that Gardano's 1541 edition of Jhan Gero's *Primo libro di madrigali italiani et canzoni francese a due voci* contained a dedication signed by Girolamo Scotto. He pointed to this as evidence that Scotto commissioned Gardano to print the book. He also turned the idea of pirated editions on its head by proposing that their frequent reprinting of each other's editions, "without incident, suggests at least an informal agreement to tolerate such reprinting."[6]

Lewis also examined some of these reprinted editions with a view to discovering the relationship between the two printers. By comparing specific pairs of editions, she discovered that the printers did not always directly copy from each other, but in some cases revised earlier editions, and in other instances used different sources for their exemplars. She concluded that "Gardano and Scotto seem neither to have colluded, nor to have been fiercely competitive, but rather to have coexisted."[7]

All of these recent scholars have made convincing arguments in favor of cooperative enterprise. By examining privileges, dedications, and related editions, they have taken the first steps in determining the relationship between the music printers. But there is another way to consider this issue, one that goes beyond the specialty of music. I propose that an examination of marketing strategies by the printing industry in general and how Scotto and Gardano's music publications reflect those procedures will shed further light on their association.

As we have seen in chapter 1, the Venetian printing industry acted as an organic unit. In order for the trade to survive, competition among its membership had to be kept to a minimum. Thus Venetian bookmen followed the basic laws of supply and demand in that only the optimal number of printers specialized in any given field. Secular vernacular literature, scientific texts, and canonical works sustained a bevy of printers, while subjects requiring special typography, such as music, could support only one or two presses. Archival documents reveal that *mercatori* in any given field

remained on friendly terms—forming partnerships, commissioning books, even sharing typographical supplies and equipment.[8]

The music editions listed in appendix A give us a good idea as to the quantity
and variety of music titles brought out by the Venetian presses. While it appears that
Scotto and Gardano issued the same musical repertories, a closer look at their output
reveals a more complicated picture. The two bookmen were driven by commercial
concerns, which, in turn, determined what music they printed. They spread their net
wide by publishing a variety of musical genres. At the same time, they issued dis-
tinctly separate repertories, often from different geographical areas, thereby avoiding
direct competition with each other. When they discovered a title that sold, however,
they eagerly reprinted each other's editions, following a practice common to the rest
of the printing industry at that time.

The reprinting of successive editions of the same work became a lucrative
enterprise for the Venetian bookmen. Gardano tended to rely more heavily on reprinted publications than Scotto (see fig. 7.2); his publication list contains a higher
proportion of reprints than Scotto's—48 percent as opposed to 35 percent for Scotto.
Indeed, even though about twenty more music editions printed by Gardano than by
Scotto survive, Scotto published more first editions than Gardano did—264 for
Scotto as opposed to 224 for Gardano. This trend prevailed throughout their publishing careers, but is particularly noticeable during the earlier period.

With an eye always toward profitability, the Venetian printers maintained a
careful balance in their production between commissioned works and reprinted editions. Two-thirds of Scotto's and over half of Gardano's extant publications were
first editions, and the vast majority of these first editions were single-composer
publications paid for by musicians and other third parties on a fixed fee basis (see
fig. 7.2). As we have seen in chap. 3, commissions provided financial opportunities
with little or no risks. They offered new music to the presses, which, in turn, might
become best-selling reprinted editions. Partnerships also proved beneficial by spread-
ing the financial risks among a group of printers and other interested parties. Both
types of publications offset speculations the printers made on independently financed
anthologies and reprinted editions.

Gardano and Scotto enhanced their financial stability by keeping competition
between themselves to a minimum. To this end they established their own separate
clientele. Composers and other third parties often favored one or the other for their
printing needs.[9] The music printers furthered this spirit of cooperative enterprise by
obtaining music from different geographical locations, and, to some extent, maintaining a division in genres they printed.

They also resorted to a variety of schemes in the presentation of their music
books. This was especially true with reprinted publications. Forever searching for a
way to provide the public with something novel, the music printers would often
alter previous editions in several ways.

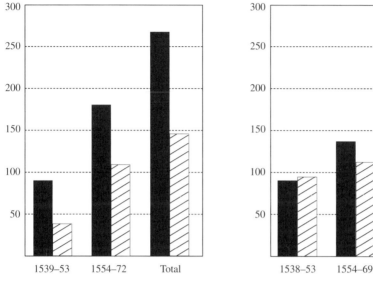

FIGURE 7.2 First and reprinted editions of music publications issued by Scotto and Gardano

SOMETHING OLD, SOMETHING NEW: REPRINTED EDITIONS

The two printers began to reprint each other's as well as their own music publications as early as 1540. Though they often duplicated certain features, rarely did Gardano and Scotto copy each other's publications exactly.[10] They frequently added works or replaced old pieces with new ones, as seen with Gardano's 1540 reprint of Jacquet of Mantua's First Book of Motets *a* 5.[11] In a few instances, they used different sources for their volumes, as observed in the "parallel" editions of Rore's Third Book of Madrigals issued by both printers in 1548.[12]

Gardano, in some cases, created "new" publications by redefining previously printed editions. By slightly altering the phrase *i madrigali da diversi perfettissimi musici* to *i madrigali di Verdelot* on the title page of his 1541 edition of *Le Dotte et eccellente compositioni*, he transformed Scotto's 1540 anthology into a single-composer edition. Gardano thus singled out Verdelot as the star composer, even though only a quarter of the madrigals in the volume were by him. He evidently realized that two books were better than one, when, in 1544, the French émigré recast two previous Scotto editions of Rore's First Book of Five-Voice Madrigals into a first and second book. Needless to say, Gardano's edition of the second book contained only a small proportion of Rore madrigals—eight out of a total of twenty-seven pieces.[13]

While Gardano created additional books of madrigals by single composers, Scotto did just the opposite in his reprinted publications. He favored the condensation of editions, by merging two or more publications into one volume. The previously mentioned 1540 edition of Verdelot's *Tutti li madrigali del primo et secondo libro a 4* was an amalgamation of two books brought out by his brother Ottaviano in 1533 and 1534. Likewise, Scotto's 1541 edition of Nola's *Canzone villanesche . . . libro primo et secondo a 3* might have originally appeared in two separate editions.[14]

Scotto also chose to reduce the number of pages in his reprinted editions. By rearranging the order of pieces found in earlier publications, he was able to retain the complete contents of the previous edition. For example, he eliminated a full gathering (eight pages) from his 1544 edition of Arcadelt's *Primo libro a 4* by squeezing three madrigals onto two-page openings for ten pages.[15]

Gardano modified some of his reprinted editions in yet another way. He would rearrange the contents of a preexistent edition to follow an ordering by clef, signature, and tonal type.[16] He carefully reconfigured Willaert's two books of four-voice motets to reflect such a plan. The organization of the contents of his 1545 editions of the two books differs drastically from the first editions of 1539 brought out by Girolamo Scotto and his second cousins, Brandino and Ottaviano di Amadio Scotto. Gardano deleted several motets found in both books, replacing them with other works. He even interchanged pieces between the two books in order to accommodate his organization.[17]

Why did Gardano and Scotto make these changes in their reprinted editions? It may be speculated that, in the case of Gardano, by rearranging the contents according to cleffing, signature, and tonal type, he sought to improve the haphazard arrangement of earlier editions to conform to higher theoretical principles of modal order.[18] But perhaps the reason for his reorganization had more to do with business practices than with abstract ideals. The changes made by both printers provided a way of getting around proffering a duplicate copy. By adding new pieces, omitting old ones, or simply changing the order of the contents, Gardano and Scotto could claim their reprints to be new and therefore better publications. The Venetian patrician Dandolo declared with reference to Willaert's *Musica nova*, that "it was common practice among printers . . . to insert previously printed material into their collections."[19] But it was also a good selling strategy to alter popular publications and then offer them as something novel, something "improved," to the public.

THE SERIES AND SINGLE-COMPOSER EDITIONS

Though it may appear that the two firms arbitrarily published whatever music they could get their hands on, Gardano and Scotto actually conceived their publications with great care. Besides recycling reprints, they presented many of their editions in multi-volume units as sets of single-composer editions or as a series of anthologies. They also realized the selling potential of single-composer editions.

Grouping together single editions to form multi-volume series was not a novel idea when Girolamo Scotto and Antonio Gardano started printing music. The concept of a series of music anthologies had been used by printers as a selling device ever since Petrucci produced his first publications of polyphonic music. Sets of volumes devoted to a single composer, however, did not emerge until the 1530s, when Ottaviano Scotto and Andrea Antico brought out the madrigal publications of Philippe Verdelot.

Both Antonio Gardano and Girolamo Scotto continued this trend in their earliest publications. As seen in appendix A, Gardano brought out five books of Arcadelt madrigals from 1539 to 1544.[20] At the same time, he organized motet and madrigal anthologies into three different series. The *Fior de Motetti*, which was a rearrangement of Moderne's earlier *Motetti del Fiore* series, and the *Motetti del Frutto* were comprised of two and three books, respectively. The *note nere* madrigal editions would eventually include four volumes.[21] Scotto moved in a different direction by bringing out single-composer editions of sacred music in pairs.

The vogue for single-composer publications and sets of editions encouraged the two printers to group other editions together. In addition to his motet and Mass publications, Scotto created a "set" of two Verdelot madrigal books in 1540 by reprinting Books One and Two of Verdelot's Four-Voice Madrigals in a single volume and the lute intabulations of selected Verdelot madrigals in another. The following year he brought out two books of Nola's three-voice canzone in one volume and three books of his own madrigals, each for two, three, and four voices.

That the two music printers viewed the series and single-composer editions as effective selling devices may be seen in Gardano's 1541 reprints of previous Scotto editions. The editions in question were Verdelot's *Tutti li madrigali del primo et secondo libro a 4* and *Le Dotte et eccellente compositioni de i madrigali da diversi perfettissimi musici a 5*. We have already noted how Gardano reworded the title of *Le Dotte* to create the allusion that his reprint was a single-composer edition of five-voice madrigals by Verdelot. Gardano also promoted *Le Dotte* as a companion volume to Verdelot's First and Second Books of Four-Voice Madrigals. Furthermore, he added another publication to create a set of three editions containing four-, five , and six-voice madrigals each. He entitled the six-voice edition *Verdelot la piu divina et piu bella musica . . . madrigali a sei voci* even though the publication was actually an anthology. Like *Le Dotte*, Verdelot's name took pride of place on the title page, and like *Le Dotte*, only a small number of the pieces (six out of the thirty-one) were attributed to the composer.[22]

Such wheeler-dealing on the part of Gardano supports the view that single-composer editions and series were useful marketing tools, especially in the selling of reprinted editions. Both Venetian printers used them to attract not only new customers but old clients. Extant binder's volumes testify to the interest collectors and bibliophiles had in acquiring complete sets of editions, rather than single publications. The 1609 inventory of books in the Arundel collection now housed in the British Library, for example, lists all five books of Arcadelt's four-voice madrigals together under a single entry.[23] The two book lists of music editions offered by the Gardano and Scotto firms dating from the 1590s also confirm this marketing strategy. Often one item will list several books by a single composer as a unit for a single price, rather than separately as individual editions (see above, fig. 4.2).

SEPARATE GEOGRAPHICAL SOURCES

Scotto and Gardano could not continue to run their music presses on reprinted editions alone. They had to seek new editions and commissions from a variety of sources. They went beyond Venice in their quest for new music, carefully cultivating connections all over the Italian peninsula and across the Alps. It is clear that from the very beginning of their printing careers, the two printers deliberately avoided direct competition by acquiring their music from completely different places.

SCOTTO'S ASSOCIATION WITH LOMBARDY

Girolamo inaugurated his career as director of the Scotto press with three sets of four- and five-voice motet books each containing the music of a major composer of the time: Adrian Willaert, *maestro di cappella* of St. Mark's, Nicolas Gombert, chapel master for Emperor Charles V, and Jacquet of Mantua, *maestro di cappella* for Cardinal Ercole Gonzaga. These editions were among the first sacred publications dedicated to the works of a single composer. The next year he launched a new series of Mass publications featuring the works of the Spanish composer Cristóbal de Morales (see app. A).

Except for the Gombert motets, Scotto's motet repertory was dominated by the music of Italian-based composers with ties mainly to Venice and Mantua. The close proximity of composers like Willaert and Jacquet should have made acquisition of their music relatively easy. The sudden appearance of several editions devoted to the music of Gombert, however, is more difficult to account for, since the Netherlandish composer was not known to have been in northern Italy around this time. Where then did Scotto obtain the Gombert motets?

Scotto must have turned to his native Lombardy for this new supply of music. As we have seen, Girolamo had strong family ties to Milan, where he posted one of his nephews as his agent. The most important Milanese patron of the Scotto press during the early 1540s was Alfonso d'Avalos, marquis of Vasto and governor-general of Milan under Charles V. Girolamo dedicated his 1539 edition of Gombert's First Book of Four-Voice Motets to d'Avalos, who, with his strong links to the Imperial court, might have been the source for Gombert's music.

Alfonso was married to Maria d'Aragona, one of the most celebrated and cultivated women of the Neapolitan court. Their own court in Milan, which flourished from 1538 until 1546, became a haven for poets, *literati*, and musicians. Alfonso d'Avalos exemplified the life of a cultivated courtier with a strong bent toward orthodox Catholicism; he was equally well versed in military affairs as in the arts and letters. He is credited with the authorship of two famous madrigal poems, *Il bianco e dolce cigno* and *Anchor che col partire*. Tutored as a child by the composer Costanzo Festa, Alfonso evidently kept up his interest in music throughout his life. His proclivity toward religiosity might account for the sacred music publications dedicated to him, which, in addition to the Gombert motets, include two other Milanese motet publications. One of them was devoted to the motets of Vincenzo Ruffo, who served at the d'Avalos court possibly from as early as 1538 until 1542.[24] Ruffo's connection with Alfonso might explain the presence of several motets and a Mass setting by the composer in collections brought out by Scotto at this time.[25] Dedications in two other important non-music editions published by the Scotto press also affirm a close connection between the Venetian firm and the Milanese court. The distinguished scholar Agostino Nifo honored, on the title page of his 1540 Aristotelian commentary, *De verissimis temporum signis Commentariolus*, Maria d'Aragona. Even more significant, Girolamo's brother, Ottaviano, addressed a dedicatory letter to Alfonso d'Avalos and Maria d'Aragona in Alessandro Piccolomini's *De la institutione di tutta la vita de l'homo nato nobile* (1542).[26]

Scotto also had connections in Piacenza, in particular with the short-lived Accademia Ortolana.[27] The works of some of the musicians belonging to this literary circle appeared among Scotto's early publications. In 1540, Claudio Veggio commissioned Scotto to print a book of his four-voice madrigals. The same year three pieces by Paolo Giacomo Palazzo turned up in Scotto's edition of Verdelot's *Tutti li madrigali del primo et secondo libro a 4*. Another member of the Piacentine academy, the writer Antonfrancesco Doni, made the most important contribution to Scotto's production when in 1544 he had Scotto print the first collection of his *Lettere* and an unusual musico-literary work, the *Dialogo della musica*. With the creation of the dukedom of Parma and Piacenza by Pope Paul III in 1545, political unrest caused the demise of the Accademia Ortolana and Scotto's link with Piacenza.

GARDANO'S ASSOCIATION WITH FERRARA

As we have seen, Ferrara already had a music press when Gardano began his publishing house. Buglhat, Hucher, and Campis inaugurated their music-printing operation in 1538 with their motet collection *Liber cantus*. By 1540 the partnership evidently had broken up, when Campis issued Alfonso dalla Viola's Second Book of Madrigals by himself. Buglhat and Hucher continued to print books in Ferrara for another eighteen years, but their music editions appeared on a sporadic basis. They were evidently unable to compete with the larger Venetian publishers, in particular Gardano, who became the favored press of musicians with ties to the Este court.

In the early years, Gardano, a foreigner relatively new to Venice, printed a limited number of first editions. His main source for new music came from Ferrara. Early commissioned editions such as Alvise Castellino's *Primo libro delle villote a 4* (1541) and Jacques Buus's *Primo libro di canzoni francese a 6* (1543) contain dedications to Duke Ercole II d'Este and his wife, Renée de France, respectively. Gardano might have even acquired the music for his *Motetti del Frutto* series from a Ferrarese source, as implied by the well-known quarrel between Gardano and the printer, Johannes de Buglhat of Ferrara, which was made public on the title pages and prefaces of their motet publications of 1538–39.[28]

In the 1550s and 60s, Antonio Gardano firmly established the tentative connections he had made with Ferrara during the 1540s. The list of dedicatees in appendix B reveals that all but three of the music editions honoring members of the Este family were printed by the Gardano firm. In 1550, Francesco dalla Viola, who first worked for Cardinal Ippolito II d'Este in Rome and then became the *maestro di cappella* for Prince Alfonso, dedicated his First Book of Four-Voice Madrigals to Alfonso's sister Leonora. Giulio Fiesco also paid homage to Leonora and Lucretia d'Este in his *Musica nova* of 1569. Cardinal Luigi d'Este received a dedication from Bertoldo Sperindio in the Second Book of Five-Voice Madrigals of 1562 as well as one from Portinaro in the Second Book of Motets of 1568.

Of all the members of the Este family, Alfonso II, who became duke of Ferrara in 1559, was the most avid in his devotion to music. We have already noted his involvement in the publication of Willaert's *Musica nova*. Many composers dedicated their music publications to Alfonso. In 1554, Guilio Fiesco paid respect to the then prince with his First Book of Five-Voice Madrigals. A year later, Francesco Manara did the same in his First Book of Four-Voice Madrigals. Both of these editions were printed by Gardano.

After Willaert's *Musica nova,* Gardano continued to hold a virtual monopoly on music publications intended for the Este court. Gardano himself signed the dedication to Duke Alfonso in Jacquet Berchem's monumental *Primo, Secondo et Terzo Libro del Cappriccio* of 1561.[29] In 1567, Lasso had the Venetian firm print his Fourth Book of Five-Voice Madrigals, which he also dedicated to Duke Alfonso.

Even after the death of its founder in 1569, the Gardano firm remained the music press of choice for musicians seeking patronage with the Ferrarese court. When they wished to dedicate their music edition to a member of the Este family, such composers as Girolamo Vespa, Alessandro Milleville, Luzzasco Luzzaschi, Paolo Isnardi, Luca Marenzio, and Giaches de Wert selected the Gardano press.[30] It was not until 1582, when Vittorio Baldini established himself as ducal printer, that exclusive patronage of the Gardano press in Ferrara ceased.[31]

SCOTTO AND THE MANTUAN–TRIDENTINE–IMPERIAL AXIS

It was during the second half of his printing career that Girolamo Scotto cultivated his commercial interest with Mantua and Trent. One of his nephews from Milan represented the Scotto firm as an agent in Mantua.[32] Composers in the service of various branches of the Gonzaga family as well as Cardinal Madruzzo in Trent utilized the Scotto press for their music publications. The bulk of the editions intended for Mantua and Trent were devoted to Latin motets, Masses, and other liturgical settings. The preponderance of sacred editions issued by the Venetian firm testifies to the reformist atmosphere that prevailed at these two centers. It also affirms the traditional allegiance Mantua and Trent had with the Imperial court. The pivotal figures in this cultural (and political) alliance were Cardinal Cristoforo Madruzzo, prince-bishop of Trent and Bressanone, Cardinal Ercole Gonzaga, bishop of Mantua, and later, Ercole's nephew, Duke Guglielmo Gonzaga.

Cristoforo Madruzzo had a meteoric career in the church. He became canon (1529), then dean (1535) of Trent. In 1539 he was named bishop of Trent and three years later bishop of Bressanone. Pope Paul III appointed him a cardinal in 1543. Madruzzo had an important connection with the Imperial court, for, as the bishop of Trent, he was also a prince (Tirol) of the Holy Roman Empire. In that capacity, Madruzzo acted as a procurator for Ferdinand, archduke of Austria. He also played a role during the early years of church reform, since Trent was the chosen site of the council. For Madruzzo, then, musical and artistic patronage was deeply rooted in the church.

Madruzzo's close friend Ercole Gonzaga became bishop of Mantua in 1520. He received his cardinal's hat in 1526, and later was appointed pontifical legate to Charles V. Upon the death of his elder brother, Duke Federico, in 1540, Ercole assumed the co-regency of the duchy with Federico's wife Margherita and his younger brother Ferrante. His advocacy of church reform had a profound influence on the Mantuan court. For forty-seven years, Ercole and then his nephew, Duke Guglielmo, exerted their own vision of the Catholic Reformation in Mantua. They emphasized patronage of the arts in the service of the church. The building and decorating of churches became the main artistic endeavor of the mid-century Gonzagas. They undertook such architectural projects as the abbey church of San Benedetto Po, the renovation of the cathedral of San Pietro, and the Palatine Basilica of Santa Barbara, which Guglielmo constructed during the 1560s.

The predilection for church reform in Trent and Mantua was also made apparent in musical patronage. Both Madruzzo and the Gonzagas tended to favor church composers who wrote little or no secular music, such as Jacquet of Mantua, Giovanni Contino, and Palestrina. Thus, most of the Venetian music publications intended for Mantua and Trent at this time were sacred, and all of them were printed by the Scotto press.

The Scotto firm's association with Mantua can be traced as far back as 1539, the very first year Girolamo assumed active management of the press. At that time,

Scotto published a pair of books devoted to four- and five-voice motets by Cardinal Ercole's private musician Jacquet of Mantua. Both editions contained lengthy dedications by the Venetian printer honoring the cardinal of Mantua.[33] For the next twenty-eight years, Girolamo Scotto was to remain Jacquet's principal printer, issuing eleven further editions of the composer's music.

During the two-year period of 1554–55, Scotto brought out an unusually high number of editions with a link to the Mantuan-Trent-Imperial axis. They included three liturgical publications: Rore and Jacquet Psalms and reprinted editions of Jacquet's two books of five-voice Masses. Hoste da Reggio, *maestro della musica* for Ferrante Gonzaga (brother of Cardinal Ercole and supreme commander of the Imperial forces), had three books of madrigals printed by Scotto in 1554. The most striking publication of this period, however, was a set of five editions with the descriptive title of the *Motetti* [or *Madrigali*] *del Laberinto*. The series included Girolamo Carli's *Motetti del Laberinto a cinque voci*, Ippolito Ciera's *Madrigali del Laberinto a quatro voci*, and three books of motets mostly by Netherlandish composers.

The Second, Third, and Fourth Books of the *Motetti del Laberinto* had the closest ties to the Mantuan-Tridentine-Imperial axis. These three volumes actually constituted one large anthology of forty-nine motets, practically all by Netherlanders connected with the Imperial court. They included Clemens non Papa, Thomas Crecquillon, Cornelius Canis, and Pierre Manchicourt. Many of the motets in the *Motetti del Laberinto* had been previously printed in collections issued by Susato and Ulhard from 1546 to 1553. Scotto, however, did not utilize the northern publications for his series, for a comparison of readings between the *Laberinto* editions and the earlier German and Netherlandish prints reveals significant variants.

Though none of the three books in the *Motetti del Laberinto* collection contains a formal dedicatory page, they all have embedded in their titles a statement of dedication by Paulus Caligopoeus addressed to Cardinal Cristoforo Madruzzo. While Madruzzo is the dedicatee of the three books, his close friend, Cardinal Ercole Gonzaga, may have been instrumental in the publication of the books, as seen in the last book of the series. Three motets by Jacquet of Mantua are placed toward the end of *Motetti del Laberinto Libro quarto*. Two of them are celebratory works with strong connections with Mantua. *Hesperiae ultimae* commemorates the visit of Philip II to Mantua in January 1549,[34] and *Dum vastos Adriae fluctus* pays homage both to Josquin and to the city of Mantua.[35]

The descriptive title of the *Motetti del Laberinto* editions as well as the woodcut of a circular labyrinth with the minotaur (see above, fig. 2.12) may also have a connection with the Mantuan court. The labyrinth had a long association with the Gonzagas. It was the device of Isabella d'Este (1474–1539), wife of Francesco Gonzaga. One of the rooms of the Palazzo Ducale in Mantua is entitled the *Sala del Laberinto*. It contains a ceiling painted blue and gold depicting a maze with the motto "Forse che si, forse che no" running through it.[36]

In the 1560s, three other composers associated with Mantua and Trent—Giovanni Contino, Giaches de Wert, and Alessandro Striggio—had their music printed by the Scotto press. Giovanni Contino, now known primarily as the teacher of Luca Marenzio, was first in the service of Cardinal Madruzzo. After spending ten years as *maestro di cappella* at the cathedral in his native Brescia, he joined the service of Duke Guglielmo Gonzaga in Mantua. At least ten editions of his music were printed by Scotto during the two-year period of 1560–61.[37]

While Giaches de Wert and Alessandro Striggio did not work at the Mantuan court during the 1560s, they nevertheless had strong connections with various members of the Gonzaga family. The Mantuan Gonzagas might have recommended the Scotto firm to Wert when he was ready to have his first book of madrigals printed. Wert dedicated his *Primo libro de madrigali a cinque voci* (1558) to Count Alfonso Gonzaga of Novellara, a member of a minor branch of the family who maintained ties with the Mantuan court. Wert's Mantuan-Milanese connection is also revealed in *Il primo libro de madrigali a quatro voci* (1561), which he dedicated to Fernando d'Avalos, marquis of Pescara and Vasto and governor of Milan. Fernando was married to Isabella Gonzaga, sister of Duke Guglielmo of Mantua. As Wert revealed in his edition, the dedication came at the suggestion of Camillo Gonzaga, the eldest brother of Count Alfonso of Novellara.

The Mantuan nobleman Alessandro Striggio also commissioned Scotto to print his madrigals. Though he entered the service of Cosimo I de' Medici, duke of Tuscany, in 1559, Striggio continued to have strong ties with the Mantuan court. After the publication of his first two books of madrigals, he sent copies of each of his editions to Duke Guglielmo Gonzaga along with a letter dated 1 June 1560.[38] Unlike Wert, who after his second book of five-voice madrigals switched to Gardano as his main printer, Striggio remained a loyal client of the Scotto press.

Other composers honored various members of the Gonzaga family with dedications of music editions printed by Scotto. Matteo Rufilo paid homage to Cesare Gonzaga, prince of Molfetta and son of Ferrante Gonzaga, duke of Guastalla in his first book of five-voice madrigals (1561). In 1562, Paolo Clerico dedicated his two books of five-voice madrigals to Cardinal Ercole Gonzaga, with the second book containing two madrigals composed by Ercole's distant cousin, Scipione Gonzaga. In his First Book of Four-Voice Madrigals (1563), the Paduan composer Francesco Portinaro praised Scipione, who was at that time a student at the University of Padua.[39]

Even when the famous Roman composer Giovanni Pierluigi da Palestrina wished to have a music edition for the Mantuan court printed, he turned to the Scotto press. From 1555 until 1572, Palestrina had his first editions printed exclusively by the Roman firm of Valerio Dorico.[40] The Dorico press ceased operations in 1572. With no viable music printer in Rome, Palestrina had to seek publication of his music elsewhere. The Second Book of Motets of 1572 was the first collection of sacred music by the Roman composer issued by a Venetian press. The choice of the Scotto firm comes as no surprise, considering that Palestrina dedicated the edition to Duke Guglielmo Gonzaga.

The composer's association with Guglielmo began as early as 1568 when they exchanged letters and their own musical compositions.[41] Palestrina presumably wrote the two eight-voice motets, *Gaude Barbara beata* and *Beata Barbara*, which appear in the Second Book of Five-Voice Motets, especially for Guglielmo's Palatine Basilica of Santa Barbara. He also included motets by his two sons, Rodolfo and Angelo, and his brother Silla in the 1572 edition. Apparently, Palestrina hoped to secure a position at the Mantuan court for his eldest son, Rodolfo. After Guglielmo received the edition, he rewarded the composer with 25 scudi and the promise of a post for Rodolfo as organist at the basilica of Santa Barbara.[42] But tragedy struck the Palestrina family, for on 20 November, only one month after the publication received a privilege, Rodolfo died of the plague. Less than two months later, his uncle, Silla, also fell victim to the plague.

SCOTTO'S CONNECTIONS WITH NAPLES AND SICILY

Girolamo Scotto not only capitalized on his associations with Mantua and Trent, he also benefited from his printing network to the south. We have seen that one of the main outposts for the Scotto firm was Naples, home of the popular *canzone villanesca alla napolitana*. Scotto's business connections in Naples (his nephew, Giovanni Maria Scotto, operated a press there from before 1548 through at least 1566)[43] presumably helped him gain access to this new genre. As early as 1541 Scotto brought out the first Venetian edition of three-voice *canzoni villanesche alla napolitana* by a Neapolitan composer. The publication of Giovanni Domenico da Nola's first and second books of *villanesche* generated a flurry of four-voice arrangements of this imported genre by resident composers in Venice, and, during the 1540s, both Scotto and Gardano regularly issued editions of three- and four-voice *canzoni villanesche* by Neapolitans and northerners.[44]

The two Venetian publishers continued to print music editions with Neapolitan connections for the next thirty years, but Scotto clearly became the prime printer for the Neapolitan market, with nearly double the extant editions as Gardano.[45] Neapolitan composers, whose works appeared in Scotto publications during the 1540s and 50s, included Heliseo Ghibel, Giandominico La Martoretta, Marc' Antonio Volpe, Gioan Battista Melfio, and Stefano Lando. Musicians from the Abruzzo such as Bernardino Carnefresca (i.e., Lupacchino), Cesare Tudino, and Marc' Antonio Mazzone of Miglionico also used the Scotto press. In the 1560s, Neapolitans who either remained in the Kingdom of Naples or left for northern Italian centers, such as Matteo Rufilo (worked for Gonzagas), Paolo Lagudio, Giovan Leonardo Primavera (lived in Venice), Giulio Ciccarelli, Michele Califano, and Massimo Troiano (lived in Treviso) sought out the Scotto firm for their publications.

The Sicilian towns of Palermo and Messina were also important trading centers for the Scotto press. As with Neapolitan composers, several musicians connected with Sicilian courts had their music printed by Scotto. Girolamo's ties with the island apparently grew stronger during the latter part of his publishing career. Giandominico La Martoretta and Salvatore di Cataldo sent their music to Scotto for publication. The most important and prolific composer was Pietro Vinci. Born in Nicosia, Vinci maintained important ties with Sicily, returning there after working in several parts of Italy. His chief appointment was as *maestro di cappella* at Santa Maria Maggiore in Bergamo from 1568 until 1580. He remained a loyal client of the Scotto firm, having nearly all of his publications printed by the press.

ORLANDO DI LASSO, THE *LIBRI DELLE MUSE,*
AND THE ROMAN CONNECTION

In addition to Ferrara, Gardano sought out other geographical areas as potential sources for his music publications. He turned his attention to Rome, where several editions of Orlando di Lasso's madrigals first appeared in the late 1550s. No other composer achieved more widespread fame in his own lifetime than Orlando di Lasso (1532–94). His works were issued by all the great Continental music-publishing houses of Munich, Nuremberg, Antwerp, Paris, Louvain, Rome, Milan, and Venice. Over 280 single-composer editions contained Lasso's music and another 250 anthologies included one or more of the famed Netherlander's works—a number that goes way beyond the publications of any other sixteenth-century composer.[46]

Lasso's Italian publishing career began in 1555 with his *Primo libro di madrigali a cinque voci.*[47] Though it has been generally assumed that Gardano was the first Italian printer to issue an edition dedicated to the Netherlander's music, Lasso's *Primo libro di madrigali a cinque voci* was probably printed first in Rome by the singer and composer Antonio Barré.[48] For the rest of the decade, Barré and another Roman printer, Valerio Dorico, issued first editions of madrigals by Lasso (Books 2 and 3 *a* 5 and Book 1 *a* 4) and several anthologies containing one or more works by the famous composer. It was natural that the Romans were among the earliest to issue Lasso's music, since Lasso lived in Rome for about three years before his departure for the north. None of these editions had a connection with the composer, for all the dedications were signed either by the printer or a third party.[49]

Though the Romans were responsible for most of the first editions of Lasso's early madrigal books, the Venetians were more instrumental in their widespread dissemination. The first two books of five-voice madrigals and the first book of four-voice madrigals became extremely popular. These three editions were reprinted in Venice, mostly by the Gardano press, some fifteen times each during the course of the next three decades.

The ties Venetian music printers had with Rome were not limited to Lasso editions, but also included other Roman music publications. The *Libri delle Muse,* a group of anthologies, reappeared as Venetian editions almost immediately after their debut in Rome. The series, first printed by Antonio Barré from 1555 to 1563, consisted of books of madrigals, *villanelle*, and motets divided by genre and number of voices.[50] It contained a repertory hitherto unknown in northern Italy by composers chiefly working in Rome, such as Palestrina, Lasso, Monte, Animuccia, Matelart, Ferro, and Barré himself. It also presented genres not yet in vogue in Venetian circles during the 1550s, in particular the four-voice *madrigale arioso*.[51] The *Libro delle Muse* series was also among the earliest collections to include a consistently large number of multi-stanza *canzone* or madrigal cycles.[52] All of these factors had a significant influence on later Venetian publications.

When Barré stopped printing music editions in the mid-60s, Gardano and other Venetian publishers continued to bring out several important first editions devoted to Lasso as well as publications containing the works of Roman-based musicians. To acquire more of Lasso's music, Gardano turned north to the Bavarian court in Munich. In 1565 the Venetian printer issued Lasso's *Sacrae lectiones ex Propheta Iob*. It contained a verse dedicated to Duke Albrecht V of Bavaria by Nicolò Stoppio, the duke's bookdealer and agent in Venice. During the following year, Gardano brought out first editions of Books Two, Three, and Four of Lasso's motets and the first Mass by Lasso to be published.[53] But the most notable publication issued by the Venetian printer during these years was the *Libro quarto de madrigali a cinque voci* of 1567.[54] The *Libro quarto* was probably the only edition printed in Italy in which the composer took an active participation. As noted in chap. 5, Lasso dedicated the work to Duke Alfonso II d'Este of Ferrara. The composer presumably oversaw part of the production of the edition, since he was in Venice in May 1567. From Venice he went to Ferrara, where on 9 June 1567 he presented his newest publication to Duke Alfonso.[55]

During this same period other Venetian presses also printed first editions of Lasso's music. Girolamo Scotto came out with the *Quinque et sex vocibus perornatae, sacrae cantiones nunc primum . . . liber secundus* in 1565. The contents of this book were completely different from the *Liber secundus* of motets issued by Gardano a year later. Both the title page and dedication inform us that Giulio Bonagiunta, a singer at St. Mark's, was responsible for the publication. In his dedication, Bonagiunta mentioned receiving the motets as a gift from Lasso, "which, thanks to the composer's courtesy, I was to use as I pleased; I decided to put them in print and publish them."[56]

Bonagiunta underwrote other editions containing Lasso's music, which Scotto and even Merulo printed during the late 60s. Lasso's name figures prominently on the title pages of Bonagiunta's two anthologies, *Primo libro de gli eterni motetti* and *Terzo libro del Desiderio madrigali a quattro voci*, printed by the Scotto press in 1567. In 1568 Merulo printed a fifth book of Lasso motets for Bonagiunta. Merulo also issued the earliest extant edition devoted exclusively to Mass settings by Lasso. Although the title, *Quinque missae suavissimis modulationibus refertae, una quinque reliquae vero quatuor vocibus . . . liber secundus*, implies the existence of a first book of Masses that no longer survives, Merulo might have considered Gardano's 1566 collection of Masses, which contains Lasso's *Missa In te domine* for six voices, as the "liber primus."[57]

While all of the city's music publishers printed and reprinted a succession of Lasso editions, Antonio Gardano remained the foremost Venetian publisher of the Netherlander's music during this period. Indeed, the significant number of first editions of Lasso's music that the Gardano press brought out during the rest of the sixteenth century point to a strong connection between the composer and the Venetian firm. But Gardano's relationship with Lasso and the court in Munich was not the only one the music printer maintained to the north. He also established important links with composers and patrons from other transalpine principalities.

GARDANO, TRANSALPINE CENTERS, AND THE
NOVUS THESAURUS MUSICUS

During the 1560s, Gardano's sources for commissioned editions extended north to various German-speaking centers. Composers working in Munich, Augsburg, and Vienna tended to favor Gardano for their publishing needs. We have already noted that Lasso, after arriving at the Bavarian court, used Gardano as his primary Venetian printer. Other musicians associated with northern patrons also sought out the Gardano press. The Netherlander Jacobus Kerle came to Venice to oversee the printing of his psalms and Magnificat settings at the Gardano press in 1561. Kerle, who spent the early part of his career in Orvieto, met Cardinal Otto Truchsess, Lord High Steward of Waldburg and bishop of Augsburg, in 1559. Cardinal Otto commissioned Kerle to write for the Council of Trent the *Preces speciales*, which Gardano printed in 1562. Kerle remained in the service of the cardinal off and on from 1562 until 1568, when he was appointed vicar-choral at Augsburg cathedral.

Composers in the service of the Imperial court in Vienna also had ties with the Gardano press. Jacobus Vaet, the *Kapellmeister* to Archduke Maximilian of Austria from 1554 until his death in 1567, had two books of motets printed by Gardano in 1562. In 1568, Philippe de Monte assumed Vaet's position at the court of Emperor Maximilian II. One of the most prolific composers of the sixteenth century, Monte had at least thirty-four books of madrigals, ten books of motets, and five books of *madrigali spirituali* published in Venice. For a time, he alternated between the two Venetian printers for his editions. Before his arrival in Vienna in 1568, two of his madrigal books were printed by Gardano. Then with his career secured, Monte embarked on an ambitious publishing program. During the four-year period of 1569–73, the Scotto firm issued at least six editions. Monte switched to the Gardano press in 1574; from that time until the composer's death in 1603, a seemingly unendless stream of his publications was printed by Angelo Gardano with only a handful of editions printed by the Scotto firm in 1580–81.

Of all the commissioned publications with ties across the Alps, the *Novus Thesaurus Musicus* was by far the most sumptuous. Printed by Gardano in 1568, the *Novus Thesaurus Musicus* was edited and compiled by Pietro Giovanelli, a member of a wealthy merchant family from Gandino. Giovanelli presumably financed the magnificent edition, which contained 254 motets, mostly by composers active in Austria at the Habsburg court chapels of the Emperor Maximilian II and his brothers, Archduke Ferdinand of Tyrol and Archduke Charles of Styria.[58] Intended as a private commemorative edition for an elite audience, it was the most ambitious music anthology published in mid-sixteenth century Venice.

The *Novus Thesaurus Musicus* was the most elaborate publication ever printed by Gardano, who used the same upright quarto format, large paper size, initials, and music and text type fonts that he had employed some ten years earlier for the *Musica nova*[59] But the comparison with the earlier publication stops here, for the *Novus Thesaurus* was far more complicated to produce. Though printed as a series of five separate books, the set was conceived as one huge edition. The Gardano press employed continuous pagination from one volume to the next, so that all five volumes might be bound together. The publication thus consisted of six partbooks with a total of 468 pages each—by far the largest single music edition issued by any sixteenth-century Italian printer. Of particular typographical interest were a number of different, specially printed presentation leaves added to several copies. These copies have their own brief dedicatory preambles addressed to such important figures as Cardinal Borromeo, the dukes of Bavaria, Saxony, and Mantua, and the bishop of Bergamo.[60]

The printing of different repertories from separate geographical sources was clearly an important business practice if not for both printers at least for Gardano. This was made clear in the case of the largest batch of new music the French émigré published at the beginning of his printing career: the madrigals of Jacques Arcadelt.

THE ARCADELT SERIES: A CONFLICT OVER REPERTORY

The most frequently named composer on the title pages of Gardano's early publications was Jacques Arcadelt, the famed northerner who spent the 1520s and 30s in Florence. As seen in app. A, Gardano published six different books of madrigals under his name, and it is no exaggeration to say that Arcadelt editions—the *Primo libro* in particular—sustained Gardano's press during its early stages. Gardano might have acquired the music for the Arcadelt editions from Florentine sources, in particular expatriates such as Ruberto Strozzi or his cousin Neri Capponi, who were living in Venice at the time,[61] or he might have gained possession of the music through his literary friend Nicolò Franco, who, in a published letter, requested Camillo Giordano to give the writer some Arcadelt madrigals in his possession.[62]

In issuing the Arcadelt repertory, Gardano decided to capitalize on the marketing concept of the single-composer, multi-volume series described above. He brought out the first edition of the *Primo libro a 4* (now lost) sometime between May and September of 1538.[63] Arcadelt's *Primo libro a 4* was Gardano's second publication, but the first to contain music never before printed.[64] Many of the fifty madrigals had already gained wide circulation in manuscript sources mainly of Florentine provenance. Thus, Gardano (or his patron) chose carefully the most popular madrigals for the first edition.[65] Arcadelt's *Primo libro*, in fact, became the best known and most often reprinted music edition of the sixteenth century. It must have been an immediate success, for in the same year a Milanese printer brought out a pirated version, which is also lost. We learn this from the dedication to the extant 1539 edition, where Gardano remarks sarcastically that "those printers who have reprinted the pieces in Milan, . . . have failed to notice some errors that were in the first edition (owing to the carelessness of my compositors rather than my own)."[66]

For the next few years, several books of Arcadelt madrigals rolled off the Venetian presses. Their quick succession (three different books in two years) suggests that Gardano had acquired enough Arcadelt madrigals to fill several publications. But before he could release a second volume, the Scotto press in collaboration with Andrea Antico brought out their *Secondo libro* sometime in January 1539. The Scotto–Antico book contained twenty-five madrigals; as with Gardano's edition of the *Primo libro*, all the pieces lacked attributions. Production of the *Secondo libro* most likely began in the fall of 1538, if not sooner, since, as with previous Scotto music publications, Antico's more time-consuming woodcut process was used to prepare the music typography. We will never know which of the Scotto brothers was responsible for publishing the *Secondo libro*. It has been generally assumed that this was the last music edition published by Ottaviano, but Girolamo Scotto could also have been in charge of the press by this time. In either case the point is moot, since, as we have seen, the two brothers maintained joint ownership of the firm until Ottaviano's death in the late 1560s, and by 1538 presumably shared equal financial responsibility of the press.

Gardano was obviously incensed by this usurpation of his repertory, for only one month after the Scotto publication appeared, he issued another edition of Arcadelt's Second Book, but with completely different contents. He entitled his edition *Il vero secondo libro* to distinguish it from the Scotto–Antico publication. In the accompanying dedication honoring Nicolò Alberto, Gardano railed against the printers of the earlier *Secondo libro* for falsely issuing madrigals by other composers under Arcadelt's name, while declaring the works in his edition "the true offspring of their father [i.e., Arcadelt]." Gardano's claim was apparently misleading, since only eight of the madrigals in the Scotto edition occur with conflicting attributions in other sources, and eleven other pieces reappeared in later Gardano editions under Arcadelt's name.[67] Gardano, in fact, was just as guilty of misattributing pieces to Arcadelt as was Scotto, for five madrigals in *Il vero secondo libro* were credited in later editions to other composers.[68]

Gardano promised his patron Leone Orsini a third book of Arcadelt madrigals in the dedication of his 1539 edition of the *Primo libro*. But again the Scotto firm beat him to the punch by bringing out the *Terzo libro* sometime between May and September of 1539. Gardano did not discredit Scotto's *Terzo libro* as he had with the *Secondo libro*; instead he recognized the edition, and issued his next edition, the *Quarto libro*, in September of 1539.[69]

One wonders why Gardano was overly disturbed by Scotto's *Secondo libro*, particularly in light of his relatively mild protest against the reprinting of his *Primo libro* by Milanese printers. Surely pirating the exact same contents of a privileged edition was a greater transgression than issuing a new edition with new madrigals. Moreover, if Gardano was so angry at Scotto for the *Secondo libro*, why did he not get upset about Scotto's publication of the *Terzo libro?*[70] A review of Gardano's earliest editions and his relationship to other printers offers an explanation for the extravagant tone of his dedications.

A tense atmosphere must have prevailed at the Gardano press during its first two years of operation. The several dedications signed by Gardano in his early editions suggest that, as a newcomer without extensive connections in the book trade, the French émigré had to rely on patronage and his own resources for the publication of his editions. He also had to compete with other music printers already established in Venice and in other northern Italian centers. He apparently had difficulty in acquiring music for his own publications, for only two of his earliest editions, the Arcadelt madrigals and the *Motetti del Frutto* collection, contained new repertory. Even with these two series, Gardano felt threatened by other printers, believing that they were pilfering music works that rightfully belonged to him. The Arcadelt editions, as already noted, were not the only publications in which Gardano vented his anger at other printers. As dramatic as his accusations of piracy and fraud in his Arcadelt editions may seem, they pale in comparison with the quarrel that he had with the Ferrarese printers Buglhat, Campis, and Hucher over the repertory found in the *Motetti del Frutto* collection (see chap. 2).

Clearly, Gardano was trying to break into the Venetian printing business, and in order to succeed, he had to take an aggressive stance. The exaggerated style of the dedicatory letters, written, as Thomas Bridges suggests, by Gardano's friend Nicolò Franco,[71] impart a belligerent, almost desperate tone. From Gardano's point of view, he was fighting not only for musical repertories, but also for the very existence of his press.

Though Gardano blasted the Scotto press in the lengthy dedication of *Il vero secondo libro*, his public contentiousness apparently waned after 1539. The reason for the cessation of the vitriolic rhetoric might have to do with an incident involving Nicolò Franco, which led to the writer's involuntary departure from Venice before June of 1540.[72] Gardano must have been affected by the scandal because a hiatus occurred in his publications from April 1540 until 1541. A more serious consequence for Gardano, however, might have been the loss of Bishop-elect Leone Orsini as his patron, since no new dedications to Orsini appeared in Gardano editions dating after May 1539. Orsini clearly lost interest in the music-printing business, for in June 1540 he became the first *principe* of the newly formed Accademia degli Infiammati in Padua, the same academy of which Pietro Aretino was a member.[73] Even more significantly, Aretino and other members of the academy, such as

Alessandro Piccolomini, had important associations with Ottaviano Scotto and the Scotto press.[74] A resolution to the dispute over the Arcadelt repertory must have occurred between the two Venetian presses very soon after the printing of the *Terzo libro*. Scotto chose not to issue any more Arcadelt books (except the lucrative *Primo libro*), and Gardano ceased writing inflammatory remarks against printers in his dedications.

The Arcadelt madrigal books offer a clear-cut example of territorial issues concerning a specific musical repertory. More often than not, Gardano and Scotto would avoid such proprietary disputes. It appears that after the Arcadelt affair, the two printers deliberately refrained from direct competition by bringing out different repertories. During the early years of their careers, Scotto emphasized sacred music editions devoted to single composers, while Gardano printed mostly motet anthologies. Gardano also continued to publish more volumes of Arcadelt madrigals, as well as a series of *note nere* madrigal books. Separation of repertories between the two presses continued for the next few decades. During the 1560s, the Scotto press specialized in the lighter Italian song form, the *canzone villanesche alla napolitana*.

CANZONI VILLANESCHE PUBLICATIONS

The Neapolitan dialect song was commonly known by several names: the *canzone villanesca alla napolitana, villanesca alla napolitana, villotte alla napolitana*, or just *napolitana*. When Girolamo Scotto introduced the genre to Venice in 1541 with his publication of Giovanni Domenico da Nola's *Canzone villanesche libro primo et secondo*, they became an instant success. Throughout the 1540s Scotto and Gardano continued to bring out *villanesche* publications by Neapolitans and northern Italians until the late 1550s, when interest in the genre apparently began to wane.[75] The 1560s witnessed a renewed interest in the publication of this lighter Italian secular form by Venetian music printers. Girolamo Scotto, in particular, printed and reprinted some fifty editions of this genre between 1560 and 1570—more than the output of the two previous decades combined.[76] The most popular series of the decades was the *Villotte alla napolitana* for three voices. Containing a large repertory of anonymous Neapolitian *villanesche*, the collection was originally conceived as a set of four books, which by the next decade grew to six volumes. Gardano issued the first three or possibly four books in 1560.[77] Though he introduced this repertory to the Venetian public, Gardano was not the first to print it. Like the *Libro delle Muse* anthologies and Lasso madrigal editions, Gardano owed the inspiration for the *villotte* series to the Roman printer Antonio Barré, whose *Secondo libro delle muse a tre voci. Canzon villanesche alla napolitana* of 1557 served as the source for Book Two of Gardano's collection.[78] The *villotte* series proved very popular and was reprinted several times throughout the decade by the Gardano firm.[79] In 1562 Scotto brought out his own edition, *Li quattro libri delle villotte alla napolitana*. As the title implies, Scotto consolidated the four books into one volume, thus producing a more economical version of the publication.[80]

The success of the *villotte* series encouraged Scotto to continue to promote publication of three-voice dialect songs, making them a specialty for his printing firm. *Villanesche* by a new generation of Neapolitan and northern Italian composers appeared in a variety of collections. Giovan Leonardo Primavera, Massimo Troiano, Marc' Antonio Mazzone di Miglionico, and the shadowy figure Nicolò Roicerandet Borgognone, who were all in Venice during the latter half of the 1560s, compiled editions containing their own *villanesche* as well as those by such Neapolitans as Giovanni Leonardo dell'Arpa, Giovanni Domenico da Nola, and Rinaldo Burno. Giulio Bonagiunta also compiled two anthologies featuring *villanesche* by northern composers associated with Venice and/or the Bavarian court such as Claudio Merulo, Vincenzo Bellavere, Ivo de Vento, Francesco Londariti, and Gioseffo Guami. The popularity of three-voice *villanesche* did not wane, but continued into the next decade with the publication of works by such lesser-known composers as Giovanni Battista Pinello, Pompilio Venturi, Giovanni Zappasorgo, Giuseppe Policreto, and Pietro Antonio Bianco, all of whom restricted themselves to the writing of dialect songs.

The revitalized *canzone villanesca alla napolitana* became one of the featured musical genres of the Scotto firm. Another specialty publication that was introduced at the Scotto press during the 1560s was a new kind of musico-literary anthology.

THE *EDIZIONE COLLETTIVA:* MUSICO-LITERARY ANTHOLOGIES

While the preferred music publication from the marketing point of view during the 1540s and 50s was the single-composer edition, by the 60s the concept of publishing an organic collection of works by several composers took hold as a viable alternative in attracting patronage.[81] Practically none of these *edizioni collettive* were sponsored by the printer. Instead, an outside party—usually a musician who had access to the works of other composers—assembled, edited, and financed the edition. The most important and most influential of these anthologizers was Giulio Bonagiunta. He inaugurated this new type of publication, when, in 1565, he launched a series of anthologies at the Scotto press. In all, he sponsored, edited, and underwrote some seventeen editions with the help of other bookmen and patrons.[82]

The concept of an anthology publication was not new in the mid-sixteenth century. Indeed, scribes before the age of printing organized their music manuscripts as miscellanies. Even after the shift from script to print, collections of individual works by a variety of composers continued as the main blueprint for music publications, as seen in the editions issued by Petrucci and other early music printers. North of the Alps, the anthology or *recueil* continued to remain the primary type of music publication for printers throughout the sixteenth century. When Venetian music printing entered the commercial age in the early 1540s, however, Gardano and Scotto quickly moved away from anthologies in favor of single-composer editions. Commercial factors played an important role in this change. Editions comprised of a miscellany of works by different composers apparently did not have enough panache to sell well on their own. Gardano and Scotto had to use different marketing ploys in order to make their anthologies more appealing. They employed fanciful titles, organized single editions into series, and even at times disguised anthologies as single-composer editions by promoting the most marketable composer in the edition on the title page.

The anthologies of the 1560s differed markedly from those of earlier decades in that the compiler, whether it be a printer or an external editor, sought to fashion the collection into a unified musico-literary work, what has been called the *edizione collettiva*.[83] Though the integrative aspect tended to vary with each anthology, the key unifying element found in all these collections was a particular musical genre— the madrigal cycle. With the madrigal cycle, the composers of the time created a large-scale musical work by setting each verse of a multi-stanza poem, such as an entire *canzone, sestina*, or series of *ottave*, to different music. Complete settings of *canzoni* first emerged in the 1540s. Jacquet Berchem's setting of the Petrarch *sestina Alla dolc'ombra delle belle frondi*, which appeared in Doni's *Dialogo della musica* (1544),[84] and Rore's twelve-part setting of *Vergine bella*, completed in 1548–49,[85] count among the earliest madrigal cycles.[86]

Throughout the 1550s, the multi-strophe form rose to prominence in single-composer publications. Ruffo, Gero, Ciera, Alessandro Romano, Lando, Spontone, and others all tried their hand at this genre. Venetian music printers shied away from using the madrigal cycle in their anthologies of the 1550s. The Roman printer and composer Antonio Barré, on the other hand, was the first to feature it in his anthology series *Libro delle Muse* (1555–63).[87] He devoted his inaugural volume of five-voice madrigals (1555) to four different madrigal cycles by Arcadelt, Berchem, Ruffo, and himself, and in his second book (1557) he introduced Lasso's five-voice setting of the Petrarch *sestina Standomi un giorno*.

The sense of musico-dramatic unity in the anthology did not occur in its full form until the mid-1560s, with the appearance of the Bonagiunta editions and other Scotto publications.[88] The degree of musical integration varied with each anthology. In some cases, it meant the presentation of several madrigal cycles by different composers as in *Gli amorosi concenti* (1568), which included two *sestine* by Andrea Gabrieli and Rossetto and a five-stanza *canzone* by Monte. In other instances, the anthology publication contained a *canzone de diversi*, that is, a collaborative setting by a group of composers of a single madrigal cycle, as in *Il Gaudio* (1567). Here, each stanza of Luigi Alamanni's *sestina Mai non voi più cantare* is set by a different composer, most of whom have some connection with Venice.[89] The selection of composers to represent the musical taste of a specific city or court also served to unify an anthology. *Musica de'Virtuosi* (1569), compiled by Massimo Troiano, for example, included only musicians associated with the court of Duke Albrecht in

Munich. It contains two *canzoni*; the first work, the thirteen-stanza *Al dolce suon del mormorar de l'onde*, begins with a stanza set by Lasso.[90]

The commemoration of a special event in a *canzone de diversi* also lent added weight to the integration of a collection or *raccolta celebrativa*.[91] *I dolci frutti* (1570), for example, contains an eleven-stanza *canzone* either celebrating the imminent formation of the Holy League against the Turks (stanzas 9 and 11, in particular, praised Pope Pius V and Philip II of Spain as well as Don John of Austria, the "noble son of Charles V," who was chosen to command the fleet), or it glorifies Margaret, duchess of Parma. Each stanza is set by a different composer. The composers are grouped according to where they live, beginning with the Venetian composers, Donato, Merulo, and Zarlino, continuing with the Roman, Animuccia, Bonardo who worked in Padua, Contino, and Wert—identified with Mantua—and ending with other composers from the Venetian Republic: the Venetian Andrea Gabrieli, the Paduan Costanzo Porta, and finally Martinengo, who was then *maestro di cappella* at Verona cathedral.

One of the most successful occasional anthologies of the period was the *Corona della morte dell'Illustre Signore . . . Anibal Caro*, a volume commemorating the death of the famous writer and humanist Anibal Caro. What is unusual about this edition is that both the sonnets and the music were commissioned especially for the volume, bringing together the contributions of several eminent writers and composers.[92] The unity of the work originates with the text, in which each stanza invokes Caro's name. Furthermore, the "corona" of the title relates specifically to the form of the poem, whereby the last line of the preceding stanza becomes the first line of the next, thus creating a cyclic form.[93]

OTHER VENETIAN MUSIC PRESSES

The late 1550s and 1560s was a period of unprecedented wealth for Venice and her merchants. For the book trade the economic boom meant an increase in the number of printing establishments. At its peak toward the end of the 1560s, the industry embraced some fifty-six presses employing 500 to 600 persons.[94] The favorable economic climate encouraged newcomers to try their hand at music printing. Pietro Pietrasanta dabbled in the field in the 1550s, while for a brief time in the 1560s, the two music presses of Claudio Merulo and Francesco Rampazetto flourished alongside the larger houses of Scotto and Gardano.

Francesco Rampazetto was active as a printer from 1553 until his death around 1577. He worked mainly on commission for other printers and booksellers. Like the Scotto firm, he printed a variety of books that covered several fields from literature and architecture to astronomy, history, and music. Most of Rampazetto's publications were in the vernacular, but he also printed Latin, Greek, and Spanish texts. During the nine-year period from 1561 to 1568, he issued at least thirty-two music editions and one theory book (see app. A). Rampazetto generally printed his books on a commission basis. Several of his music publications such as Razzi's *Libro primo delle laudi spirituali* (1563) for the Florentine publisher, Jacopo and Filippo Giunti; the *Terzo libro delle muse a 4* (1563) for the Roman music printer, Antonio Barré; and Pietro Vinci's *Secondo libro de madrigali a 5* for the Venetian printer, Giovanni Comencino, confirm Rampazetto's status as a printer who worked on contract for both private individuals and other publishers. The rest of his first editions were printed at the request of composers or third parties. In 1566, Filippo Zusberti, a singer at St. Mark's, commissioned Rampazetto to print Zarlino's six-voice motets. The same year, Giulio Bonagiunta, another singer at St. Mark's, underwrote an anthology of five- and six-voice madrigals by Hettor Vidue, Alessandro Striggio, and others. Rampazetto also reprinted popular single-composer editions by Arcadelt, Rore, Lassus, and Morales, as well as volumes from such well-known anthologies as the *Mottetti del Fiore* and *Madrigali . . . a note negre*.

The other newcomer of the sixties was Claudio Merulo da Correggio. Better known as a composer and the first organist at St. Mark's, Merulo entered the music printing business in 1566, when he joined three other partners, in establishing a press.[95] After only one year the partnership dissolved, leaving Merulo to continue printing music on his own until 1570. Unlike Rampazetto, who printed books in several subjects, Merulo confined himself to the field of music. Some thirty-four music editions survive from his press—an impressive number given the brief four-year history of the firm (see app. A).

Merulo's repertory differed markedly from that of the two major Venetian presses. Whereas the publications of Gardano and Scotto were international in scope, Merulo's output was more parochial. It included an impressive array of first editions, reflecting the organist's ties with composers living in or near the Venetian orbit as well as his professional association with the church and with northern Italian courts, particularly that of Mantua.

Merulo's own music naturally took pride of place among the publications. He planned to issue at least eleven editions of his own music, of which only three survive.[96] The organist also capitalized on his personal connections with various musicians. He referred to Constanzo Porta as "carissimo amico mio" in the dedication to one of the two books of Introits he printed in 1566. Merulo had a close association with the actor, playwright, and businessman, Antonio Molino, whose *I dilettevoli madrigali a 4* he printed in 1568.[97] In the same year, Merulo printed an edition of Lasso's *Quintus liber . . . motetos a 5, 6, & 8* underwritten by Giulio Bonagiunta, a fellow member of the chapel at St. Mark's. Giovan Leonardo Primavera, Domenico Micheli, and other composers living in the Veneto at that time also had their works published by Merulo.

The town of Mantua figured prominently as a source for patronage and publications for the Merulo press. Guglielmo Testori, Giaches de Wert, and Giovanni Maria Rosso, all musicians working at the Mantuan court and cathedral, had their music issued by Merulo. Two letters dated 1566 from Merulo to Duke Guglielmo Gonzaga, moreover, reveal an established business rapport between the organist/printer and the Mantuan court.[98]

The rising demand for music publications in the 1560s dictated the need for additional printers; yet even during such opportune times, neither Rampazetto nor Merulo could succeed without the cooperation of at least one of the two major presses. Typographical and archival evidence support the notion of an association between Scotto and both of the smaller presses.

Rampazetto worked for the Scotto firm as early as 1555/56, when two music editions published under Scotto's name employed the music font and initials that ultimately belonged to Rampazetto in the 1560s. Even after establishing his own press, Rampazetto borrowed a variety of typographical materials from the Scotto firm.[99] It was, moreover, no accident that Rampazetto succeeded Scotto as the elected Prior of the Guild of Booksellers and Printers in 1572, for all the officers of the guild at one time or another held partnerships with the House of Scotto.[100]

As seen in chapter 3, Fausto Bethanio, Merulo's partner, also had ties with the Scotto press. Two years before the establishment of their press, Bethanio referred to himself as a printer at the Scotto press ("stampator in venetia alla di Scotti"). Be-thanio presumably learned the technique of music printing by working either as a journeyman or apprentice at the Scotto firm, and then joined Merulo and two others to found another press.

Certain music editions brought out by Rampazetto and Merulo also link the two new presses with the two larger firms. Two of Rampazetto's publications continue a series of editions by individual composers who exclusively patronized the Scotto press, notably Primavera's Third Book of Five- and Six-Voice Madrigals (1566) and Vinci's Second Book of Five-Voice Madrigals (1567) (see app. A). Rampazetto printed a madrigal publication underwritten by Giulio Bonagiunta, whose other editions Scotto issued at this time. Scotto evidently farmed out some of his overflow business to Rampazetto.[101]

Merulo might have had a similar relationship with Antonio Gardano, since he also issued later volumes of series begun by that press. They include Micheli's Third Book of Five-Voice Madrigals (1567) and Lasso's Fifth Book of Five to Eight-Voice Motets (1568) (see app. A). Finally when Merulo gave up his printing concern in 1570, he turned to Gardano's heirs to print many of his own works up through the 1590s.

IT IS CLEAR THAT A SPIRIT of cooperative enterprise endured among Venetian music printers throughout the sixteenth century. Scotto and Gardano learned early on that in order to succeed, they had to follow procedures observed by the printing industry at large. They carefully struck a balance in the production of commissioned works, independently financed publications, and reprinted editions.

Certain marketing strategies played a key role in minimizing competition be-tween the two music presses. They also defined the musical repertories published in

Venice. We have seen how Scotto and Gardano altered the editions they reprinted. They would rearrange the order, omit and/or add new pieces, separate or combine whole editions, or simply retitle their reprinted editions. These changes may be perceived as promotional tactics whereby the printer could proffer improved even new editions to the public. Another marketing ploy was the multi-volume series. By arranging their anthologies and single-composer volumes into sets, the two printers created an effective selling device, particularly for "repeat" customers and biblio-philes who were interested in collecting complete series of editions.

The two most telling business strategies observed by Scotto and Gardano were sub-specialization in certain repertories and the cultivation of different geographical sources from where they obtained their new editions and commissions. From the very beginning of their careers, the two printers deliberately avoided direct com-petition by bringing out different repertories. Scotto emphasized sacred music edi-tions devoted to single composers, while Gardano mostly printed motet anthologies. Gardano's other repertories included the Arcadelt madrigals and the *note nere* an-thologies. In the 1560s, Scotto featured the lighter *villote alla napolitane* and the musico-literary madrigal anthology. Gardano, on the other hand, continued to stress single-composer editions.

That proprietorship of new repertories was taken very seriously by printers can be observed in the case of the Arcadelt madrigals. Gardano was the first printer to issue an edition of Arcadelt madrigals. When the Scotto press released a second book containing an entirely new repertory of Arcadelt madrigals, Gardano became furious. His rage had nothing to do with the reprinting of music, rather it concerned the right of exclusive ownership of a specific musical repertory that he believed belonged to him.

The crucial business practice that enabled the two printers to publish distinct repertories was the acquisition of music from separate locations. During his long publishing career, Gardano maintained an important association with the duchy of Ferrara. In later years, he also had significant connections with Rome and with German-speaking centers across the Alps. Scotto, on the other hand, looked west-ward to his native Lombardy, and then to Mantua and Trent. He also had established links with Naples and Sicily.

Cooperative enterprise among the printers continued to prevail even when Clau-dio Merulo and Francesco Rampazetto established their own music presses in Venice in the 1560s. It is clear that neither of the new firms could have brought out as many music publications as they did without the tacit consent of the two major music presses. Indeed, the music publications, typography, and archival documents all sup-port the notion that the smaller presses maintained close relationships with either Gardano or Scotto.

By the 1570s, the Venetian music printing industry underwent significant changes. Antonio Gardano's heirs assumed control of the firm, and Claudio Merulo ceased operation of his press. Girolamo Scotto's death in 1572 initiated a slow but steady decline of that dynastic press. While the firms of Gardano and Scotto continued to operate into the seventeenth century, the deaths of their *mercatori* signaled the end of an important era in Venetian music printing.

The near monopoly that the Gardano and Scotto firms had on Italian music printing began to wane in the 1580s with the establishment of several new music presses across the Italian peninsula. In Venice, Giacomo Vincenti and Ricciardo Amadino brought out music publications first in partnership and then separately. The hundreds of music books they printed rivaled that of the Gardano firm. Production of Venetian music books, in general, continued to flourish, reaching several peaks until its decline in the 1630s.[102]

Music printing also assumed greater importance in other Italian centers during the last two decades of the century. Florence secured her first music printer in 1583 with the founding of the Marescotti press.[103] Music printing began to take off in Rome and Milan in 1583 and 1598, respectively.[104] Further south in Naples, the specialty became firmly established around 1602.[105]

In some respects, Girolamo Scotto and Antonio Gardano's successors exceeded what the mid-century printers had achieved. But it was the two giants of the Venetian music printing industry who, through their business acumen, played a pivotal role in establishing their specialty as a successful commercial venture. In the spirit of cooperative enterprise, they produced separate repertories, commissioned works, reprinted popular editions, and devised all sorts of marketing schemes—from the creation of series with fanciful titles to the refashioning of reprinted editions—to sell their music books. By streamlining their production methods and tapping into Venice's trade routes, they were able to disseminate music to a larger and more diverse audience than hitherto imagined. In so doing, they transformed the Venetian music press from a narrowly focused artistic endeavor into an international business, which influenced composers and patrons alike. Scotto and Gardano also had a profound impact on our modern world, for, by producing an enormous body of musical works for all occasions, they bequeathed an important legacy that has enabled us to expand our knowledge of the life and culture of Cinquecento Europe.

NOTES

1. *Biographisch-bibliographiches Quellen-Lexikon der Musiker and Musiklehrten* (Leipzig, 1899–1904), 4: 149.

2. *The Italian Madrigal*, trans. Alexander H. Krappe, Roger H. Sessions, and Oliver Strunk (Princeton, 1949; repr. 1971), 1: 166.

3. Articles on "Gardane" and "Scotto" in *MGG*, 4: 1376–77; 12: 435.

4. *Pierre Attaingnant*, 159–60.

5. Richard J. Agee, "The Venetian Privilege and Music-Printing in the Sixteenth Century," *Early Music History* 3 (1983): 1–42 at 19–21.

6. Bridges, "Publishing of Arcadelt's First Book," 1: 131–32. For more on the Gero edition see chap. 3.

7. "Twins, Cousins, and Heirs: Relationships among Editions of Music Printed in Sixteenth-Century Venice," in *Critica Musica: Essays in Honor of Paul Brainard*, ed. John Knowles (Amsterdam, [1996]), 193–224 at 216.

8. Cooperation existed, for example, between Aldus Manutius and Zacharias Callierge, the two printers of Greek texts; see Lowry, *World of Aldus Manutius*, 126. The same holds true for the Scotto press, which formed partnerships and remained on friendly terms with Giovanni Griffio, Damiano Zenaro, and Giovanni Maria Bonelli—the only other printers who specialized in the sub-field of Latin translations of commentaries dealing with Aristotle's texts in logic and natural philosophy. See chap. 1.

9. Though not exclusively, first editions of works by Willaert, Gombert, Jacquet of Mantua, and later Monte, Contino, Striggio, and Vinci were brought out by the Scotto press, while publications by Arcadelt, Andrea Gabrieli, Kerle, and Lasso tended to be issued first by Gardano's firm.

10. This is not to say that no first editions were used as exemplars for reprinted publications. Among the earlier publications, Gardano's 1542 edition of Gombert's Second Book of Motets *a 4* clearly used the Scotto 1541 edition as the printer's copy. The 1546 unsigned Scotto edition of Arcadelt's *Primo libro* copied verbatim the 1545 Gardano publication. See also Lewis, "Twins, Cousins, and Heirs."

11. Lewis, *Antonio Gardano*, 1: 250.

12. Lewis, "Rore's Setting of Petrarch's 'Vergine Bella'," 382–83.

13. Lewis, *Antonio Gardano*, 1: 435–40.

14. The format of two books in one volume of the Nola edition suggests that two separate editions may have been printed earlier, possibly issued in Naples. See J. Bernstein, *Music Printing in Renaissance* Venice, 274–75.

15. Ibid., 296.

16. There are several examples. Among the earliest are the 1541 reprinted editions of Gombert's First Book of Motets *a 4* (Lewis, *Antonio Gardano*, 1: 289) and Verdelot's *Primo e secondo libri a 4* (ibid., 1: 306) as first noted by Chapman, "Andrea Antico," 339. On the ordering of contents in Gardano editions, see Lewis, Antonio Gardano, 2: 123–49.

17. Both Chapman, "Andrea Antico," 396–405 and Adrian Willaert, *Opera omnia*, ed. Hermann Zenck (CMM 3; AIM, 1950–), 1: 9 present a comparative study of the two editions. Lewis also mentions them in "Antonio Gardane's Early Connections with the Willaert Circle," in *Music in Medieval and Early Modern Europe: Patronage, Sources and Texts*, ed. Iain Fenlon (Cambridge, 1981), 209–26 at 224.

18. Gardano, however, was not always consistent in altering the contents of his reprinted editions to follow modal ordering. In his 1544 reprint of Rore's First Book of Five-Voice Madrigals (Lewis, *Antonio Gardano*, 1: 429), he rearranged the pieces from the strict modal series of the 1542 Scotto edition to a random ordering.

19. "nonostate si usi tutto di tra stampatori . . . de inserire nelle loro scielte alle volte del stampato." As cited in Anthony Newcomb, "Editions of Willaert's *Musica Nova*: New Evidence, New Speculations," *JAMS* 26 (1973): 132–45 at 137–38, and Jessie Ann Owens and Richard J. Agee, "La stampa della 'Musica nova'," 272, doc. 43.

20. Anthologies published by Gardano also reflect the "series" concept. In addition to his two motet collections, Gardano also issued in 1542–43 a group of three madrigal anthologies, two of which consisted of pieces in the new *note nere* style (Lewis, *Antonio Gardano*, 1: 348; 351; 395).

21. On the *note nere* anthologies see Don Harrán, ed. *The Anthologies of Black-Note Madrigals* (CMM 73; AIM, 1978–81), 1/1: pp. xi–xxx and Haar, "The *Note nere* Madrigal."

22. On the Verdelot six-voice madrigals see Alexandra Amati-Camperi, "An Italian Genre in the Hands of a Frenchman: Philippe Verdelot as Madrigalist, with Special Emphasis on the Six-Voice Pieces" (Ph.D. diss., Harvard University, 1994).

23. "Madrigali d'Archadelt a quatre, 5 libris et volum. Venetiis 1541," in Sears Jayne and F. R. Johnson, eds., *The Lumley Library: The Catalogue of 1609* (London, 1956), no. 2577.

24. On the d'Avalos court with particular reference to Ruffo, see Lewis Lockwood, *Counter-Reformation*, 19–26.

25. Five Ruffo motets appear anonymously in Scotto's 1541 edition of Gombert's First Book of Five-Voice Motets; Ruffo's *Missa Alma redemptoris* occurs in the *Missae cum quatuor vocibus paribus decantandae, Morales Hispani, ac aliorum* of 1542.

26. Scotto had links with other Milanese nobility. One emerges in the dedication found in the 1541 Gardano edition of the Gero *Duos*, with which Scotto honors a member of the Visconti family. See Gero, *Il primo libro*, ed. Bernstein and Haar.

27. Grendler, *Critics of the Italian World*, 50–54.

28. The fight was presumably over competition for the same repertory—a repertory which might have emanated from Ferrarese sources. Details of the entire affair appear in several sources, such as: Lewis, *Antonio Gardano*, 1: 31–32; Fenlon and Haar, *The Italian Madrigal*, 70; and Bridges, "Publishing of Arcadelt's First Book," 1: 90–91. See chap. 2 for further discussion of the title pages.

29. On the edition see James Haar, "The *Capriccio* of Giachet Berchem: A Study in Modal Organization," *Musica disciplina* 42 (1988): 129–56.

30. A list of madrigal editions relating to Ferrara from 1559 onwards appears in Newcomb, *The Madrigal at Ferrara*, 1; 251–52, app. 4.

31. On Baldini see Cavicchi, "Baldini, Vittorio."

32. See chap. 4.

33. It is clear from the dedication of the four-voice motet book, however, that Scotto did not know Ercole personally, since he mistakenly referred to him as Cardinal Ippolito Gonzaga (possibly mixing him up with Cardinal Ippolito II d'Este).

34. Albert Dunning, *Die Staatsmotette*, 1480–1555 (Utrecht, 1970), 265–67.

35. Dunning, "Josquini antiquos, Musae, memoremus amores," *Acta musicologica* 41 (1969): 108–16.

36. Mario Praz, "The Gonzaga devices," in *Splendours of the Gonzaga*, Catalogue of Exhibition held 4 November 1981–31 January 1982, Victoria and Albert Museum, ed. David Chambers and Jane Martineau (London, 1981), 65. A reproduction of the ceiling appears in Sergio Bertelli, Franco Cardini, and Elvira Zorzi, *Le corti italiane del Rinascimento* (Milan, 1985), 100.

37. On Contino's life see, Paolo Guerini, "Giovanni Contino di Brescia," *Note d'archivio* 1 (1924), 130–42; Steven Ledbetter, "Marenzio's Early Career," *JAMS* 32 (1979), 304–18; and most recently the introductions to Giovanni Contino, *Modulationum quinque vocum . . . liber primus (Venice, 1560)*, ed. Richard Sherr (Sixteenth-Century Motet 25; New York and London, 1994) and *Il primo libro de' madrigali a cinque voci (1560)*, ed. Romano Vettori (Monumenti musicali italiani 13; Rome, 1987).

38. Butchart, "First Published Compositions of Striggio," 27.

39. On Scipione as a music patron see Fenlon, "Cardinal Scipione Gonzaga (1542–93): 'Quel padrone confidentissimo'," *Journal of the Royal Music Association* 113 (1988): 223–49.

40. For an account of the printing of Palestrina's editions see Jane A. Bernstein, "The Publication of Palestrina's Music in Sixteenth-Century Rome and Venice," in *Atti del convegno di studi palestriniani: 6–9 ottobre 1994* (Rome, in press).

41. Transcriptions of the correspondence appear in Bertolotti, *Musici alla corte dei Gonzaga*, 47–52. See also Oliver Strunk, "Guglielmo Gonzaga and Palestrina's *Missa Dominicalis*," *The Musical Quarterly* 33 (1947): 228–39, reprinted in id. *Essays on Music in the Western World* (New York, 1974), 94–107; Knud Jeppesen, "Pierluigi da Palestrina, Herzog Guglielmo Gonzaga und die neugefundenen Mantovaner-Messen Palestrinas, ein ergänzender Bericht." *Acta Musicologica* 25 (1953): 132–79; and Fenlon, *Music and Patronage*, 1: 90–92.

42. Cametti, *Palestrina*, 158.

43. See chap. 4.

44. Cardamone, *The Canzone villanesca*, 1: 13.

45. A complete list of music editions with connections to Naples appears in Keith Larson and Angelo Pompilio, "Le edizioni musicali napolitane," in *Musica e cultura a Napoli dal XV al XIX secolo*, ed. Lorenzo Bianconi and Renato Bossa (Quaderni della Rivista 9; Florence, 1983), 103–39 at 107–111. See also Larson, "The Unaccompanied Madrigal in Naples from 1536 to 1654" (Ph.D. diss., Harvard University, 1985) for more detailed information on individual Neapolitan composers, patrons, and editions.

46. Figures are drawn from James Erb, *Orlando di Lasso: A Guide to Research* (New York and London, 1990), p. xvi.

47. In the same year Dorico printed in Rome his *Villanelle d'Orlando di Lassus e d'altri . . . libro secondo*. None of the pieces has an attribution, but apparently only one of the dialect songs can be attributed to Lasso; see Cardamone, *The Canzone villancesca*, 21.

48. Haar comes to the same conclusion in "The Early Madrigals of Lassus," *Revue belge de musicologie*, 39–40 (1985–86): 17–32 at 23. Though the wording of title page ("novamente stampato et datto in luce") implies that this volume is the first edition of Lasso's *Primo libro di madrigali a 5*, the possibility that it had already been printed in Rome by Antonio Barré cannot be ruled out. The clause "newly printed and brought to light", normally signifying a first edition, also appears on Gardano's reprinted editions of Lasso's Second and Third Books of Five-Voice Madrigals and First Book of Four-Voice Madrigals. All of these early madrigal books, however, were first issued in Rome by Barré with dedications. Gardano was not totally dishonest in using the phrase that normally designated first editions. For Gardano, the statement "Novamente stampato et dato in luce" denoted that his publication was printed in Venice for the first time. In that sense, it was a first edition *for Venice*. For a different opinion, see Lewis, *Antonio Gardano*, 2:35.

49. In one of the editions, the sponsor of the book states that he came in possession of many madrigals in Spoleto where he held onto them for a while. Barré, in the dedication of the Third Book of Five-Voice Madrigals (1563), reports that he has diligently searched for works by the composer, presumably after Lasso left Italy. The complete dedication appears in Maureen Buja, "Antonio Barré and Music Printing in Mid-Sixteenth-Century Rome" (Ph.D. diss., University of North Carolina, 1996), 363.

50. For a list of the series with their reprints see Haar, "The *'Madrigale Arioso'*: A Mid-Century Development in the Cinquecento Madrigal," *Studi musicali* 12 (1983): 203–19 at 204 n. 3. Discussion of the series also appears in Buja, "Antonio Barrè," 75–100.

51. Haar, "The *'Madrigale Arioso'*," 203–19.

52. Madrigal cycles did appear in earlier Venetian publications such as Doni's *Dialogo della musica* (1544) and Rore's *Terzo libro delle madrigali a 5* (1548), and several Venetian publications of single-composer editions of the 1550s contained madrigal cycles, but the consistency and profusion of multi-stanza *canzone* in anthologies did not take hold until the *Libri delle Muse* series. For a discussion of the *canzone* during the 1550s see Lewis, *Antonio Gardano*, 2: 45–63.

53. The Mass appeared in the collection *Liber missarum quatuor cum quinque et sex vocum . . . liber primus* (1566), which also included Mass settings by Rore and Annibale Padovano.

54. A detailed discussion of the edition appears in Haar, "Le muse in Germania: Lasso's Fourth Book of Madrigals," in *Orlandus Lassus and his Time. Colloquium Proceedings Antwerpen 24–26. 08, 1994*, ed. Ignace Bossuyt, Eugeen Schreurs, and Annelies Wouters (Peer, 1995), 49–72.

55. The Venetian Senate granted Gardano a privilege for the edition on 26 June 1567,

after he printed the edition and Lasso presented it to Alfonso in Ferrara (Gardano started the process on May 26). For transcriptions of the documents see Agee, "The Privilege and Venetian Music Printing," 263–65.

56. "cum ab Orlando Lasso . . . magistro cantiones aliquae, vulgo Mottetta, nuncupata mihi donata fuissent, quibus authoris liberalitate mihi pro meis uti licet, typis mandare, ac tui praeclarissimi nominis inscriptione illustrata emittere, publicareque volui. . . ." See J. Bernstein, *Music Printing in Venice*, 663 for the complete dedication.

57. Another anthology, *Praestatissimorum divinae musices auctorum missae decum, quatuor, quinque & sex vocum . . .* (1570) containing three Lasso Masses was issued by Pierre Phalèse in Louvain. See Vanhulst, *Catalogue des éditions*, 153.

58. See Pietro Giovanelli, comp., *Novus Thesaurus Musicus* (1568), ed. Albert Dunning (CMM 64; AIM, 1974), 5: p. vii.

59. The physical description of the edition is based on Lewis's discussion in "The Printed Music Book in Context," 907–12.

60. For an example of one of these presentation leaves see ibid., 911.

61. Gardano's connection with the Florentine court is documented by his 1539 edition of *Musiche fatte nelle nozze del . . . Duca di Firenze* (Lewis, *Antonio Gardano*, 1: no. 14), a work presumably commissioned by the Medici for the wedding of Cosimo de' Medici to Eleanor of Toledo. Stanley Boorman, "What Bibliography Can Do: Music Printing and the Early Madrigal," *Music & Letters* 72 (1991): 236–58 at 238–41, further speculates on a strong involvement by the Strozzi family in the patronage and financial backing of early Venetian madrigal publications, particularly by Scotto and Antico. The Orsini connection is suggested by Bridges, "Publishing of Arcadelt's First Book," 1: 69–70. On Florentine patronage in Venice see Feldman, *City Culture*, 24–46.

62. *Le Pistole Vulgari di M. Nicolo Franco* (Venice: Gardano, 1539), fols. 67–67ᵛ. The letter, dated 6 April 1538, is transcribed and discussed in Bridges, "Publishing of Arcadelt's First Book," 1:103–04; 2:381–82.

63. Bridges, "Publishing of Arcadelt's First Book," 1:70.

64. Gardano's first publication, *Venticinque canzoni francese*, was devoted to French chansons, the vast majority of which had previously appeared in anthologies printed in Paris by Pierre Attaingnant; see Lewis, *Antonio Gardano*, 1:178.

65. Fenlon and Haar, *Italian Madrigal*, 240.

66. ". . . quegli Stampatori che ristampatigli in Milano, non si sono aveduti d'alcuni errori ch'erano ne la prima stampa, piu tosto per incuria de i miei compositori, che mia." English translation taken from Bridges, "Publishing of Arcadelt's First Book," 1:68. The complete dedication appears in several secondary sources, including ibid., 2: app. D, plate 3b; Lewis, *Antonio Gardano*, 1: 183, and Fenlon and Haar, Italian Madrigal, 241.

67. Bridges, "Publishing of Arcadelt's First Book," 1:87; Chapman, "Andrea Antico," 352–54; Lewis, *Antonio Gardano*, 1:209–10; Fenlon and Haar, *Italian Madrigal*, 249.

68. Bridges, "Publishing of Arcadelt's First Book," 1:87.

69. Bridges, "Publishing of Arcadelt's First Book," 1:94–96 and Fenlon and Haar, *Italian Madrigal*, 257 speculate that the *Quarto libro* could have been Gardano's third book. Jacobus Arcadelt, *Opera omnia*, ed. Albert Seay (CMM 31; AIM, 1965–70), 2:xvi and Lewis, *Antonio Gardano*, 1:213, claim that in the interim Gardano came out with a third book which is now lost.

70. Fenlon and Haar, *Italian Madrigal*, 245–46, 250 n. 6, also wonder about Gardano's anger in his dedication. They propose a chronology in the printing of the series whereby *Il vero secondo libro* appears as the fifth book (after his publication of book four); thereby suggesting that Gardano, who had planned a second book, was taken by surprise by Scott's *Secondo libro* and needed time to assemble his own independent volume. Lewis, *An-*

tonio Gardano, 1:75–77, has, through bibliographical evidence, finally laid to rest the issue of dating of the *Vero secondo libro*. She and Boorman, "What Bibliography Can Do," 253 n. 51, agree with Bridges, "Publishing of Arcadelt's First Book," 1:88, that the edition was printed early in the year 1539, and the date February 1539 that appears in the edition should *not* be read *more veneto*, as suggested by Chapman, "Andrea Antico," 167, 174, Ester Pastorello, *Tipografi, editori, librai*, pp. viii–ix, and Fenlon and Haar, *Italian Madrigal*, 249 n. 1.

The order of the editions then appears as follows: *Libro primo* (Gardano, 1538? lost); *Libro secondo* (Scotto/Antico, January 1539); *Il vero secondo libro* (Gardano, February 1539); *Libro primo* (Gardano, May 1539); *Libro terzo* (Girolamo Scotto, 1539); *Libro quarto* (Gardano, September 1539). This chronology follows Bridges, but differs from Haar and Fenlon, 250 n. 6 in the placement of *Il vero secondo libro*, and from Lewis, 1: 213 in the omission of a "lost" edition of *Libro terzo* by Gardano in 1539.

71. "Publishing of Arcadelt's First Book," 1:99.

72. For the complete story see ibid., 1:105, and above, chap. 6.

73. Samuels, "Benedetto Varchi," 604–06; both Bridges, "Publishing of Arcadelt's First Book." 1:106, and Lewis, *Antonio Gardano*, 1:23 mention that Aretino was among the first members of the academy.

74. See chap. 6.

75. The publication history of the genre appears in Cardamone, *The Canzone villanesca*, 1: 5–31.

76. Ibid., 1:29.

77. Since the wording of the title pages is the same for his 1562 reprints, it is possible that Gardano brought out all four books in 1560, of which only the first three survive.

78. Gardano might also have appropriated other volumes of *villanesche* from Barré's *Libro delle Muse* series, in particular the first and possibly the third and fourth books, which are now lost.

79. See Cardamone, *The Canzone villanesca*, 2: app. C, pt. 3 for a table illustrating the relationships of the editions for the first five books.

80. See J. Bernstein, *Music Printing in Renaissance Venice*, 612.

81. Haar notes this phenomenon, particularly in its later phases in the 1580s, in *Essays on Italian Poetry and Music*, 130 n. 16. For an overview of printed madrigal anthologies, see Franco Piperno, "L'antologia madrigalistica a stampa nel Cinquecento," in *Gli Eccellentissimi musici della città di Bologna con uno studio sull'antologia madrigalistica del Cinquecento* (Florence, 1985), 1–197.

82. For a discussion of the financial aspects of Bonagiunta's editions see chap. 5. On the editions themselves, see Ongaro, "Venetian Printed Anthologies," 43–69.

83. Bianconi, "Il Cinquecento e il Seicento," 342 n. 21.

84. Haar, *Essays on Italian Poetry and Music*, 91 and Einstein, *Italian Madrigal*, 1: 432. Gardano reissued Berchem's cycle in his 1555 edition of *Il primo libro de le muse*.

85. Lewis, "Rore's Setting of Petrarch's 'Vergine Bella'."

86. Giaches de Ponte's *Cinquanta Stanze del Bembo* . . . (Venice: Gardano, 1545) should also be mentioned.

87. Haar makes a fascinating correlation between the cyclic madrigal and the melodic formulae of *improvvisatori* in *Essays on Italian Poetry and Music*, 92. In addition to featuring cyclic madrigals in his anthologies, Antonio Barré also published a series of volumes devoted to the *madrigale arioso*, a genre which emulated the stock melodies of the *improvvisatori*.

88. See Piperno, "L'Antologia madrigalistica," 12–16; also Ongaro, "Venetian Printed Anthologies," 43–46.

89. The composers in question are Claudio Merulo, Francesco Bonardo, Antonio Greco,

Leandro Mira, and Daniele Grisonio; see J. Bernstein, *Music Printing in Renaissance Venice*, 727–29. Piperno, "L'antologia madrigalistica," 15, suggests that the *canzone de diversi* served as a type of competition between the composers involved.

90. See J. Bernstein, *Music Printing*, 727–29.

91. The term is borrowed from Amedeo Quondam, *Il naso di Laura* (Ferrara, 1991), 136, as cited by Ongaro, "Venetian Printed Anthologies," n. 8.

92. Among the literary contributors were Caro's nephew, Giovanni Battista, who helped to write and assemble the text, Battista Zuccarino, Domenico Venier, Girolamo Fenarolo, and Cardinal Boba. The impressive array of composers requested to set each sonnet included Merulo, Andrea Gabrieli, Palestrina, Zarlino, Grisonio, Schietti, Comis, Anville, Adriani, Ghibel, Bellavere, Raimondo, Sperindio Bertoldo, and Rinaldi. See J. Bernstein, *Music Printing*, 761–64.

93. I am grateful to Giulio Ongaro for sharing this observation with me.

94. Grendler, *Roman Inquisition*, 3 n. 3.

95. On the archival documents concerning Merulo's partnership and music printing business see Edwards, "Claudio Merulo," 159–210.

96. The table of contents of Merulo's *Ricercari d'intavolature d'organo . . . libro primo* (1567) lists twelve organ books nine of which contained works by Merulo. The organist apparently printed only two of the twelve: the *Ricercari d'intavolatura d'organo . . . libro primo* dedicated to Count Marcantonio Martinengo Villachiara and the *Messe d'intavolatura d'organo . . . libro quarto* (1568) dedicated to Antonio Altoviti, Archbishop of Florence. He dedicated his third publication, *Il primo libro di madrigali a 5*, to his future patron, Ottavio Farnese, Duke of Parma (see app. B).

97. For the connection between Molino and Merulo see Edwards, "Claudio Merulo," 220–23.

98. Bertolotti, *Musici alla corte dei Gonzaga in Mantova*, 56; also cited by Edwards, "Claudio Merulo," 189.

99. See chap. 3.

100. Brown, *The Venetian Printing Press*, 252. Giovanni Griffio, Damiano Zenaro, Lodovico Avanzo, Giovanni Antonio Bindoni, and Pietro da Fino are named in the minutes of the guild, see chap. 1.

101. Nielson, "Rampazetto," *Music Printing and Publishing*, 384.

102. Angelo Pompilio, "Strategie editoriali delle stamperie veneziane tra il 1570 e il 1630," in *Atti del XIV congresso della Società Internazionale di Musicologia, Bologna, 27 agosto-settembre 1987*, ed. A. Pompilio, D. Restani, L. Bianconi, and F. A. Gallo (Turin, 1990), 1: 254–71.

103. Carter, "Music-Printing in Late Sixteenth- and Early Seventeenth-Century Florence," 27–72.

104. On music printing in Milan see Mariangela Donà, *La stampa musicale a Milano fino all'anno 1700* (Florence, 1961). For a valuable introduction on Rome in the late sixteenth and early seventeenth centuries, see Bridges, "The Publishing of Arcadelt's First Book," 1: 250–74.

105. Pompilio, "Editoria musicale a Napoli e in Italia nel Cinque-Seicento," 79–102.

Appendix A

TABLE OF VENETIAN
MUSIC EDITIONS
(1538–1572)[1]

KEY

Small capital = first edition
Lower-case = reprint by same printer
Lower-case italic = reprint by different printer
* = title issued by two printers in the same year, first edition unclear
† = first edition no longer survives

SCOTTO	GARDANO
1538	
	MOTTETTI DEL FRUTTO 5 VV, BK. 1
	VENTICINQUE CANZ. FRAN. A 4, BK. 1
1539	
ARCADELT, MADR. A 4, BK. 2	†Arcadelt, Madr. a 4, Bk. 1
ARCADELT, MADR. A 4, BK. 3	Arcadelt, Madr. a 4, "Vero" Bk. 2
GOMBERT, MOTETS 4 VV, BK. 1	ARCADELT, MADR. A 4, BK. 4
GOMBERT, MOTETS 5 VV, BK. 1	GARDANO, CANZONI FRANCESE A 2
JACQUET, MOTETS 5 VV, BK. 1	MOTETTI DEL FRUTTO 6 VV, BK. 1
JACQUET, MOTETS 4 VV, BK. 1	*Fior de Mottetti 5 vv, Bk. 2*
WILLAERT, MOTETS 4 VV, BK. 1	*Fior de Mottetti 4 vv, Bk. 1*
WILLAERT, MOTETS 4 VV, BK. 2	MOTTETTI DEL FRUTTO 4 VV, BK. 1
WILLAERT, MOTETS 5 VV, BK. 1	MUSICHE FATTE NELLE NOZZE A 6
1540	
Quinque Missae 5 vv, Bk. 1	*Jacquet, Motets 5 vv, Bk. 1*
Masses 4 vv, Bk. 1	
Veggio, Madr. a 4	
Verdelot, Intavolatura	
Verdelot, Madr. a 4, Bk. 1–2	
LE DOTTE, MADR. A 5	
GERO, MADR. & CANZ. FRAN. A 2, BK. 1	

1. This table lists extant editions of vocal and instrumental polyphonic music and keyboard and lute intabulations, but omits liturgical chant books and music theory publications. The inventory of Gardano editions is based on the preliminary checklist in Lewis, "Antonio Gardane and his Publications of Sacred Music," 2.589-679, and Agee, *The Gardano Music Printing Firms*, 200-08.

SCOTTO	GARDANO
1541	
Arcadelt, Madr. a 4, Bk. 1	*Arcadelt, Madr. a 4, Bk. 1
Gombert, Motets 4 vv, Bk. 1	Arcadelt, Madr. a 4, Bk. 1
Gombert, Motets 5 vv, Bk. 1	Arcadelt, Madr. a 4, Bk. 2
GOMBERT, MOTETS 5 VV, BK. 2	*Arcadelt, Madr. a 4, Bk. 3*
GOMBERT, MOTETS 4 VV, BK. 2	Arcadelt, Madr. a 4, Bk. 4
SCOTTO, MADR. A 3	CASTELLINO, VILLOTTE A 4, BK. 1
SCOTTO, MADR. A 2, BK. 1	MAISTRE JHAN, MADR. 4 VV, BK. 1
NOLA, CANZONI NAPOL. A 3, BK. 1–2	*Gero, Madr. & Canz. francese a 2, Bk. 1*
	Gombert, Motets 4 vv, Bk. 1
	PASSETTO, MADR. A 4, BK. 1
	VERDELOT, MADR. A 6, BK. 1
	Le Dotte, Madr. a 5
	Verdelot, Madr. a 4, Bk. 1 & 2
	FESTA, MADR. A 3, BK. 1
1542	
SEX MISSAE 5 VV	ARCADELT MADR A 3 BK 1
MISSAE VOCIBUS PARIBUS 4 VV	FERABOSCO, MADR. A 4, BK. 1
MORALES, MAGNIFICATS 4 VV, BK. 1	*Gombert, Motets 4 vv, Bk. 2*
RORE, MADR. A 5	WILLAERT, MOTETS 6 VV, BK. 1
SCOTTO, MADR. A 4, BK. 1	MADR. DE DIVERSI A 5, BK. 1
WILLAERT, HYMNS 4 VV	MADR. DE DIVERSI A NOTE NERE A 4, BK. 1
1543	
MAISTRE JHAN, MOTETS 4 VV	Arcadelt, Madr. a 3, Bk. 1
*LUPACCHINO, MADR. A 4	*Arcadelt, Madr. a 4, Bk. 2*
QUINQUE MISSAE 5 VV	*Arcadelt, Madr. a 4, Bk. 3*
MORALES, MOTETS 4 VV	BUUS, CANZONI FRANCESE A 6, BK. 1
REULX, MADR. A 4	Festa, Madr. a 3, Bk. 1
MOTETS PARIBUS VOCIBUS 5 VV	*Gero, Madr. & Canz. Francese a 2*
	*LUPACCHINO MADR. A 4
	Reulx, Madr. a 4
	MOTETS 3 VV
	Madr. diversi a note nere a 4, Bk. 1
	MADR. DE DIVERSI A NOTE NERE A 4, BK. 2
	MADR. DE DIVERSI A 2, BK. 1
	Gero–Janequin, Madr. & Canz. Fran. a3 Bk 1
1544	
Arcadelt, Bk. 1 Madr. a 4	ARCADELT, MADR. A 4, BK. 5
BOYLEAU, MOTETS 4 VV	BERTOLDO, MADR. A 4, BK. 1
CORTECCIA, MADR. A 4, BK. 1	Colin, Masses 4 vv, Bk. 3
DONI, DIALOGO DELLA MUSICA	Gardano, Canzoni francese a 2, Bk. 1
Jacquet, Motets 4 vv, Bk. 1	*MORALES, MASSES 4 VV, BK. 2
MARTINENGO, MADR. A 4	*Quinque Missae 4 vv, Bk. 4*
*MORALES, MASSES 4 VV, BK. 2	RORE, MOTETS 5 VV, BK. 1
ARETINO, RESPONSORIES 4 VV	*Rore, Madr. cromatici a 5, Bk. 1*
RAGAZZONI, MADR. A 4	*Rore, Madr. a 5, Bk. 2*
RORE, MADR. A 5	Verdelot, Madr. a 4, Bk. 1–2
*QUINQUE MISSAE 1 VV, BK. 1	SEX MISSAE 4 VV. BK. 1
WILLAERT–CORTECCIA, CANZ. NAPOL. A 4	

SCOTTO	GARDANO
1545	
PERISSONE CAMBIO, MADR. A 5	Arcadelt, Madr. a 4, Bk. 1
Gero, Madr. & Canz. fran. a 2, Bk. 1	Arcadelt, Madr. a 4, Bk. 4
NOLA, MADR. A 4	PERISSONE CAMBIO, CANZ. NAP. A 4
Rore, Motets 5 vv	CIMELLO, CANZ. NAP. A 3, BK. 1
RUFFO, MADR. A 4, BK. 1	FONTANA, CANZ. NAP. A 3, BK. 1
Verdelot, Madr. a 4, Bk. 1–2	*Jacquet, Motets 4 vv, Bk. 1*
Morales, Magnificats a 4, Bk. 1	JANEQUIN, LA BATAGLIE A 4
	LICINO, DUO CROMATICI, BK. 1
	Morales, Magnificats 4 vv, Bk. 1
	Nola, Canz. nap. a 3, Bk. 1
	Nola, Canz. nap. a 3, Bk. 2
	PONTE, 50 STANZE DEL BEMBO A 4
	RORE, MOTETS 5 VV
	Veggio, Madr. a 4, Bk. 1
	Willaert, Motets 4 vv, Bk. 1
	Willaert, Motets 4 vv, Bk. 2
	Willaert, Canz. nap. a 4
	Flox florum, Motets 4 vv, Bk. 1
1546	
Arcadelt, Madr. a 4, Bk. 1	ABONDANTE, INTABULATURA, BK. 1
GHIBEL, MOTETS 5 VV, BK. 1	Arcadelt, Madr. a 4, Bk. 1
G. B. CREMA, INTABULATURA, BK. 3	BERCHEM, MADR. A 5, BK. 1
VICENTINO, N., MADR. A 5, BK. 1	BIANCHINI, INTABULATURA, BK. 1
BARBERIIS, INTABULATURA, BK. 4	CANDONIO, MADR. A 4, BK. 1
BARBERIIS, INTABULATURA, BK. 5	*F. Da Milano, Intabulatura, Bk. 2*
BARBERIIS, INTABULATURA, BK. 6	*F. Da Milano, Intabulatura, Bk. 1*
DA MILANO, INTABULATURA, BK. 2	*G. B. Crema, Intabulatura, Bk. 1*
ROTTA, INTABULATURA BK. 1	LICINO, DUOS, BK. 2
	LUPACCHINO, MADR. A 4, BK. 2
	MAIO, CANZONE NAPOL. A 3, BK. 1
	Morales, Motets 4 vv
	NOVELLO, MASCHERATE A 4, BK. 1
	ARETINO, LAMENTATIONS 4 VV
	PARABOSCO, MADR. A 5
	PIFARO, INTABULATURA, BK. 1
	REULX, MADR. A 4, BK. 2
	Rotta, Intabulatura, Bk. 1
	Ruffo, Madr. note nere a 4, Bk. 1
	Verdelot, Madr. a 6, Bk. 1
	VINDELLA, INTABULATURA, BK. 1
	Madr. de diversi a note nere a 4
1547	
Madr. de diversi a note nere a 4, Bk. 1	ANIMUCCIA, MADR. A 4–6, BK. 1
Festa–Fogliano, Madr. a 3, Bk. 1	BIFETTO, MADR. A 4, BK. 1
	BUUS, RECERCARI A 4, BK. 1
	PERISSONE CAMBIO, MADR. A 4 BK. 1
	Corteccia, Madr. a 4, Bk. 1
	CORTECCIA, MADR. A 4, BK. 2
	CORTECCIA, MADR. A 5–6, BK. 1
	EL CONTE, MOTETS 5 VV

(Continued)

SCOTTO	GARDANO
1547 *(Continued)*	GINTZLER, INTABULATURA, BK. 1
	Sex Missae 5 vv
	HOSTE DA REGGIO, MADR. A 4, BK. 1
	LUCARIO, MOTETS 4 VV, BK. 1
	LUPACCHINO, MADR. A 5, BK. 1
	Quinque Missae 5 vv
	F. da Milano–Fiorentino, Intabulatura
1548	
ABONDANTE, INTABULATURA, BK. 2	Arcadelt, Madr. a 4, Bk. 1
BORRONO, INTABULATURA, BK. 8	BIFETTO, MADR. A 4, BK. 2
GHIBEL, MOTETS 5 VV, BK. 1	CAUSSIN, MOTETS 5 VV
LA MARTORETTA, MADR. A 4	CIMELLO, CANZONI NAPOL. A 4, BK. 1
MARTINENGO, MADR. A 4, BK. 2	Janequin, Canzoni fran. a 4, Bk. 2
MADR. DE LA FAMA A 4	NASCO, MADR. A 5
RORE, MADR. A 5, BK. 3	PORTINARO, MOTETS 5 VV, BK. 1
Willaert, Canzon a 4	PIONNIER, MOTETS 5 VV, BK. 1
F. DA MILANO, INTABULATURA, BK. 7	*Rore, Madr. a 5, Bk. 3*
	Willaert, Canzon a 4
	Madr. de diversi a note neri a 4, Bk. 1
	Madr. de la Fama a 4
1549	
ALBERTI, MASSES 5 VV, BK. 1	BODEO, MADR. A 4, BK. 1
GERO, MADR. A 4, BK. 1	BUUS, RECERCARI A 4, Bk. 2
GERO, MADR. A 4, BK. 2	BUUS, INTABULATURA D'ORGANO, BK. 1
MENON, MADR. A 4	BUUS, MOTETS 4 VV, BK. 1
NOLA, MOTETS 5 VV, BK. 1	DORATI, MADR. A 5, BK. 1
ARETINO, MADR. CROM. A 4, BK. 1	LUPINO, MOTETS 4 VV, BK. 1
SCHAFFEN, MADR. A 4	WERRECORE, LA BATAGLIA A 4
SCOTTO, MADR. A 3	*Rore, Motets 5 vv, Bk. 3*
TIBURTINO, MUSICA A 3	*VERDELOT, ELLETIONE MOTETTI 4 VV*
Verdelot, Madr. a 4, Bk. 1–2	*Le Dotte, Madri. a 5*
MOTETTI 6 VV, BK. 1	ZARLINO, MOTETS 5 VV, BK. 1
Motetti del Frutto 5 vv, Bk. 1	Motetti del Frutto 6 vv, Bk. 1
MOTETTI 5 VV, BK. 1	Motetti del Frutto 5 vv, Bk. 1
*MOTETTI PARIBUS VOCIBUS 4 VV	*Motetti paribus vocibus 5 vv*
Motets del Frutto 4 vv, Bk. 1	*MOTETS PARIBUS VOCIBUS 4 VV
Elettione de Motetti 3 vv, Bk. 1	Motets del Frutto 4 vv, Bk. 1
ELETTIONE DE MOTETTI 3 VV, BK. 2	MADR DIV. A NOTE NERE A 4, "VERO" BK. 3
*VERDELOT, ELLETIONE MOTETS 4 VV	*Rore, Madr. a 5, Bk. 3*
MADR. DE DIVERSI A NOTE NERE A 4, BK. 3	
TIBURTINO, FANTASIE A 3	
BARBERIIS, INTABULATURA, BK. 9	
BARBERIIS, INTABULATURA, BK. 10	
Canzon francese a 4, Bk. 2	
Rore, Madr. a 5, Bk. 3	
1550	
BUUS, CANZ. FRANC. A 5, BK. 1	Arcadelt, Madr. a 4, Bk. 1
DONATO, CANZ. & MADR. A 4	Arcadelt, Madr. a 4, Bk. 5

(Continued)

SCOTTO	GARDANO
1550 *(Continued)*	
Gombert, Motets 5 vv, Bk. 1	BARGES, VILLOTTE A 4, BK. 1
Werrecore, La Bataglia a 4	PERISSONE CAMBIO, MADR. A 5, BK. 2
Janequin, Premier livre a 4	*Donato, Canzone a 4, Bk. 1*
Willaert, Motets 5 vv, Bk. 1	PORTINARO, MADR. A 5, BK. 1
Willaert, Hymns	F. DALLA VIOLA, MADR. A 4, BK. 1
Madr. de diversi a note nere a 4, Bk. 1	WILLAERT–JACQUET, PSALMS
Gombert, Motets 5 vv, Bk. 1	
1551	
DONATO, CANZON A 4, BK. 1	Arcadelt, Madr. a 4, Bk. 1
†Ghibel, Madr. a 3, Bk. 1	Perissone Cambio, Canzone a 4
Scotto, Madr. a 2, Bk. 1	*Gombert, Motets 4 vv, Bk. 1*
Festa, Madr. a 3, Bk. 1	MAISTRE JHAN, LAMENTATIONS A 4
Gero–Janequin, Madr. & Canz. fran. a 3	Maio, Madr. a 4, Bk. 1
	Ponte, 50 Stanze del Bembo
	Rore, Madr. a 4, Bk. 1
	Rore, Madr. a 5, Bk. 2
	Willaert, Fantasie Recercari a 3
	Motets 3 vv
	MADR. A 3
	DIVERSI AUTORI INTABULATURA
1552	
Gero, Madr. & Canz. Fran. a 2	Arcadelt, Madr. a 4, Bk. 2
Verdelot, Madr. a 4, Bk. 1–2	*Donato, Canzone a 4, Bk. 1*
Madr. de diversi a note nere a 4, Bk. 1	Gardano, Canzoni fran. a 2
Madr. de diversi a note nere a 4, Bk. 2	*Gero, Madr. & Canz fran. a 2, Bk. 1*
Madr. de diversi a note nere a 4, Bk. 3	*Ghibel, Madr. a 3, Bk. 1*
	Gombert, Motets 5 vv, Bk. 1
	Gombert, Motets 5 vv, Bk. 2
	LA MARTORETTA, MADR. A 4, BK. 2
	Werrecore, La Bataglia a 4
	Phinot, Motets 5 vv, Bk. 1
	Rore, Madr. a 4, Bk. 1
	Rore, Madr. cromatici a 5, Bk. 1
	Rore, Madr. a 5, Bk. 2
	Rore, Madr. a 5, Bk. 3
	Ruffo, Madr. cromatici a 4, Bk. 1
	Madr. de diversi a note nere a 4, Bk. 1
1553	
Arcadelt, Madr. a 4, Bk. 1	Arcadelt, Madr. a 4, Bk. 1
	BENDUSI, OPERA DE BALLI A 4
	DONATO, MADR. A 5–6, BK. 1
	Gero, Madr. a 3
	Jacquet, Motets 5 vv, Bk. 1
	RUFFO, MADR. A 5, BK. 1
	Willaert, Canz. nap.. a 4
	Madr. de diversi a 2, Bk. 1

SCOTTO	GARDANO	OTHER PRESSES
1554		
CARLI, MOT. DEL LABERINTO 5 VV	Arcadelt, Madr. a 4, Bk. 1	
CIERA, MADR. DEL LABERINTO A 4	BALLETTI, INTABULATURA, BK. 1	
FESTA, MAGNIFICATS 4 VV	Bianchini, Intabulatura, Bk. 1	
GHIBEL, MADR. A 4, BK. 1	*Donato, Canz. nap. a 4, Bk. 1*	
JACQUET, MASSES 5 VV, BK. 1	FIESCO, MADR. A 4, BK. 1	
HOSTE DA REGGIO, MADR. A 5, BK 1	GHIBEL, CANZ. NAP. A 3, BK. 1	
HOSTE DA REGGIO, MADR. A 4, BK 2	LA MARTORETTA, MADR. A 4, L. 3	
HOSTE DA REGGIO, MADR. A 4, BK 3	NASCO, MADR. A 4, BK. 1	
A. ROMANO, LE VERGINI A 4	PORTINARO, MADR. A 5, BK. 2	
RORE, MADR. CROMATICI A 5, BK. 1	RUFFO, MADR. A 5, BK. 2	
RORE, MADR. A 4, BK. 1	*Ruffo, Madr. a 5, Bk. 3*	
RUFFO, MADR. 6–8	*Le Dotte, Madr. a 5*	
RUFFO, MADR. A 5, BK. 2	MADR. DE DIVERSI A NOTE NERE A 4, BK. 4	
TUDINO, MADR. A 4		
MOTETTI LABERINTO 4 VV, BK. 2		
MOTETTI LABERINTO 4 VV, BK. 3		
MOTETTI LABERINTO 5 VV, BK. 4		
RORE–JACQUET, PSALMS 4 VV		
PHINOT, PSALMS 4 VV, BK. 1		
1555		
†?BERCHEM, MADR. A 4, BK. 1	*Cavazzoni, Intabulatura, Bk. 1*	
Gero, Motets 5 vv, Bk. 1	CORVO, MOTETS 5 VV, BK. 1	
Gero, Motets 5 vv, Bk. 2	†*Lasso, Madr. a 5, Bk. 1*	
LHÉRITIER, MOTETS 4 VV, BK. 1	MANARA, MADR. A 4 BK. 1	
PEREGO, MADR. A 4	Nasco, Madr. a 4, Bk. 1	
Phinot, Psalmi 4 vv, Bk. 1	*Phinot, Motets 5 vv, Bk. 2*	
RUFFO, MOTETS 6 VV	*Phinot, Psalmi 4 vv, Bk. 1*	
Verdelot, Madr. a 4, Bk. 1–2	PORTA, MOTETS 5 VV, BK. 1	
VOLPE, MADR. A 4, BK. 1	PORTA, MADR. A 4, BK. 1	
JACQUET, MASSES 5 VV, BK. 2	Ruffo, Madr. a 5, Bk. 1	
	RUFFO, MADR. A 4, BK. 2	
	WILLAERT, PSALMS 4 VV	
	Libro delle Muse, Madr. a 5, Bk. 1	
	Madr. de diversi a 3	
1556		
MELFIO, MADR. A 4, BK. 1	PADOVANO, RICERCAR A 4, BK. 1	
Ruffo, Madr. a 4, Bk. 1	*Arcadelt, Madr. a 4, Bk. 3*	
Arcadelt, Madr. a 4, Bk. 1	*Berchem, Madr. a 4, Bk. 1*	
Donato, Canzone a 4, Bk. 1	Festa, Madr. a 3, Bk. 1	
VILLANCICOS DE DIVERSOS	*F. da Milano, Intabulatura, Bk. 1*	
†Nasco, Canz. nap. a 4, Bk. 1	†Gero, Madr. a 3, Bk. 2	
	Hoste da Reggio, Madr. a 4, Bk 1	
	Ruffo, Madr. a 4, Bk. 1	
	RUFFO, MADR. A 5, BK. 4	
	Verdelot, Madr. a 4, Bk. 1–2	

SCOTTO	GARDANO	OTHER PRESSES

1557	AZZAIOLO, VILLOTTE A 4, BK. 1
	Lasso, Madr. a 5, Bk. 1
	Morales, Masses 4vv, Bk. 2
	NASCO, CANZONE A 6
	NASCO, MADR. A 5, BK. 2
	PORTINARO, MADR. A 5, BK. 3
	Rore, Madr. a 4, Bk. 1
	RORE, MADR. A 4, BK. 2
	RORE, MADR. A 5, BK. 4
	RUFFO, MASSES 5 VV
	Ruffo, Madr. a 5, Bk. 2
	Willaert–Jacquet, Psalms
	Madr. de diversi a note neri a 4,
	   Bk. 1
	Libro delle Muse, Madr. a 4,
	   Bk. 1
		<u>PIETRASANTA</u>
		Arcadelt, Madr. a 4, Bk. 1
		Donato, Madr. a 5–6, Bk. 1
		Rore, Madr. a 5, Bk. 3
		Verdelot, Madr. a 4,
		   Bks. 1–2

1558
LANDO, MADR. A 4, BK. 1
ARETINO, MADR. A 5–8
Ponte, 50 Stanze del Bembo
MONTAGNANA, CANZONE A 4,
   BK 1
Scotto, Madr. a 2, Bk. 1
SPONTONE, MADR. A 4 BK. 1
VINCI, MOTETS 5 VV, BK. 1
WERT, MADR. A 5, BK. 1
Madr. de diversi a note nere a 4,
   Bk. 1
Libro delle Muse, Madr. a 4,
   Bk. 1
	Arcadelt, Madr. a 4, Bk. 1
	Donato, Canz. nap. a 4, Bk. 1
	Nasco, Canz. nap. a 4, Bk. 1
	Ruffo, Madr. a 5, Bk. 4	

1559
Arcadelt, Madr. a 4, Bk. 1
DORATI, MADR. A 5, BK. 2
Lasso, Madr. a 5, Bk. 1–2
Rore, Madr. cromatici a 5, Bk. 1
Ruffo, Madr. a 5, Bk. 4
CATALDO, TUTTI I PRINCIPII A 4
Scotto, Madr. a 2, Bk. 2
Libro delle Muse, Madr. a 4,
   Bk. 2
Madr.de diversi a 3
Festa, Madr. a 3, Bk. 1
	Arcadelt, Madr. a 3, Bk. 1
	AZZAIOLO, VILLOTTE A 4, BK. 2
	Gero, Madr. a 3, Bk. 1
	Lasso, Madr. a 5, Bk. 2
	Morales, Magnificats 4 vv
	LIBRO DELLE MUSE, MADR. A 5,
	   BK.2
	PETRUCCI, PSALMS 5 VV, BK. 1
	PORTA, MOTETS 4 VV, BK. 1
	PORTA, MADR. A 5, BK. 1
	RUFFO, MAGNIFICATS 5 VV
	Willaert, Fantasie Recercar a 3
	WILLAERT, MUSICA NOVA
	Libro delle Muse, Madr. a 4,
	   Bk. 1
	†Lupacchino–Tasso, Bk. 1 a 2	

1560 CONTINO, INTROITS 5 VV CONTINO, MOTETS 6 VV, BK. 1	*Arcadelt, Madr. a 4, Bk. 2* CHAMATERÒ, MADR. A 5, BK. 1	*(Continued)*

SCOTTO	GARDANO	OTHER PRESSES
1560 *(Continued)*		
CONTINO, MOTETS 5 VV, BK. 1	Donato, Madr. a 5–6, Bk. 1	
CONTINO, MOTETS 5 VV, BK. 2	Janequin, Canz. fran. a 4, Bk. 2	
CONTINO, MADR. A 5, BK. 1	LAMBERTINI, MADR. A 4, BK. 1	
Lasso, Madr. a 5, Bk. 1	*Lasso, Madr. a 4, Bk. 1*	
Lasso, Madr. a 5, Bk. 2	PORTINARO, MADR. A 5, BK. 4	
Monte, Madr. a 5, Bk. 1	*Rore, Madr. a 5, Bk. 3*	
RAIMONDO, MADR. A 4, BK. 1	ROSSETTO, MADR. A 4, BK. 1	
Ruffo, Madr. a Note nere a 4,	ROSSETTI, MADR. A 5, BK. 1	
Bk.1	RUFFO, MADR. A 4, BK. 3	
†Striggio, Madr. a 5, Bk. 1	*Striggio, Madr. a 5, Bk. 1*	
Striggio, Madr. a 5, Bk. 1	*†Striggio, Madr. a 6, Bk. 1*	
VINCI, MUSICA A 2, BK. 1	*Libro delle Muse, Madr. a 4,*	
Madr. de diversi a note nere a 4,	*Bk. 2*	
Bk. 1	*†Libro delle Villotte a 3, Bk. 1*	
Azzaiolo, Villotte a 4, Bk. 1	*Libro delle Villotte a 3, Bk. 2*	
Lupacchino–Tasso, Bk. 1 a 2	*†Libro delle Villotte a 3, Bk. 3*	
1561		
Arcadelt, Madr. a 4, Bk. 1	Arcadelt, Madr. a 4, Bk. 1	
CONTINO, MASSES 4 VV, BK. 1	BERCHEM, CAPRICCIO A 4,	
CONTINO, LAMENTATIONS	BKS. 1–3	
CONTINO, HYMNS	BERTOLDO, MADR. A 5, BK. 1	
Jacquet, Masses 5 vv, Bk. 1	CHAMATERÒ, MADR. A 4, BK. 1	
Jacquet, Masses 5 vv, Bk. 2	CIERA, MADR. A 5, BK. 1	
Nasco, Canz. nap. a 4, Bk. 1	DORATI, MADR. A 5, BK. 3	
RUFILO, MADR. A 5, BK. 1	ESSENGA, MADR. A 5, BK. 2	
VINCI, MADR. A 5, BK. 1	*F. da Milano, Intabulatura, Bk. 2*	
Wert, Madr. a 5, Bk. 1	GORZANIS, INTABOLATURA BK. 1	
Wert, Madr. a 5, Bk. 2	KERLE, MAGNIFICATS 4 VV	
WERT, MADR. A 5, BK. 2	KERLE, PSALMS 4 VV	
WERT, MADR. A 4, BK. 1	NASCO, LAMENTATIONS 4 VV	
Libro delle Muse, Madr. a 5,	Nasco, Madr. a 4, Bk. 1	
Bk. 1	Verdelot, Madr. a 6	
Libro delle Muse, Madr. a 5,	RORE–PADOVANO MADR. A 4,	
Bk. 2	BK.5	
Striggio, Madr. a 6, Bk. 1	SPONTONE, MADR. A 5, BK. 1	
	Willaert, Psalms 4 vv	
	LIBRO DELLE MUSE, MADR. A 5,	
	BK. 3	
	Madr. de diversi a 3	
1562		
CLERICO, MADR. A 5, BK. 1	BERTOLDO, MADR. A 5, BK. 2	<u>RAMPAZETTO</u>
CLERICO, MADR. A 5, BK. 2	F. da Milano, Intabulatura, Bk. 3	*Lasso, Madr. a 5, Bk. 1*
GARUGLI, MOTETS 5 VV, BK. 1	KERLE, PRECES SPECIALES 4 VV	*Libro delle Muse, Madr.*
Gero, Madr. & Canz. fran. a 2,	KERLE, MASSES 4 VV, BK. 1	*a 4, Bk. 1*
Bk. 1	*Lasso, Motets 5 vv, Bk. 1*	
Lasso, Madr. a 5, Bk. 1	*Lasso, Madr. a 4, Bk. 1*	
Lasso, Madr. a 5, Bk. 2	*Hoste da Reggio, Madr. a 3,*	
Rore, Madr. crom. a 5, Bk. 1	*Bk. 1*	
Rore, Madr. a 5, Bk. 3	Lupacchino–Tasso, Bk. 1 a 2	
Rore, Madr. a 5, Bk. 4	*A. Romano, Le Vergini a 4*	
	MONTE, MADR. A 4, BK. 1	*(Continued)*

SCOTTO	GARDANO	OTHER PRESSES
1562 *(Continued)*	Nasco, Canzone & Madr. a 6	
Scotto, Libro delle Muse, Madr. a 3, Bk. 2	ROUSSEL, MADR. A 5, BK. 1	
Willaert, Lib. delle Muse a 3, Bk. 3	Ruffo, Madr. a 5, Bk. 1	
Motets del Frutto 4 vv, Bk. 1	VAET, MOTETS 5 VV, BK. 1	
I DOLCI ET HARMONIOSI A 5, BK.1	VAET, MOTETS 5–6 VV, BK. 2	
I DOLCI ET HARMONIOSI A 5, BK. 2	*Wert, Madr. a 4, Bk. 1*	
LIBRO DELLE MUSE, MADR. A 3, BK. 1	LIBRO DELLE VILLOTTE A 3, BK. 1	
Lasso, Madr. a 4, Bk. 1	LIBRO DELLE VILLOTTE A 3, BK. 2	
Rore, Madr. a 5, Bk. 2	LIBRO DELLE VILLOTTE A 3, BK. 3	
Scotto, Madr. a 2, Bk. 1	LIBRO DELLE VILLOTTE A 3, BK. 4	
Scotto, Madr. a 2, Bk. 3		
Quatro Libri delle Villotte a 3		
1563		
Borrono, Intabulatura de lauto	Abondante, Intabulatura, Bk. 1	RAMPAZETTO
Bianchini, Intabulatura, Bk. 1	GIACOMINI, MADR. A 5, BK. 1	*Morales, Masses 4 vv, Bk.*
FIESCO, MADR. A 4, 5, 6, 7, 8	GIGLIO, MOTETS 4 VV, BK. 1	*2* LASSO–RORE, MOTETS
GORZANIS, INTAB., BK. 2	*Phinot, Psalmi 4 vv*	4 VV, BK. 1
LAGUDIO, MADR. A 5, BK. 1	MONTAGNANA, MOT. 5VV, BK. 1	RAZZI, LAUDI SPIRITUALI
Lasso, Madr. a 5, Bk. 3	*Rore, Madr. crom. a 5, Bk. 1*	*Madr. note nere a 4, Bk. 1*
Morales, Quinque Missarum a 5	*Rore, Madr. a 5, Bk. 2*	*Lib. delle Muse a 4, Bk. 3*
Aretino, Lamentations 4 vv	*Rore, Madr. a 5, Bk. 4*	*Lasso, Madr. a 5, Bk. 2*
PESCIOLINI, MADR. A 5–6, BK. 1	WERT, MADR. A 5, BK. 3	*Morales, Magnificats 4 vv*
PORTINARO, MADR. A 4, BK. 1		*Rore, Madr. a 5, Bk. 1*
RUFILO, MADR. A 4, BK. 1		*Rore, Madr. a 4, Bk. 1*
SCHIAVETTO, MADR. A 4 & A 5		*Ruffo, Madr. a 5, Bk. 4*
VAROTO, MASSES 6 VV, BK. 1		
Vinci, Madr. a 5, Bk. 1		
WILLAERT, MADR. A 4		FARRI
RORE, MOTETS 4 VV		G. M. BONARDO, MADR.
MUSICA SPIRITUALE A 5, BK. 1		A 3, BK. 1
F. da Milano, Intabulatura, Bk. 1		
F. da Milano, Intabulatura, Bk. 2		
Intabulatura de lauto de diversi		
F. da Milano–Perino, Intabulatura Bk.. 3		
Aretino, Responsories 4 vv		
Morales, Masses 4 vv, Bk. 1		
1564		
Azzaiolo,Villotte a 4, Bk. 1	PADOVANO, MADR. A 5, BK. 1	RAMPAZETTO
Azzaiolo,Villotte a 4, Bk. 2	Azzaiolo, Villotte a 4, Bk. 1	*Motetti del Fiore 4 vv, Bk.*
RAGAZZO, MADR. A 4, BK. 1	Festa, Madr. a 3, Bk. 1	*1* DELLA FAYA, MADR. A 5,
SCHAFFEN, MOTETS 5 VV, BK. 1	Gardano, Canzoni francese a 2	BK. 1
SCHAFFEN, MOTETS 5 VV, BK. 2	GORZANIS, INTABULATURA, BK. 3	LONDARITI, MOTETS 6 VV,
SCHIAVETTO, MOTETS 5 –6 VV	*Lasso, Madr. a 5, Bk. 3*	BK. 1
	MENTA, MADR. A 5, BK. 1	*MORALES,
	MICHELI, MADR. A 5, BK. 1	LAMENTATIONS
	MICHELI, MADR. A 5, BK. 2	4–6 VV
	BLESSI, GREGHESCHE, BK. 1	*Aretino, Responsories 4 vv, Bks. 1–2*
		(Continued)

SCOTTO	GARDANO	OTHER PRESSES
1564 *(Continued)*	PAEN, MADR. A 2, BK. 1	
	Palestrina, Motets 4 vv, Bk. 1	
	PORDENON, MADR. A 5, BK. 1	
	Rore, Madr. a 4, Bk. 1	
	Striggio, Madr. a 5, Bk. 1	
	TAGLIA, MADR. A 5, BK. 2	
	Vinci, Madr. a 5, Bk. 1	
	Wert, Madr. a 4, Bk. 1	
	Wert, Madr. a 5, Bk. 1	
	Wert, Madr. a 5, Bk. 2	
1565	BONARDO, MADR. A 4, BK. 1	RAMPAZETTO
Jacquet, Motets 5 vv, Bk. 1	CORFINI, MADR. A 5, BK. 1	ASOLA, INTROITS 4 VV
Jacquet, Motets 4 vv, Bk. 1	GABRIELI, MOTETS 5 VV, BK. 1	*Willaert, Psalmi 4 vv*
Jacquet, Motets 5 vv, Bk. 2	*Gorzanis, Intabulatura, Bk. 2 G.*	
LASSO, MOTETS 5–6 VV, BK. 2	GUAMI, MADR. A 5, BK. 1	
Nasco, Canzone a 4, Bk. 1	*Lasso, Motets 5 vv, Bk. 1*	
FERRARESE, PASSIONES 4 VV	LASSO, SACRAE LECTIONES 4 VV	
PRIMAVERA, MADR. A 3, BK. 1 2	*Lasso, Madr. a 4, Bk. 1*	
PRIMAVERA, CANZ. NAP. A 3,	*Lasso, Madr. a 5, Bk. 2*	
BK. 1	A.ROMANO, MADR. A 5, BK. 1	
LE VIVE FIAMME, MADR. A 5,	ORTIZ, HYMNS, BK. 1	
BK. 1	*Rore, Madr. a 4, Bk. 1*	
WAELRANT, CANZ. NAP. A 4	*Ruffo, Masses 5 vv*	
Quatro Libri Villotte a 3	*Striggio, Madr. a 6, Bk. 1*	
Bonagiunta, Canz. nap. a 3,	*Verdelot, Madr. a 4, Bks. 1–2*	
BK. 1	*Madregali ariosi a 4*	
Lupacchino-Tasso, Bk. 1 a 2		
1566	ESSENGA, MADR. A 4, BK. 1	RAMPAZETTO
JACQUET, HYMNS 4–5 VV	GABRIELI, MADR. A 5, BK. 1	*Villotte a 4, Bk.1*
Lasso, Motets a 5, Bk. 1	LA MARTORETTA, MOTETS 5 VV,	*Lasso, Madr. a 5, Bk. 2*
ARPA, CANZONE NAP. A 3, BK. 1	BK. 1	PRIMAVERA, MADR. A 5,
Primavera, Canzone nap. a 3	LASSO, MOTETS 5–6 VV, BK. 2	BK. 3
+Striggio, Madr. a 6, Bk. 1	LASSO, MOTETS 5–6 VV, BK. 3	*Rore, Madr. a 5, Bk. 3*
Striggio, Madr. a 5, Bk. 1	LASSO, MOTETS 6–8 VV, BK. 4	+Striggio, Madr. a 6, Bk. 1
Vinci, Madr. a 5, Bk. 1	Lasso, Madr. a 5, Bk. 1	VIDUE–STRIGGIO, MADR.
IL DESIDERIO, MADR. A 4, BK. 1	*Lasso, Madr. a 5, Bk. 3*	A 5–6
IL DESIDERIO, MADR. A 5, BK. 2	LONDARITI, MOTETS 5 VV, BK. 1	*Arcadelt, Madr. a 4, Bk. 1*
Villotte a 3	NEUSIDLER, INTAB., BK. 1	*Lasso, Motets 5 vv, Bk. 1*
BONAGIUNTA, CANZ. NAP. A 3,	NEUSIDLER, INTAB., BK. 2	*Lasso, Madr. a 5, Bk. 1*
BK. 2	RORE, MADR. A 5, BK. 5	ZARLINO, MOTETS 6 VV
ARPA, CANZONE NAP. A 3, BK. 2	Wert, Madr. a 5, Bk. 3	
Musica a 3, Bk. 1	RORE–PADOVANO, MASSES	MERULO
	4–6 VV	MERULO, MADR. A 5, BK.1
	Villotte a 3, Bk. 2	PORTA, INTROIT 5 VV, BK. 1
	Rore–Padovano, Madr. a 4	PORTA, INTROIT 5 VV, Bk. 2
		Primavera, Canz. nap. a 3,
		Bk. 2

SCOTTO	GARDANO	OTHER PRESSES
1567		
CALIFANO, CANZ. NAP. A 3, BK. 1	ALCAROTTO, MADR. A 5–6, BK. 1	<u>RAMPAZETTO</u>
FERRETTI, CANZON A 5	PADOVANO, MOTETS 5–6 VV,	VINCI, MADR. A 5, BK. 2
JACQUET, ORATIONES 4 VV	BK.1	
Lasso, Madr. a 5, Bk. 1	BELLAVERE, MADR. A 5, BK. 1	<u>MERULO</u>
Lasso, Madr. a 5, Bk. 2	CARLI, MADR. A 5, BK. 1	BASTINI, MADR. A 5–6,
Lasso, Madr. a 5, Bk. 3	DORATI, MADR. A 5, BK. 4	BK. 1
ROSSETTO, IL LAMENTO	LASSO, MADR. A 5, BK. 4	CONFORTI, MADR. A 5,
STRIGGIO, IL CICALAMENTO A 5	MAGIELLO, MADR. A 5, BK. 1	BK. 1
TROIANO, CANZ. NAP. A 3, BK. 3	MONTE, MADR. A 5, BK. 2	FIESCO, MADR. A 5, BK. 2
LIB. DE ETERNI, MOTETS 5–6 VV,	PORDENON, MADR. A 5, BK. 2	MERULO, RICERCAR
BK. 1	RENALDI, MADR. A 4–5, BK. 1	INTAV.
LIB. FIAMME, MADR. A 5 –6,	RICCIO, MADR. A 5, BK. 1	MICHELI, MADR. A 6, BK. 3
BK. 2	RICCIO, MADR. A 6, BK. 1	
Madr.de diversi a note nere a 4,	SPONTONI, MADR. A 5, BK. 2	NOLA, VILLANELLE A 3–4,
Bk. 1	WERT, MADR. A 5, BK. 4	BK. 1
Madr.de diversi a note nere a 4,	*Villotte a 3, Bk. 3*	ORSO, MADR. A 5, BK. 1
Bk. 2		ROSSO, MADR. A 4, BK. 1
IL DESIDERIO, MADR. A 4, BK. 3		ROSSO, MOTETS 5 VV, BK 1
Canzone nap. a 3, Bk. 1		
IL GAUDIO, MADR. A 3		<u>SESSA</u>
		Ponte, 50 stanze del
		Bembo
1568		
ADRIANI, MADR. A 6, BK. 1	COMA, MADR. A 5, BK. 1	<u>RAMPAZETTO</u>
Arcadelt, Madr. a 4, Bk. 1	CORFINI, MADR. A 5, BK. 2	*Arcadelt, Madr. a 4, Bk. 1*
BECCHI, INTABULATURA, BK. 1	*Donato, Madr. a 4, Bk. 2*	RUFFO, PSALMS 4 VV
CASULANA, MADR. A 4, BK. 1	FLECCIA, MADR. A 4–5, BK. 1	
CICCARELLI, MOTETS 5 VV A 5	ISNARDI, MASSES 5 VV	<u>MERULO</u>
DATTARI, VILLANELLE A 3–5	ISNARDI, MADR. A 5, BK. 1	LASSO, MOTETS 5–8 VV,
DONATO, MADR. A 4, BK. 2	*Lasso, Madr. a 5, Bk. 2*	BK. 5
Ferretti, Canzone a 5	MAGIELLO, MADR. A 5, BK. 2	*Lupacchino-Tasso, a 2,*
GALILEI, FRONIMO	PORTINARO, MOTETS A 6–8, BK 2	*Bk. 1*
PORTINARO, LE VERGINI A 5–7	Rore, Madr. a 5, Bk. 5	MERULO, MESSE
PRATONERI, MADR. A 5, BK. 1	Wert, Madr. a 5, Bk. 4	INTABULATURA, BK. 4
†Troiano, Canzone a 3, Bk. 1–2	GIOVANELLI, NOVI THES. BK. 1	MOLINO, MADR. A 4, BK. 1
Troiano, Canzone a 3, Bk. 3	GIOVANELLI, NOVI THES. BK. 2	*Morales, Magnificats 4 vv*
LIB. FIAMME MADR. A 5, BK. 3	GIOVANELLI, NOVI THES. BK. 3	*Palestrina, Madr. a 4, Bk 1*
GLI AMOROSI MADR A 4, BK.1	GIOVANELLI, NOVI THES. BK. 4	*Festa, Madr. a 3, Bk. 1*
CORONA DELLA MORTE	GIOVANELLI, NOVI THES. BK. 5	
1569		
BARBETTA, INTAVOLATURA, BK. 1	ALCAROTTI, MADR. A 5–6, BK. 2	
BONIZZONI, CANZONI A 4, BK. 1	AZZAIOLO, VILLOTTE A 4, BK. 3	
CHAMATERÒ, MASSES 5–7 VV,	COSSA, MADR. A 4, BK. 1	
BK. 1	FAA, MADR. A 5, BK. 1	
CHAMATERÒ, MADR. A 5, BK. 2	FIESCO, MUSICA NOVA A 5, BK. 1	
CHAMATERÒ, MADR. A 5, BK. 3	ISNARDI, PSALMS 4 VV	
CHAMATERÒ, MADR. A 5, BK. 4	*Lasso, Motets 5 vv, Bk. 1*	
CHAMATERÒ, MADR. A 4, BK. 2	Lasso, Motets 5–6 vv, Bk. 2	
FERRETTI, CANZON A 5, BK. 2	Lasso, Motets 5–6 vv, Bk. 3	
LAMBERTINI, PSALMS 4 VV	Lasso, Motets 6–8 vv, Bk. 4	
MAZZONE, MADR. A 5, BK. 1	Lasso, Motets 6–8 vv, Bk. 5	
MAZZONE, MADR. A 4, BK. 1	MASSAINO, MADR. A 4, BK. 1	

(Continued)

SCOTTO	GARDANO	OTHER PRESSES

1569 *(Continued)*
MAZZONI, CANZ. NAP. A 3, BK. 1
MONTE, MADR. A 6, BK. 2
MONTE, MADR. A 4, BK. 2
PRIMAVERA, CANZ. NAP. A 4,
  BK. 1
PRATONERI, PSALMS 6 VV
Rore, Libro delle Fiamme,
  Madr. a 4–5, Bk. 1
Striggio, Il Cicalamento a 5
TROIANO, CANZ. NAP. A 3, Bk. 4
MUSICA DE' VIRTUOSI A 5, BK. 1
Ferretti, Canzon a 5, Bk. 1
	MICHELI, MADR. A 5, BK. 4
	MOLINO, MADR. A 4, BK. 2
	MORTA, MADR. A 5, BK. 2
	Portinaro, Le Vergini a 6, Bk. 5
	RENALDI, MADR. A 4, BK. 1
	Rore, Madr. a 4, Bk. 1
	Striggio, Madr. a 5, Bk. 1
	Striggio, Madr. a 6, Bk. 1
	TASTAVIN, MADR. A 5, BK. 1
	Motets 3 vv
	Libro delle Muse, Madr. a 5,
	  Bk. 3
	Madregali ariosi a 4
	Madr. de diversi a 3
	Lasso, Madr. a 4, Bk. 1
		MERULO
		Lasso, Motets 5 vv, Bk. 6
		Lasso, Madr. a 4, Bk. 1
		Nola, Canz. nap. a 3–4,
		  Bk. 1
		†Monte, Madr. a 6, Bk. 1
		ARETINO, MAGNIFICATS
		  5 VV
		Rore, Madr. a 4, Bk. 2
		Motets 5 vv, Bk. 1
		
		ZORZI/ZANTANI
		LA ELETTA, MADR. A 4–5

1570
ADRIANI, MADR. A 5, BK. 1
ADRIANI, MADR. A 5, BK. 2
Arcadelt, Madr. a 4, Bk. 1
BACCUSI, MASSES 5 VV, BK. 1–6
CASULANA, MADR. A 4, BK. 2
DORATI, LE STANZE A 4
DUC, MADR. A 4, BK. 1
FERRETTI, NAPOL. A 5, BK. 3
MAZZONI, CANZ. NAP. A 3, BK. 2
A. ROMANO, CANZ. NAP. A 5,
  BK. 1
Monte, Madr. a 5, Bk. 1
Monte, Madr. a 5, Bk. 2
Monte, Madr. a 6, Bk. 1
MONTE, MADR. A 5, BK. 3
Nola, Villanelle a 3–4, Bk. 1
Primavera, Canz. napol. a 3,
  Bk. 1
*Primavera, Canz. napol. a 3,
  Bk. 2*
†Primavera, Villotte a 3, Bk. 3
SCOTTO, MADR. A 3
STRIGGIO, MADR. A 5, BK. 2
TORTORA, MADR. A 5–6, BK. 1
*Libro delle Fiamme, Madr.
  a 5–6, Bk. 2*
I DOLCI FRUTTI, MADR. A 5, BK. 1
PRIMA STELLA DE MADR. A 5
JUSTINIANE A 3, BK. 1
CORONA DELLE NAPOL. A 3–4
RACCOLTA DI NAPOL. A 3, BK. 1
GORZANIS, NAPOL. LEUTO, BK. 1
TURTURINO, NAPOL. LEUTO,
  BK. 1
	AGOSTINI, MADR. A 5, DK. 1
	ASOLA, MASSES 5 VV, BK. 1
	ASOLA, MASSES, BK. 2
	BACCUSI, MADR. A 5–6, BK. 1
	BALBI, MADR. A 4, BK. 1
	CORTECCIA, RESPONSORIES, Bk 1
	CORTECCIA, RESPONSORIES, Bk 2
	FALCIDIO, MASSES 5 VV, BK. 1
	FIDELIS, MADR. A 4, BK. 1
	GABRIELI, MADR. A 5, BK. 2
	Gero, Madr. a 3, Bk. 1
	GUERRERO, MOTETS 5 VV, BK. 1
	Lasso, Madr. a 5, Bk. 1
	Lasso, Madr. a 5, Bk. 3
	Lasso, Madr. a 5, Bk. 4
	SABINO, MADR. A 5, BK. 1
	VESPA, MADR. A 5, BK. 1
	Wert, Madr. a 4, Bk. 1
	VILLOTTE A 3, BK. 5
	VILLOTTE A 3, BK. 6
		MERULO
		LASSO, MASSES 5 VV, BK. 2
		Rore–Jacquet, Psalmi 4 vv

SCOTTO	GARDANO	OTHER PRESSES
1571		
CANDIDO, MASCHERATE A 3–5	AGOSTINI, ENIGMI A 6, BK. 1	ANGELIERI/MERULO
CORFINI, MOTETS 5–8 VV, BK. 1	ANTEGNATI, MADR. A 4, BK. 1	ROCCIA, MADR. A 4, BK. 1
Ferretti, Canzoni a 5, Bk. 1	ASOLA, LE VERGINI A 3	
Ferretti, Canzoni a 5, Bk. 2	CORTECCIA, MOTETS 5 VV, BK. 1	ROCCA
FERRETTI, NAPOL. A 5, BK. 4	CORTECCIA, MOTETS 6 VV, BK. 1	*G. M. Bonardo, Madr. a 3,*
FIORINO, LA NOBILTÀ A 3	FAA, MADR. A 5–6, BK. 2	*Bk. 1*
GORZANIS, NAPOL. A 3, BK. 2	GABRIELI, GREGHESCHE, BK. 1	
A. ROMANO, NAPOL. A 5, BK. 2	ISNARDI, PSALMS 4 VV	
Monte, Madr. a 6, Bk. 2	MARINO, MADR. A 5, BK. 1	
MONTE, MADR. A 5, BK. 4	MASSAINI, MADR. A 5, BK. 1	
PINELLO, CANZONI A 3, BK. 2	MAURO, MADR. A 4, BK. 1	
SCOTTO, CORONA CANZ. A 3,	MAURO, MADR. A 5, BK. 1	
BK. 2	*Palestrina, Motets 4 vv, Bk. 1*	
SCOTTO, CORONA CANZ. A 3,	PESCIOLINI, MADR. A 6, BK. 2	
BK. 3	PORDENON, MADR. A 5, BK. 3	
Striggio, Madr. a 5, Bk. 2	PORTA, MOTETS 6 VV, BK. 1	
STRIGGIO, MADR. A 6, BK. 2	Rore, Madr. a 4, Bk. 2	
VENTURI, VILLANELLE A 3, BK. 2	SESSA D'ARANDA, MADR. A 4,	
VINCI, MADR. A 5, BK. 3	BK. 1	
VINCI, MADR. A 6, BK. 1	*Wert, Madr. a 5, Bk. 1*	
ZAPPASORGO, NAPOL. A 3, BK. 1	WERT, MADR. A 5–7, BK. 5	
POLICRETO, NAPOL. A 3, BK. 1	Willaert, Psalms 4 vv	
	Villotte a 3, Bk. 1	
	Villotte a 3, Bk. 2	
	Villotte a 3, Bk. 4	
1572		
BACCUSI, MADR. A 5, BK. 2	AGOSTINI, MADR. A 4, BK. 2	
BACCUSI, MADR. A 6, BK. 2	AGOSTINI, CANONES A 6. BK. 1	
BIANCO, CANZONI A 3, BK. 1	CASENTINI, MADR. A 5, BK. 1	
CAVATONI, MADR. A 4–5	Gabrieli, Motets 5 vv, Bk. 1	
CONVERSO, CANZONI A 5, BK. 1	Gabrieli, Madr. a 5, Bk. 1	
COTTONE, MADR. A 5, BK. 1	Gabrieli, Madr. a 5, Bk. 2	
Ferretti, Napolitane a 5, Bk. 3	GABRIELI, MASSES 6 VV, BK. 1	
A. Romano, Canzoni a 5, Bk. 1	INGEGNERI, MADR. A 5, BK. 2	
MONTE, MOTETS 5 VV, BK. 1	ISNARDI, LAMENTATIONS 5 VV	
PALESTRINA, MOTETS 5–8 VV,	Lasso, Motets 5–6 vv, Bk. 2	
BK. 2	Payen, Madr. a 2, Bk. 1 (Le	
PINELLO, CANZONI A 3, BK. 3	Vergine)	
Scotto, Madr. a 2, Bk. 1	PORTINARO, MOTETS. 5 VV, BK. 3	
VINCI, MOTETS 5 VV, BK. 2	STABILE, MADR. A 5, BK. 1	
Corona Napolitane a 3–4, Bk. 1	VICTORIA, MOTETS 4–8 VV	
Justiniane a 3, Bk. 1	Wert, Madr. a 5, Bk. 3	
	ZACCHINO, MOTETS 4 VV	

Appendix B

TABLE OF DEDICATEES
ITALIAN MUSIC EDITIONS
(1536–1572)

Dedicatee	Title	Year	Printer
Accademia degli Elevati, Padua	Portinaro, Madrigali a 5, Bk. 4	1560	Gardano
Accademia Filarmonica, Verona	Baccusi, Madrigali a 6, Bk. 2	1572	Scotto
	Cavatoni, Scielta de madrigali a 4–5	1572	Scotto
	Chamaterò, Madrigali a 5, Bk. 3	1569	Scotto
	Nasco, Madrigali a 5	1548	Gardano
	Ruffo, Madrigali a 6–8	1554	Scotto
	Wert, Madrigali a 5, Bk. 5	1571	Gardano
Accademici Costanti, Vicenza	Portinaro, Madrigali a 5–6, Bk. 3	1557	Gardano
	Nasco, Canzone et madrigali a 6	1557	Gardano
Acciaioli, Bernardo	Palestrina, Madrigali a 4, Bk. 1	1555	Dorico
	Palestrina, Madrigali a 4, Bk. 1	1568	Merulo
Acquaviva d'Aragona, Alberto	Sabino, Madrigali a 5, Bk. 1	1570	Gardano
Acquaviva d'Aragona, Gio. Girolamo, Duke of Atri	Tudino, Madrigali a 5, Bk. 1	1565	Dorico
Acque, bishop of (Petrus Faunus Costaciarus)	Trossarello, Madrigali a 6, Bk. 1	1570	Ponzio
Alarcon, Hernando d'	Orso, Madrigali a 5, Bk. 1	1567	Merulo
Albano, Gian Girolamo, count	Alberti, Missae 5 vv, Bk. 1	1549	Scotto
	Martinengo, Madrigali a 4	1544	Scotto
Alberto I, dean of Treviso	Troiano, Villanesche a 3, Bk. 3	1567	Scotto
Alberto, Nicolò	Arcadelt, Madrigali a 4, Bk. 2	1541	Gardano
	Arcadelt, Madrigali a 4, Bk. 2	1539	Gardano
Albrecht V, duke of Bavaria	Contino, Motetti 6 vv, Bk. 1	1560	Scotto
	Gabrieli, Motetti 5 vv, Bk. 1	1565	Gardano
	Gabrieli, Missae 6 vv, Bk. 1	1572	Gardano
	Lasso, Sacrae lectiones 4 vv	1565	Gardano
	Lasso, Motetti 5 vv, Bk. 1	1566	Rampazetto
	Londariti, Motetti 6 vv, Bk. 1	1564	Rampazetto
	Musica de'virtuosi, Madrigali a 5, Bk. 1	1569	Scotto
Aldrovandi, Teseo, abbot	Porta, Madrigali a 5, Bk. 2	1569	Gardano
Alessi, Gionforte de	Vinci, Madrigali a 5, Bk. 2	1567	Rampazetto
Allencastro, Dionisio de	Lusitano, Motetti 6–8 vv	1551	Dorico

DEDICATEE	TITLE	YEAR	PRINTER
Altoviti, Antonio, archbishop of Florence	Animuccia, Motetti 5 vv, Bk. 1	1552	Dorico
	Merulo, Messe d'intavolatura, Bk. 4	1568	Merulo
Anguissola, Federico	Veggio, Madrigali a 4	1540	Scotto
Arcimboldo, Antonello	Ruffo, Missae 4 vv	1570	Antoni
Avalos, Alfonso d', marquis of,	Gombert, Motetti 4 vv, Bk. 1	1539	Scotto
Vasto; governer-general of	Motetti 5 vv, Bk. 1	1543	Castiglione
Milan	Ruffo, Motetti 5 vv, Bk. 1	1542	Castiglione
Avalos, Ferdinando Francesco d', marquis of Pesaro and Vasto	Wert, Madrigali a 4, Bk. 1	1561	Scotto
Avalos, Inico d'Aragona d'	Giglio, Motetti 4 vv, Bk. 1	1563	Gardano
	Libro delle Muse, Madrigali a 4, Bk. 3	1562	Barré
Ayerbe,Michele da, count of Simmeri	Lagudio, Madrigali a 5, Bk. 1	1563	Scotto
Arezzo, bishop of. *See* Minerbetti			
Balbo, Aloysio	Zarlino, Motetti 5 vv, Bk. 1	1549	Gardano
Bardi, Pandolfo, count	Mauro, Madrigali a 5, Bk. 1	1571	Gardano
Barrese, Pietro, Marquis of Pietrapretia	Havente, Madrigali a 4, Bk. 1	1556	unsigned
Barozzi, Lorenzo	Portinaro, Madrigali a 5, Bk. 3	1561	Gardano
Bartolini, Nofri, archbishop of Pisa	Arentino, Lamentations	1546	Gardano
Bembo, Pietro, cardinal	G. Cavazzoni, Intavolatura d'organo	1543	B. V.
Bembo, Torquato	Barberiis, Intavolatura de leuto, Bk. 9	1549	Scotto
	Portinaro, Madrigali a 5, Bk. 1	1550	Gardano
Benzoni, Benzon de	Corona delle napolitane a 3–4	1570	Scotto
	Corona delle napolitane a 3–4	1572	Scotto
Bergamo, Regents of La Misericordia	Vinci, Motetti 5 vv, Bk. 2	1572	Scotto
Bernardini, Alessandro	Dorati, Madrigali a 5, Bk. 4	1567	Gardano
Bernardini, Gioseffo	Corfini, Madrigali a 5, Bk. 1	1565	Gardano
	Dorati, Madrigali a 5, Bk. 2	1559	Scotto
Bernardo, Francesco	Martorello, Madrigali a 5, Bk. 1	1547	Fabriano & Bindoni
Bianchi, Gaspar, count	Azzaiolo, Villotte del Fiore a 4, Bk. 2	1559	Gardano
Bianchini, Giovan Battista, and Ludovico Leggerini	Il Gaudio, Madrigali a 3	1567	Scotto
Bollano, Domenico, bishop of Brescia	Contino, Introitus et Haleluia 5 vv	1560	Scotto
Bonaldi, Francesco. *See* Vergelli			
Bonvisi, Gioseffo, and Ludovico Penitesi	Guami, Madrigali a 5, Bk. 1	1565	Gardano
Bonvisi, Lorenzo	Bastini, Madrigali a 5–6, Bk. 1	1567	Merulo
Borgasi, Sigismondo, canon	Mazzoni, Canzoni napolitane a 3, Bk. 1	1569	Scotto
	Bk. 1 de gli eterni motetti 5–6 vv	1567	Scotto
Borromeo, Carlo, cardinal	Boyleau, Magnificats 4–6 vv	1566	Pozzo
Bottrigari, Ercole	Spontone, Madrigali a 4, Bk. 1	1558	Scotto
Bracelli, Giovan Battista	Taglia, Madrigali a 4, Bk. 1	1555	Moscheni
Bragadino, Girolamo	Berchem, Madrigali a 5, Bk. 1	1546	Gardano
Brandolini, Brandolino, count of Valmareno	Baccusi, Madrigali a 5, Bk. 2	1572	Scotto
Brescia, canons of	Contino, Hymni	1561	Scotto
	Contino, Threni Jeremiae	1561	Scotto
Buontempi, Alessandro	Cossa, Madrigali a 4, Bk. 1	1569	Gardano
Buonvisi, Benedetto	Dorati, Madrigali a 5, Bk. 3	1561	Gardano
Buotrono, Girolamo	Maiotro Jhan, Madrigali a 4, Bk. 1	1541	Gardano
Calina, Barbara	Contino, Madrigali a 5, Bk. 1	1560	Scotto
Calmo, Andrea	Agostini, Musica rime di Calmo a 4	1567	Pozzo

DEDICATEE	TITLE	YEAR	PRINTER
Cambi, Alfonso	Animuccia, Madrigali a 5, Bk. 2	1551	Blado
Camaldolese Religion	Porta, Introitus 5 vv	1566	Merulo
Campeggio, Lorenzo, archdeacon of Bologna	Micheli, Madrigali a 6, Bk. 3	1567	Merulo
Campeggio, Pietro, bishop of Feltre	Raimondo, Madrigali a 4, Bk. 1	1560	Scotto
Candia (Crete), archbishop of (Filippo) Mocenigo	Ciera, Madrigali del Laberinto a 4, Bk. 1	1554	Scotto
Capodiferro, Tiberio, and Gaspari Cincio, canons of Vatican Basilica	Animuccia, Magnificats	1568	Dorico
Capreolo, Comiti Alfonso	Riccio, Madrigali a 5, Bk. 1	1567	Gardano
Capua, Giovanni di, count of Altavilla	Nola, Madrigali a 5, Bk. 2	1564	Salviano
Cornaro, Giorgio, bishop of Treviso	Jacquet, Hymns 4–5 vv	1566	Scotto
Cornaro, Jacopo, abbot and Andrea	Pordenon, Madrigali a 5, Bk. 2	1567	Gardano
Caracciolo, Colantonio, marquis of Vico	Monte, Madrigali a 4, Bk. 1	1562	Gardano
Caracciolo, Francesco	Nola, Motetti 5 vv, Bk. 1	1549	Scotto
Carbone, Giovan'Antonio	Rufilo, Madrigali a 4, Bk. 1	1563	Scotto
Carbone, Giovanni Bernardino	Lucario, Motetti 4 vv, Bk. 1	1547	Gardano
Carrafa, Hippolita Gonzaga	Hoste da Reggio, Madrigali a 3, Bk. 1	1554	Moscheni
Casa, Giovanni della	Rore, Madrigali a 5, Bk. 3	1548	Gardano
Casali, Michele	Spontone, Madrigali a 5, Bk. 1	1561	Gardano
Castelletta, Vittoria	A. Romano, Canz. napolitane a 5, Bk. 2	1571	Scotto
Casulana, Maddalena	Molino, Madrigali a 4, Bk. 1	1568	Merulo
Cavenago, Lucilio	Vicentino, Madrigali a 5, Bk. 5	1572	Ponzio
Celso, Lorenzo	Monte, Madrigali a 5, Bk. 2	1567	Gardano
Cerasi, Gio. Pietro and Tiberio	Agostini, Enigmi Musicali a 6, Bk. 1	1571	Gardano
Cesarina, Cleria Farnese	Venturi, Villanelle a 3, Bk. 2	1571	Scotto
Charles, archduke of Austria	Gorzanis, Canzoni napolitane a 3, Bk. 2	1571	Scotto
	Zacchino, Motetti 4 vv, Bk. 1	1572	Gardano
	Gabrieli, Missae 6 vv, Bk. 1	1572	Gardano
	Padovano, Motetti 5–6 vv, Bk. 1	1567	Gardano
	Padovano, Madrigali a 5, Bk. 1	1564	Gardano
Chiericata, Lucretia	Vicentino, Madrigali a 5, Bk. 1	1546	Scotto
Chiossa, Giovanni Battista	Fidelis, Madrigali a 4, Bk. 1	1570	Gardano
Ciardi, Francesco	Canacci, Madrigali a 5, Bk. 1	1564	Dorico
Cincio, Gaspari. *See* Capodiferro			
Colonna, Fabritio	Cimello, Canti a 4, Bk. 1	1548	Gardano
Colonna, Felice Orsina	Libro delle Muse, Madrigali a 4, Bk. 1	1555	Barré
Colonna, Marc'Antonio	Martelli, Madrigali a 4, Bk. 1	1564	Blado
Coloredo, Carlo, dean of Udine	Ciera, Madrigali a 5, Bk. 1	1561	Gardano
Compagnia delli signori Constanti	Bonardo, Madrigali a 4, Bk. 1	1565	Gardano
Contarini, Alessandro	Il Desiderio, Madrigali a 5, Bk. 2	1566	Scotto
Contarini, Benedetto	Passetto, Madrigali a 4, Bk. 1	1541	Gardano
Contarini, Luigi	Primavera, Canzone napol. a 3, Bk. 1	1565	Scotto
Corno, abbot of	Tiburtino, Musica a 3	1549	Scotto
Correlli, Giovanni Paolo	Bk. 1 della raccolta di Napoli a 3	1570	Scotto
Costanzo, Tucci	Boyleau, Madrigali a 4, Bk. 1	1546	Fabriano & Bindoni
Crec, Oliviero, abbot of Jovis	Libro delle Muse, Canzoni napolitane a 3, Bk. 2	1557	Barré
Cremona, Alessandro	Taglia, Madrigali a 5, Bk. 1	1557	Moscheni
Cupis, Bernardino de, Monsignor	Bodeo, Madrigali a 4, Bk. 1	1549	Gardano
	Porta, Motetti 5 vv, Bk. 1	1555	Gardano
Curto, Gasparo	Nasco, Madrigali a 4, Bk. 1	1554	Gardano

Dedicatee	Title	Year	Printer
Dandino, Anselmo, abbot	A. Romano, Madrigali a 5, Bk. 1	1565	Gardano
	Micheli, Madrigali a 5, Bk. 2	1564	Gardano
	Conforti, Madrigali a 5, Bk. 1	1567	Merulo
Della Rovere, Giulio, cardinal	Brassart, Madrigali a 4, Bk. 1	1564	Barré
	Lupino, Motetti 4 vv, Bk. 1	1549	Gardano
	Porta, Motetti 6 vv, Bk. 1	1571	Gardano
Della Rovere, Guidobaldo, duke of Urbino	Ferabosco, Madrigali a 4, Bk. 1	1542	Gardano
	Porta, Motetti 4 vv, Bk. 1	1559	Gardano
	Rosso, Madrigali a 4, Bk. 1	1567	Merulo
Dietrichstein, Moritz II von	Gorzanis, Intabulatura di lauto, Bk. 2	1563	Scotto
Doria, Giacomo	Motetti del Frutto a 6, Bk. 1	1539	Gardano
	Canzone francese a 2	1539	Gardano
Dorimbergo, Vito di	Balbi, Madrigali a 4, Bk. 1	1570	Gardano
	Gli amorosi concenti, Madrigali a 4, Bk. 1	1568	Scotto
Dotto, Daulo, dal Gigante	Pordenon, Madrigali a 5, Bk. 1	1564	Gardano
Durandi, Carlo	Antegnati, Madrigali a 4, Bk. 1	1571	Gardano
Erbere, Arrigo	Perissone Cambio, Canz. napolitane a 4	1545	Gardano
Este, Alfonso II d', duke of Ferrara	Corfini, Motetti 5–8 vv, Bk. 1	1571	Scotto
	Berchem, Capriccio a 4 , Bk. 1– 3	1561	Gardano
	Willaert, Musica Nova	1559	Gardano
	Lasso, Madrigali a 5, Bk. 4	1567	Gardano
	Manara, Madrigali a 4, Bk. 1	1555	Gardano
	Fiesco, Madrigali a 4, Bk. 1	1554	Gardano
Este, Ercole II d', duke of Ferrara	Castellino, Villotte a 4, Bk. 1	1541	Gardano
Este, Ippolito d', cardinal	Palestrina, Motetti 5–7 vv, Bk. 1	1569	Dorico
	Rosello, Madrigali a 5, Bk. 1	1563	Dorico
Este, Laura d'	Bertoldo, Madrigali a 4, Bk. 1	1544	Gardano
Este, Leonora d'	F. Dalla Viola, Madrigali a 4, Bk. 1	1550	Gardano
Este, Lucretia d'	Fiesco, Madrigali a 5, Bk. 2	1567	Merulo
	Vespa, Madrigali a 5, Bk. 1	1570	Gardano
Este, Lucretia and Leonora d'	Fiesco, Musica Nova a 5, Bk. 1	1569	Gardano
Este, Luigi d', cardinal	Portinaro, Motetti 6–8 vv, Bk. 2	1568	Gardano
	Bertoldo, Madrigali a 5, Bk. 2	1562	Gardano
Este, [Renée of France], duchess of Ferrara	Buus, Canzoni francese a 6, Bk. 1	1543	Gardano
Fano, Canons and Convent of	Garugli, Motetti 5 vv, Bk. 1	1562	Scotto
Fantuzzi, Carlo Antonio	Lupacchino, Madrigali a 5, Bk. 1	1547	Gardano
Farnese, [Alessandro], cardinal	Corvo, Motetti 5 vv, Bk. 1	1555	Gardano
Farnese, Margherita, duchess of Parma	Alcarotti, Madrigali a 5–6, Bk. 2	1569	Gardano
Farnese, Ottavio, duke of Parma	Renaldi, Madrigali a 4–6, Bk. 1	1569	Scotto
	Wert, Madrigali a 5, Bk. 2	1561	Scotto
	Vinci, Madrigali a 6, Bk. 1	1571	Scotto
	Merulo, Madrigali a 5, Bk. 1	1566	Merulo
	Massaini, Madrigali a 5, Bk. 1	1571	Gardano
	Wert, Madrigali a 5, Bk. 2	1564	Gardano
	Renaldi, Madrigali a 4, Bk. 1	1569	Gardano
Farnese, Ranuccio. *See* Sant'Angelo, cardinal of			
Fenarolo, Girolamo	Barges, Villotte a 4, Bk. 1	1550	Gardano
Ferdinand, archduke of Austria	Buus, Canzoni francese a 5, Bk. 1	1550	Scotto
	Casentini, Madrigali a 5, Bk. 1	1572	Gardano
Feria, Baldasar	Rore, Motetti 5 vv	1545	Gardano
Fernandez di Cordova, Consalvo	Wert, Madrigali a 5, Bk. 3	1563	Gardano
Fernando, Garcia	Arpa, Todino, etc., Canz. nap. a 3, Bk. 1	1566	Scotto
Ferrero, Pierfrancesco, bishop of Vercelli	Lasso, Libro delle Muse, Madrigali a 5, Bk. 2	1557	Barré

DEDICATEE	TITLE	YEAR	PRINTER
Ferrier, Dum	Arpa, Todino, Nola., Canzoni napolitane a 3, Bk. 2	1566	Scotto
Ferro, Giovanni, count of Macerata	Adriani, Madrigali a 6, Bk. 1	1568	Scotto
	Donato, Madrigali a 4, Bk. 2	1568	Scotto
	Corona della morte a 5	1568	Scotto
	Striggio, Il cicalamento a 5	1567	Scotto
	Ferretti, Canzoni napolitane a 5, Bk. 2	1569	Scotto
Foggia, Cesare, bishop of Umbriatico	Melfio, Madrigali a 4, Bk. 1	1556	Scotto
Fontani, Giovanni Filippo	Essenga, Madrigali a 4, Bk. 1	1566	Gardano
Fontego de' Tedeschi, merchants of	Bianchini, Intabolatura di leuto, Bk. 1	1546	Gardano
Foppa, Cesare	Villanova, Canzoni napolitane a 3, Bk. 2	1568	Pozzo
Fornari, Cristoforo	Hoste da Reggio, Madrigali a 4, Bk. 3	1554	Scotto
Forno, Annibale del	Le vive fiamme a 5, Bk. 1	1565	Scotto
Gadda delli Elefantuzzi, Camillo	Dattari,Canzoni napolitane a 4	1563	Moscheni
Gaddi, Cav.	Rosselli, Madrigali a 4, Bk. 1	1565	Dorico
Galerato, Lodovico, count	Caimo, Madrigali a 4, Bk. 1	1564	Moscheni
Gallio, Tolomeo, Archbishop of Sipontino	Zoilo, Madrigali a 4-5, Bk. 2	1563	Blado
Gallo, Sulpitio	Matelart, Intavolatura di lauto	1559	Dorico
Gambacorti, Mario	Giglio, Motetti 4 vv, Bk. 1	1563	Gardano
Gattinario, Antonio, count of Castro	Ghibel, Motetti 5 vv, Bk. 1	1546	Scotto
	Ghibel, Motetti 5 vv, Bk. 1	1548	Scotto
Giacobilli, Giulio	Adriani, Madrigali a 5, Bk. 1	1570	Scotto
Girolamo, Prevosto de la Scala	Ragazzoni, Madrigali a 4	1544	Scotto
Giulij, Gioan Francesco de	Justiniane a 3, Bk. 1	1570	Scotto
Giustiniani, Gios.	Rossetto, Madrigali a 5, Bk. 1	1560	Gardano
Gonzaga, Alfonso, count of Novellara	Carli, Madrigali a 5, Bk. 1	1567	Gardano
	Wert, Madrigali a 5, Bk. 1	1558	Scotto
	Wert, Madrigali a 5, Bk. 1	1564	Gardano
Gonzaga, Cesare, duke of Ariano, prince of Molfetta	Boyleau, Madrigali a 4–8	1564	Moscheni
	Chamaterò, Madrigali a 5, Bk. 4	1569	Scotto
	Rufilo, Madrigali a 5, Bk. 1	1561	Scotto
Gonzaga, Ercole, cardinal	Clerico, Madrigali a 5, Bk. 1	1562	Scotto
	Clerico, Madrigali a 5, Bk. 2	1562	Scotto
	Jacquet, Motetti 5 vv, Bk. 1	1539	Scotto
	Jacquet, Motetti 4 vv, Bk. 1	1539	Scotto
	Hoste da Reggio, Madrigali a 4, Bk. 1	1547	Gardano
	Portinaro, Motetti 5 vv, Bk. 1	1548	Gardano
Gonzaga, Ferrando	Hoste da Reggio, Madrigali a 5, Bk. 1	1554	Scotto
Gonzaga, Guglielmo, duke of Mantua	Baccusi, Madrigali a 5–6, Bk. 1	1570	Gardano
	Coma, Madrigali a 5, Bk. 1	1568	Gardano
	Faa, Madrigali a 5, Bk. 1	1569	Gardano
	Isnardi, Madrigali a 5, Bk. 1	1568	Gardano
	Palestrina, Motetti 5–8 vv, Bk. 2	1572	Scotto
	Wert, Motetti 5 vv, Bk. 1	1566	Merulo
	Wert, Madrigali a 4, Bk. 5	1567	Gardano
Gonzaga, Isabella	Hoste da Reggio, Madrigali a 4, Bk. 2	1554	Scotto
Gonzaga, Lucrezia	G. M. Bonardo, Madrigali a 3, Bk. 1	1563	Farri
Gonzaga, Luigi	Fiesco, Madrigali a 4–8, Bk. 1	1563	Scotto
Gonzaga, Scipione	Portinaro, Madrigali a 4, Bk. 1	1563	Scotto
Gonzaga, Vincenzo, duke of Mantua	Faa, Madrigali a 5–6, Bk. 2	1571	Gardano
Gonzaga, Vincenzo, prior of Barileta	Riccio, Madrigali a 6, Bk. 1	1567	Gardano
	Primavera, Madrigali a 5, Bk. 3	1566	Rampazetto
Grandonio, Davit. *See* Milano			

DEDICATEE	TITLE	YEAR	PRINTER
Grandonio, Gioseffe, and Camillo Trivisano	Vidue, Striggio, Madrigali a 5–6, Bk.1	1566	Rampazetto
Grassi, Giuseppe	Converso, Canzoni a 5, Bk. 1	1572	Scotto
Grimaldi, Luca	Ruffo, Motetti 6 vv	1555	Scotto
	Ruffo, Madrigali a 5, Scielta 2	1554	Scotto
Grimani, Alvise. *See* Milano			
Grisone, Antonio	Mazzone, Madrigali a 4, Bk. 1	1569	Scotto
Grossi, Battista Giovanni de, bishop of Reggio	Carli, Motetti del Laberinto 5 vv, Bk. 1	1554	Scotto
Guarna, Benedetto	Licino, Duo cromatici, Bk. 2	1546	Gardano
Guevara, Alfonso, count of Potenza	Melfio, Madrigali a 4, Bk. 1	1564	Dorico
Guidobono, Francesco	Lasso, Villanelle a 3, Bk. 2	1555	Dorico
Guise, cardinal de	Lasso, Madrigali a 4, Bk. 1	1560	Dorico
Hanna, Paolo di	Buus, Intabolatura d'organo, Bk. 1	1549	Scotto
Ingrignetta, Ferrante	Menta, Madrigali a 4, Bk. 1	1560	Barré
Isolani, Giovanni Francesco, count	Azzaiolo, Villotte a 4, Bk. 3	1569	Gardano
Johannes Jacopo, archbishop of Salzburg	Lasso, Missae 4–5 vv, Bk. 2	1570	Merulo
Iulius III, pope	Palestrina, Missae 1–5 vv, Bk. 1	1554	Dorico
Kiesel, Giorgio, di Kaltenbrunn	Gorzanis, Napolitane in Leuto, Bk. 1	1570	Scotto
	Gorzanis, Intabolatura di lauto, Bk. 1	1561	Gardano
La Martoretta, Giandomenico	La Martoretta, Madri. a 4, Bk. 2	1552	Gardano
Lando, Francesco	Bertoldo, Madrigali a 5, Bk. 1	1561	Gardano
Langnauer, Giovanni	Neusidler, Intabolatura di lauto, Bk. 1	1566	Gardano
Lazzarini, Benedetto de	Ferretti, Canzone napolitane a 5	1567	Scotto
Lecalsi, Nicolano, Joanni Merullo, Francesco Joannis, Joanni Antonio Politio, Antonio Gotho, jurists of Messina	Ghibel, Introits, Bk. 1	1565	Dorico
Leggerini. *See* Bianchini			
Leze, Andrea de	Arcadelt, Madrigali a 4, Bk. 5	1544	Gardano
Lezze, Giovanni da	Boyleau, Motetti 4 vv	1544	Scotto
	Padovano, Ricercari a 4, Bk. 1	1556	Gardano
Linck, Melchior	Neusidler, Intabolatura di lauto, Bk. 2	1566	Gardano
Locatello, Eustachio, bishop of Reggio	Pratoneri, Harmonia Psalmos 6 vv	1569	Scotto
Locatello, Roberto	Ghibel, Madrigali a 4, Bk. 1	1554	Scotto
Lonata, Laura Ruscha	Boyleau, Madrigali a 4, Bk. 2	1558	Moscheni & Pozzo
Londonio, Antonio	Vinci, Madrigali a 5, Bk. 3	1571	Scotto
	Contino, Missae 5 vv, Bk. 1	1572	Pozzo
	Casulana, Madrigali a 4, Bk. 2	1570	Scotto
Lucchis, Vincentio, bishop of Ancona	Lasso, Motetti 5–8 vv, Bk. 5	1568	Merulo
Madruzzo, Cristoforo, cardinal	Gintzler, Intabolatura di lauto, Bk. 1	1547	Gardano
	Contino, Motetti 5 vv, Bk. 1	1560	Scotto
	Contino, Missae 4 vv, Bk. 1	1561	Scotto
Madruzzo, Cristoforo, cardinal, choir of	Motetti del Laberinto 4 vv, Bk. 2	1554	Scotto
	Motetti del Laberinto 4 vv, Bk. 3	1554	Scotto
	Motetti del Laberinto 5 vv, Bk. 4	1554	Scotto
Maffetti, Ventura	Adriani, Madrigali a 5, Bk. 2	1570	Scotto
Malaspina, Lepido, abbot	Ruffo, Madrigali a 4, Bk. 2	1555	Gardano
Mandosio, Orazio	Stabile, Madrigali a 5, Bk. 1	1572	Gardano
Manrique, Giovanni	Cottone, Madrigali a 5, Bk. 1	1572	Scotto
	Troiano, Canzoni napolitane a 3, Bk. 4	1569	Scotto
Mantova, Marco da	Barberiis, Intabolatura di lauto, Bk. 6	1546	Scotto
Marchesi, Francesco Maria della	Primavera, Canzoni napolit. a 3, Bk. 2	1566	Merulo

DEDICATEE	TITLE	YEAR	PRINTER
Marini, Giovanbattista	Della Faya, Madrigali a 5, Bk. 1	1564	Rampazetto
Mario, Giuliano de	Burno, Elletione de canzone a 3	1546	Fabriano & Bindoni
Marra, Giovanni de la	Nola, Villanelle a 3–4, Bk. 1	1567	Merulo
Marsigli, Marc'Antonio Colonna	Micheli, Madrigali a 5, Bk. 1	1564	Gardano
Martinengo, Marc'Antonio de	Merulo, Ricercari Intavolatura, Bk. 1	1567	Merulo
Villachiara	Ruffo, Capricci a 3	1564	Moscheni
Marzato, Andrea	Berchem, Madrigali a 4, Bk. 1	1555	Scotto
Maximilian II, Emperor	Portinaro Le Vergini a 6	1568	Scotto
	Portinaro Le Vergini a 6, Bk. 5	1569	Gardano
	Fleccia, Madrigali a 4–5, Bk. 1	1568	Gardano
	Monte, Motetti 5 vv, Bk. 1	1572	Scotto
	Monte, Madrigali a 5, Bk. 4	1571	Scotto
	Monte, Madrigali a 6, Bk. 2	1569	Scotto
	Ingegneri, Madrigali a 5, Bk. 2	1572	Gardano
Medici, Alessandro de'	Willaert, Missae 4 vv, Bk. 1	1536	Marcolini
	Galilei, Intavolatura, Bk. 1	1563	Dorico
Medici, Cosimo I de', duke of	Corteccia, Madrigali a 4, Bk. 1	1544	Scotto
Tuscany	Corteccia, Madrigali a 4, Bk. 1	1547	Gardano
	Corteccia, Madrigali a 5, Bk. 1	1547	Gardano
	Corteccia, Madrigali a 4, Bk. 2	1547	Gardano
	Corteccia, Responsoria, Bk. 1	1570	Gardano
	Corteccia, Responsoria, Bk. 2	1570	Gardano
	Morales, Missae 4–6 vv, Bk. 1	1544	Dorico
Medici, Fernando de', cardinal	Palestrina, Motetti 4 vv, Bk. 1	1571	Gardano
	Pesciolini, Madrigali a 6, Bk. 2	1571	Gardano
Medici, Francesco de'	Aretino, Madrigali a 5–8	1558	Scotto
Medici, Giulio de'	Corfini, Madrigali a 5, Bk. 2	1568	Gardano
Melchiori, Pietro	Bianco, Canzoni napolitane a 3, Bk. 1	1572	Scotto
Melchiorri, Marcello	Ferretti, Napolitane a 5, Bk. 3	1570	Scotto
Merulo, Claudio. *See* Vergelli			
Milano, Marco; Davit Grandonio;	Bonagiunta, Canzoni napolitane a 3,	1566	Scotto
and Alvise Grimani	Bk. 2		
Minerbetti, Bernardetto, bishop of	Aretino, Responsoria 4 vv	1544	Scotto
Arezzo	Aretino, Responsoria 4 vv, Bk. 1 & 2	1564	Rampazetto
Miranda, Aloysio, abbot	Lasso, Rore, Motetti 4 vv, Bk. 1	1563	Rampazetto
Mocenigo, Filippo. *See* Candia			
Modena, Antonio	Montagnana, Canzone & madrigali a 4,	1558	Scotto
	Bk. 1		
Mola, Francesco della	Libro delle Muse, Canzoni moresche	1555	Barré
	a 3, Bk. 2		
Molino, Antonio	Gabrieli, Madrigali a 5, Bk. 2	1570	Gardano
	Monte, Madrigali a 5, Bk. 3	1570	Scotto
Molino, Luigi, canon	Renaldi, Madrigali a 4–6, Bk. 1	1567	Gardano
Monadeschi della Cervara, Luca	Kerle, Hymns 4 vv	1558	Barré
Monadeschi della Cervara,	Libro delle Muse, Madrigali a 4, Bk. 2	1557	Barré
Monaldo	Lasso, Libro delle Muse, Madrigali a 5,		
	Bk. 3	1563	Barré
	Tortora, Madrigali a 5–6, Bk. 1	1570	Scotto
Moncada, Francesco, count of	La Martoretta, Madrigali a 4	1548	Scotto
Calataniscetta			
Moncada, Giulia, marchioness of	Cataldo, Tutti i principii de' canti	1559	Scotto
Pietroprezia	dell'Ariosto a 4		
Montalto d'Aragona, Antonio	Vinci, Madrigali a 5, Bk. 1	1561	Scotto
Montilio, Carlo	Calitano, Canzoni napolitane a 3, Bk. 1	1567	Scotto
Morone, Giovanni, cardinal	Varoto, Missae 6 vv, Bk. 1	1563	Scotto
Nero, Giovanni Nicolo de'	Animuccia, Madrigali a 4–6, Bk. 1	1547	Gardano
Nero, Marco and Piero de'	Animuccia, Madrigali a 3, Bk. 1	1565	Dorico

Dedicatee	Title	Year	Printer
Neroni, Alessandro	Mauro, Madrigali a 5, Bk. 1	1571	Gardano
Noia, Carlo della	Menta, Madrigali a 5, Bk. 1	1564	Gardano
Noia, Orazio della	Fiorino, La nobiltà di Roma a 3	1571	Scotto
Noia, Pompeo della	Sessa d'Aranda, Madrigali a 4, Bk. 1	1571	Gardano
Occagna, Gottardo	Perissone Cambio, Madrigali a 5	1545	Scotto
	Novello Mascherate a 4, Bk. 4	1546	Gardano
	Rore, Madrigali a 5, Bk. 3	1548	Scotto
Orio, Girolamo	Gabrieli, Greghesche a 3, Bk. 1	1571	Gardano
Orsina, Isabella de' Medici	Casulana, Madrigali a 4, Bk. 1	1568	Scotto
	Rossetto, Lamento di Olimpia	1567	Scotto
	Rossetto, Madrigali a 6, Bk. 1	1566	Merulo
	Rossetto, Musica Nova a 5	1566	Dorico
Orsini, Leone, bishop of Fréjus	Arcadelt, Madrigali a 4, Bk. 1	1539	Gardano
	Arcadelt, Madrigali a 4, Bk. 1	1541	Gardano
	Venticinque canz. francese a 4	1538	Gardano
Orsino, Flavio, cardinal	Tastavin, Madrigali a 5, Bk. 1	1569	Gardano
Orsino, Ludovico	Micheli, Madrigali a 5, Bk. 4	1569	Gardano
Orsino, Paolo, duke of Bracciano	Giacomini, Madrigali a 5, Bk. 1	1563	Gardano
Ottobono, Gabrielle	Bonagiunta,Canzoni napol a 3 Bk 1	1565	Scotto
Padua, canons of	Porta, Introitus Sanctorum 5 vv	1566	Merulo
Palavicino, Francesco	Buus, Motetti 4 vv, Bk. 1	1549	Gardano
	Motetti del Frutto 5 vv, Bk.. 1	1538	Gardano
Palavicino, Lodovico, Marchese	Perego, Madrigali a 4	1555	Scotto
Pampuro, Andrea, abbot	Paolo Ferrarese, Passiones 4 vv	1565	Scotto
Parthi, Stefano	Libro delle Muse, Madrigali a 5, Bk. 3	1561	Gardano
Paruta, Domenico, abbot	A. Gabrieli, Madrigali a 5, Bk. 1	1572	Gardano
	Lasso, Motetti 5 vv, Bk. 1	1565	Scotto
Passero, Marcantonio	Barberiis, Intabulatura di lauto, Bk. 5	1546	Scotto
Paul III, pope	Morales, Missae 4–5 vv, Bk. 2	1544	Dorico
Penitesi. *See* Bonvisi			
Pepoli, Giulio, count	Dattari, Le villanelle a 3–5	1568	Scotto
Pesaro, Francesco	Molino, Madrigali a 4, Bk. 2	1569	Gardano
Petra, Girolamo	Schaffen, Madrigali a 4	1549	Scotto
Philip II, king of Spain	Palestrina, Missae 4–6 vv, Bk. 2	1567	Dorico
	Palestrina, Missae 4–6 vv, Bk. 3	1570	Dorico
Piccolomini, Indico d'Aragona, duke of Amalfi, marquis of Capistrano,count of Celano	Libro delle Muse, Madrigali a 4, Bk. 3	1563	Rampazetto
Pierfrancesco, majordomo of duke of Tuscany	Dorati, Madrigali a 5, Bk. 1	1549	Gardano
Pignatello, Camillo	Monte, Madrigali a 4, Bk. 2	1569	Scotto
Pignatta, Gasparo	I Dolci frutti, Madrigali a 5, Bk. 1	1570	Scotto
	Il Turturino, Napolitane in lauto, Bk. 1	1570	Scotto
Pinello, Galeatio	Ciccarelli, Motetti 5 vv	1568	Scotto
Pio, Rudolfo, cardinal	Palestrina, Motetti 4 vv, Bk. 1	1563	Dorico
Pisani, Francesco, cardinal	Barberiis, Intabulatura di lauto, Bk. 4	1546	Scotto
Pius V, pope	Guerrero, Motetti 5 vv, Bk. 1	1570	Gardano
Podocattaro, Abbate	Animuccia, G., Laudi spirituale, Bk. 2	1570	Blado
Poggi, Cristoforo	Ferretti, Napolitane a 5, Bk. 4	1571	Scotto
Quaini, Girolamo	Policreto, Napolitane a 3, Bk. 1	1571	Scotto
Ramuino, Alessandro	Abondante, Intabolatura di lauto, Bk. 2	1548	Scotto
Rangona, Giulia Orsina	Massaino, Madrigali a 4, Bk. 1	1569	Gardano
Ravasciero, Gian Girolamo	Nola, Madrigali a 4	1545	Scotto
Ravenna, cardinal of	G. Cavazzoni, Intabulatura d'organo, Bk. 2	154?	unsigned
Renée of France. *See* Este			

DEDICATEE	TITLE	YEAR	PRINTER
Ribera, Perafan, duke of Alcalá	Ortiz, Hymni, Bk. 1	1565	Gardano
Ricci, Suor Caterina	Razzi, Laudi spirituali, Bk. 1	1563	Rampazetto
Ricci, Provost Pierfrancesco	Pesciolini, Madrigali a 5–6, Bk. 1	1563	Scotto
Romeo, Cesare	Ruffo, Madrigali a 4, Bk. 3	1560	Gardano
Roncalli, Domenego	Perissone Cambio, Madr. a 5, 7, 8, Bk. 2	1550	Gardano
Ronchale, Antonio	Il Desiderio, Madrigali a 4, Bk. 1	1567	Scotto
Rossi, bishop of	A. Romano, Le Vergini a 4	1554	Scotto
Rossi, Federico, abbot	Chamaterò, Madrigali a 5, Bk. 2	1569	Scotto
Roverelli, Girolamo, count	Agostini, Madrigali a 4, Bk. 2	1572	Gardano
Ruggiero, count of Callepio	Bifetto, Madrigali a 4, Bk. 1	1547	Gardano
	Bifetto, Madrigali a 4, Bk. 2	1548	Gardano
Ruini, Carlo, Lelio, and Lucio	Lambertini, Madrigali a 4, Bk. 1	1560	Gardano
Sagramosi, Orazio	Ruffo, Armonia celeste a 5, Bk. 4	1556	Gardano
Salernitano, Tomaso	Mazzone, Madrigali a 5, Bk. 1	1569	Scotto
Salviati, Genevra	Libro delle Fiamme, Madrigali a 5, Bk. 3	1568	Scotto
Saminiati, Gigli and Benedetto	Caussin, Motetti 5 vv	1548	Gardano
San Bonifazio, Ercole da	Barberiis, Intabolatura, Bk. 10	1549	Scotto
San Marco, Procuratori of	Zarlino, Motetti 6 vv	1566	Rampazetto
San Salvatore, Prior of	Jacquet, Orationes complures 4 vv	1567	Scotto
Sanseverina, Barbara, countess of Sala	Chamaterò, Madrigali a 4, Bk. 2	1569	Scotto
Sanseverino, Francesco, count of Colorno	Bonizzoni, Canzoni a 4, Bk. 1	1569	Scotto
Sanseverino, Pietro Antonio, prince of Bisignano	Gero, Motetti 5 vv, Bk. 1	1555	Scotto
Santa Pau, Francesco	Vinci, Musica a 2, Bk. 1	1560	Scotto
Santa Pau, Francesco and Imara	Vinci, Motetti 5 vv, Bk. 1	1558	Scotto
Sant'Angelo, cardinal of (Ranuccio Farnese)	Donato, Madrigali a 5–6, Bk. 1	1553	Gardano
Sanvitali, Giberto, count of Sala	Chamaterò, Madrigali a 5, Bk. 1	1560	Gardano
Saraceno, Ambrosio	Madrigali misura breve a 4, Bk. 1	1542	Gardano
Saraceno, Carlo	Madrigali de diversi a 5, Bk. 1	1542	Gardano
Saraceno, (Giovanni Michele), cardinal	Volpe, Madrigali a 4, Bk. 1	1555	Scotto
Saravalli, Giovanni	Mazzoni, Canzoni napolitane a 3, Bk. 2	1570	Scotto
Savorgnano, Giacobo	Candonio, Madrigali a 4, Bk. 1	1546	Gardano
Savorgnano, Girolamo, bishop of Šibenik	Schiavetto, Madrigali a 4–5	1563	Scotto
	Schiavetto, Motetti 5–6 vv	1564	Scotto
Schleinitz, Joannes Hugoldo	Barbetta, Intavolatura di lauto, Bk. 1	1569	Scotto
Scotto, Honorio, count	Balletti, Intabolatura, Bk. 1	1554	Gardano
Sermoneta, (Nicolaus Caietanus), cardinal	Conforti, Ricercari a 4, Bk. 1	1558	Dorico
Sertori, Giovanni	Pordenon, Madrigali a 5, Bk. 3	1571	Gardano
Sforza, Guido Ascanio	Animuccia, Laudi 4 vv, Bk. 1	1563	Dorico
Sigismund August, king of Poland	Rodio, Missae 4–6 vv, Bk. 1	1562	Dorico
Signori Fiamenghi	Duc, Madrigali a 4, Bk. 1	1570	Scotto
Singlitico, Piero	La Martoretta, Madrigali a 4, Bk. 3	1554	Gardano
Sinibaldi, Alessando	Porta, Madrigali a 4, Bk. 1	1555	Gardano
Spinola, Antonio	Essenga, Madrigali a 5, Bk. 2	1561	Gardano
Spinola, Giovan Battista	Donato, Canzone & madrigali a 4	1550	Scotto
Stampa, Gaspara	Perissone Cambio, Madrigali a 4, Bk. 1	1547	Gardano
Steinhussen, Jacob Pinsonio	Testori, Madrigali a 5, Bk. 1	1566	Merulo
Stellini, Don Pellegrino	Verdelot, Madr. a 4, Bks.1–2	1566	Merulo
Superchio, Girolamo	El Conte, Motetti 5 vv	1547	Gardano
Thosco, Roberto	Libro delle Muse, Madrigali a 5, Bk. 2	1559	Gardano
Tiene, Leonora	Pinello, Canzoni napolitane a 3, Bk. 2	1571	Scotto

DEDICATEE	TITLE	YEAR	PRINTER
Tiene, Theodoro, count	Pinello, Canzoni napolitane a 3, Bk. 3	1572	Scotto
Torniello, Romagnolo	Alcarotto, Madrigali a 5–6, Bk. 1	1567	Gardano
Torre, Giovanni Battista della	Ruffo, Madrigali a 5, Bk. 1	1553	Gardano
Torre, Guido della, count	Primavera, Canz. napolitane a 4, Bk. 1	1569	Scotto
	Roccia, Madrigali a 4, Bk. 1	1571	Angelieri
Tradel, Ridolfo	Candido, Mascherate a 3– 5	1571	Scotto
Trevisano, Marco	Willaert, Motetti 6 vv, Bk. 1	1542	Gardano
Trivisano, Camillo. *See* Grandonio			
Trivultio, Catelano, bishop of Piacenza	Doni, Dialogo della musica	1544	Scotto
Trivultio, Giovangiacomo	Chamaterò, Madrigali a 4, Bk. 1	1561	Gardano
Trivultio, Giovangiacomo, marquis of Vigevano	Tudino, Madrigali a 4	1554	Scotto
Trivultio, Giovanni, count	Martinengo, Madrigali a 4, Bk. 2	1548	Scotto
Trono, Michel	Il Desiderio, Madrigali a 4, Bk. 1	1566	Scotto
Truchsess, Otto, cardinal	Contino, Motetti 5 vv, Bk. 2	1560	Scotto
	Lambertini, Septem Psalmi 4 vv	1569	Scotto
	Victoria, Motetti 4–8 vv, Bk. 1	1572	Gardano
Urries Pedro d'	Ortiz, Trattado de Glossa	1553	Dorico
Uttinger, Hieronimo	Buus, Ricercari a 4, Bk. 1	1547	Gardano
	Buus, Ricercari a 4, Bk. 2	1549	Gardano
	Rore, Motetti 5 vv, Bk. 1	1544	Gardano
Valiero, Zacharia	Magiello, Madrigali a 5, Bk. 2	1568	Gardano
Varana, Virginia Feltrin	Porta, Madrigali a 5, Bk. 1	1559	Gardano
Vatican Basilica, canons of	Animuccia, Missae 4–6 vv, Bk. 1	1567	Dorico
Verallo, Girolamo, papal legate	Arcadelt, Madrigali a 4, Bk. 3	1539	Scotto
Vergelli, Paolo, Claudio Merulo, and Francesco Bonaldi	Blessi [Molino], Greghesche a 4–8, Bk. 1	1564	Gardano
Vida, Girolamo, bishop of Alba	Ragazzo, Madrigali a 4, Bk. 1	1564	Scotto
Vigili, Honofrio	Animuccia, Madrigali a 5	1554	Dorico
	Monte, Madrigali a 5, Bk. 1	1554	Dorico
	Libro delle Muse, Madrigali a 5, Bk. 1	1555	Barré
Villabruna, Antonio	Libro delle Fiamme, Madrigali a 5–6, Bk. 2	1567	Scotto
	Zappasorgo, Napolitane a 3, Bk. 1	1571	Scotto
Visconti, Battista	Intabulatura di lauto	1536	Castiglione
Visconti, Cesare	Gero, Madrigali et canzone francese a 2, Bk. 1	1541	Gardano
Visconti, Giovanbattista	Vindella, Intavolatura di lauto, Bk. 1	1546	Gardano
Visconti, Paulo and Prospero	Bellavere, Madrigali a 5, Bk. 1	1567	Gardano
	Caimo, Canzoni napolitane a 3, Bk. 1	1566	Porro
Wilhelm II, duke of Bavaria	Galilei, Fronimo Dialogo	1568	Scotto
Zamberti, Alessandro	Werrecore, La bataglia a 4	1549	Gardano
Zampesco, Brunoro	Primavera, Madrigali a 5–6, Bk. 1 & 2	1565	Scotto
Zantani, Antonio	La eletta di tutta la musica, Bk. 1	1569	Zorzi/ Zantani
Zerbinati, Tomaso	Agostini, Madrigali a 5, Bk. 1	1570	Gardano
Zino, Francesco, canon	Asola, Introits a 4	1565	Rampazetto
Zuccello, Andrea	Nasco, Madrigali a 5, Bk. 2	1557	Gardano

BIBLIOGRAPHY

Adams, Herbert Mayrow, ed. *Catalogue of Books Printed on the Continent of Europe 1501–1600 in Cambridge Libraries.* 2 vols. Cambridge, 1967.

Agee, Richard J. "Filippo Strozzi and the Early Madrigal." *JAMS* 38 (1985): 227–37.

———. *The Gardano Music Printing Firms, 1569–1611.* Rochester, N.Y., 1998.

———. "The Privilege and Venetian Music Printing in the Sixteenth Century." Ph.D. diss., Princeton University, 1982.

———. "Ruberto Strozzi and the Early Madrigal." *JAMS* 36 (1983): 1–17.

———. "A Venetian Music Printing Contract in the Sixteenth Century." *Studi musicali* 15 (1986): 59–65.

———. "The Venetian Privilege and Music-Printing in the Sixteenth Century." *Early Music History* 3 (1983): 1–42.

———, and Jessie Ann Owens. "La stampa della 'Musica nova' di Willaert." *Rivista italiana di musicologia* 24 (1989): 219–305.

Albrecht, Otto E. "Collections.'" *New Grove* 4: 541.

Amati-Camperi, Alexandra. "An Italian Genre in the Hands of a Frenchman: Philippe Verdelot as Madrigalist, with Special Emphasis on the Six-Voice Pieces." Ph.D. diss., Harvard University, 1994.

Amram, David W. *The Makers of Hebrew Books in Italy. Being Chapters in the History of the Hebrew Printing Press.* Philadelphia, 1909.

Anglés, Higinio. "El Archivo musical de la Catedral de Valladolid." *Anuario musical* 3 (1948): 59–108.

Annibaldi, Claudio. "Il mecenate 'politico': ancora sul patronato musicale del cardinale Pietro Aldobrandini (1571–1621)." *Studi musicali* 16 (1987): 33–93, and 17 (1988): 101–78.

———, ed. *La musica e il mondo: mecenatismo e committenza musicale in Italia tra Quattro e Settecento.* Bologna, 1993.

Aquilecchia, Giovanni. "Pietro Aretino e altri poligrafi a Venezia." In *Storia della Cultura Veneta.* Vol. 3, Part 2: *Dal primo Quattrocento al Concilio di Trento*, edited by Girolamo Araldi and Manlio Pastore Stocchi, 61–98, Vicenza, 1980.

Arcadelt, Jacobus. *Opera omnia.* Edited by Albert Seay. CMM 31. AIM, 1965–70.

Aretino, Pietro. *Del secondo libro de le lettere di M. Pietro Aretino.* Paris, 1609.

———. *The Letters of Pietro Aretino.* Edited by Thomas C. Chubb. New York, 1940; reprint, Hamden, Conn., 1967.

Argellati, Filippo. *Bibliotheca scriptorum Mediolanensium.* 2 vols. in 4. Milan, 1745.

Armstrong, Elizabeth. *Robert Estienne, Royal Printer*. Cambridge, 1954.

Ascarelli, Fernanda, and Marco Menato. *La tipografia del '500 in Italia*. Florence, 1989.

Balsamo, Luigi, and Alberto Tinto. *Origini del corsivo nella tipografia italiana nel Cinquecento*. Milan, 1967.

Barachetti, Gianni, and Carmen Palamini. *La stampa a Bergamo nel Cinquecento*. Bergamo, 1989.

Benjamin, Walter. "The Work of Art in the Age of Mechanical Reproduction." In *Illuminations*, edited by Hannah Arendt, 217–51. New York, 1970.

Bernstein, Jane A. "The Burning Salamander: Assigning a Printer to Some Sixteenth-Century Music Prints." *Music Library Association Notes* 42 (1985/86): 483–501.

———. "Buyers and Collectors of Music Publications: Two Sixteenth-Century Music Libraries Recovered." In *Music in Renaissance Cities and Courts: Studies in Honor of Lewis Lockwood*, edited by Jessie Ann Owens and Anthony Cummings, 21–34. Warren, Mich., 1997.

———. "Financial Arrangements and the Role of Printer and Composer in Sixteenth-Century Italian Music Printing." *Acta musicologica* 62 (1990): 39–56.

———. "Girolamo Scotto and the Venetian Music Trade." In *Atti del XIV congresso della Società Internazionale di Musicologia, Bologna, 27 agosto-1 settembre 1987*, edited by A. Pompilio, D. Restani, L. Bianconi, and F. A. Gallo, 1: 295–305. Turin, 1990.

———. "Lassus in English Sources: Two Chansons Recovered." *JAMS* 27 (1974): 315–25.

———. "Printing and Patronage in Sixteenth-Century Italy." In *Actas del XV congreso de la Sociedad Internacional de Musicología: "Culturas Musicales del Mediterraneo y sus Ramificaciones,"* Madrid, 3-10/IV/1992, 5: 2603–13. Madrid, 1993.

———. "The Publication of Palestrina's Music in Sixteenth-Century Rome and Venice." In *Atti del convegno di studi palestriniani: 6–9 ottobre 1994*. Rome, in press.

———. "Scotto, Girolamo and Ottaviano." In *Music Printing and Publishing*, 420–22.

———, ed., *Adrian Le Roy, Premier livre de chansons en forme de vau de ville (1573), Nicolas de la Grotte,Chansons de P. de Ronsard, Ph. Desporte, et autres (1580), Premier livre de chansons à deux parties (1578), Chansons by Antonio Gardane Published by LeRoy and Ballard*. Sixteenth-Century Chanson 15. New York and London, 1992.

———, ed. *Pierre Santerre, Alessandro Striggio, Touteau, Philippe Verdelot, Johnnes Verius, Antoine de Villiers, Chansons Published by LeRoy and Ballard*. Sixteenth-Century Chanson 22. New York and London, 1991.

Bernstein, Lawrence F. "The Bibliography of Music in Conrad Gesner's *Pandectae* (1548)." *Acta musicologica* 45 (1973): 119–63.

———. "*La courone et fleur des chansons a troys*: A Mirror of the French Chanson in Italy in the Years between Ottaviano Petrucci and Antonio Gardano." *JAMS* 26 (1973): 1–68.

———, ed. *La Courone et fleur des chansons a troys*. 2 pts. Masters and Monuments of the Renaissance 3. New York, 1984.

Bertelli, Sergio, Franco Cardini, and Elvira Zorzi. *Le corti italiane del Rinascimento*. Milan, 1985.

Bertolotti, Antonino. *Musici alla corte dei Gonzaga dal secolo XV al XVIII*. Milan, [1890].

Berz, Ernst-Ludwig. *Die Notendrucker und ihre Verleger in Frankfurt am Main von den Anfängen bis etwa 1530. Eine bibliographische und drucktechnische Studie zur Musikpublikation*. Kassel, 1970.

Bianconi, Lorenzo. "Il Cinquecento e il Seicento." In *Letteratura italiana,* edited by Alberto Asor Rosa, 6: 319–63. Turin, 1986.

———. "Weitere Ergänzungen zu Emil Vogels 'Bibliothek der gedruckten weltlichen Vocalmusik Italiens, aus den Jahren 1500–1700' aus italienischen Bibliotheken." *Analecta musicologica* 9 (1970): 142–202.

Black, Christopher F. *Italian Confraternities in the Sixteenth Century.* Cambridge, 1989.

Blackburn, Bonnie J. "Josquin's Chansons: Ignored and Lost Sources." *JAMS* 29 (1976): 30–76.

———. "The Printing Contract for the *Libro primo de musica de la salamandra* (Rome, 1526)." *Journal of Musicology* 12 (1994): 345–56.

Bloch, Joshua. "Venetian Printers of Hebrew Books." *Bulletin of the New York Public Library* 36 (1932): 71–92.

Boccazzi, Franca Zara. *La Basilica dei Santi Giovanni e Paolo in Venezia.* Padua, 1965.

Boetticher, Wolfgang. *Orlando di Lasso und seine Zeit.* Kassel, 1958.

Bongi, Salvatore. *Annali di Gabriel Giolito de' Ferrari.* 2 vols. Rome, 1890–97; repr. Rome, n.d.

Boorman, Stanley H. "A Case of Work and Turn Half-Sheet Imposition in the Early Sixteenth Century." *The Library,* 6th ser., 8 (1986): 301–21.

———. Glossary to *Music Printing and Publishing,* 487–550.

———."Early Music Printing: Working for a Specialized Market." In *Print and Culture in the Renaissance,* edited by Erald P. Tyson and Sylvia S. Wagonheim, 222–45. Newark, Del., 1986.

———. "Magni," In *Music Printing and Publishing,* 329–30.

———. "Petrucci." In *Music Printing and Publishing,* 365–69.

———. "Petrucci at Fossombrone: A Study of Early Music Printing with Special Reference to the Motetti de la Corona (1514–1519)." Ph.D. diss., University of London, 1976.

———. "Printed Music Books of the Italian Renaissance from the Point of View of Manuscript Study." In *Actas del XV congreso de la Sociedad Internacional de Musicología: "Culturas Musicales del Mediterraneo y sus Ramificaciones,"* Madrid, 3–10/IV/1992, 5: 2587–602. Madrid, 1993.

———. "The Salzburg Liturgy and Single-Impression Music Printing." In *Music in the German Renaissance: Sources, Styles and Contexts,* edited by John Kmetz, 235–53. Cambridge, 1995.

———. "Some Non-conflicting Attributions, and Some Newly Anonymous Compositions, from the Early Sixteenth Century." *Early Music History* 6 (1986): 109–57.

———. "What Bibliography Can Do: Music Printing and the Early Madrigal." *Music & Letters* 72 (1991): 236–58.

Bouwsma, William J. *Venice and the Defense of Republican Liberty: Renaissance Values in the Age of the Counter Reformation.* Berkeley and Los Angeles, 1968.

Bowers, Fredson. *Principles of Bibliographical Description.* Princeton, 1949.

Brauner, Mitchell P. N. "The Parvus Manuscripts: A Study of Vatican Polyphony (ca. 1535–1580)." Ph.D. diss., Brandeis University, 1982.

———. "Traditions in the Repertory of the Papal Choir in the Fifteenth and Sixteenth Centuries." In *Papal Music and Musicians in Late Medieval and Renaissance Rome,* edited by Richard Sherr, 168–78. Oxford, 1998.

Brennecke, Wilfried. "Kerle, Jacobus de." *New Grove* 9: 873.

Brésard, Henri. *Les Foires de Lyon au XVᵉ et au XVIᵉ siècle.* Lyons, 1914.

Bridges, Thomas W. "The Publishing of Arcadelt's First Book of Madrigals." 2 vols. Ph.D. diss., Harvard University, 1982.

———. "Gardano." *New Grove* 7: 158–59.

————. "Scotto." *New Grove* 17: 85–87.

British Museum. *Catalogue of Books Printed in the XVth Century Now in the British Museum. Part V. Venice*. Edited by Julius Victor Scholderer. London, 1924.

Brown, Horatio. *The Venetian Printing Press 1469–1800*. London, 1891.

Brown, Howard Mayer. *Instrumental Music Printed before 1600: A Bibliography*. Cambridge, Mass., 1965.

Brulez, Wilfrid. *Marchands flamands à Venise, I (1568–1605)*. Études d'histoire économique et sociale 6. Rome and Brussels, 1965.

Bryant, David. "Alcuni osservazioni preliminari sulle notizie musicali nelle relazioni degli ambasciatori stranieri a Venezia." In *Andrea Gabrieli e il suo tempo. Atti del convegno internazionale (Venezia, 16–18 settembre 1985)*, edited by Francesco Degrada, 181–92. Florence, 1990.

Buja, Maureen. "Antonio Barrè and Music Printing in Mid-Sixteenth-Century Rome." Ph.D. diss., University of North Carolina, 1996.

Burke, Peter. *Culture and Society in Renaissance Italy, 1420–1540*. London, 1972.

Butchart, David, "The First Published Compositions of Alessandro Striggio." *Studi musicali* 12 (1983): 17–33.

Caffi, Francesco. *Storia della musica sacra nella già cappella ducale di San Marco in Venezia dal 1318 al 1797*. 2 vols. Venice, 1854.

Cairns, Christopher. *Pietro Aretino and the Republic of Venice: Researches on Aretino and his Circle in Venice, 1527–1556*. Florence, 1985.

Cambio, Perissone. *Madrigali a cinque voci (Venice, 1545)*. Edited by Martha Feldman. Sixteenth-Century Madrigal 2. New York and London, 1990.

Camerini, Paolo. *Annali dei Giunti, Volume I, Venezia, Parte I e II*. Bibliografica Italica, nos. 26, 28. Florence, 1962–63.

Cametti, Alberto. *Palestrina*. Milan, 1925.

Carapetyan, Armen. "The *Musica Nova* of Adriano Willaert." *Journal of Renaissance and Baroque Music* 1 (1946/47): 200–21.

Cardamone, Donna. *The Canzone villanesca alla napolitana and Related Forms, 1537–1570*. Studies in Musicology 45. 2 vols. Ann Arbor, Mich., 1981.

————. "*Madrigali a Tre et Arie Napolitane*: A Typographical and Repertorial Study." *JAMS* 35 (1982): 436–81.

————, ed. *Adrian Willaert and His Circle: Canzone Villanesche alla Napolitana and Villotte*. Recent Researches in the Music of the Renaissance 30. Madison, Wis., 1978.

————, and David L. Jackson. "Production with Multiple Formes in Susato's First Edition of Lasso's 'Opus 1'." *Music Library Association Notes* 46 (1989): 7–24.

Carli, Girolamo. *Motetti del laberinto (Venice, 1554)*. Edited by Richard Sherr. Sixteenth-Century Motet 24. New York and London, 1995.

Carroll, Linda L. *Angelo Beolco (Il Ruzante)*. Boston, 1990.

Carter, Harry. *A View of Early Typography up to about 1600*. Oxford, 1969.

Carter, Tim. "Music and Patronage in Later Sixteenth-Century Florence: The Case of Jacopo Corsi (1561–1602)." *I Tatti Studies in the Renaissance* 1 (1985): 57–104.

————. "Music-Printing in Late Sixteenth- and Early Seventeenth-Century Florence: Giorgio Marescotti, Cristofano Marescotti and Zanobi Pignoni." *Early Music History* 9 (1989): 27–72.

————. "Music Selling in Late Sixteenth-Century Florence: The Bookshop of Piero di Giuliano Morosi." *Music & Letters* 70 (1989): 483–504.

————. "The Music Trade in Later Sixteenth-Century Florence." In *Atti del XIV congresso della Società Internazionale di Musicologia, Bologna, 27 agosto–1 settembre*

1987, edited by A. Pompilio, D. Restani, L. Bianconi, and F. A. Gallo, 1: 288–94. Turin, 1990.

Casali, Scipione. *Annali della tipografia veneziana di Francesco Marcolini da Forlì.* Forlì, 1861; Reprint, Bologna, 1953, with a new introduction by Luigi Servolini.

Castellani, Carlo. "Watermarks." In *Early Venetian Printing Illustrated.* Compiled by Ferdinando Ongania. New York, 1895.

Cavicchi, Adriano. "Baldini, Vittorio." In *Music Printing and Publishing,* 158–59.

Cecchetti, B. "Altri stampadori ed altri librai." *Archivio Veneto* n.s., 29 (1885), 412–13.

Cerretta, Florindo. "An Account of the Early Life of the Accademia degli Infiammati in the Letters of Alessandro Piccolomini to Benedetto Varchi." *Romanic Review* 48 (1957): 249–64.

———. *Alessandro Piccolomini: letterato e filosofo senese del Cinquecento.* Siena, 1960.

Chambers, David S. *The Imperial Age of Venice, 1380–1580.* London, 1970.

———, and Brian Pullan, eds. with Jennifer Fletcher. *Venice: A Documentary History, 1450–1630.* Oxford, 1992.

Chapman, Catherine Weeks. "Andrea Antico." Ph.D. diss., Harvard University, 1964.

———. "Printed Collections of Polyphonic Music Owned by Ferdinand Columbus." *JAMS* 21 (1968): 34–84.

Chartier, Roger. *The Culture of Print: Power and the Uses of Print in Early Modern Europe.* Translated by Lydia G. Cochrane. Princeton, 1989.

———. *The Order of Books: Readers, Authors, and Libraries in Europe between the Fourteenth and Eighteenth Centuries.* Translated by Lydia G. Cochrane. Stanford, 1994.

Chubb, Thomas. *Aretino, Scourge of Princes.* New York, 1940.

Cicogna, Emmanuele A. *Delle inscrizioni veneziane.* 6 vols. Venice, 1834–61.

Coldwell, Charles P. "The Printing of Lute Tablature." Paper presented at the annual meeting of the American Musicological Society, Louisville, Kentucky, 28 October 1983.

Contino, Giovanni. *Modulationum quinque vocum . . . liber primus (Venice, 1560).* Edited by Richard Sherr. Sixteenth-Century Motet 25. New York and London, 1994.

———. *Il primo libro de' madrigali a cinque voci (1560).* Edited by Romano Vettori. Monumenti musicali italiani 13. Rome, 1987.

Corteccia, Francesco. *The First Book of Madrigals for Four Voices.* Edited by Frank A. D'Accone. CMM 32, vol. 8. AIM, 1981.

Cox, Virginia. *The Renaissance Dialogue: Literary Dialogue in its Social and Political Contexts, Castiglione to Galileo.* Cambridge, 1992.

Cranz, F. Edward. *A Bibliography of Aristotle Editions 1501–1600.* 2d ed. Edited by Charles B. Schmitt. Baden-Baden and Geneva, 1984.

Cusick, Suzanne. *Valerio Dorico, Music Printer in Sixteenth-Century Rome.* Studies in Musicology 43. Ann Arbor, Mich., 1980.

Cuyler, Louise E. "Musical Activity in Augsburg and its *Annakirche,* ca. 1470–1630." In *Cantors at the Crossroads: Essays in Church Music in Honor of Walter E. Buszin,* edited by Johannes Riedel, 33–43. St. Louis, 1967.

Dalbanne, Claude. "Robert Granjon, imprimeur de musique." *Gutenberg Jahrbuch* 14 (1939): 226–32.

Darbellay, Étienne, ed. *Le Toccate e i Capricci di Girolamo Frescobaldi: genesi delle edizioni e apparato critico.* Monumenti musicali italiani 2–4, supplement. Milan, 1988.

Davies, Hugh William. *Devices of the Early Printers.* London, 1935.

DeFord, Ruth. "Ruggiero Giovanelli and the Madrigal in Rome 1572–1599." Ph.D. diss., Harvard University, 1975.

Di Filippo Bareggi, Claudia. "L'editoria veneziana fra '500 e '600." In *Storia di Venezia dalle origini alla caduta della Serenissima.* Vol. 6: *Dal Rinascimento alla Barocca,* edited by Gaetano Cozzi and Paolo Prodi, 615–48, Rome, 1994.

———. *Il mestiere di scrivere. Lavoro intellecttuale e mercato librario a Venezia nel Cinquecento.* Rome, 1988.

Donà, Mariangela. *La stampa musicale a Milano fino all'anno 1700.* Florence, 1961.

Donati, Lamberto. "Le iniziali iconografiche del XVI secolo." In *Studi bibliografici,* 219–39. Florence, 1967.

Doni, Antonfrancesco. *Dialogo della musica.* Edited by G. Francesco Malipiero and Virginio Fagotto. Collana di musiche veneziane inedite o rare 7. Vienna, 1964.

———. *La libraria.* Venice, 1550.

———. *L'opera musicale.* Edited by Anna Maria Monterosso Vacchelli. Instituta e monumenta, ser. 2, vol. 1. Cremona, 1969.

Dowling, M. "The Printing of John Dowland's Second Booke of Ayres." *The Library,* 4th ser., 12 (1932): 365–80.

Draudius, Georg. *Bibliotheca librorum germanicorum classica.* Frankfurt, 1611.

Duggan, Mary Kay. *Italian Music Incunabula.* Berkeley and Los Angeles, 1992.

Dunning, Albert. "Josquini antiquos, Musae, memoremus amores." *Acta musicologica* 41 (1969): 108–16.

———. *Die Staatsmotette, 1480–1555.* Utrecht, 1970.

Durling, Richard J., comp. *A Catalogue of Sixteenth-Century Printed Books in the National Library of Medicine.* Bethesda, 1967.

Le edizioni italiane del XVI secolo: censimento nazionale. Edited by Maria Sicco and M. A. Baffio. Istituto centrale per il catalogo unico delle biblioteche italiane e per le informazioni bibliografiche. 4 vols. to date. Rome, 1985-.

Edwards, Rebecca A. "Claudio Merulo: Servant of the State and Musical Entrepreneur in Later Sixteenth-Century Venice." Ph.D. diss., Princeton University, 1990.

Ehrman, Albert, and Graham Pollard. *The Distribution of Books by Catalogue from the Invention of Printing to A.D. 1800.* Cambridge, 1965.

Einstein, Alfred. "The 'Dialogo della musica' of Messer Antonio Francesco Doni." *Music & Letters* 15 (1934): 244–53.

———. *The Italian Madrigal.* 3 vols. Translated by Alexander H. Krappe, Roger H. Sessions, and Oliver Strunk. Princeton, 1949; repr. 1971.

Eisenstein, Elizabeth L. *The Printing Press as an Agent of Change: Communications and Cultural Transformations in Early Modern Europe.* 2 vols. Cambridge, 1979.

———. *The Printing Revolution in Early Modern Europe.* Cambridge, 1983.

Eitner, Robert, et al. *Bibliographie der Musik-Sammelwerke des XVI. und XVII Jahrhunderts.* Berlin, 1877; repr. Hildesheim, 1963.

———. *Biographisch-bibliographisches Quellen-Lexikon der Musiker und Musikgelehrten.* 10 vols. Leipzig, 1899–1904; 2d rev. ed. Graz, 1959–60.

Engel, Hans. *Luca Marenzio.* Florence, 1956.

Erb, James. *Orlando di Lasso: A Guide to Research.* New York and London, 1990.

Essling, Victor Massena. *Études sur l'art de la gravure sur bois à Venise. Les livres à figures vénitiens de la fin du XVe siècle et du commencement du XVIe.* Paris, 1907–14.

———. *Les Missels imprimés à Venise de 1481 à 1600.* Paris, 1892.

Estienne, Henri. *The Frankfurt Book Fair.* Translated by J. W. Thompson. Chicago, 1911.

Fahy, Conor. "The 'Index prohibitorum' and the Venetian Printing Industry in the Sixteenth Century." *Italian Studies* 35 (1980): 52–61.

Favaro, Elena. *L'Arte dei Pittori in Venezia e i suoi statuti.* Florence, 1975.

Febvre, Lucien, and Henri-Jean Martin. *The Coming of the Book: The Impact of Printing 1450–1800*. Translated by David Gerard. Edited by Geoffrey Nowell-Smith and David Wooton. London, 1976. Originally published as *L'Apparition du livre* (Paris, 1958).

Feldman, Martha. "The Academy of Domenico Venier, Music's Literary Muse in Mid-*Cinquecento* Venice." *Renaissance Quarterly* 44 (1991): 476–512.

———. *City Culture and the Madrigal at Venice*. Berkeley and Los Angeles, 1994.

Fenlon, Iain. "Cardinal Scipione Gonzaga (1542–93): 'Quel padrone confidentissimo'." *Journal of the Royal Music Association* 113 (1988): 223–49.

———. "Il foglio volante editoriale dei Tini circa il 1596." *Rivista italiana di musicologia* 12 (1977): 231–43.

———. "*In destructione turcharum:* The Victory of Lepanto in Sixteenth-Century Music and Letters." In *Andrea Gabrieli e il suo tempo. Atti del convegno internazionale (Venezia, 16–18 Settembre 1985)*, edited by Francesco Degrada, 293–317. Florence, 1987.

———. "Lepanto: The Arts of Celebration in Renaissance Venice." *Proceedings of the British Academy* 73 (1987): 201–36.

———. *Music and Patronage in Sixteenth-Century Mantua*. 2 vols. Cambridge, 1988.

———. *Music, Print and Culture in Early Sixteenth-Century Italy*. The Panizzi Lectures, 1994. London, 1995.

———. "Venice: Theatre of the World." In *Man and Music: The Renaissance from the 1470s to the End of the 16th Century,* edited by Iain Fenlon, 102–32. Englewood Cliffs, N.J., 1989.

———, and James Haar. *The Italian Madrigal in the Early Sixteenth Century: Sources and Interpretation*. Cambridge, 1988.

Fischer, Hans. "Conrad Gesner (1516–1565) as Bibliographer and Encyclopaedist." *The Library,* 5th ser., 21 (1966): 119–33.

Forcella, Vincenzo. *Iscrizioni delle chiese e degli altri edifici di Milano dal secolo VIII ai giorni nostri*. 12 vols. in 6. Milan, 1889–93.

Forney, Kristine K. "Orlando di Lasso's Opus 1: The Making and Marketing of a Renaissance Music Book." *Revue belge de musicologie* 39–40 (1985–86): 33–60.

———. "Tielman Susato, Sixteenth-Century Music Printer: An Archival and Typographical Investigation." Ph.D. diss., University of Kentucky, 1978.

Francesco Canova da Milano. *Intavolatura de viola o vero lauto (Naples, 1536)*. Facs. ed., introduction by Arthur Ness. Geneva, 1988.

———. *The Lute Music*. Edited by Arthur J. Ness. 2 vols. Cambridge, Mass., 1970.

Frisi, Anton Francesco. *Memorie storiche di Monza e sua Corte*. 3 vols. Milan, 1794.

Fulin, Rinaldo. "Documenti per servire alla storia della tipografia veneziana." *Archivio veneto* 23 (1882): 84–212.

———. "Nuovi documenti per servire alla storia della tipografia veneziana." *Archivio veneto* 23 (1882): 390–405.

Fumagalli, Giuseppe. *Lexicon Typographicum Italiae*. Florence, 1905.

Garbelotto, Antonio. *Il Padre Costanzo Porta da Cremona, O.F.M. Conv., grande polifonista del '500*. Rome, 1955.

Gardano, Antonio. *Canzoni francesi*. Edited by Virginio Fagotto and G. Francesco Malipiero. Collana di Musiche Veneziane Inedite o Rare, 8. Milan, 1973.

Gaskell, Philip. *A New Introduction to Bibliography*. Oxford, 1972.

Gaspari, Gaetano. *Catalogo della biblioteca del Liceo Musicale di Bologna*. 5 vols. Bologna, 1890–1943.

Gasparinetti, A. F. "Notes on Early Italian Papermaking." *The Paper Maker* 27 (1958): 25–32.

Gero, Jhan. *Il primo libro de' madrigali italiani et canzon francese a due voci.* Edited by Lawrence Bernstein and James Haar. Masters and Monuments of the Renaissance 1. New York, 1980.

Gerulaitis, Leonardas. *Printing and Publishing in Fifteenth-Century Venice.* London, 1976.

Gesner, Conrad. *Pandectarum sive Partitionum Universalium . . . Libri XXI.* Zurich, 1548.

Getz, Christine. "Music and Patronage in Milan, 1535–1555, and Vincenzo Ruffo's First Motet Book." Ph.D. diss., University of North Texas, 1991.

Ghibel, Heliseo. *Helysei Gibelli musici eccellentissimi motetta super plano cantu cum quinque vocibus et in festis solennibus decanenda liber primus (Venice: s.n., 1546).* Edited by Richard Sherr. Sixteenth-Century Motet 21. New York and London, 1993.

Giazotto, Remo. *Harmonici concenti in aere veneto.* Rome, 1954.

Gilbert, Felix. "Venice in the Crisis of the League of Cambrai." In *Renaissance Venice,* edited by John R. Hale, 274–92. London, 1973.

Gilmore, Myron. "Myth and Reality in Venetian Political Theory." In *Renaissance Venice,* edited by John R. Hale, 431–44, London, 1973.

Giovanelli, Pietro, comp. *Novus Thesaurus Musicus (1568).* Edited by Albert Dunning. CMM 64. AIM, 1974.

Giraud, Yves. "Deux livres de tablature inconnus de Francesco da Milano." *Revue de musicologie* 55 (1969): 217–19.

Glixon, Jonathan. "Music at the Venetian Scuole Grandi, 1440–1540." In *Music in Medieval and Early Modern Europe: Patronage, Sources and Texts,* edited by Iain Fenlon, 193–208. Cambridge, 1981.

———. "A Musicians' Union in Sixteenth-Century Venice." *JAMS* 36 (1983): 392–421.

Göhler, Albert. *Verzeichnis der in den Frankfurter und Leipziger Messkatalogen der Jahre 1564 bis 1769 angezeigten Musikalien.* Leipzig, 1902.

Gottwald, Clytus. *Die Musikhandschriften der Staats- und Stadtbibliothek Augsburg.* Handschriftenkataloge der Staats- und Stadtbibliothek Augsburg 1. Wiesbaden, 1974.

Greenblatt, Stephen. *Renaissance Self-Fashioning: From More to Shakespeare.* Chicago, 1980.

Grendler, Paul F. "Chivalric Romances in the Renaissance." *Studies in Medieval and Renaissance History* 10 (1988): 57–102.

———. *Critics of the Italian World, 1530–1560: Anton Francesco Doni, Nicolò Franco, and Ortensio Lando.* Madison, Wis., 1969.

———. "The Destruction of Hebrew Books in Venice, 1568." *Proceedings of the American Academy for Jewish Research* 45 (1978): 103–30.

———. "Form and Function in Italian Renaissance Popular Books." *Renaissance Quarterly* 46 (1993): 451–85.

———. "Francesco Sansovino and Italian Popular History, 1560–1600." *Studies in the Renaissance* 16 (1969): 139–80.

———. "Printing and Censorship." In *The Cambridge History of Renaissance Philosophy,* edited by Charles B. Schmitt and Quentin Skinner. 25–53, London, 1973.

———. *The Roman Inquisition and the Venetian Press, 1540–1605.* Princeton, 1977.

———. *Schooling in Renaissance Italy: Literacy and Learning, 1300–1600.* Baltimore, 1989.

Griffiths, John, and Warren E. Hultberg. "Santa Maria and the Printing of Instrumental Music in Sixteenth-Century Spain." In *Livro de homenagem a Macario Santiago Kastner.* Edited by M. F. Cidrais Rodrigues, M. Morais, and R. Veiera Nery, 347–60. Lisbon, 1992.

Grigolato, Gilda, comp., and A. Zecca Laterza, indexer. *Musiche della Cappella di Santa Barbara in Mantova*. Conservatorio di Musica "Giuseppe Verdi," Catalogo della biblioteca . . . Fondi speciali I. Florence, 1972.

Guerini, Paolo. "Giovanni Contino di Brescia." *Note d'archivio* 1 (1924): 130–42.

Haar, James. "Arie per cantar stanze ariotesche." In *L'Ariosto: la musica, i musicisti*, edited by Maria Antonella Balsano, 31–46. Florence, 1981.

———. "Perissone Cambio." *New Grove* 14: 535.

———. "The *Capriccio* of Giachet Berchem: A Study in Modal Organization." *Musica disciplina* 42 (1988): 129–56.

———. "The Early Madrigals of Lassus." *Revue belge de musicologie*, 39–40 (1985–86): 17–32.

———. *Essays on Italian Poetry and Music in the Renaissance, 1350–1600*. Berkeley and Los Angeles, 1986.

———. "The *Libraria* of Antonfrancesco Doni." *Musica disciplina* 24 (1970): 101–25.

———. "The 'Libro Primo' of Costanzo Festa." *Acta musicologica* 52 (1980): 47–55.

———. "The '*Madrigale Arioso*': A Mid-Century Development in the Cinquecento Madrigal." *Studi musicali* 12 (1983): 203–19.

———. "Le muse in Germania. Lasso's Fourth Book of Madrigals." In *Orlandus Lassus and his Time. Colloquium Proceedings Antwerpen 24–26. 08. 1994*. Edited by Ignace Bossuyt, Eugeen Schreurs, and Annelies Wouters, 49–72. Peer, 1995.

———. "The *Note nere* Madrigal." *JAMS* 18 (1965): 22–41.

———. "Notes on the 'Dialogo della Musica' of Antonfrancesco Doni." *Music & Letters* 47 (1966): 198–224.

Haebler, Konrad. *The Study of Incunabula*. Translated by Lucy Eugenia Osborne. New York, 1933.

Hale, John R., ed. *Renaissance Venice*. Totowa, N.J., 1973.

Hall, James. *Dictionary of Subjects and Symbols of Art*. New York, 1974.

Harrán, Don, ed. *The Anthologies of Black-Note Madrigals*. CMM 73. AIM, 1978–81.

Harvard, Steven. *Ornamental Initials: The Woodcut Initials of Christopher Plantin, a Complete Catalogue*. New York, 1974.

Heartz, Daniel. " 'Au pres de vous'—Claudin's Chanson and the Commerce of Publishers' Arrangements." *JAMS* 24 (1971): 193–225.

———. *Pierre Attaingnant, Royal Printer of Music*. Berkeley and Los Angeles, 1969.

Herzog, Emil. *Chronik der Kreisstadt Zwickau*. 2 vols. Zwickau, 1839.

Hirsch, Rudolf. *Printing, Selling and Reading, 1450–1550*. Wiesbaden, 1967.

Howard, Deborah. *Jacopo Sansovino: Architecture and Patronage in Renaissance Venice*. New Haven, 1975.

Hoyoux, J. "Les Moyens d'existence d'Erasme." In *Bibliothèque d'Humanisme et Renaissance* 6 (1944): 7–59.

Il Verso, Antonio. *Madrigali a tre e a cinque voci (libro XV, opera XXXVI, 1619)*. Edited by Lorenzo Bianconi. Musiche rinascimentali siciliane 8. Florence, 1978.

Index Aureliensis: Catalogus Librorum Sedecimo Saeculo Impressorum. Baden-Baden and Geneva, 1962-.

Jackson, Alfred Forbes. *Type Designs, their History and Development*. London, 1959.

Jackson, Margaret H., ed. *Catalogue of the Francis Taylor Pearson Plimpton Collection of Italian Books and Manuscripts in the Library of Wellesley College*. Cambridge, Mass., 1929.

Jayne, Sears, and F. R. Johnson, eds. *The Lumley Library: The Catalogue of 1609*. London, 1956.

Javitch, Daniel. *Proclaiming a Classic: The Canonization of Orlando Furioso*. Princeton, 1991.

Jedin, Hubert. *A History of the Council of Trent.* Translated by E. Graf. 2 vols. London, 1957–61. Originally published as *Geschichte des Konzils von Trient.* 2 vols. (Freiburg, 1949–51).

Jeppesen, Knud, "Pierluigi da Palestrina, Herzog Guglielmo Gonzaga und die neugefundenen Mantovaner-Messen Palestrinas, ein ergänzender Bericht." *Acta Musicologica* 25 (1953): 132–79.

Johnson, Alvin H. "The 1548 Editions of Cipriano de Rore's Third Book of Madrigals." In *Studies in Musicology in Honor of Otto E. Albrecht,* edited by John W. Hill, 110–24. Kassel, 1980.

Judd, Robert F. "The Use of Notational Formats at the Keyboard: A Study of Printed Sources of Keyboard Music in Spain and Italy c. 1500–1700." D.Phil. thesis, Oxford University, 1988.

Kapp, Friedrich. *Geschichte des deutschen Buchhandels.* 2 vols. Leipzig, 1886.

Kévorkian, Raymond H. *Catalogue des "incunables" arméniens (1511–1695) ou Chronique de l'imprimerie arménienne.* Geneva, 1986.

King, A. Hyatt. *Four Hundred Years of Music Printing.* London, 1968.

———. "The Significance of John Rastell in Early Music Printing." *The Library,* 5th ser., 26 (1972). 197–214.

King, Margaret L. *Venetian Humanism in an Age of Patrician Dominance.* Princeton, 1986.

Kristeller, Paul Oskar. *Renaissance Thought and its Sources.* Edited by Michael Mooney. New York, 1979.

Krummel, D. W. *English Music Printing 1553–1700.* London, 1975.

———. "Oblong Format in Early Music Books." *The Library,* 5th ser., 26 (1971): 312–24.

Lane, Frederic C. "Family Partnerships and Joint Ventures." In *Venice and History: The Collected Papers of Frederic C. Lane,* 36–55. Baltimore, 1966.

———. "Venetian Bankers, 1496–1533." In *Venice and History: The Collected Papers of Frederic C. Lane,* 69–86. Baltimore, 1966.

———, *Venice: A Maritime Republic.* Baltimore, 1973.

Larson, Keith. "The Unaccompanied Madrigal in Naples from 1536 to 1654." 2 vols. Ph.D. diss., Harvard University, 1985.

———, and Angelo Pompilio. "Le edizioni musicali napolitane." In *Musica e cultura a Napoli dal XV al XIX secolo,* edited by Lorenzo Bianconi and Renato Bossa, 103–39. Quaderni della Rivista, no. 9. Florence, 1983.

Ledbetter, Steven. "Marenzio's Early Career." *JAMS* 32 (1979): 304–18.

Lehmann-Haupt, Hellmut. *Peter Schoeffer of Gernsheim and Mainz, with a List of his Surviving Books and Broadsides.* Rochester and New York, 1950.

Leschinkohl, F. "Venedig, das Druckzentrum serbischer Bücher im Mittelalter." *Gutenberg Jahrbuch* (1957): 116–21.

Lesure, François. *Anthologie de la chanson parisienne au XVIᵉ siècle.* Monaco, 1953.

———, and Geneviève Thibault. *Bibliographie des éditions d'Adrian Le Roy et Robert Ballard (1551–98).* Paris, 1955.

———. "Bibliographie des éditions musicales publiés par Nicolas Du Chemin (1549–1576)." *Annales musicologiques* 1 (1953): 269–373.

Leuchtmann, Horst. *Orlando di Lasso: Sein Leben.* Wiesbaden, 1976.

Lewis, Mary S. "Antonio Gardane and his Publications of Sacred Music, 1538–55." Ph.D. diss., Brandeis University, 1979.

———, "Antonio Gardane's Early Connections with the Willaert Circle." In *Music in Medieval and Early Modern Europe: Patronage, Sources and Texts,* edited by Iain Fenlon, 209–26. Cambridge, 1981.

————. *Antonio Gardano, Venetian Music Printer, 1538–1569: A Descriptive Bibliography and Historical Study.* Vol. 1: *1538–49;* Vol. 2: *1550–1559.* New York and London, 1988–1997.

————. "Buglhat, Johannes de." In *Music Printing and Publishing,* 189.

————. "The Printed Music Book in Context: Observations on Some Sixteenth-Century Editions." *Music Library Association Notes* 40 (1990): 899–918.

————. "Rore's Setting of Petrarch's 'Vergine Bella': A History of its Composition and Early Transmission." *Journal of Musicology* 4 (1985–86): 365–409.

————. "Twins, Cousins, and Heirs: Relationships among Editions of Music Printed in Sixteenth-Century Venice." In *Critica Musica: Essays in Honor of Paul Brainard,* edited by John Knowles, 193–224. Amsterdam, [1996].

Lippmann, Friedrich. "Giovanni de Macque fra Roma e Napoli: nuovi documenti." *Rivista italiana di musicologica,* 13 (1978): 245–79.

Litta, Pompeo, ed. *Le famiglie celebri italiane.* 15 vols. Milan, 1819–1902.

Le Livre arménien a travers les ages. Catalogue de l'exposition tenue au Musée de la marine, Marseille, 2–21 octobre 1985. Marseille, n.d.

Lockwood, Lewis. *The Counter-Reformation and the Masses of Vincenzo Ruffo.* Vienna, 1970.

————, and Jessie Ann Owens. "Willaert, Adrian." *New Grove* 20: 421–28.

Logan, Oliver. *Culture and Society in Venice, 1470–1790: The Renaissance and its Heritage.* New York, 1972.

Lorenzetti, Giulio. *Venice and its Lagoon: Historical-Artistic Guide.* Translated by John Guthrie. Trieste, 1926; repr. 1975.

Lowinsky, Edward E. *Music in the Culture of the Renaissance and Other Essays.* Edited by Bonnie J. Blackburn. 2 vols. Chicago, 1989.

Lowry, Martin. *Nicholas Jenson and the Rise of Venetian Publishing in Renaissance Europe.* Oxford, 1991.

————. *The World of Aldus Manutius: Business and Scholarship in Renaissance Venice.* Ithaca, N.Y., 1979.

Ludwig, Gustav. "Contratti fra lo stampador Zuan di Colonia ed i suoi soci e inventario di una parte del loro magazzino." *Miscellanea di storia veneta, Reale deputazione veneta di storia patria,* 2d ser., 8 (1902): 45–48.

Lunelli, Renato. "Contributi trentini alle relazioni fra l'Italia e la Germania nel Rinascimento." *Acta musicologica* 21 (1948): 41–70.

Luzzaschi, Luzzasco. *Madrigal per cantare e sonare a uno, due e tre soprani (1601).* Edited by Adriano Cavicchi. Monumenti di musica italiana, ser. 2: Polifonia, 2. Brescia and Kassel, 1965.

Mackenney, Richard. *Tradesmen and Traders: The World of the Guilds in Venice and Europe c. 1250–c. 1650.* Totowa, N.J., 1987.

McKenzie, D. F. "Printers of the Mind: Some Notes on Bibliographical Theories and Printing-House Practices." *Studies in Bibliography (Papers of the Bibliographical Society of the University of Virginia)* 22 (1969): 1–75.

McLuhan, Marshall. *The Gutenberg Galaxy: The Making of Typographic Man.* Toronto, 1962.

Manzi, Pietro. "Annali tipografici di Giovanni Maria Scotto (1559–1566)." In *La tipografia napoletana nel '500.* [3] *Annali di Giovanni Paolo Suganappo, Raimondo Amato, Giovanni de Boy, Giovanni Maria Scotto et tipografi minori (1533–1570),* 159–206. Florence, 1973.

Marciani, Corrado. "Editori, tipografi, librai veneti nel regno di Napoli nel Cinquecento." *Studi veneziani* 10 (1968): 457–554.

———. "I Vuković tipografi-librai slavi a Venezia nel XVI secolo." *Economia e storia* 19 (1972): 342–62.

Martin, Henri-Jean. *The History and Power of Writing*. Translated by Lydia G. Cochrane. Chicago, 1994.

Mauroner, Fabio. *Le incisioni di Tiziano*. Padua, [1943].

Maylender, Michele. *Storia delle accademie d'Italia*. 5 vols. Bologna, 1926–30.

Mazzone, Marc'Antonio. *Il primo libro delle canzoni a quattro voci*. Edited by Maria Antonietta Cancellaro. Musiche del Rinascimento italiano 2. Florence, 1990.

Meissner, Uta. *Der Anterwerpener Notendrucker Tylman Susato: Eine bibliographische Studie zur niederländischen Chansonpublikation in der ersten Hälfte des 16. Jahrhunderts*. 2 vols. Berlin, 1967.

Meyer-Baer, Kathi. *Liturgical Music Incunabula*. London, 1962.

Miller, Beth. "Antico, Andrea." In *Music Printing and Publishing*, 143–46.

Milsom, John. "The Nonsuch Music Library." In *Sundry Sorts of Music Books: Essays on the British Library Collections presented to O. W. Neighbour on his 70th Birthday*, edited by Chris Banks, Arthur Searle, and Malcolm Turner, 146–82. London, 1993.

———. "Songs and Society in Early Tudor London." *Early Music History* 16 (1998).

Mischiati, Oscar. *Indici, cataloghi e avvisi degli editori e librai musicali italiani dal 1591 al 1798*. Florence, 1984.

———. *La prassi musicale presso i Canonici regolari del Ss. Salvatore nei secoli XVI e XVII e i manoscritti polifonici della Biblioteca musicale "G. B. Martini" di Bologna*. Rome, 1985.

Mohler, Ludwig, *Kardinal Bessarion als Theologe, Humanist und Staatsmann: Funde und Forschungen*. 3 vols. Paderborn, 1923.

Morell, Martin. "Georg Knoff: Bibliophile and Devotee of Italian Music in Late Sixteenth-Century Danzig." In *Music in the German Renaissance: Sources, Styles and Contexts*, edited by John Kmetz, 103–26. Cambridge, 1995.

Morelli, A. "Nuovi documenti frescobaldiani: i contratti per l'edizione del primo libro di Toccate." *Studi musicali* 17 (1988): 255–63.

Moro, Giacomo. "Insegne librarie e marche tipografiche in un registro veneziano del '500." *La Bibliofilia* 91 (1989): 51–80.

Mortimer, Ruth, comp. *Harvard College Library, Department of Printed Books and Graphic Arts. Catalogue of Books and Manuscripts. Part II. Italian 16th Century Books*. 2 vols. Cambridge, Mass., 1974.

Music Printing and Publishing. Edited by D. W. Krummel and Stanley Sadie. New York and London, 1990.

Myers, Patricia Ann. "An Analytical Study of the Italian Cyclic Madrigals Published by Composers Working in Rome ca. 1540–1614." Ph.D. diss., University of Illinois, 1971.

Nardi, Bruno. *Saggi sull'aristotelismo padovano dal secolo XIV al XVI*. Florence, 1958.

Ness, Arthur. "Barberiis, Melchior." *New Grove* 2: 136.

Newcomb, Anthony. "Editions of Willaert's *Musica Nova*: New Evidence, New Speculations." *JAMS* 26 (1973): 132–45.

———. *The Madrigal at Ferrara, 1579–1597*. 2 vols. Princeton, 1980.

Nielson, Clare Ianotta. "Rampazetto." In *Music Printing and Publishing*, 384.

Nugent, George. "Anti-Protestant Music for Sixteenth-Century Ferrara." *JAMS* 43 (1990): 228–91.

———. "The Jacquet Motets and their Authors." Ph.D. diss., Princeton University, 1973.

Nuovo, Angela. *Alessandro Paganino* (Padua, 1990).

————. "Il Corano arabo ritrovato (Venezia, P. e A. Paganini, tra l'agosto 1537 e l'agosto 1538)." *La bibliofilia* 89 (1987): 237–71.

Olschki, Leo S. *Choix de livres anciens rares et curieux,* vol. 12. Florence, 1940.

Ongaro, Giulio Maria. "The Chapel of St. Mark's at the Time of Adrian Willaert (1527–1562): A Documentary Study." Ph.D. diss., University of North Carolina at Chapel Hill, 1986.

————. "The Library of a Sixteenth-Century Music Teacher." *Journal of Musicology* 12 (1994): 357–75.

————. "Venetian Printed Anthologies of Music in the 1560s and the Role of the Editor." In *The Dissemination of Music: Studies in the History of Publishing,* edited by Hans Lenneberg, 43–69. Lausanne, [1994].

Osborn, J. M., ed. *Autobiography of Thomas Whythorne.* London, 1962.

Owens, Jessie Ann. "Il Cinquecento." In *Storia della musica al Santo di Padova,* edited by Sergio Durante and Pierluigi Petrobelli, 27–92 and 285–338. *Fonti e studi per la storia del Santo Padova* 6. Vicenza, 1990.

————. "La cappella musicale della Basilica del Santo: alcune forme di mecenatismo." In *La cappella musicale nell'Italia della controriforma: Atti del Convegno internazionale di studi nel iv Centenario di fondazione della Cappella Musicale di S. Biagio di Cento, 13–15 ottobre 1989,* ed. Oscar Mischiati and Paolo Russo, 251–63. Florence, 1993.

Paganuzzi, E., C. Bologna, L. Rognini, G. M. Cambié, and M. Conati, eds. *La musica a Verona.* Verona, [1976].

Panzer, Georg. *Annales typographici ab artis inventae origine ad annum 1500.* 8 vols. Nuremberg, 1800.

Pastorello, Ester. Catalogue of books printed in Venice, 1469–1600 held in selected northern Italian libraries. Sala dei Manoscritti, Biblioteca Nazionale Marciana, Venice

————. *Tipografi, editori, librai a Venezia nel secolo XVI.* Florence, 1924.

Pesenti, Tiziana. "Stampatori e letterati nell'industria editoriale a Venezia e in Terraferma." In *Storia della Cultura Veneta.* Vol. 4, part 1: *Il Seicento,* edited by Girolamo Araldi and Manlio Pastore Stocchi, 93–129, Vicenza, 1983.

Petrucci Nardelli, Franca. *La lettera e l'immagine, le iniziali "parlanti" nella tipografia italiana (secc. XVI–XVII).* Florence, 1991.

Picker, Martin, ed. *The Motet Books of Andrea Antico.* Monuments of Renaissance Music 8. Chicago, 1988.

Piperno, Franco. "L'antologia madrigalistica a stampa nel Cinquecento." In *Gli Eccellentissimi musici della città di Bologna con uno studio sull'antologia madrigalistica del Cinquecento,* 1–197. Florence, 1985.

Pitoni, Giuseppe Ottavio. *Notitia de' contrapuntisti e compositori di musica.* Edited by Cesare Ruini. Florence, 1988.

Poguc, Samuel F. *Jacques Moderne: Lyons Music Printer of the Sixteenth Century.* Geneva, 1969.

————. "A Sixteenth-Century Editor at Work: Gardane and Moderne." *Journal of Musicology* 1 (1982): 217–38.

Pompilio, Angelo. "Editoria musicale a Napoli e in Italia nel Cinque-Seicento." In *Musica e cultura a Napoli dal XV al XIX secolo,* ed. Lorenzo Bianconi and Renato Bossa, 79–102. Florence, 1983.

————. "Strategie editoriali delle stamperie veneziane tra il 1570 e il 1630." In *Atti del XIV congresso della Società Internazionale di Musicologia, Bologna, 27 agosto–1 settembre 1987,* edited by A. Pompilio, D. Restani, L. Bianconi, and F. A. Gallo, 1: 254–71. Turin, 1990.

Powers, Harold S. "Tonal Types and Modal Categories in Renaissance Polyphony." *JAMS* 34 (1981): 428–70.

Primo catalogo collettivo delle biblioteche italiane. Edited by Centro nazionale per il catalogo unico delle biblioteche italiane e per le informazioni bibliografiche. 9 vols. Rome, 1962–79.

Prizer, William. *Courtly Pastimes: The Frottole of Marchetto Cara.* Ann Arbor, Mich., 1980.

Pozza, Neri. "L'editoria veneziana da Giovanni da Spira ad Aldo Manuzio. I centri editoriali di Terraferma." In *Storia della Cultura Veneta.* Vol. 3, part 2: *Dal primo Quattrocento al Concilio di Trento,* edited by Girolamo Araldi and Manlio Pastore Stocchi, 215–44, Vicenza, 1980.

Praz, Mario, "The Gonzaga devices." In *Splendours of the Gonzaga.* Catalogue of Exhibition held 4 November 1981–31 January 1982, Victoria and Albert Museum, London, edited by David Chambers and Jane Martineau, 65–72, London, 1981.

Pullan, Brian. "Occupations and Investments of the Venetian Nobility." In *Renaissance Venice,* ed. John R. Hale, 379–408. London, 1973.

———. *Rich and Poor in Renaissance Venice: The Social Institutions of a Catholic State to 1620.* Oxford, 1971.

———, ed. *Crisis and Change in the Venetian Economy in the Sixteenth and Seventeenth Centuries.* London, 1958.

Quondam, Amedeo. *Le "carte messagiere": retorica e modelli di comunicazione epistolare, per un indice dei libri di lettere del Cinquecento.* Rome, 1981.

———. "Mercanzi d'onore, 'Mercanzia d'utile': produzione libraria e lavoro intellectuale a Venezia nel Cinquecento." In *Libri, editori, e pubblico nell'Europa moderna: guida storica e critica,* ed. Armando Petrucci, 51–104. Rome, 1977.

———. *Il naso di Laura.* Ferrara, 1991.

Radke, Hans. "Rotta, Antonio." *New Grove* 16: 260.

Renouard, Antoine. *Annales de l'imprimerie des Alde, ou Histoire des trois Manuce et de leurs éditions,* 3d ed. Paris, 1834.

Rice, Eugene. "Recent Studies on the Population of Europe, 1348–1620." *Renaissance News* 18 (1965): 180–87.

Richardson, Brian. *Print Culture in Renaissance Italy, The Editor and The Vernacular Text, 1470–1600.* Cambridge, 1994.

Rooses, M., and J. Denucé, eds. *Correspondance de Christophe Plantin.* Antwerp, 1833–1918.

Rosand, David. *Painting in Cinquecento Venice: Titian, Veronese, Tintoretto.* New Haven, 1982.

Rosand, Ellen. "Music in the Myth of Venice." *Renaissance Quarterly* 30 (1977): 511–37.

Rose, Paul Lawrence. "The *Accademia Venetiana*: Science and Culture in Renaissance Venice." *Studi veneziani* 11 (1969): 191–242.

Rosenthal, Margaret F. *The Honest Courtesan: Veronica Franco, Citizen and Writer in Sixteenth-Century Venice.* Chicago, 1992.

Samuels, Richard S. "Benedetto Varchi, the *Accademia degli Infiammati,* and the Origins of the Italian Academic Movement." *Renaissance Quarterly* 29 (1976): 599–633.

Sartori, Claudio. *Bibliografia della musica strumentale italiana stampata in Italia fino al 1700.* 2 vols. Biblioteca di bibliografia italiana 23 and 56. Florence, 1952–68.

———. *Bibliografia delle opere musicali stampate da Ottaviano Petrucci.* Biblioteca di bibliografia italiana 18. Florence, 1948.

———. "Una dinastia di editori musicali." *La bibliofilia* 58 (1956): 176–208.

———. *Dizionario degli editori musicali italiani.* Florence, 1958.

————. "La famiglia degli editori Scotto." *Acta musicologica* 36 (1964): 19–30.

————. "Scotto." *MGG* 12: cols. 435–37.

Saxl, Fritz. "Veritas Filia Temporis," In *Philosophy and History: Essays Presented to Ernst Cassirer.* Edited by Raymond Klibansky and H. J. Paton, 197–222. Oxford, 1936.

Schaal, Richard. "Die Musikbibliothek von Raimund Fugger d.J.: Ein Beitrag zur Musiküberlieferung des 16. Jahrhunderts." *Acta musicologica* 29 (1957): 1–137.

Schmitt, Charles B. *Aristotle and the Renaissance.* Cambridge, Mass., 1983.

————. "Philosophy and Science in Sixteenth-Century Italian Universities." In *The Renaissance: Essays in Interpretation,* ed. André Chastel, 287–336. London, 1982.

Scholderer, Victor. "Printing at Venice to the End of 1481," in *Fifty Essays,* 74–89.

————. *Fifty Essays in Fifteenth- and Sixteenth-Century Bibliography,* ed. Dennis E. Rhodes. Amsterdam, 1966.

Schütz, E. "The Evolution of Armenian Typographic Art in the West-European Period (16th–17th Centuries)." In *Atti del quinto simposion internazionale di arte armena,* 449–58. Venice, 1991.

Schulz, Juergen. *Venetian Painted Ceilings of the Renaissance.* Berkeley and Los Angeles, 1968.

Scotti, Giovanni. "L'antica famiglia verennate degli Scotti." *Periodico della Società Storica della Provincia e antica Diocesi di Como* 22 (1915): 65–97.

Shaaber, M. A., ed. *Sixteenth-Century Imprints in the Libraries of the University of Pennsylvania.* Philadelphia, 1976.

Sherr, Richard. "The Publications of Guglielmo Gonzaga." *JAMS* 31 (1978): 118–25.

Short-Title Catalogue of Books Printed in Italy and of Books in Italian Printed Abroad 1501–1600 Held in Selected North American Libraries. Edited by Robert G. Marshall. 3 vols. Boston, 1970.

Short-Title Catalogue of Books Printed in Italy and of Italian Books Printed in Other Countries from 1465 to 1600 now in the British Museum. London. 1958.

Slim, H. Colin. "The Music Library of Hans Heinrich Herwart." *Annales musicologiques* 7 (1964–77): 67–79.

Steinberg, S. H. *Five Hundred Years of Printing.* London, 1955.

Stellfeld, J. A. *Bibliographie des éditions musicales plantiniennes.* Brussels, 1949.

Stevenson, Robert. *Spanish Cathedral Music in the Golden Age.* Berkeley and Los Angeles, 1961.

Straeten, Edmond vander. *La Musique aux Pays-Bas avant le XIXe siècle.* 8 vols. Brussels, 1867–88.

Strunk, Oliver. "Guglielmo Gonzaga and Palestrina's *Missa Dominicalis.*" *The Musical Quarterly* 33 (1947): 228–39. Reprinted in id. *Essays on Music in the Western World,* 94–107. New York, 1974.

Tenenti, Alberto. "Luc Antonio Giunti il giovane, stampatore e mercante." In *Studi in onore di Armando Sapori,* 2: 1021–60. Milan, 1957.

Thibault, Geneviève. "Deux catalogues de libraires musicaux: Vincenti et Gardane (Venise 1591): *Revue de musicologie* 10 (1929): 177–83; 11 (1930): 7–18.

Tinto, Alberto. *Annali tipografici dei Tramezzino.* Florence, 1968.

Tucci, Ugo. "The Psychology of the Venetian Merchant in the Sixteenth Century." In *Renaissance Venice,* ed. John R. Hale, 346–78. London, 1973.

Turrini, Giuseppe. *L'Accademia Filarmonica di Verona dalla fondazione (maggio 1543) al 1600 e il suo patrimonio musicale antico.* Atti e memorie della Accademia di Agricoltura, Scienze e Lettere di Verona 18. Verona, 1941.

————. *Catalogo delle opere musicali: Città di Verona. Biblioteca della Società Accademia Filarmonica di Verona. Fondo musicale antico.* Bolletino dell'Associazione dei Musicologi Italiani 14. Parma, 1935–36.

Vaccaro, Emerenziana. *Le marche dei tipografi ed editori italiani del secolo XVI nella Biblioteca Angelica di Roma.* Biblioteca di bibliografia italiana 98. Florence, 1983.

Vanhulst, Henri. *Catalogue des éditions de musique publiées à Louvain par Pierre Phalèse et ses fils 1545–1578.* Brussels, 1990.

————. "Lassus et ses éditeurs: remarques à propos de deux lettres peu connues." *Revue belge de musicologie* 39–40 (1985–86): 80–100.

————. "Suppliers and Clients of Christopher Plantin, Distributor of Polyphonic Music in Antwerp (1568–1578)." In *Musicology and Archival Research. Colloquium Proceedings Brussels 22–23.4.1993,* ed. B. Haggh, F. Daelemans, and A. Vanrie, 558–604. Archives et Bibliothèques de Belgique 46. Brussels, 1994.

Vasconcellos, Joaquim, ed. *Primeira parte do index da livraria de musicado muyto alto, e poderos Rey Dom João o IV . . . Por ordem de sua Mag. por Paulo Crasheck. Anno 1649.* Porto, 1874–76.

Vettori, Romano. "Note storiche sul patronato musicale di Cristoforo Madruzzo cardinale di Trento (1512–1578)." *Rivista italiana di musicologia* 20 (1985): 3–43.

Victoria, Tomás Luis de. *Opera omnia.* Edited by F. Pedrell. Leipzig, 1902–13.

Vidal, Gore. *Vidal in Venice.* New York, 1985.

Vitali, Carlo. " 'La scuola della virtù delle Zitelle': insegnamento e pratiche musicali fra Sei e Ottocento presso il Conservatorio degli Esposti di Bologna." In *I Bastardini: patrimonio e memoria di un ospedale bolognese.* Bologna, 1990.

Voet, Leon. *The Golden Compasses: A History and Evaluation of the Printing and Publishing Activities of the Officina Plantiniana at Antwerp.* 2 vols. Amsterdam, 1972.

Volpati, Carlo. "Gli Scotti di Monza, tipografi-editori in Venetia." *Archivio storico lombardo* 49 (1922): 365–82.

Weale, William H. J., and Hans Bohatta. *Bibliographia liturgica: catalogus missalium ritus Latini, ab anno M.CCCC.LXXIV Impressorum.* London, 1928.

Weaver, Robert. *A Descriptive Bibliographical Catalog of the Music Printed by Hubert Waelrant and Jan de Laet.* Warren, Mich., 1994.

————. *Waelrant and Laet, Music Publishers in Antwerp's Golden Age.* Warren, Mich., 1995.

Wegman, Rob C., "From Maker to Composer: Improvisation and Musical Authorship in the Low Countries, 1450–1500," *JAMS* 49 (1996), 409–79.

Weiss, Piero. *Letters of Composers through Six Centuries.* Philadelphia, 1967.

Willaert, Adrian. *Opera omnia.* Edited by Hermann Zenck, Walter Gerstenberg, and Helga Meier. CMM 3. AIM, 1950-.

Willer, Georg. *Die Messkataloge Georg Willers Herbstmesse 1564 bis Herbstmesse 1573.* Facs. ed., *Die Messkataloge des sechszehnten Jahrhunderts,* vol. 1. Edited by Bernhard Fabian. Hildesheim and New York, 1972.

Zappella, Giuseppina. *Le marche dei tipografie degli editori italiani del Cinquecento,* 3 vols. Milan, [1986].

Zorzi, Marino. "La circolazione del libro. Biblioteche private e pubbliche." In *Storia di Venezia dalle origini alla caduta della Serenissima.* Vol. 6: *Dal Rinascimento alla Barocca,* edited by Gaetano Cozzi and Paolo Prodi, 589–613, Rome, 1994.

————. "Dal manoscritto al libro," In *Storia di Venezia dalle origini alla caduta della Serenissima. Vol. 4: Il Rinascimento politica e cultura,* edited by Alberto Tenenti and Ugo Tucci, 817–958, Rome, 1996.

INDEX